# JIMSHOES IN VIETNAM

# JIMSHOES IN VIETNAM

## Orienting a Westerner

## James R. Klassen

HERALD PRESS
Scottdale, Pennsylvania
Kitchener, Ontario
1986

**Library of Congress Cataloging-in-Publication Data**

Klassen, James R., 1947-
    Jimshoes in Vietnam.

    Bibliography: p.
    1. Vietnam—Description and travel.   2. Mennonites—
Missions—Vietnam.   3. Klassen, James R., 1947-   —
Journeys—Vietnam.   4. Missionaries—Vietnam—
Biography.   5. Missionaries—United States—Biography.
I. Title.
DS556.38.K62   1986          915.97044          86-9801
ISBN 0-8361-3412-5 (pbk.)

JIMSHOES IN VIETNAM
Copyright © 1986 by Herald Press, Scottdale, Pa.  15683
    Published simultaneously in Canada by Herald Press,
    Kitchener, Ont.  N2G 4M5. All rights reserved.
Library of Congress Catalog Card Number: 86-9801
International Standard Book Number: 0-8361-3412-5
Printed in the United States of America
Design by Gwen Stamm

91 90 89 88 87 86  10 9 8 7 6 5 4 3 2 1

*dedicated to all
who let the light shine
including especially
Jesus the Christ*

# CONTENTS

# AUTHOR'S PREFACE

*Jimshoes in Vietnam*

JIMSHOES. They may be cowboy boots or tennis shoes, but when I wear them, they become Jimshoes. I can't help it! In a similar way, this book is my book, even though it involves other people. I am just an ordinary guy wearing ordinary shoes, and—who knows?—maybe the shoes will fit you, too.

IN. "In," as well as "to" and "from." "For," not "against," Vietnam. "For"/"In." Foreign? I went as a stranger, but the Vietnamese accepted me as a friend.

VIETNAM. In the news. Out of the news. Vietnam: my home from October 1972 until April 1976. Vietnam: often the focus of my thoughts, prayers, words, and deeds prior to 1972 as well as after 1976, too.

*Orienting a Westerner*

"Orienting"—because living is learning. Vietnam broadened and reshaped my perspective. Sometimes Vietnam overturned my ideas, but the positive impact of friends and the negative impact of war strengthened and solidified my commitment to peace. In the following pages, while sharing my experiences in the Orient, I have also described relevant—but less obvious—factors.

"A"—singular, not plural. These pages present one primary perspective: mine. I have tried to maintain a wide, balanced view—seeing both the flowers and the barbed wire—but I can not claim to be unbiased. I certainly prefer flowers to barbed wire.

"Westerner"—because I was born and nourished in a Mennonite home on the sunny plains of central Kansas. I acknowledge

# JIMSHOES IN VIETNAM

# Chapter 1

# JONAH IN JIMSHOES

*A Christmas Marathon*

1968. Vietnam: war. The United States: fragmented. Martin Luther King, Jr.: shot. Bobby Kennedy: shot.

That fall, I entered my senior year at Bethel College, North Newton, Kansas. Half a million U.S. soldiers swarmed across Vietnam. As a pacifist, I felt restless. Richard Nixon won the November election for president.

My prayers for peace in Vietnam boomeranged. God unexpectedly tapped me on the shoulder, calling me to serve there in a constructive role. I tried to ignore the feeling. I ran from God, but running drained my energy. I was no athlete—neither physically nor spiritually. Although arguing while running is impractical, at Christmas in 1968 I finally tried that, too.

The Lord: "Jim, I think you should go to Vietnam."

James: "Wait a minute. I think you're talking to the wrong guy."

The Lord: "No, Jim. I mean you."

James: "But, Lord, I'm just a young guy. I'm just a farm boy from Kansas. I don't know very much about this old world yet. How can I go?"

The Lord: (Silence.)

James: "Lord, I'm part of a very close-knit family. People have said we're one in a million. How could I leave?"

The Lord: (More silence.)

James: "Vietnam is far away. Why, it's halfway around the world. It's got a different language. Everything would be strange. How can I go there?"

The Lord: (Silence, again.)

James (trying a final sprint to win): "Besides all that, Lord, I'd like to remind you that there's a war going on in Vietnam. It isn't very safe to be in a war, you know. Why should I go there?"

The Lord: (Silence.)

James (bargaining): "Okay. Just let me finish college and go through three years of seminary, and then I'll go."

The Lord: "Thanks, Jim."

The gnawing inner turmoil disappeared. Good-bye, Jonah. I was ready to walk humbly with God again—at least for a while!

### War and Peace

Earlier in 1968, a "Tet Offensive" had convinced President Lyndon Johnson, commander in chief of half a million U.S. troops in Vietnam, to withdraw from the presidential campaign. More than ten years later, I heard the U.S. lieutenant who had been in charge of security at the Bien Hoa military base explain the Tet Offensive.

> It was country-wide. It was the turning point. The VC and NVA attacked every major military installation in South Vietnam. Bien Hoa was the head of Military Region III. How could they get regiments into that small place without our knowing it? When it started, I was at the command post where we had a map of the whole country. One light after another lit up as military bases were attacked. The systematic wave was moving southward.

His voice tightened as he continued.

> We fought from 10:00 p.m. till 2:00 p.m. the next day. That's when I became convinced the whole thing was insane. Finally, we didn't know at whom we were shooting, and we didn't care. They lost militarily, but they made their point: no military force could stop that nationalism. After the Tet Offensive we could see the handwriting on the wall. The Vietnamese were looking for a reunified Vietnam.

In 1968, though, I had never heard of Bien Hoa or Military Region III. Even without knowing that geography, I advocated peace in my orations at speech contests. As a math major, I enjoyed noting which famous mathematicians were pacifists. Three clippings in my files captured the irrationality of the war.

Although U.S. government officials regularly announced that

the end of the war was near, my first clipping—titled "The High Cost of Fantasy," by Emmet John Huges in a 1965 Newsweek— revealed a credibility gap.

We have turned the corner in Vietnam.
—*Department of Defense, May 1963*

It will be a long war.
—*Robert McNamara, November 1965*

Yet nothing dismays so much as the haziness of true American purpose—the final, justifying goal. In *public,* the official vision of the future is laudable and ludicrous: a safe and severed South Vietnam, governing itself democratically and guarding itself invulnerably. In *private,* however, the highest U.S. officials always have conceded the best of all possible Vietnamese worlds to be only this: an avowedly Socialist or Communist state groping for freedom from Peking. . . . [1]

The second clipping, by *Newsweek* Senior Editor Borchgrave in 1966, noted,

Amateur statisticians have computed the cost of killing one VC at $375,000. . . . The three-year period mentioned in Washington as that needed to win in Vietnam seems wildly optimistic. Five to seven years would appear more realistic—assuming, of course, that China does not enter the conflict. [2]

Based on polls, the third clipping reported, "Americans Can't Name Vietnam Enemy." Stanford social scientists worked with the National Opinion Research Center in Chicago to test a representative sample: less than 30 percent of the people polled knew that the "Vietcong" were South Vietnamese. In another poll, less than 5 percent of the people in Iowa knew that those South Vietnamese Vietcong (VC)—not North Vietnamese—constituted more than 90 percent of the forces fighting the U.S. soldiers in Vietnam. [3] I felt dejected: as a Christian pacifist, I knew more about the identity of the Vietnamese soldiers than most people in the United States did. How could the United States know why it was fighting in Vietnam, if it did not even know whom it was fighting there?

For several years, while claiming to want negotiations and peace talks, President Johnson escalated the war and denied that Hanoi ever expressed any interest in peaceful solutions. Johnson had been lying: Hanoi had offered to negotiate a political settlement. President Nixon lacked credibility, too.

I felt empty listening to politicians' hollow words of war. I knew that Jesus called his followers to be peacemakers and to pray for their enemies. Although his call to peacemaking provided the basic orientation for my life, struggling with the specific nature of that call had surprised me. The end of my marathon had clarified one thing: after completing seminary, I would go to Vietnam shod with the Good News of peace, not with any army boots.

*Applying Myself*

I glanced at the clock: past midnight. The morning of May 4, 1972, had arrived. My fingers stood poised on the keyboard of my manual typewriter; a bent paper clip substituted for a center ribbon holder—patent pending! Heavily-edited, handwritten notes on scratch paper blanketed the unfinished term papers and open books which were piled on the desk and on half of the bed in my narrow dormitory room at the Associated Mennonite Biblical Seminaries, Elkhart, Indiana.

I was searching for words to answer the Personnel Information Form for Mennonite Central Committee (MCC), a relief and social work organization sponsored by the Mennonite and Brethren in Christ Churches. "Name the locations in which you are interested. . . . " "Locations" was plural; my interest singular.

My eyes focused on the typewriter carriage. I felt drops of sweat inch their way down from my armpits. I concentrated on each letter: ". . . Vietnam."

My heart lay exposed. I explained:

I have friends (and one relative) who have served in Vietnam—some in the U.S. military forces, some in MCC and IVS (International Voluntary Service). . . . I do not hold any glamorous ideas of what I would be able to accomplish. . . . I want to learn the language . . . and do a lot of listening. . . . Of course, I would hope . . . to contribute in other ways too—not by imposing myself, but by sharing myself and those skills and resources which I have. . . . I also realize that there are other areas of need (including the United States!), but by . . . going precisely to Vietnam without the military obligation forcing me there, I hope to invite my close friends and relatives in military service to seriously consider an alternative lifestyle.

Question 40 on the application asked, "What do you feel are your strengths and weaknesses in these areas (of your assignment interest)?" I discovered that each strength implied a corresponding weakness.

Number one was a sense of humor which allowed me to relate to people without adopting their lifestyle. Weakness lurked in not moving beyond the humor.

The next strength and weakness: I was not married. Was being single an advantage or a disadvantage? Both.

"Total Commitment." One of my final seminary term papers stretched fifty-four pages, single-spaced. Perhaps being a mathematics major in college had pushed me to become a perfectionist, or perhaps vice versa.

> Family Ties. Strength: In a world that longs for community, I am tremendously grateful to my parents for ... home life ... dialogue, love, respect, discipline, high ideals.... Our strong family ties should provide a helpful context from which to understand and appreciate Vietnamese family structures. Weakness: danger of overdependence....

After answering all the questions, I stopped typing. My eyes felt strained, my arms limp. Sweat had painted huge, wet, irregular blotches on my faded shirt. I needed a few hours of sleep.

After sunrise, I reread the entire application. "What does Christ and the Christian faith mean to you?" My answer—not the graduation ceremony—climaxed my last days in seminary.

> In Jesus the Word became flesh, in my life there must also be an integrity of word and deed: the lofty words must become hands joyfully outstretched to the neighbor, the winged words must become feet willing to cross the hot dry desert, the loving words must become strong shoulders to help bear the burdens of others.

### Wait, Watch, Pray

For the first time in my life, I had promised to join a "peace demonstration"—a silent vigil at the Elkhart Post Office later that morning. In my heart, I had also promised to mail my application to Mennonite Central Committee at Akron, Pennsylvania, as a symbolic, yet concrete, action before participating in the vigil. In the vigil, one person carried a towering sign which declared our opposition to the war in Vietnam. Two others stepped from the line to distribute leaflets or to talk with those who stopped to question or comment.

I remained silent. Standing in line exactly two years after the Ohio National Guard killed four students at a peace demonstration at Kent State University, I thought about the form I had just sent to MCC. I had written, "Peace stands at the heart of the biblical message. I believe that peace is a lifestyle. . . . " Yes, I would remember. On May 4, 1972, my Jimshoes walked to the post office twice: once as a repentant Jonah to quietly mail a letter, once as a bearded Klassen to quietly pray for peace. I did not know whether MCC needed any personnel in Vietnam. I also did not know how the Elkhart community would respond to silent public prayers for peace. Preliminary answers arrived quickly.

At the post office, most people accepted a leaflet as they passed. Some also stopped to talk. A few pedestrians silently averted their gaze and shook their heads. Some opponents shouted four-letter-word protests at us from their cars as they cruised past. My prayer for peace included them.

Within a week, my five-page application form with its nine additional pages of typed information brought a response from MCC: a request for more information. A month later, while I was in Canada as a summer youth worker, MCC sent me another letter. One sentence struck me: "...possible participation in an assignment in Vietnam beginning in January 1973 might be plausible." That was it!

How could I keep calm? My four-year-old covenant with the Lord had taken one huge step closer to fulfillment. Besides wanting to go to Vietnam, as a Mennonite, I wanted to serve with MCC rather than with any other relief or social work organization. I felt radiant enough to warm the whole cool, Canadian shoreline of Lake Huron where I was working. My body seemed weightless. I called my parents in Kansas to share the good news.

At the beginning of August, I suddenly received a letter recommending a mid-September orientation and an arrival in Pleiku soon after that to serve as a hospital coordinator. The letter asked, "What would be the earliest possible date you would consider beginning an assignment like this?" The plausibility for the next year had turned into an urgency for the next month! I had agreed to work in Canada into September. In addition to the passport application, vaccinations, packing, and farewells, I needed time for writing a summer report, reading about Vietnam, and meditating. I figured October 1 was the earliest I could arrive in Pennsylvania for orientation.

Though sponsored by Mennonite Central Committee, I agreed to serve under Vietnam Christian Service (VNCS) for my first months. Three church organizations composed VNCS: MCC, Lutheran World Relief, and Church World Service.

*Pack, Plan, Wave*

Max Ediger, a friend of mine from Bethel College days, wrote me directly from Vietnam. He had typed single-spaced on both sides of a single sheet of lightweight, legal-size, onionskin paper. The dark words from the back side could easily be read from the front side (reading backwards, from right to left, like Hebrew). Fortunately, most lines showing through from the back sat sandwiched perfectly between the lines typed on the front. Consequently, I read between the lines on both sides.

Max, an MCC worker, wrote about Pleiku and the rainy weather there, about the Mennonites and their peace witness in Vietnam, about traveling and things to pack into my suitcase.

I came with one small suitcase, and I could have come with less. Why travel with a lot of junk which just causes worries and costs money? Come light and enjoy your trip.

Above all bring love, a good sense of humor, respect for other religions and a different culture, a lot of patience, an open mind, a desire to learn, strength to take some abuse and the ability to turn the other cheek, acceptance of others (this I have found especially difficult when I meet some deeply religious military lifers whose duty it is to operate the CIA program), but not the silence that means agreement, a good personal understanding of Christian reconciliation, and the willingness to share your life and time with a lot of others at the most undesirable times. These things won't clog up your suitcase, but will certainly make your term here more exciting.

Try not to bring preconceived ideas about the situation here, fantastic dreams of what you are going to accomplish, or the idea that language study is going to be easy. These things won't clog up your suitcase either, but they will certainly clog up your adjustment. . . .

Several days before I left for orientation, I received a two-page hand-written letter on official letterhead from the Pleiku Evangelical Clinic.

Dear Mr. James Reed Klassen—
   Hi. Maynard Shirk here. We got this note here from MCC saying you may be joining the Pleiku unit. Great! We welcome you! Pleiku's a beautiful place! (when it's not raining)....
   Maybe I should see if I can comment accurately on Bob's job (as hospital coordinator) yet a little. Bob takes care of all unit finances. (Hence, he needs training as an accountant)—he also is responsible for keeping the medicine warehouse organized & medicines in stock (hence, he needs to know medicines and warehousing)—then he also services the 2 cars, a Land Rover & Toyota 4 wh. dr. (hence he must be a mechanic)—also he sees that lights work, doors close, and screens keep flies out at the hospital (hence he must be familiar with maintenance, electrician & plumber trades) ... his business transactions & friendships will demand Vietnamese (hence, a linguist). And he must be ready to drop anything he's doing anytime and go help anybody else who has a minor (or major) emergency—or even just request for routine help. In his spare time he takes people to the airport (or meets incoming people), takes patients to Province hospital ... etc. etc.
   In case you lack training in any of the areas mentioned (or not mentioned) please don't sign up for crash courses. Come over here and we'll give you a 3 year course in it all—guaranteed to be a tremendous lesson in living!

After reading Maynard's letter, I looked forward to meeting him. With that welcome from Vietnam, as well as tangible and intangible support from family and friends in the United States, and with the Prince of Peace, I would not be alone in Vietnam.

On Sunday, September 17, my home church commissioned me. The congregation sang "God of Grace and God of Glory." There, in the Alexanderwohl Mennonite Church near Goessel, Kansas, the third stanza became my special prayer.

Cure Thy children's warring madness;
Bend our pride to Thy control;
Shame our wanton, selfish gladness,
Rich in things and poor in soul.
Grant us wisdom, grant us courage,
Lest we miss Thy kingdom's goal....

One week later, at the United Methodist Church in Lebanon, Kansas, where I was an associate member, the Sunday school superintendent read the twelfth chapter of Romans to commission me. That chapter became a favorite of mine.

> Bless those who persecute you;
> bless and do not curse them. . . .
> Repay no one evil for evil. . . .
> Beloved, never avenge yourselves. . . .
> No, "if your enemy is hungry, feed him;
> if he is thirsty, give him drink. . . ."
> Do not be overcome by evil,
> but overcome evil with good.

In the midst of packing for a three-year term, I bade farewell to many people—including my older, married brother Don, his wife Roine, and their daughter Rachel. Rachel, that charming, young niece of mine, asked, "Uncle Jim, when will you come back?"

"It won't be long," I replied. "I'll be back in three years."

She responded immediately, indignantly. "It is too a long time! Why, I'm almost eight, so I'll be eleven by then!"

Finally, on October 9, my parents, youngest sister, and I stood holding hands in the middle of our Kansas living room, ready to leave for the airport. In our circle, each one shared a Scripture verse.

My father started with Proverbs 3:5-6, " 'Trust in the Lord with all thine heart; and lean not unto thine own understanding. In all thy ways acknowledge him, and he shall direct thy paths.' "

My mother spoke next, crisply. " 'The Lord shall fight for you, and ye shall hold your peace.' Exodus 14:14."

Cynthia, my youngest sister, hesitated. "Dad used the exact verses from Proverbs that I had in mind, but I'm still going to share them because they're worth repeating. 'Trust in the Lord. . . .' "

I concluded with my paraphrase of the last half of 1 John 4:16. " 'God is love, and those who dwell in love dwell in God, and God in them.' "

After punctuating the "Amen" of our prayer by squeezing hands in a chain reaction around the circle, we scurried through the front door. Dad paused on the front porch, looked me squarely in the eyes, and shared one more parting thought. "We don't know if we'll see you again on this earth, but we'll see you in heaven for sure."

As that Monday morning dawned, the Salina airport waited 120 miles away. Dad and Cynthia both missed classes: Dad, as a high school teacher; Cynthia, as a high school student. Work also waited for Mom because she had agreed to type the final copy of my summer report and send it to Canada.

At the airport, the boarding call signaled parting time. My married sister, Vernell, and her husband, Paul, had also driven to Salina for my departure. "Good-bye. God bless." The words seemed to echo. "Good-bye. God bless."

"ONLY PASSENGERS BEYOND THIS POINT." The sign stood firm. Then brisk commands diverted me with several other passengers.

"This way, please. Empty your pockets. Place everything on the tables."

I scanned the cramped room. All the others called aside were clean-shaven U.S. soldiers; I alone was a bearded pacifist. Why was I classified with them? The airport security guards frisked us and searched our carry-on luggage.

That official "detour" made me one of the last to board the silver DC-3. At the top of the portable ramp, I waved good-bye before boarding my first commercial flight. I found a window seat. The engines started; the plane began to taxi. I waved once more. "I'll be back in three years," I had promised my niece. I wondered what lay ahead for me and for the rest of the family.

I had tried to prepare carefully for Vietnam. In my luggage destined for Pleiku, I carried a set of screwdrivers, a pliers, and a six-inch Vise-Grip. My briefcase bulged with books, including my Bible, *Jesus, the Son of Man* by Gibran, and *Vietnam: A Crisis of Conscience* by Brown, Heschel, and Novak. Three file folders also stood squeezed in my briefcase. One crinkled folder which was labeled "personal pilgrimage" held college and seminary term papers. Another faded folder held "challenging thoughts"—poems, meditations, and proverbs. The third folder—a new one, with "MCC" penciled on the tab—clutched the correspondence of the past five months.

Perhaps only my shoes looked unusual. Max, Maynard, and

MCC memos—all mentioned rain in Pleiku, so this Kansas farm boy invested in waterproof, jet-black, felt-lined, slip-on knee-boots. A swatch of disconcerting army-green rubber reinforced the toes. Wanting to avoid everything army-green, I had used a felt-tipped marker to make the reinforcements match the rest of the black boots. With the legs of my slacks pulled down over the top, the rubber boots appeared rather fashionable. Because they weighed too much to ship in my suitcase, I wore them on the planes all the way from Kansas to Vietnam. After arriving in Vietnam, I only wore the boots once—and it was not muddy then.

During the last leg of my 12,000 mile flight to Saigon, while I was still wearing those knee-high Jimshoes, the stewardesses served each passenger a harmless Oriental fortune cookie with a late evening snack. My hollow cookie held a folded, pale green slip of paper: "Your wish is out of reach; do not try to gain it." As if to deny the assertion of that printed "fortune" from a crumby cookie, I carried that narrow, pale green piece of paper in my pocket everywhere I went in Vietnam. I had stopped running from the Lord. No little words on paper could make me start running again—at least not for a long time!

# Chapter 2

# GREEN BANANAS

*Beyond Me*

No one deplaned at the Saigon airport until the security guards had completed their hurried search of the aircraft. As I disembarked, the howling jet engines symbolized the tension of the dark night. The engines never relaxed. Their piercing whine soon intensified for a quick takeoff, leaving the trouble spot as far behind as fast as possible. But I had just arrived.

Unaware of any deadline, I took last place in line and scanned the handful ahead of me—mostly men, foreigners like myself. I wondered why they had come.

One by one, the new arrivals faced an official who wore a blue-gray shirt with a cloth badge on one sleeve. After his nod of approval, the new-comers split into two lines for stamping visas. My turn finally came. What took so long? I peered over the counter. A gigantic book, with pages twelve inches wide and twenty-four inches long, lay open in front of the official. Names—lists of names—filled the book. He was searching under "K." My name was not there! MCC had received my entry visa for Vietnam just before I left the U.S.

"Try looking under 'James,' " I suggested. My heart beat faster. I read "JAMES" upside down: one JAMES after another, JAMES this, JAMES that, but no JAMES REED KLASSEN!

"Try looking under 'Reed,' " I urged. Where was my name? What was wrong? The group at the airport dwindled to nearly zero. I spotted a lanky American man standing on the other side of the pipe railings beyond the customs tables. I peered over the counter again. My name was not in that book! The official shut the book and then waved me on with a toss of his head. What a relief!

The next official stamped my visa in red. Stamping the opposite page in English, he wrote "17/10/72" beside the word "Arrived." Wednesday, October 17, 1972. Halfway around the world, my niece celebrated her eighth birthday.

After customs cleared me, the man who had been waiting leaned toward me. "Are you James Klassen?" he asked.

"Yes," I replied. "Are you from Vietnam Christian Service?"

"I'm Roger Getz, the director. I've got a car outside. It's getting close to curfew. Is this all of your luggage? Let's go."

We sped along nearly deserted streets. In Kansas my directions had always been clear; here my mind groped for directions in the darkness. Frustrated, I felt we were going north. "Excuse me, what direction are we going?"

Getz explained, "The streets angle, but we're basically going south."

Oh, no! I was wrong. I concentrated on going south.

"We knew your plane was delayed," Getz continued, "because we had people out here several times to meet you. Finally we were told your flight was canceled. Nobody else thought you would come in tonight anymore, but I just got home from a meeting at church and decided I would check once more."

"I'm sure glad you did!"

My brain still insisted that we were going north.

Max Ediger, whose letter stood squeezed into my briefcase, was waiting for me at the VNCS guest house. He had left central Vietnam a few days earlier for a business trip to Saigon and stayed for my arrival. A thousand questions, more or less, flew back and forth between us.

Conduit on whitewashed walls in my bedroom linked a bulky control box to a ceiling fan which rocked perilously. Besides counteracting heat and humidity, the churning air discouraged mosquitoes from taking blood samples at night.

*Eye-openers*

Rumbling trucks, sputtering motorcycles, and the irregular roar of traffic filtered into my room, awaking me at 6:30 a.m. My first acculturation test sat waiting for me at breakfast on the covered patio: green bananas. No one else seemed to mind them, but I liked yellow bananas, not green ones. Okay, I told myself, you wanted to come to Vietnam, so now eat a green banana. I expected a flat, dry taste. Surprise! The banana was ripe and delicious.

The predominance of green struck me when Max and I toured the Saigon area. The luscious, tropical green lay neglected in the background. Battle fatigues—green military uniforms worn with bulky boots—seemed to be everywhere: riding, walking, buying, guarding. Many Vietnamese soldiers looked like boys in their early teens. Guns cluttered the view wherever soldiers were stationed. Barbed wire, too, served as a trademark there.

That evening, I learned that the war also used propaganda as a trademark. "The South Vietnam government talks of refugees fleeing from the 'VC' (Viet Cong—Vietnamese Communists)," someone explained, "but the refugees really are afraid of the bombs that would fall on their villages when the 'ar-vin' hears that the 'VC' were there." ('Ar-vin,' spelled ARVN, referred to the Army of the Republic of Vietnam under Thieu.)

The informal orientation continued, further negating propaganda about the "VC." "Like the evacuated hospital at Kontum," a social worker from there said. "When the 'VC' took over the city, they left the hospital alone, but the ARVN retook it and then destroyed $10,000 worth of medicines."

So that is how the Thieu government with U.S. support "helps" the people, I thought. I wondered, what is truth? How could I combat propaganda?

I did not know if breakfast the next morning included "green bananas"; I slept right through it. My body was still adjusting to the twelve or thirteen-hour time difference between Kansas and Vietnam.

Ninh, Personnel Director for VNCS, spent the day guiding me through a maze of forms in the Vietnam Christian Service (VNCS) office. A blank application for a MACV card forced me to learn more acronyms. MACV, derived from Military Assistance Command Vietnam and pronounced "mac-vee," stood directly under the U.S. Joint Chiefs of Staff and the U.S. President. A MACV card entitled its bearer to buy goods at subsidized prices on the U.S. military base in a general store and supermarket operated for U.S.

military personnel. Only card-carrying U.S. citizens could make purchases there.

"I won't need one of those cards," I remarked.

Ninh chuckled. "Oh, you're a good Mennonite."

Few people in Vietnam ever knew I refused a MACV card, but declining the card served as a symbol distinguishing my commitment from that of the U.S. government and the U.S. military. Some U.S. pacifists in Vietnam had a card: they, like the Apostle Paul, decided to take advantage of their citizenship.

I quit working on forms and walked with Max to the Mennonite Mission headquarters next door where he introduced me to James Stauffer, Luke Martin, and Don Sensenig. James and his wife Arlene, sponsored by the Eastern Mennonite Board of Missions and Charities, had started Vietnam Mennonite Mission in 1957. Luke and Mary had arrived in 1962; Don and Doris in 1963.

"Where can I get a Vietnamese Bible?" I asked.

In one swoop, Don pivoted, snatched a Bible, and handed it to me. His words flew as fast as he moved. "This one has a blemish on the cover. We couldn't sell it that way. Take it. It's yours from the Mennonite Mission."

Besides welcoming me, the Mission shattered my negative stereotype of missionaries. I had thought missionaries were only evangelists and MCC only emphasized service, but James Stauffer directed a service center for VNCS.

Sunday afternoon, as a faithful son, I wrote to my parents, telling them of my safe arrival. I learned later that they never received that letter.

Sunday evening, Roger Getz, the VNCS director, invited several other VNCS workers and me to his house for supper—"dinner," as city folks called it.

"Is that thunder?" I thought rain seemed imminent in the muggy weather.

"No, those are bombs you hear. There must be a B-52 bombing raid not too far from Saigon." The conversation turned to questions about my arrival.

"Man, was I ever sweating at the airport when they couldn't find my name in that big book!" I recounted. "I sure was glad when they let me in anyhow."

"No! You don't want them to find your name in that big, black book. It's a list of people who aren't allowed into Vietnam." They chuckled.

"No kidding!" I said. "I even tried to help the guy find it in there."

Later that night, I suddenly awoke. What was that unusual sound? Above the systematic swish of the ceiling fan, I heard more bombing. The house seemed to tremble. I looked at my watch: 4:00 a.m. Monday.

At supper, I heard more bombing. I had slept through thunderstorms in Kansas, but that night "thunder" woke me up again. That bombing at 2:00 a.m. marked the beginning of my seventh day in Vietnam. Later, the talkative VNCS business manager explained, "Some Americans put in air conditioners so they can sleep. The noisy air conditioner drowns out the sound of the bombing."

Two days later, two newspaper articles dealt specifically with bombing. A publication for the U.S. Armed Forces asserted,

> President Nixon has quietly curtailed the bombing of North Vietnam . . . during the current critical peace talks, it was learned Tuesday. . . . Monsoons have already begun over the north and would have cut into American airstrikes anyhow. . . . The air strikes (were down) from the usual average of 300 or more per day.[1]

A UPI article in *The Saigon Post,* an English daily, presented a different view.

> U.S. navy jets bombed North Vietnam's heartland Monday but 'heavy thunderstorms' and monsoon rains cut American air strikes to their lowest number in three weeks, U.S. officers said Tuesday. The U.S. command diverted several missions of heavy B52 bombers from their usual targets in North Vietnam to the South, spokesmen said. The eight-engine jets hit with their heaviest strikes of the entire Indochina war in South Vietnam. . . . Asked if the Nixon administration had ordered a cutback in the raids to aid negotiations for peace, one source said that 'there is no information that would lead one to that conclusion' at U.S. command headquarters.[2]

I gave the rain—not the aloof incumbent presidential candidate Richard Nixon—credit for reducing bombing in the North. Rather than being grounded, however, the bombers dumped their thundering payload in the South. I had heard the results. "Curtailed the bombing of North Vietnam" merely meant a change of focus, not an overall reduction in the bombing.

What could a peacemaker do when the bombs were falling? I felt handicapped because I could not speak or understand Vietnamese yet.

The sun still rose in the west and set in the east every day until I left Saigon for the Vietnam Inter-mission Language School in Dalat. Having wrong directions in Saigon, though, did not worry me because I thought my home would be Pleiku. My initial orientation ended. Eating green bananas seemed natural already. I did not yet know that yellow bananas held surprises, too.

# Chapter 3

# DON'T REPEAT YOURSELF, DON'T REPEAT YOURSELF

*On My Own*

Only a small, faded picture beside the wardrobe broke the monotony of the bare, blue walls. Drawn, dark maroon curtains hid metal grids inside the window panes and also hid the darkness outside the panes.

After unpacking my meager belongings, I sat alone at a narrow desk in this rented room, my new home. Overhead, a single, unshielded bulb lit the square room as I began writing in my journal. "Tues, Nov 7, Dalat, 9:30 p.m...."

Two days earlier Ninh, the personnel director from Vietnam Christian Service, had accompanied me to the city of Dalat to find accommodations for my next three months of full-time language study. "In Vietnam you need friends," he had remarked, and through his friends, he had found this room. Down the hall, a room barely larger than mine housed three university students. When Ninh and I finalized arrangements for room and board, I excitedly shook hands with both the landlord and the landlady. I had forgotten that in Vietnam, men rarely shake hands with women. It was not my first mistake, nor my last.

After writing in my journal about gunshots from the previous two nights, I recalled the beggars I had seen. I was unprepared for so many: young children in rags, old men in tattered clothes, shabbily dressed women with sick babies. "When hands are held out to me to beg for money," I wrote, "I try to ignore them, but I can't. My stomach feels hollow. I shake my head. I look straight ahead— but something gnaws at me inside.... Jesus said, 'Blessed are the poor'—does that mean beggars?" My journal held no answer. How

33

much longer could I rely on my lack of language skills as an excuse for not responding?

I paused. The weight of language study and of being on my own immobilized me. After answering my final questions about Dalat, Ninh had left earlier in the evening. For the first time since arriving in Vietnam, I was alone.

Dalat, nestled comfortably around a lake in the tree-studded hills of Central Vietnam, was colder than Saigon. Without a fan to keep the malaria-carrying mosquitoes from bugging me at night, a mosquito-net canopy hovered over my bed. Giving the room a festive air, blue cords—"streamers"—anchored the canopy to the wardrobe, door jam, metal window grid, and to a corner nail.

I slept soundly and awoke too late for breakfast. I hiked through the front gate, up and then down the winding road to the central market.

Riding the bus was simple: board the correct bus at the beginning of the bus line and get off at the end, directly in front of the Chi-Lang military compound. I saw the overloaded Chi-Lang bus leaving. The next bus would leave in about fifteen minutes, but I lacked that much extra time. Assuming no one on the bus knew English, how could I ask it to stop? As a bookworm, I had read about people dashing to catch a bus, but the rationale—so far removed from my life in central Kansas—had eluded me. Suddenly, under pressure, as if by instinct, I stumbled across the right expression in an international language: I broke into a trot to try to catch the bus. The bus stopped.

The alert bus boy who collected the money for the trip hollered something to the driver while I quickly wiggled a toehold next to two men perched on the ladder mounted outside the back of the bus. Right hand grasping a ladder rung, left hand clutching my bulky language books, left foot dangling—I hung on tightly, awkwardly. The bus loaded more passengers. Then another guy—a fully equipped soldier with grenades hanging from his belt—wedged onto the ladder beside me. Detesting that ride, I resolved never to get up so late again.

At the compound, the gate for vehicles stood closed, forcing me through a narrow entrance and past Vietnamese soldiers in a guardhouse. I glanced toward the soldiers. My blond hair, blue eyes, and pale skin served as my pass. I puffed as I reached the top of the rise, passing a dilapidated bunker which crouched near another gate before I reached the school buildings inside the compound. I arrived at the language school just before the bell rang.

*Bite-size Study*

    "*Chao ong* Jim"—"Hello, Mr. Jim." The teachers greeted me in typical Vietnamese style, using my given name instead of my family name. The school format was repetition: repeat after the teacher, repeat after the tape, repeat together, repeat individually. Listen, then repeat. "*Chao; chao*"—"Hello; hello." Vietnamese tradition thousands of years old required addressing people by title when greeting them, so we practiced, "*Ong; ong*"—"Sir; sir." Then we made our first sentence: "*Chao ong; chao ong*"—"Hello, sir; hello, sir."

    That first day, I rode another snub-nosed, squatty bus home for lunch. Food service for me from the family kitchen did not start till the next day. Lacking enthusiasm to venture to a restaurant, I peeled an orange. That was my lunch. I rested a few minutes before trekking to board the bus for three more forty-five-minute class periods in school.

    Listen and repeat. "Hello, sir. How are you?" One word at a time—sometimes one phoneme—then two words, a sentence, and finally a dialogue.

    After the dismissal bell, I boarded the bus through its back door, like the other passengers. Two benches, separated by a center isle, ran the length of the bus. Since I rode to the end of the line, I sat down behind the driver, away from the bustle of the back door. Just like the previous times that day, when I stepped off the bus, I handed the bus boy correct change without a word.

    I knew one restaurant had a menu in English, but I felt unwilling to tackle the Dalat restaurant establishment at suppertime. Staying home seemed so much easier. My food supply consisted of one apple. That was my supper.

    The next morning, I scribbled two words into my diary: "Hunger pangs." Someone brought cookies for the tea break at school: good fortune without any printed proverbs to complicate matters. I still eagerly awaited lunch.

After I arrived at the villa where I stayed, a boy promptly brought my lunch upstairs to my room. I bowed my head. *"Komm, Herr Jesú"* The German table grace which I had learned at home in Kansas also invited the Lord to be my guest in Vietnam. I riveted the chopsticks into my right hand and grasped a piece of white meat which had neat suction cups on one side. I found it spongy and delightful. Later, I confirmed my hunch: squid tentacles. Another saucer held curried potatoes with beef tidbits. I switched the chopsticks to my left hand; it was as clumsy as my right hand. I finished the meat dishes, lettuce, banana, and tea before returning to school for the final classes.

*The First Test*

After the last afternoon session, I sauntered down the hill to the waiting, faded yellow bus and greeted the young bus boy in Vietnamese. The driver, who was next on my "practice list," angled sideways across the driver's seat with his right foot propped against the top of the engine housing beside his seat. That uncomfortable position had one advantage: he could observe the passengers directly, instead of using the mirror.

Because I was taller than most Vietnamese people, the low bus ceiling forced me to stoop slightly as I walked to the front. I sat just behind the bulky pipe railing that separated the awkwardly perched driver from the passengers. I smiled, nodded to him, and recited as clearly as I could, *"Chao ong."*

He perked up. *"Chao ong,"* he responded with a smile. Then— in a classic illustration of the predicament facing beginning language students—he said, or maybe asked, something I could not understand. I felt helpless, but assumed he might have asked what I was doing in Dalat. Since my vocabulary included no words for *school* or for *study,* I showed him my textbook and demonstrated the learning process: *"Chao, chao; ong, ong; chao ong, chao ong."* Apparently he realized the narrow limits of my vocabulary. We both chuckled.

The bus boy collected the twenty-piaster fare as the passengers stepped off the bus at the last stop. After handing him a five hundred piaster bill (worth about one U.S. dollar), I held out my hand for the change. The minor business transaction succeeded. Although I had practiced saying "thank you" in school, I lacked confidence to try it in public. I simply said good-bye again.

My landlady had requested my Saigon address as a reference. The teachers at school had told me how to ask whether someone was home; I practiced the question several times. The landlady's extended family living in the villa where I stayed included Hue, her teenage granddaughter. Since Hue had studied English, she served as our resident translator. After finding the landlady, I asked as clearly as I could in Vietnamese: "Is Miss Hue at home?"

One of Hue's brothers immediately scampered to call her. While waiting in the kitchen, the landlady invited me to have a snack. She selected a boiled sweet potato, still steaming, and peeled it about halfway. She ate the exposed part, dipping it into a platter of salt after each nibble. Then she peeled the remainder. I followed her example, but juggled my hot potato because my fingertips on one hand could not tap dance fast enough to stay cool.

After we finished the tasty treats, the landlady ushered me into the front parlor. Clear plastic protected the bright red cushions on the easy chairs. Instead of leaning back and crossing my legs American-style, I sat on the front half of the seat cushion and leaned forward in polite Vietnamese fashion. Sipping tea filled gaps in our stiff conversation. The other grandchildren stood respectfully behind us or hovered in the hallway.

"Here is my address in Saigon." Relying on my forensics experience, I spoke slowly in English, enunciating each word.

"Do you live here?" She pointed to the address.

"No," I said, "that is the office for Vietnam Christian Service."

"Where do you live?"

"I have no home in Saigon," I explained. "In three months, when I leave Dalat, I will go to Pleiku."

"You go to Pleiku?"

"Yes, I will go to Pleiku."

"When do you go to Pleiku?"

"In three months—at the end of January." On a sheet of scrap paper I printed "Nov Dec Jan," penciled a box around all three, and then wrote "Dalat" inside the box. Outside the box, I printed "Feb" and "Pleiku."

"I will study in Dalat for three months and then go to Pleiku."

I jotted "study" into the box enclosing the three months. Several of the curious children who had inched closer nodded their heads.

"In Pleiku, what will you do?"

"I will work in a hospital."

A couple of grandchildren thought their older sister was translating too slowly and quickly rendered my response in Vietnamese for their grandmother.

The petite frail-framed grandmother, my landlady, seemed content with my answer, but she did not relax. "Will you teach the children English?"

In a flash I remembered Max's warning: "You will probably get a pile of requests to teach English, but don't agree to any until you are out of language school. Your priority in Dalat is learning Vietnamese, not teaching English."

I sipped my tea. "I can speak English." Then gently shaking my head, I added, "But I am not a teacher."

Grandmother persisted. "The children have books. They study hard. You teach them one hour every day, okay?"

How could I negotiate? "Is forty-five minutes okay?"

"Okay." Grandmother accepted the compromise. As she and I sipped tea, the younger children edged closer to this Kansas farm boy in their midst. I glanced at them and smiled. I would teach them, not on the basis of my Vietnamese, but on the strength of the English they already knew. I had also silently decided to turn my time with the children into a two-way street: I would help improve their English, they would help me learn Vietnamese.

When should we start? The question was never asked.

*Building Bridges*

At 7:30 that evening, I pattered downstairs, carrying a notebook, a clipboard, and my two new dictionaries. The children were playing with brown puppies and a plump kitten. One boy handed me a puppy. The puppy tried unsuccessfully to back out of the bargain; its wide eyes regarded me with suspicion. My farm background had taught me to avoid making sudden moves near strange animals. The tense puppy gradually relaxed as I stroked it. When I handed it back to the boy, his Grandma barked something in Vietnamese. A younger boy immediately pointed at the door and said in English, "You may go." They dared not detain me because my pile of books implied an important meeting.

"I'm not going anywhere," I said. "Do you want. to study English?"

They responded immediately: "Yes, Sir!" They had understood my English.

They explained the situation to their grandmother. She strode to the stairway and flipped on the lights, obviously wanting us to study upstairs in my room. The three boys and I complied.

They practiced my name; I practiced theirs. Then they dutifully opened their English textbook to Lesson Six, on telling time. After drilling a simple question-answer dialogue, we counted minutes. They stumbled over the initial "th" in "thirty." No Vietnamese words required sticking out the tongue because that was impolite. The boys bravely stuck out their tongues. I demonstrated it. "Thirty; thirty." Listen, then repeat.

I closed the English book and opened my hefty Vietnamese textbook to Lesson One. Although they knew the familiar pattern of listening and repeating, they felt awkward as teachers. I smiled reassuringly. They soon enjoyed their new role. Hiep, the oldest of the three, decided the printed dialogue lacked tact at one point and recommended a more polite alternative.

Bored by the discussion, Huy asked me, "How old are you?"

"I'm twenty-five. How old are you?"

"Eight."

"Hiep, how old are you?"

"I am nine."

Then I looked at the youngest one. He grinned. "Six."

Other communication limped along. They looked up words in my Vietnamese dictionary with English explanations. I used the companion volume to find the Vietnamese for English words. Their curiosity prompted countless questions.

"Why did you come to Vietnam?"

"I came to Vietnam to work at a hospital in Pleiku," I replied.

"Are you a doctor?"

"No, I'm not a doctor."

"What will you do?"

"I will help buy medicine and fix things that break."

The boys drew funny faces. I sketched a bee stinging a man on the nose. The boys chuckled and fired new questions at me.

"Are you afraid of ghosts?"

"Do you like *nuoc mam* (fish sauce)?"

"How many brothers and sisters do you have?"

"Are you married?"

"Do you snore?"

"Do you use special medicine to grow your beard?"

They demonstrated different styles of snoring and tried to teach me a Vietnamese tongue-twister about beards. I gave up.

Several explosions thundered nearby. The boys remained calm, so I concluded that the artillery fire was "outgoing"—aimed away from us.

"Are you a soldier?"

"No," I explained, "I'm not a soldier. I like peace. I do not like war, so I am not a soldier."

An idea suddenly struck Huy. He requested a clean sheet of white paper and tore it carefully to form a square. He deftly folded it this way and that way. A tail and two wings, a sturdy body and stocky neck, a head and beak appeared. The paper bird in the palm of his hand looked like a white dove.

He just called it a bird, though, and gladly taught me the steps, steps more complex than any of my paper airplanes had ever needed. Not wanting to be outdone, his brothers busily folded a frog, a boat, a horse, and a dog.

Was that paper folding a waste of time and a regression to childish ways? Perhaps not. That evening, I had experienced paper folding as more than an art: it had become an open door, enabling us to communicate without words. I had preached sermons on the importance of little things, but these young boys had given me a practical demonstration. If swords can be turned into plowshares, I thought, maybe pentagon papers can be turned into doves.

When the boys' grandmother came upstairs at 10:30 to call them, she brought me a delicate vase with fragrant flowers. Although I managed a polite "thank you" in Vietnamese, I wished I could have said more. The boys seemed sad to leave. Hiep, the oldest one, served as spokesman. "We go now. Good-bye." Then the other two chimed in. "Good-bye." "Good-bye."

I acknowledged each one. "Good-bye. Goodnight. Good-bye." Then, with the slightest bow of my torso and a polite nod of my head, I said good-bye to the grandmother in Vietnamese.

In my journal I called the evening "a breakthrough." The next morning—Saturday—tested the strength of the new relationship.

*Watershed*

I slept late Saturday. Since someone at the language school recommended that Americans stay off the streets—maintain a "low profile"—during the weekend, I planned to stay home. Two thirds of the young trio appeared in my doorway ready for more paper folding, interrupting my review of my Vietnamese lesson. After a couple hours their grandmother—my landlady—appeared in the doorway to teach me a lesson I had not read about in any books.

"Please come," one of the boys urged me.

I obliged. We all followed the grandmother to the rest room at the end of the hall. She tore a small piece of clean paper and threw it into the stool. She shook her head disapprovingly as she glared at me and waved one hand, palm down, over the stool. With only a handful of English words in her vocabulary, she chose one noted for its clarity: "No!"

She tore another piece of clean paper and threw it on top of some crumpled newspaper in an open-weave wire basket next to the stool. "Okay," she announced soberly and nodded her head. I understood. I remembered when catalogs served a dual purpose in the wooden outhouse on the farm where I grew up. In my experience, though, indoor flush toilets had always been able to de-vour toilet paper, but I knew I would never flush toilet paper here again.

I returned to my room for my dictionary and clipboard. To translate "I'm very sorry" into Vietnamese, I arbitrarily chose one rendering for each English word, copied them onto my clipboard, and then spoke to the landlady.

Her wrinkled face broke into a smile. "Okay," she replied. A university student from across the hall heard us and joined the group in time to hear my apology. The student explained that the words I had chosen meant not simply, "I'm very sorry," but rather, "I'm deeply regretful," as if I had committed a major crime.

*Sunday Prayers*

Since anti-U.S. demonstrations in the areas of Vietnam under Thieu's control had been planned for Saturday, some U.S. official had decided that U.S. citizens should keep a low profile for their own safety on Sunday, too. What should I do on Sunday morning instead of attending the local Protestant church?

Since my journal entries began in the middle of a blue notebook, I opened the notebook to page one, which was blank. On the top line I wrote, "Our Father who art in heaven." Then, writing only one phrase at the top of each successive page, I continued entering the familiar prayer from Matthew, chapter six. After finding the passage in my Greek-English New Testament, I copied the Greek phrase by phrase with word-for-word English equivalents.

Leaving several blank lines for Hebrew, I said the prayer in German, but spelling several words puzzled me. Then I opened my Vietnamese Bible to "Ma-thi-o." I entered one Vietnamese word at a time, pausing to find the English translation and recording it before proceeding. Years later, my translation of the Vietnamese text looked as awkward as my German spellings, and the lines for Hebrew still stared blankly.

That Sunday morning in Dalat, I also paraphrased the prayer in English.

> Our Father
>     who smiles wherever there is beauty and hope
>     who dwells wherever there is simplicity and reverence
>     who lives wherever there is love and peace. . . .

That night as I lay in bed listening to the artillery guns unloading their hollow hells, I prayed again that God's will might be done on earth as it is in heaven. Arriving like a thief at night, the impersonal payload of explosives entered homes without knocking. War seemed so insane. Something inside me winced each time I heard gunfire. I hoped—I prayed—that the gunfire would not hit any person or animal. Unfortunately, the guns spoke the language of violence fluently. I listened to the guns repeat the pattern again and again: BOOM! SSSWOOOoooshhh—for about twenty-five seconds, loud at first, then diminishing. Silence. Five seconds later, a distant explosion. Then another "BOOM!" started the cycle again. The guns thundered their greetings in unmistakable terms, and like the Vietnamese language, the greeting could also mean good-bye. The guns, however, intended the greetings—so loud and clear—to be a last good-bye when they hit home. Their language knew no nuances: though their good-bye carried an air of finality, the guns never meant farewell.

*Farther Along*

I walked to school several times that week, sometimes pausing to take photographs of barbed wire or sunflowers along the three-mile route. When Sunday dawned, I expected smooth sailing for the quarter mile to church. I knew I just needed to follow the paved, winding street behind the market.

I left home ten minutes before the worship service, allowing five minutes to walk and five minutes to spare if I had trouble finding the church. With Bible and dictionaries in hand, I rounded the curves at cruising speed. Suddenly, I faced an unexpected fork in the street. Baffled, I peered along both branches, but the church building played hide-and-seek. I did not know how to ask directions. One street climbed abruptly, perhaps to the military compound which fired the artillery rounds. I picked the lower, level route and resumed speed, urgently sweeping the landscape with my eyes. Where was the church?

There! Across the valley, I spotted the church building. It seemed far away. I rounded the corner facing an ornate Buddhist pagoda. More than two-thirds of the distance to the church still lay ahead. While circling the rim of the valley, I scanned the houses huddled in the valley for alternate routes. I searched in vain. As I arrived at the front entrance to the church, I realized this church was Roman Catholic, not Protestant. I had never looked back. Under the welcoming archway, I glanced over my left shoulder.

Oh, no! There, back across the valley, just above the street I had taken, stood the Protestant church where teachers, staff, and the other students from the langauge school were expecting me. Deflated and sweaty, I began trudging back. Desperate, I charged into the valley, trying to find a shortcut. After zigzagging through alleys in the valley, I passed the ornate pagoda again.

The rugged road up to the church lead me past the main entrance. Unfortunately, I arrived just as the worship service ended.

Everyone asked the same question: "Where have you been?"

Too tired to be very embarrassed, I gazed across the valley and pointed out the "five-minute" route that had taken me one and a half hours.

### Learning at Lunch

At school, only two teachers—one tall, one short—bravely traded responsibilities throughout the day, repeating the elementary phrases. Because I knew so few people in Dalat, whenever they happened to board the bus that I was riding to school, the chilly morning atmosphere felt friendlier.

Once they invited me to lunch at a small cafe just outside the military compound. When we arrrived at the bottom of the hill, the guards in the cramped, dilapidated, wooden guardhouse stopped us to check the identification cards of the two teachers. I wondered again, why the mission language school rented buildings on a military compound even though the rent was minimal. I was unconvinced that economic advantages alone should determine the location of the school. I felt the current location blurred the missionaries' message of good news. Many foreign missionaries, however, did not sense any problem.

The cafe, with its specialty of Hue-style beef-noodle soup, lay a few yards beyond the pillbox guardhouse. In the cafe, the teachers continued teaching wholeheartedly: each time they asked me a question, they first asked it in Vietnamese. When I looked puzzled, the shorter teacher translated the words I did not understand. Both teachers helped me answer in Vietnamese. The Hue-style soup teemed with hot peppers. The petite, red, hot peppers, or their smaller green cousins, appeared innocent, but packed an unforgettable punch. Their flat, round seeds, floating on the surface of the soup or resting unobserved behind some noodles, were cruelest of all—pure wallop in concentrated form! I blew my nose and wiped the sweat from my forehead. The teachers showed me how to politely remove the seeds from the soup.

Trang, the tall teacher, asked, "Why did you want to come to Vietnam?"

"Many U.S. soldiers are forced to come to Vietnam, but I am

not a soldier. I volunteered to come to Vietnam because I believe that love and peace are the Jesus way, not war and hate." I tried to keep my answer simple, yet clear. The teachers—Christians— seemed to understand.

Sen, the short teacher, pointed to Trang. "Her younger brother must go to the army. My husband must go to the army, too. We are very sad."

Soon the conversation turned to other topics. "Have you been to Nhatrang yet?" Trang asked.

They laboriously translated the question into English. Proud of myself, I said the Vietnamese word for "no" without fumbling. The teachers, however, explained that "not yet" was generally more tactful and specifically more appropriate than a flat "no" in answering this question format.

Trang continued, "Nhatrang is very beautiful. It is my home."

"I hope I will be able to visit Nhatrang someday." I knew that Mennonite Central Committee and the Evangelical Church of Vietnam cosponsored a hospital there. I did not know that Nhatrang would someday be my home.

"Do you like the ocean?" Sen asked.

"Yes, I like the ocean, but my home in Kansas is very far from the ocean."

In typical Western fashion, I had planned to pay for my soup. The teachers insisted "No!" clearly, flatly, absolutely. I failed to understand. Many times after that, when invited out by other friends, I offered to pay for part or all of the bill. They never accepted my offer either. Finally, after about two years, I discovered the simple solution: if I wanted to pay the bill, then I needed to issue the initial invitation.

After paying for the soup, the teachers presented their identification cards to the guards at the front gate of the military compound again. My blond hair, blue eyes, and bushy beard again served as my I.D. card. I felt uncomfortable. The situation seemed illogical. The soldiers acted as if I were their commander, not merely a lunch guest. How ironic! Perhaps I should have ordered them to lay down their guns, go home, and grow rice; but I lacked the skill and the courage to say that.

The barbed wire fence next to the school towered higher than I could reach. That afternoon the barbed wire seemed even higher, colder, uglier, and crueler than before. The barbed wire symbolized the barriers between people. I resolved to study the Vietnamese language even harder in order to transcend and tear down some of those barriers.

*Tuning In*

About a week earlier, the assistant principal at the school had complimented me, "It seems easy for you to learn the langauage compared to the other students." It was not easy. Studying— including mathematics, Bible, and Vietnamese—always required hard work from me. I jotted a few reflections:

> Maybe I am able to learn somewhat readily however
> because I am used to smiling great big
> which is necessary for some vowels
> or because I am used to enunciating precisely
> in my public speaking
> or because I studied German and Hebrew and Greek
> or because I had some preliminary tutoring in Saigon
> or because I am willing to memorize the tones
> or because I realize how vital language is
> or because so many people are praying for me.

Perhaps God gave me not the gift of language ability, but rather the gift of patience to listen and repeat, hour after hour, day after day, week after week. Words carried potential like sunflower seeds. I studied hard, determined to plant healthy flowers that would outlast barbed wire barriers.

The young paper folding experts filed into my room again to study English. They sang "Clementine" in Vietnamese! "Sir, can you sing it in English?"

Singing solo in public frightened me: I could not carry a tune. I used my "best" (i.e., worst) nasal twang to camouflage my lack of musical talent and hoped my enthusiasm would overshadow the dissonance of my musical debut.

"Sing it again! Sing it again!" they chorused.

I began teaching them the words, but they resented the boring process. "You sing it. We will not sing."

Even building simple bridges became difficult, especially when the young workers were on strike. I took heart: they had requested an encore. To embellish the chorus, I sniffled and pretended to wipe tears from my eyes.

I asked the boys to write the Vietnamese words and soon sang the chorus with them. I had never anticipated a cultural exchange project like that.

"Don't repeat yourself. Don't repeat yourself," my college roommate had admonished me with a grin in Kansas. The language school in Vietnam, however, forced me to disregard the wisdom of his words. Listen and repeat. After practicing all day in school, I practiced at home in the evening. Sometimes my class in school sounded like a broken record, but gradually those words and phrases and sentences from Lesson One became spontaneous. My language school class did set one record: in the entire history of the school (even after we left), no class ever spent more weeks working on Lesson One than we did. No class ever spent more weeks working on Lesson One than we did.

# Chapter 4

# MERRY CHRISTMAS?

*A Soldier's Compliment*

"Where are you from?" the young Vietnamese soldier asked me in English as he sat down beside me on the bus.

"I'm from the United States, from Kansas. Where are you from?"

His home was not one of the few cities in Vietnam I could recognize.

"What are you doing here?" he added.

"I'm studying at a language school. After I finish, I will probably work at a hospital in Pleiku." More passengers boarded the faded, yellow bus. "You speak English very well. Did you study English in school?"

"No, I just learned it from the Americans because they have been in Vietnam so long. I couldn't go to school. I had to go to the army." He paused. "I do not like the United States government because it is only concerned about the United States and not about my country."

I looked down. "I know. Since I came to Vietnam, I have been surprised because many things our government said about Vietnam are not true."

"I think your government only likes dollars," he said. "Many men who come to Vietnam—army officers—only want dollars."

"In the United States there is a draft which forces young men to join the army," I explained, "but as a Christian I do not like war, so I refused to join the military. It makes me very sad to see so much U.S. military in Vietnam."

"I understand. I like your words." He smiled and stood to leave.

*49*

The bus stopped. He left, but his last sentences lingered. "I understand. I like your words." What more could he have said? My words had communicated a message of peace, now what would my actions communicate?

I pondered the implications. Christians recognize an integrity in the life of Jesus. Unless the lives of Christians also reflect integrity, the words that Christians speak ring as hollow as government propaganda.

*Juxtaposition*

Without a translator on Sunday, December 17, I only caught the gist of the sermon: God's call to Samuel. Two months in Vietnam only demonstrated how much I did not know. Jeremiah— the weeping prophet—came to mind. I had been reading his words for my devotions, feeling his anguish over his people's sins.

Noticing the shiny, miniature cross on the pastor's lapel, I prayed silently. "So many of your children have watered down the cross by endorsing the military. Open their eyes, Lord! Let them see that war and violence is not the way of the cross. Let them see that the way of the cross is the way of peace and love, the way of absorbing suffering instead of inflicting it...."

A thought flashed across my consciousness: the barbed wire in Vietnam was like a crown of thorns. However, in the midst of that barbed wire, flowers bloom—a juxtaposition like an awful crucifixion followed by a glorious resurrection. How long would barbed wire stand as a symbol of death in Vietnam?

*Christmas Commentary*

On the radio, the perfectly clear seven o'clock evening news on December 19, 1972, brought no surprise: resumed and stepped up U.S. bombing all over Vietnam. Nixon had ordered the most intensive bombing campaign in world history. At eight o'clock I heard Marvin Kalb's commentary: "When words fail, bombs are supposed to be eloquent." Harsh? Yes. Harsh enough? No.

Nixon had telegrammed Vietnam on October 22, agreeing to sign the completed Peace Accords in Paris on October 31.[1] Then Nixon reneged on his promise to sign.[2] He and his Secretary of State Henry Kissinger had already sabotaged the October peace agreement by the time Thieu voiced his own opposition.[3]

On October 26, two weeks before the 1972 elections, Kissinger declared, "Peace is at hand." He was deliberately misleading: his statements negated items already negotiated and implied that the U.S. had never agreed to sign.[4]

On November 20, instead of accepting the completed agreement, Kissinger demanded 69 revisions; on November 25, he demanded additional major revisions.[5]

> Publicly, Mr. Kissinger has said this was not so. Privately, however, he has told friends that he did put Washington's maximum demands "on the table".... [6]

Then when negotiations broke down in December 1972, Kissinger blamed the North Vietnamese, but he was lying again.[7] He had precipitated the impasse by his November demands, but by the end of December he was willing to return to the October agreement.[8] *The New York Times* reported events during the breakdown.

> ... President Nixon decided that he would put up with no more of what was called 'a (North Vietnamese) charade' before the American people ... and the extraordinarily heavy bombing began.[9]

> Administration officials have said that President Nixon ordered the raids because he felt Hanoi was stalling at the peace negotiations.... There has been no explanation for the massive scale of the bombings. It was the first time that B-52's ... had been used so extensively.... The planes carry 20 to 30 tons of bombs and drop them from a height of five to seven miles in a pattern roughly half a mile wide and a mile and a half long.... More than 100 ... B-52's were being sent over the North each day.[10]

During "the twelve days of Christmas"—December 18-29, 1972—the U.S. bombed North Vietnam, including Hanoi, so heavily that the bomb tonnage equaled a Hiroshima-size atomic blast every two days![11] Tad Szulc concluded,

> Agreement with Hanoi was probably possible in December 1972 without ... the Christmas bombings. The differences between the October 1972 and January 1973 texts do not appear to be sufficiently substantive to justify the death and destruction wrought by American planes.... [12]

The late afternoon sun cast long shadows when my elderly landlady called me aside. She animated the words in her limited English vocabulary. "Bomb." She shook her head. "No!" She shook her right index finger emphatically. She pointed to herself: "North Vietnam." She pointed to an elaborately carved, antique wooden wardrobe: "North Vietnam." Squinting through her tinted glasses, she wrote "1 9 5 4" on a scrap of paper and then with a sweeping gesture, indicated travel from north to south. Obviously, she and her family had been refugees from the North in 1954, and they had carried the prized wardrobe with them. She uttered English once more, pointing north, "Bomb. North Vietnam. No!" She shook her head vigorously. "Nixon. Bad."

I agreed with her, but what could I say? "Bomb. No good." Then palm down, slicing the air away from my body, I added, "Nixon. Bad."

Besides a Roman Catholic Christmas mass in Vietnamese, I attended four Protestant celebrations: one in Vietnamese, one in Koho (a Montagnard language), and two in English. I wondered if my attendence was right or not. Jesus never commanded anyone to organize big Christmas celebrations, but the Prince of Peace did give a clear call to peacemaking and cross-bearing. Charming children, tasty treats—nothing dislodged the dull ache from my heart.

*Come and Dine*

If I must celebrate Christmas, then I will celebrate it year-round. After all, we receive God's Christmas presence all year long.

In mid-January, the Dalat post office notified me that a package from Kansas had arrived. Stopping for it after school, I opened the package under the scrutiny of the official behind the counter. Peppernuts from my parents! The neat marble-sized German Christmas cookies were not contraband, so the inspector nodded his approval.

Formal Christmas celebrations had ended. The awful Christmas bombing had ended. The appropriate time to celebrate had arrived. Vietnamese university students across the hall gingerly sampled the tiny treasures. In our conversation, I learned the Vietnamese word for *German*. For a language student, nearly every conversation brings the opportunity to learn new words.

Downstairs, I squeezed out the Vietnamese words in proper sequence.

"Cookies. Christmas. German. Please have some."

"What kind of cookies?" The grandmother looked puzzled.

"Cookies of German people. Christmas cookies," I explained again. "Please have some." They each took one. I passed the peppernuts again.

"Sir, you made them?" asked one of the boys.

"No, my parents made them."

"Very delicious." Grandmother set the pace, and the other heads all nodded their approval. "Very delicious," chimed in several of the grandchildren.

"Please have some more." I offered the plate to them once more.

Grandmother declined on behalf of the family. "They are too precious. Your parents sent them to you. We have eaten enough. They are very delicious. Thank you very much." That was final.

Yes, the peppernuts were precious. My father's parents had brought the peppernut recipes as part of their German heritage when immigrating to the U.S. in the late 1800s. A few years later, my mother's parents, with a Swiss German background, settled in another community in Kansas near my father's home.

Delicious and precious. As the nuggets released their pent-up flavor, a feeling of gratitude overwhelmed me. I felt the love with which my parents had made and sent them. The tiny peppernuts suddenly seemed like communion bread.

*Pray for Peace*

I switched on the five-band radio just in time for the news. The new U.S. deputy defense secretary said he would support Nixon if Nixon would use nuclear weapons in Vietnam. I agonized in prayer for peace several times after that.

I had regularly joined the foreign missionaries for a weekly prayer meeting at the Christian and Missionary Alliance headquarters on the outskirts of Dalat, but none of the missionaries there were pacifists. Consequently, I felt part of my mission was sharing a prayer for peace with them.

That night, for the first time, I prayed audibly at the prayer meeting. I prayed for peace. My heart pounded. My body trembled. My voice shook. Why? I did not know. Was I praying so fervently? Or was I afraid to pray for peace in public? I had known most of those Christians for nearly three months, but praying with them still drained my energy.

Simple, bold letters stood in front of my closed eyes. The words refused to move until I had prayed them audibly. Then they slid quietly from right to left like weather warnings drawn across the bottom of a television screen.

> Tonight, oh God, I feel a heavy burden to pray for peace.
> We are grateful that you sent the Prince of Peace. . . .
> Purify our lives so that we may be true witnesses for you.
> Forgive us for
>     marveling at the blindness of the Germans under Hitler
>     and for closing our own eyes
>         to the U.S. saturation bombing under Nixon.
> Forgive us for putting our faith
>     in the leaders of our nation instead of in you.
> Help us to realize that being born again means that
>     we must love with your heart
>     and rise above narrow nationalism.
> Grant that the words of Jesus might not be too hard for us.
> Help us to love all men.
> This I pray in the name of the Prince of Peace
>     whom you sent to show us the way.

*What Is Relevant?*

The peppernuts awaited me at home after the prayer meeting; so did my speech for Saturday. The Vietnamese American Association (VAA) had invited me to join a panel discussing "Social Work in the U.S. and Its Relevance to Vietnam." Each panel member had five minutes for a short, introductory speech.

I had briefly worked with Spanish-American migrants in Indiana. After emphasizing their hard work and low pay in my speech, I noted their lack of education, lack of housing, lack of medical care, and lack of financial resources. (They also lacked legal aid.) Because migrant children had to begin earning money as soon as possible, the vicious cycle caught them, too.

In my conclusion, I pointed beyond their urgent physical needs.

I was involved in attempting to relieve some of the unsatisfactory housing and medical conditions and to break down some of the prejudices, but most of all I tried to be a friend and brother. . . .

It is in that same spirit . . . that I come to Vietnam. Although I am part of the Mennonite Church which from its very beginning has rejected bullets and bombs as the solution to local and international problems, I certainly don't have all the answers. . . . Today I have spoken in English and you have listened. Soon I hope to listen . . . as you speak Vietnamese, because . . . listening is an important part of friendship and an important part of the alternatives to hostility and prejudice. . . .

After practicing the speech, I tugged another pair of jeans over the ones I was wearing and slid into my lightweight jacket. Then in bed, I rolled myself tightly into my only two blankets. Early in December, I had taped the cracks around all the windows and around the ill-fitting porch door in my room. The tape blocked the north wind, but the coolness still penetrated. The temperature outside felt like the Farenheit fifty's or forty's, and because the villa had no heat, the temperature inside felt almost as cold.

An inner voice prayed the Lord's Prayer in German while an inner ear listened. That German prayer had been part of my family's evening devotions in Kansas, so it became a debt of gratitude I repaid nightly in my own devotions. I wanted to pray it again in unison with my parents upon my return home.

*Prevention*

Mornings, hating to pry my eyes open, I allowed minimum time to dress for school. Bananas and peppernuts sounded like a fine breakfast. Still half asleep, I swung the mosquito netting aside, then stopped.

Ants! Those peewee busybodies had sniffed their way to the third floor of the villa and were banqueting on my peppernuts. Their expressway stretched across the floor in my room, up the table leg, and directly to the carton. I admired their accident-free rush-hour traffic, but I resented their thievery. Did they pray, "Give us this day our daily bread"? Did the wideness of God's mercy on their behalf demand eating sacraments from my table?

I emptied the carton. With no time to spare, I dared not leave the ants in charge of the peppernuts all day. One by one, I tossed the peppernuts back into the carton. To prevent the ants from finding them again, I dangled the peppernut container from a colorful string anchoring the mosquito net.

After school, I swung open my door and strode to the tempting treasure. It was still safe. I slept well, but overnight the ants formed a tight-rope catering service. Emergency lights flashed in my head. I was angry.

I sorted the peppernuts again and practiced my speech, eating peppernuts to break the monotony. Later, a student loaned me an airtight container to keep the ants out. Competition, even with ants, raised too many questions.

The Vietnamese American Association organized programs for advanced English students. In closing the afternoon panel discussion, Gene, the moderator, emphasized, "The only way for social work to be effective in Vietnam is to strive now toward the prevention of social problems, particularly, for example, in the cramped quarters of the refugees at Danang. The real problems haven't come yet."

One panel member had noted that refugees comprised one third of the population, so the final remarks about prevention seemed ironic and left my feelings dangling. The best way to prevent social problems? Stop creating refugees. But both the Saigon government and the U.S. government deliberately created refugees so that the people and the land could be controlled more easily.

*Wounds*

During the Saturday panel discussion, Gene had mentioned the refugees at Danang. The 10:30 news on Sunday evening mentioned them, too. U.S. bombs struck Danang by accident again, this time hitting a refugee camp. Nearly a week earlier, bombs had hit the Danang airbase by mistake in the foggy weather, but military reports logged at that time recorded the bombing as on target. I thought, avoid the social problems, avoid the bombing mistakes. End the war!

In Dalat, the men in green bore physical wounds that looked ordinary enough for a hospital waiting room: amputated arms, amputated legs, a badly scarred face, blinded eyes, a bandaged hand, a foot in a cast. Later, I would see the morgue near Saigon where anxious families covered their noses to soften the stench while searching the rows of unidentified dead soldiers.

The war also left invisible—but real—wounds. On January 17, three months after arriving in Vietnam, I sat outside the language school, reading in the warm noon sunshine. Another student, Rex, walked up.

"What are you reading?" he asked.

"*Viet Nam,* edited by Gettleman." I showed him the cover. "It's amazing how the U.S. government feeds us half-truths. For example, here is a State Department document written in 1965 to prove 'Agression from the North,' but I. F. Stone's careful analysis destroys the State Department's assertions."

He sat beside me and shared his story. "I served a year with the military here in Vietnam. I tried to pick up a few words of Vietnamese, but the average GI didn't care about Vietnamese society. In fact, their attitude was literally 'damn gooks' and '——— Vietnam.' "

"I think it's great you at least tried to learn the language."

"I had to come back to Vietnam." He talked faster. "I had enrolled in school. I tried to study, but I couldn't. Vietnam was always in the back of my mind. I didn't come back to try to give America a good name. I came back so I can live with myself. I've got to try to right some of the wrongs I saw."

I nodded. "I sure respect you for coming back."

"I really didn't have a choice. I had to come back. You know, my home church didn't like it when I told them what the 'good American boys' were doing over here. I had long talks with my pastor, but he believed that the American soldiers were ideal examples of the virtuous life as they fought for freedom.

"Oh, no," Rex continued, "he wouldn't believe me when I told him it was standard practice to shoot wounded, helpless enemy soldiers in the head."

*Dogmatic*

Kenny reflected his parents' fervor for the war. He, his sister, his parents, and I had set the record as the slowest class in the language school. The Language School Director offered us a ride one afternoon to save the bus fare, so we and the two Vietnamese teachers squeezed into the back of the British Landrover. Jostling our way downtown, our first stop would be a house guarded by a German shepherd police dog.

The dog excited Kenny. "You know what? You're going to get to see that big police dog!" He thought I should be impressed, too. I recoiled inwardly.

The Landrover swerved to avoid huge chuckholes. Kenny prattled on, unaware: "You know, the one I told you about that killed six VC. There! That's the one!" He pointed with a pudgy finger as we entered the driveway, then looked at me, "Don't worry. It won't hurt you. It won't hurt Americans."

I wondered how our Vietnamese teachers felt about Kenny's way of reassuring me. The German shepherd looked strong and fierce, but I still was unimpressed. "How did it know those six people were 'VC'?" I asked.

"Oh, it knew!" Kenny shot back. "It was trained."

Kenny's confidence failed to convince me. The dog probably could distinguish large foreigners from petite Vietnamese, but I doubted that the dog had more insight than that. To many minds, though, the six dead Vietnamese were obviously "VC" because the dog killed them. I distrusted the missionaries' dog as much as I distrusted their dogmatic philosophy which attributed such keen political insights to the four-legged killer. I should have asked whether anyone could train that dog to differentiate between Republicans and Democrats. Then how many U.S. citizens would stake their lives on the dog's training?

*Presidential Power*

I doubted the dog. I doubted President Nixon, too. Even when he declared, "Let me make this perfectly clear," his message garbled the truth. The Paris Peace Agreement recognized two parties—two administrations, two governments—in South Vietnam. I listened to Nixon by radio on January 24 when he broke that first major premise of the Paris Agreement by announcing, "The United States will continue to recognize the Government of the Republic of Vietnam as the sole legitimate government of South Vietnam." Then he piously asserted, "We shall do everything the agreement requires of us."

All of the other U.S. presidents who were part of my conscious memory had been dishonest regarding Vietnam, too. Why should Nixon have been an exception? President Dwight Eisenhower, whose boyhood home lay some sixty miles from mine, sent U.S. military aid to the Diem government in direct violation of both the Geneva Accords and the unilateral declaration made by the United States at the end of the Geneva Conference.[13] In his memoirs *Mandate for Change,* as ex-president, Eisenhower acknowledged that possibly 80 percent of the people in Vietnam would have voted for Ho Chi Minh (a "communist") rather than for former emperor Bao Dai and his running mate Diem.[14] Consequently, if the elections in Vietnam had been held in 1956 (as the Geneva Accords stipulated), Ho Chi Minh would have defeated Diem at the ballot box. Diem and the United States hated that prospect and therefore thwarted majority rule and democratic elections.

In 1954, as senator, John F. Kennedy "feared the Republicans might permit a negotiated peace leading to a compromise government in which ('communist') Ho Chi Minh would be represented. He opposed Ho's participation in the governing of Vietnam, while conceding Ho's popular support. . . . "[15] By April 28, 1961, as U.S. President, Kennedy had "already indicated that we will not consider ourselves bound by any limitations imposed by the 1954 Geneva Agreements."[16] Among the many possible reasons why the U.S. withdrew its support from Diem, one little-publicized reason is crucial: President Diem had nearly completed negotiating a peace agreement with the "communists." He was killed in a military coup before the peace agreement was signed.[17]

Under President Johnson, " 'an elaborate program of covert military operations against the state of North Vietnam' began on Feb. 1, 1964."[18] These unpublicized and provocative actions included kidnapping North Vietnamese citizens and sending U.S. destroyer patrols deep into the Gulf of Tonkin along the coast of North Vietnam.[19] Then, in January 1965, Johnson's secretary of state insisted that since November 1964 the 325th Division (400 men) of North Vietnam's Army had invaded South Vietnam, but the claim was one hundred percent fabricated.[20] Although North Vietnam (the Democratic Republic of Vietnam) indicated its willingness to negotiate, President Johnson denied receiving any overtures and preferred instead to escalate U.S. involvement.[21] The "credibility gap," as journalists politely called it,[22] craved camouflage: the next president, Richard Nixon, and Secretary of State Kissinger obliged it, too.

*Bitter Fruit*

The day after hearing Nixon's radio announcement, I saw eight two-and-a-half-ton army trucks roar through Dalat. They had the right-of-way, and no one dared to challenge the shriek of their blood-curdling air horns. Each ugly green "deuce-and-a-half" carried a load of soldiers—perhaps fifty or more.

On the bus, a young soldier sat near me. Bandages covering half his face explained his absence from the army trucks.

After school, I boarded the waiting bus. A lady boarded, too, and sat directly across from me. We had often ridden the same bus, but I noticed a difference this time. Tears lingered in her eyes. She bit her lower lip to keep from crying. She gazed toward the front of the bus. I glanced away.

As we waited for the bus to leave, two children boarded. A glimpse told me too much. Brother and sister? Perhaps. The girl's dirty face, stringy hair, and torn, soiled, once-white blouse and slacks matched the younger boy's raggedy condition. She did not pass his hat—a hopeless, visorless, sailor-style thing with a turned-down brim. No, she just stood there, a battered plastic cup in one hand and one of his unwashed hands in the other.

Max had told me that some people chose to beg or sent their children to beg; they could earn more money by taking advantage of compassionate hearts than by being employed. Were these children destitue? I did not know.

Their sad silhouettes inched closer. The girl mumbled a sentence or two at each stop on their painful promenade. I overheard the words without trying. I had just passed the test on Lesson Four in school earlier that day. I understood too much of the langauge. "Uncle, please give us some money."

I barely shook my head. I stared past the bus driver. But I knew they stood silently waiting beside me. I sat motionless. They did not move either.

How long could I pretend not to see the bandaged bodies, the truckloads of soldiers, the eyes trying to blink back tears, the outstretched hands with an empty cup? I was rich compared to many Vietnamese. MCC paid my food, lodging, and school expenses. The additional spending allowance by itself—twenty-five dollars per month—was more than the monthly income of some Vietnamese families in the Mennonite Church on the outskirts of Saigon.

I wondered how long the children would continue standing there in front of me. I refused to give them anything. Finally, they moved on.

Two coins hit the bottom of the cup with a one-two punch as someone near the front made a puny contribution. That contribution relieved me. Words, too quiet for me to catch, followed the gift: the girl probably said thanks.

The engine started. The children turned to leave. They caught my eyes scanning them. She reached the cup toward me, again. I shook my head once more. I shifted my focus again. The driver ground the transmission into gear. As soon as the beggars stepped to the ground, the bus rolled toward downtown Dalat. Those five or ten minutes of waiting on the bus seemed far longer than the hours of study in school that day.

That night as I sat writing in my journal, outgoing artillery fire interrupted my thoughts. Harassment and Interdiction fire—"H & I"—discouraged people from populating the countryside: soldiers aimed the gigantic guns at random and then fired. The Saigon Government fired 80 percent of its munitions without having specific targets. I began recording the repetitious interruptions:

One of the hardest things to believe is the militarism of (one of the big guns just went off) the (another loud boom, another, another, another, another, another another, another, another, another, another, another, another another, another, another, another) . . . foreign missionaries. Tonight (another loud boom, another, another, another, another another, another, another, another another, another, another, another) was (another) prayer meeting. . . . No one came to pick . . . (me) up. Maybe there wasn't any prayer meeting tonight. Maybe (another, another another, another another, another, another another) they didn't appreciate my way (another another, another another, another another, another, another) of praying for peace.

Earlier, I had asked a university student about her brother who had stayed across the hall from me. I had missed him for some time. "The military," she began, then paused. She never finished the sentence. She did not have to.

After Vietnam defeated the French troops at Dien Bien Phu, the 1954 Geneva Accords set a timetable for reuniting Vietnam. U.S. defiance of the 1954 Geneva Accords and Nixon's stance disregarding the new Paris Accords cast heavy shadows over the prospects for peace. Nevertheless, I hoped that the United States would let peace come to Vietnam. I finished writing in my journal as the midnight siren signaled the beginning of the curfew.

*Peace?*

The outgoing, heavy artillery seemed unaware of the time on Sunday morning. At eight o'clock, January 28, 1973, according to the Paris Peace Agreement, the ceasefire should have begun. The fighting around Dalat had intensified during the preceeding days. Maybe the artillery operators, deafened by the loud blasts, had not heard about the ceasefire. Their commanders—also "hard of hearing"—deliberately ignored the ceasefire.

U.S. officials had told Dalat missionaries that Americans should keep a "low profile" again. The U.S. command feared that angry Vietnamese under the Thieu government, feeling the U.S. had deserted them, might attack U.S. citizens. I wondered, is that how allies treat each other? In fact, I heard someone use the word *bloodbath* to describe what might happen to us foreigners. That comment revealed the unhealthful nature of U.S. aid to Vietnam. Although I discounted the rumor, I decided to stay at home.

Geysje, the Indonesian nurse, was the only person from our villa who attended a worship service that morning. After she returned, she told us that many people had cried in church.

I waited until evening before writing my questions into my journal. Why couldn't the peace agreement have come sooner? How could I pray for militarists? "Father, forgive them because they don't know what they are doing. . . . Grant that . . . they may . . . change their ways."

In 1954, the U.S. promised not to become involved militarily in Vietnam. Why had the U.S. violated its promise? Grateful that the ceasefire finally came, but grieved because it could have come much sooner, I breathed a sigh of relief. No one was cheering in the streets in Dalat.

Only crying and prayers of gratitude had filled the church. But when Nixon piously declared a day of prayer and thanksgiving, he desecrated the meaning of the words. Didn't he know that Christians had been praying without ceasing for an end to the war? Jesus, not Nixon, taught me to pray.

Nixon proclaimed, "Peace with honor." Peace with honor? The honor already rang hollow. The peace, too, was questionable.

Although unaware that Nixon planned to bomb Vietnam again after the ceasefire, I felt he deserved his nickname, "Tricky Dicky." Only Watergate prevented him from implementing those devious bombing plans.[23]

# Chapter 5

# A COMPASS FOR HOMEWORK

*Dalat Departure*

At school on Monday, January 29, 1973, hopes for an honest ceasefire crisscrossed my mind, but few people at school mentioned the ceasefire. Perhaps hopes ran too deep for words. I had bought cookies at the market for coffee break: farewell cookies, not fortune cookies.

"Pleiku is a dangerous place," one missionary warned. Then as if to reassure me, he quickly added, "But it's not as bad as Kontum."

I had made friends during my three months in Dalat. Saying good-bye saddened me. Tuesday evening, the landlord's family gave me homemade coconut candy for the Lunar New Year. Then the two Vietnam Christian Service workers in the villa held an informal farewell party for me. I started packing at midnight. Before I left on Wednesday morning, Vietnamese university students from the villa and other students living nearby came to bid me farewell.

The weight of my stuffed suitcase in one hand and my overloaded briefcase in the other tore at my shoulder sockets and mashed the crepe soles of my shoes to the pavement. Worried about being late, I trudged as fast as I could.

My luggage soon sat comfortably by my side in the Chi-Lang bus. The empty bus implied that a bus had just left on this route. I sat and waited—calm outside, restless inside. I still could take a taxi, but I was too miserly.

A few more people boarded. The bus driver glanced at his watch and started the engine. I stood as we neared the station, but before I could use the words I had practiced to stop the bus, the alert bus boy signaled the driver to stop.

A dilapidated jeep, half hidden by weeds, sat abandoned at one corner of the station, symbolizing the normal activity there. I hauled my luggage into the crowded station. Surprised by the bustle, I nervously joined the waiting line for the only check-in counter. The line inched forward deceptively: it simply bulged in the middle. More people boarded the huge, old, blue-and-white transfer bus for the ride down the mountains to the airport. I overheard the destinations of people ahead of me. Why did all these people check in so early for their flights?

Only people with an airplane boarding pass could board the bus. When I heard its engine start, three or four people still stood between the counter and me. I desperately reached my ticket toward the counter.

"Pleiku."

The man behind the counter stopped. His head swung my direction. His wide eyes locked me in. He grabbed my ticket.

"Pleiku?" He fired the question at me.

I nodded: "Pleiku." He bounded to the side door, clutching my ticket and gesturing for me to follow.

Too late! The bus, already lumbering down the road, did not stop.

The ticket agent scurried to a van, motioning for me to follow. He barked something to the driver and heaved my luggage onto the other luggage in back.

"It's okay," the ticket agent assured me, handing back my ticket.

"Thank you, sir. Thanks a lot!"

The driver started the engine. I was his only passenger.

Rows of barbed wire lined every stream we crossed. Besides the soldiers and barbed wire guarding each tiny bridge, pointed posts also defended several larger bridges along the way. Visualizing stockades in the Wild West, I decided that people on neither side were all good or all bad.

More barbed wire and guardhouses marked the perimeter of the airport. A guard stopped the van, checked my ticket, and then cleared me for entry.

I trotted directly to the ticket counter with my load. Everyone else had already checked in. I sent my blue-gray suitcase as accompanied baggage.

My briefcase—full of books—hung like a pendulum weight from one of my arms. Like a trail of ants heading for a banquet, the passengers soon hustled to the plane—the only one in sight. En route to Pleiku, a stewardess served cold tea and rolls. I enjoyed the snack, thankful to be on the plane.

*Pleiku*

Having heard about Pleiku for six months, I looked forward to seeing it. The plane entered a tight, steep landing pattern. I spotted big buildings and wondered whether one was the Pleiku Evangelical Clinic. A cluster of tin roofs reflected the bright sunlight. Several rows of helicopters, with their long rotors anchored parallel to the fuselages, sat quietly a few feet north of the runway. A fleet of bombers squatted under individual round-topped shelters.

Maynard Shirk, smiling contagiously, stood waiting for me outside the tiny terminal, just beyond the gate and fence. In my briefcase, I carried the friendly letter he had written me when I was still in Kansas.

"Welcome to Pleiku!" He had a solid build.

"Thanks. It's good to be here."

"We've been looking for you. Got any more bags?"

"Yeah, one heavy beast." Heavy for me, not for him.

While we waited for the luggage, he asked, "You have a nice flight?"

"Yeah, fine. We seemed to come in pretty steep when we landed, though."

"Standard procedure. All the planes here do that. Yeah, that's Pleiku. Planes in the landing pattern are vulnerable targets."

"Say, what were all those tin roofs I could see from the air?"

"Refugee camps. There's one close to the airport. We'll drive by it on the way into town. There's barbed wire around them, but you couldn't see that from the air. To me, they always seem more like a concentration camp."

My orientation to Pleiku had begun. I spotted my suitcase.

"Here, I'll get it." Maynard grabbed it effortlessly with a burly hand.

We swung my luggage into the back of the British-made Landrover. I noticed a red cross and "Chan Y Vien Tin Lanh Pleiku" painted on the Landrover. Maynard zigzagged the Landrover between the staggered barriers on the road from the terminal. We cleared the last checkpoint. A short, open stretch of highway lay ahead of us before we reached the city limits of Pleiku.

"Man, I couldn't believe all those planes at the airport," I said. "At Dalat I saw exactly one—the one I came on."

"You landed right in the middle of M-R-Two Headquarters," he replied.

"What's that mean?"

"It's the headquarters for this whole chunk of the central highlands, which is called Military Region Two. Ever heard of Kontum? I've got to get some medicines up to the Pat Smith Hospital there this week—we've been using a chopper to get them there since the roads haven't been too safe—and I was wondering if you'd like to go along. We'd probably spend Tet up there."

"Sure! Sounds great!" Why not accept a helicopter ride? Why not spend Tet, the Lunar New Year, in Kontum? I trusted Maynard's discretion more than the bad reputation of Kontum I had heard from missionaries in Dalat.

"I can't guarantee it, but I'll try. It just depends on how much room there is. We'll check it out tomorrow when I have to bring a Montagnard woman out to the Field Hospital for minor surgery. The hospital is close to the runway where you landed and is also part of the military base."

He turned onto a road angling into town. Then as we headed west on a dusty road, Maynard continued. "There's one thing about Pleiku, and as long as you're here, you'll never get away from it: red dirt. In the rainy season it's red mud; in the dry season it's red dust. It's everywhere. Even after you leave Pleiku, it takes a week to get the reddish stain off your feet."

The reddish tint reminded me of Oklahoma soil. Kansas and Oklahoma were neighbors, so red dirt was no problem.

The houses ended abruptly. Concertina barbed wire lined the ditches. A school compound lay to the south, a military compound to the north. About two thirds of the way up the hill, Maynard turned onto a lane that broke the monotony of the barbed wire.

Ready to block the entrance if necessary, another ruffle of the barbed wire loops lay stretched beside the lane.

"Well, here we are," he announced. "This is it." A red and white sign over the main entrance defined the long, low building: "Chan Y Vien Tin Lanh Pleiku"—the Pleiku Evangelical Clinic. On the other side of the road, the military compound reached farther west.

"We'll go right on up to the house so you can get unpacked." He guided the Landrover up the steep incline on a nonexistant road. The normal driveway to "the Doctor's house" paralleled the clinic entrance.

"That's the medicine warehouse over there." Maynard used his head to indicate a building across the yard. "You'll be responsible for it. Everything that leaves there has to be signed out, but don't worry. I'll show you how."

Maynard welcomed me to Pleiku for another reason besides celebrating Tet together in a few days. Abandoning his work as roving Mennonite Mission mechanic, he had been pinch-hitting as hospital coordinator in Pleiku since October. Because he hoped to visit other places and fix other vehicles before his term expired in midsummer, he wanted me to feel at home as soon as possible. With his warm welcome, Pleiku already felt like home. I planned to stay.

That evening Maynard, several others from the hospital staff, and I visited the Tet market downtown. If the red dust was like Oklahoma, the Tet market was like the Kansas State Fair. People clustered and crowded. Vendors hawked their wares: flowers, trinkets, snacks. No other celebration rivaled Tet. I suddenly understood: Tet had prompted the bustle at the Dalat station.

Dalat already seemed far away. I was grateful for every lesson I had learned there. At the Pleiku Clinic, only Maynard and Dr. Pradhan, the medical doctor from India, spoke English fluently. Since they both knew Vietnamese, that was the predominant language. Pleiku immersed me in Vietnamese, but the three months of language study in Dalat kept me from drowning.

*Kontum*

The helicopter hovered a few feet above the Pleiku parking pad. Then we spiraled upwards to gain altitude over the military base before starting cross-country over contested jungle terrain. From the doorless cargo bay, I admired the direct—but windy— view of forested hills unfolding below us as we flew. The throbbing engine noise eliminated all conversation. I grinned at Maynard. He, the medicine, and I rode silently.

A solemn reminder stood in the middle of the open chopper doorway: the mounting post and bracket for a machine gun. Fortunately, neither gun nor gunner blocked the doorway to mar the view.

Beyond a ridge of hills, though, we watched single-engine bombers diving to drop their thundering payload, made in the U.S., delivered by the Thieu government. We saw, but heard nothing, like watching a silent movie. The pounding helicopter engine drowned the sound of the explosions in the distance. I wondered what a ceasefire meant?

Wind from the whirling chopper blades blasted the dust and whipped the semi-sparse tufts of grass as we landed next to the Pat Smith Hospital. Barbed wire marking the perimeter and shade trees left barely enough room to land.

Mangy dogs prowled the premises. Inside the overpopulated, understaffed, bungalow-style building, hospital beds squeezed the aisles.

Shortly after our arrival, a refugee from the hills—a Montagnard man—died. Maynard and I accompanied the body to the man's family. Mary Lou Refugee Camp and Village lay on a parched, barren stretch of land south of Kontum. Other than the name "Mary Lou," nothing was pleasant. We bounced across the packed, uneven ground between rows of houses. Fifty thousand people lived in this desolate place. A crowd watched us unload the lifeless, covered form.

The Thieu government was building wooden houses on that unproductive ground for the refugees. If refugees accepted a house, official statistics no longer reported them as refugees: they had been "resettled," even though they had no land and no income. They were caught in an unhealthy game.

During the afternoon, I helped unpack, sort, and inventory the medicines from Pleiku. That evening, New Year's Eve on the lunar calendar, Maynard and I visited with the doctors in their modest accommodations on the compound of a Roman Catholic Church. Occasional artillery fire punctuated our conversation. The old year blended into the new one without any perceptible difference.

Maynard, the mechanic, tackled a car alignment problem on New Year's Day. I gave him plenty of free advice, much of it well worth the price.

Purple morning glories softened the harsh reality of the barbed wire on the church compound and begged me to take their photograph. Even if they were only bindweed blossoms, I still appreciated them.

The outside wall of my bedroom on the compound also deserved a photograph. Irregular, gray, plaster polka dots decorated the fading yellow paint. Warring factions had alternately seized control of Kontum, or part of it, several times during the past years. The fighting had always taken its toll. Some buildings, like this one with gray patch-plaster, could be repaired; some could not. Wounded people, like battered buildings, faced the same two bleak options.

I saw more bombers diving in the distance to deliver their bombs. Obviously, the words on paper about a ceasefire had not stopped the war.

In the main aisle of the hospital, a priest conducted a Sunday morning worship service for patients and their families. That afternoon, a windy helicopter rearranged the loose objects beside the hospital once more. Maynard and I instinctively ducked to avoid the whirling blades as we braved the rotor-made storm and climbed through the open doorway into the chopper.

Our flight back to Pleiku in the chopper provided an excellent, but disturbing, view of bomb craters. Portions of the landscape, once picturesque, looked barren like the moon.

*What's Afoot?*

Monday morning a handwritten telegram from Max waited for me in the clinic mail: "request klassen come saigon immediately for important work stop cable arrival date ediger." What kind of important work? A temporary assignment elsewhere? A special peace project? A visit to Hanoi? Maynard booked me an Air Vietnam flight for the next day.

Later, as Maynard and I passed the Montagnard refugee camp on the northern outskirts of Pleiku, several men standing on the highway waved frantically. We stopped. A young man lay moaning on a makeshift stretcher. Blood still oozed from the gap on his mangled foot where three toes should have been. The conversation flew too fast for me. Maynard flipped the Landrover tailgate open. After loading the stretcher, the men hopped in beside it.

"Where'd he get hurt? Right in the camp?" I popped questions at Maynard.

"Yeah."

"How could he get hurt like that in a refugee camp?"

Maynard honked the horn and dodged pedestrians before answering. "That used to be where Thieu kept prisoners of war. Apparently not all the security junk has been cleaned up yet."

The men in back jumped out while the Landrover was still rolling up to the emergency entrance. Grabbing the stretcher, they called their thanks to us.

The explosive had been impartial, unable to distinguish young or old, male or female, "friend" or "foe." Someone had to "foot the bill."

Tuesday morning, Maynard and I toured the Evangelical Clinic for my orientation. The so-called Clinic functioned as a hospital. Two friendly young Montagnard ladies working at the reception counter stood to greet us.

After our introductions and a brief stop at the nursing station, Maynard and I sauntered down the ward. Following the policy of many other Vietnamese hospitals, each patient's family prepared meals for the patient, so we checked the cooking area adjacent to the hospital. Back inside the hospital, I peeked into the room used for dental work. In the next compact room, I scanned the medicines on the shelves. Since we did not want to disturb the doctor, nurse, and patient in the examining room, we toured the operating room and sterilizing room. The X-ray room across the hall finished my introductory tour. I looked back: everything except the kitchen lay under one long roof.

All of my belongings traveled with me when I left for Saigon, except my tall rubber boots. My special assignment probably would not need them.

*Saigon Schedule*

When I arrived in Saigon, Max was visiting Quang Ngai. A solid, single-spaced page of instructions from him greeted me in his absence. It defined my special assignment: open business letters, meet people at the airport, help with bookkeeping, answer telegrams, give assignments to the secretary, and make arrangements. In short, he expected me to be acting director while he was gone. I did not know when I would see Pleiku again, but the memorandum promised a discussion upon Max's return.

Max had become the director of the MCC Vietnam program on January 1, 1973, when Mennonite Central Committee withdrew from Vietnam Christian Service (VNCS) by mutual agreement. (Church World Service and Lutheran World Relief continued carrying the VNCS umbrella.) Max still preferred to be in Quang Ngai where he had been working with students, farmers, and refugees.

Traffic jams immobilized vehicles with three or more wheels, but—like thick syrup—scooters and bicycles inched this way and that way around the larger vehicles until passing the bottleneck. Consequently, the handiest transportation in Saigon was a motorscooter. I practiced driving, wobbling back and forth between the rows of bicycles parked around our office.

The bicycles belonged to students studying English in the Student Center above the MCC office. The Vietnam Mennonite Mission and the Vietnam Mennonite Church established the Center to build rapport with students.

I used first gear, only occasionally—gingerly—shifting into second when running errands on the scooter. Then James Stauffer, a Mennonite missionary, invited me to visit a social service center across town. He lead; I followed. That arrangement was a mistake. As a long-term Saigon resident and an experienced scooter driver, he knew all the shortcuts. Afraid of getting lost, I ran my scooter at top speed, or so it seemed, to keep him in sight. He weaved; I wove. After that nerve-wracking trip, I, too, was an experienced driver.

In February, I bought my first pair of sandals. I read thinned U.S. weekly news magazines, wondering why Thieu government censors had ripped out pages. I helped pack medicines for the Evangelical Clinic at Nhatrang and attended the dedication of the new Gia Dinh Mennonite Church building, unaware that I would soon be linked to the church and to the medicine work long-term.

Paul Longacre, from the main MCC office in Akron, Pennsylvania, arrived in Vietnam in mid-February on an administrative visit. While he and Max visited Pleiku, James Stauffer suggested that I stay in Saigon and begin teaching Bible classes for the Mennonite Mission. Teaching looked interesting, but improbable; I assumed Max and Paul were arranging for my work in Pleiku. I was wrong.

Max and Paul reduced the role of MCC in the Pleiku Clinic. Then they proposed a half-time MCC and half-time Mennonite Mission assignment for me in Saigon. Like a compass, all of my previous discussions with MCC had pointed to Pleiku. Having grown up on a farm, I preferred the rural atmosphere of Pleiku to the crowded hustle of Saigon. My heart was in Pleiku. So were my boots.

With my brief exposure to Vietnam, I felt inadequate to teach Bible. Besides, after completing nineteen years of formal education, I had come to Vietnam expecting to work with my hands and to work with people, not to spend time with books preparing lessons. I had chosen to serve in Vietnam with Mennonite Central Committee rather than with any missionary organization for another reason. Missionaries, I had thought, are inherently arrogant when they provide answers to deep religious questions. To avoid arrogance, I wanted to quietly replace burned out light bulbs and repair sagging screen doors at the Pleiku Clinic. Pleiku, however, had lost its viability.

Wrestling with the new job proposal, I slowly realized that anyone can be arrogant. Agriculturalists with new technology can be arrogant. Community development workers with new concepts can be arrogant. Social work organizations solving financial problems with dollars can be arrogant. Governments trying to solve political problems with bullets and bombs can be arrogant. Anyone, not just missionaries, can arrogantly hand out all the answers.

I realized that life is a two-way street. If I could teach Bible without claiming to have all the answers, then I would be willing to stay in Saigon and teach Bible in the midst of a predominantly Buddhist culture.

On Paul's last day in Vietnam, I agreed, "Okay, I'll stay in Saigon."

Paul smiled. "You know, Mennonite Mission wrote to the Elkart seminary to ask whether they had a student who would be a prospective Bible teacher for the Mennonite Church in Saigon. The seminary wrote back, 'He's already there.' "

I wondered whether this was why God had called me to Vietnam. Paul and I discussed my assignment and then turned to the general situation in Vietnam.

"When Max and I were in Pleiku," Paul said, "we heard about an American soldier who was wounded in fighting near the Cambodian border two weeks after the ceasefire. He hadn't heard about the ceasefire before he arrived at the U.S. Army hospital in Pleiku.

And just this morning, I was told that the ARVN soldiers are firing fifteen times as many bullets as the PRG (Provisional Revolutionary Government) soldiers are." Despising all the opposition (including the PRG) as "VC," the U.S. kept the ARVN soldiers well supplied.

When starting as director in January, Max used just one column for the three basic MCC financial accounts: a dollar checking account in the U.S., a piaster checking account in Vietnam, and a piaster cashbox account. By early February, we had graduated to three columns, one for each account. Due to our inexperience, bookkeeping headaches still plagued us.

With a sinking feeling, we changed our bookkeeping system two more times. We tried our fifth accounting system early in March. It, too, failed. We finally hired an accountant, but after six months, the mess from those early months of 1973 still baffled him. In desperation one day, he said, "We will not worry about those months any more." We agreed.

My role as half-time administrative assistant brought me a special assignment in March. After Geysje, an Indonesian nurse, finished her language study in Dalat, MCC assigned her to the Evangelical Clinic in Pleiku. Since I had been there once before and she had not, I was an expert of sorts. Consequently, Max asked me to accompany her to Pleiku.

Pleiku still felt like home when Geysje and I arrived. I would have gladly stayed. After all, my boots were still there. I took the front drive shaft out of the old Landrover so Maynard and I could replace the worn-out universal joint. The next day, I sadly packed my rubber boots into my suitcase and flew to Saigon. Though not sure that I would wear the boots in Saigon, I knew Pleiku would not be my long-term home. Good-bye, Pleiku, good-bye.

## Why?

Peering through the airplane window before takeoff in Pleiku, I noticed new recruits being trained. Drafting soldiers after the cease-fire seemed illogical. Both nights in Pleiku, I had heard man-made thunder—bombing—perhaps near the Cambodian border west of Pleiku. Occasionally during the day, too, the sickening sounds of bombing and artillery violated the cease-fire.

The war, in one way or another, also confronted me daily in Saigon. A poem from a Vietnamese friend who worked with MCC described the haunting agony.

Why has peace been denied my country?
Why can't people see that life is beautiful?
I have never known a time when my country was at peace.
Why was war allowed to enter the dictionary of mankind?
"I must hope because I must live"
and so hope becomes a friend and an enemy.
Why can't people see that love makes life beautiful?

Mid-March tested my public speaking skills. One Monday evening, I received an unexpected request: preaching at the Gia Dinh Mennonite Church that next Sunday.

Determined to deliver the sermon in Vietnamese, I quickly selected John 15 as my text and began studying it in Vietnamese. Jesus told his disciples, "Follow me," and "Love each other as I have loved you." Wednesday evening when I finished writing the rough draft, it stared at me, still untranslated.

The MCC secretary and I spent all day Thursday translating as simply as possible. By the end of the day, I accepted defeat: delivering the sermon in Vietnamese proved impossible for my limited language skills. Heavyhearted and exhausted, I still planned to introduce the sermon, read the Scripture, and give the closing prayer in Vietnamese. Sunday morning my stomach felt tighter than when I competed in national forensics tournaments in college.

The Mennonite Mission asked me to teach two English courses at the Student Center, to lead Friday Bible studies for the Church Leadership Training Group, and to teach a course on evangelism for the Gia Dinh Mennonite Church.

Feeling swamped, I requested a definition of "half-time work." I learned the hard way: no one could define half-time work. I had prepared myself to face issues of war and peace in Vietnam. I was unprepared to handle two full-time jobs, and my inclination toward thoroughness and perfection surrounded me like quicksand. Since the Mennonite missionaries in Saigon also all seemed overloaded with work, I joined them as a workaholic. In spite of my efforts, I often felt trapped by work until the last day of April 1975—two years later.

*Quang Ngai*

Max and I flew to Quang Ngai in April 1973, giving me a break and enabling him to check the MCC scholarship programs there. We visited a hill nicknamed "Buddha Mountain," which gave us a commanding view. On the riverbank below us, thatched huts housed refugees. The river flowed east into the ocean.

We strolled east along a wall with an archway. They had stood there hundreds, perhaps thousands, of years. A grove of trees clustered beyond the wall at the edge of the flat-topped hill. Below us to the northeast, about one third of the way to sea, lay the village of My Lai. Five years earlier U.S. soldiers had massacred over five hundred men, women, and children there. My Lai finally made the headlines; other villages in Quang Ngai Province (where similar massacres occurred) never did.

We silently surveyed the scene. Huge artillery in a fenced area beside the grove of trees began firing. Those artillery shells would also fail to make headlines, but they made an impact. Then a Buddhist monk in a pagoda near the weathered wall struck a giant gong in a slow, deliberate rhythm.

Max photographed the walls and archway. I shot the barbed wire and flowers by the pagoda. Each of us captured a slice of reality on film, but compared to our feelings, that slice seemed so thin.

## Jumping to Conclusions

A new MCC family greeted me when I arrived in Saigon. The telegram, sent to tell of their coming, arrived the next day.

Since Max had detoured to Nhatrang for a hospital board meeting, I oriented the new family. Five months in Vietnam had not turned me into an expert, so the Vietnamese MCC staff helped me with the orientation.

Before Max returned from Nhatrang, his apartment lease expired. He hoped to live with university students, but had not yet completed the arrangements. I moved our belongings, splitting them between the MCC office and the VNCS guesthouse room where I planned to stay overnight. Bananas in the guesthouse looked tempting. I broke a short, fat banana from the stem. The thin-skinned, unusually sweet banana was new to me. I liked the unique, chewy consistency.

Wham! In my mouth! A broken tooth? On a banana? Incredible! I mushed the banana around in my mouth, carefully searching for the tooth fragment. There. I grabbed it with my fingers.

A hard, black, round pit lay in my hand. A freak, I thought. I began chewing again. Shock waves hit the other side of my jaw. The broken tooth or another pit? Another pit. Bananas in Kansas had never jarred me like this.

Disecting the uneaten portion, I found more hidden pits. I had learned my lesson. Neither green nor yellow bananas would shock me again.

The next day, I moved in with a Vietnamese family—just as I had hoped. Ninh, who was serving as administrative assistant for MCC in Vietnam, had helped me find a home with his friends—the Hieu family. Ninh introduced me to them and helped make the necessary arrangements for me to join the Hieu family each evening for supper in their home.

Mrs. Hieu's younger brother Vinh and I moved into a nearby house which the family owned. Night after night, as sole occupants of the new house for rent, we discussed everything from politics to religion, oblivious to the bare walls and empty rooms. Since Vinh's English was excellent and since his short, slender body housed a warm, happy heart, we soon became devout friends. Though work and miles would test that bond, nothing could break it.

Mr. and Mrs. Hieu's four childern eagerly awaited my arrival for suppers. As often as possible, I took time to play with them. In order to play their games, though, I needed to understand the rules. My limited Vietnamese matched their limited English, so Oanh, the oldest, became my teacher. One evening, she begged, *"Nhay giay,* Mr."

"Please say that again," I requested in Vietnamese.

*"Nhay giay,* Mr."

"How do you spell that?" I asked.

She spelled it.

Hanh, the second oldest, asked, "Aren't you ready to play yet?"

"Shhh!" Oanh was educating me as fast as she could.

I turned to Hanh. "Not yet." I asked Oanh, *"Nhay*—what does it mean?"

She shrugged her shoulders. Even a first grader should know. She bravely tried to explain it to the dumb foreigner anyhow. *"Nhay* means *nhay. Nhay* means '*nhay* across.' Like this...." She jumped across a rubber band rope that stretched from the coffee table to the front door to a corner of the divan and then back to the coffee table, forming a triangle.

I understood: *nhay* meant *jump.* I jumped across the flexible barrier. Jumping the rope, a favorite game for the children, soon limbered my bones.

Each of the three older children demonstrated the rules: hook the first side of the triangle with the ankles, jump across the second side, and then release the first side while jumping across the the third side. One more rule became obvious: after all of us completed a successful round, they raised the rope. Oanh, a third-grader, won easily. With my expanded vocabulary, I was a winner, too. We had all jumped across not just a rubber band rope that evening, but across barriers of age, language, and culture.

# Chapter 6

# SPRING INTO SUMMER

*Remember Me*

One weekend in mid-April 1973 held a new role: chauffeur. Early Saturday morning, Max and I each picked up a vanload of new Christians from a tribal refugee camp located near Saigon and drove to the seashore at Vung Tau for their water baptism ceremony.

A rocky stretch of shoreline just a few yards from the highway provided water deep enough for immersion. The waves glistened in the bright sunshine and gently lapped at the rugged rocks. In that picturesque setting, 53 candidates each accepted the powerful symbolism of death and new life.

By most standards, the sea was calm. But the waves kept moving restlessly. So did my spirit. Survival in the refugee camp required a strong spirit, but the refugees being baptized were materially poor—incredibly poor. As helpless victims of an inhumane war which left them struggling for enough food every day, they dared not even dream of owning shoes, yet the preacher who baptized them walked right into the ocean with shiny leather shoes still on his feet. Wearing shoes into the salty seawater seemed illogical. Did he have to maintain such a high status that he dared not remove his shoes and socks?

The caravan of four packed vans—averaging nearly seven people per seat—carried 88 people, including the 53 newly baptised believers. Back at the Montagnard refugee camp, we all celebrated the Lord's Supper using inexpensive rectangular cookies broken into squares as communion bread and a locally made soda pop as the communion drink. I thanked God for the simplicity of the service. Sitting on the last row of flat, backless benches, I also thanked God for the sacrificial life of Jesus and remembered that he called us to follow his example.

Two days later, a missionary invited me to accompany him for a visit to a Montagnard village near the Dalat airport. As he and I sat drinking tea in the home of Pastor Sau, our short-legged stools rocked crookedly on the uneven dirt floor whenever we shifted our position. When we stood to leave, Pastor Sau selected a brass bracelet and turned to me. "These used to be status symbols for our people: the more bracelets, the higher the status. Now we are Christians, and we don't use them that way anymore. We use them as a symbol of friendship." He bent the bracelet around my right wrist. "Though we may be many miles apart, this will symbolize our friendship. All I ask is that you remember to pray for me and for my people."

"Yes, I'll remember. Thank you very much." I have worn the bracelet every day since then, and I have remembered.[1]

*What's the Difference?*

Back in Saigon by Friday—"Good Friday"—I unlocked the front door at home. I bounced my MCC Lambretta scooter up the single step and over the sill into the living room to keep it safe overnight.

The only time I had worn shoes since coming to Saigon three months earlier was the Sunday morning when I preached in Gia Dinh. (Someone had hinted that I should wear shoes for that occasion, but what was the difference between the pulpit and the seawater?) Biblical accounts of foot washing gained new meaning and integrity. At the Last Supper, Jesus told Peter, "After bathing, only the feet need washing." My sandaled feet, like Peter's, needed washing.

Dawn was softening the shadows as I drove the scooter into the churchyard shortly before 6:00 a.m. on Easter Sunday. I joined the congregation on the flat rooftop of the Gia Dinh Mennonite Church building. Crisp air and a glowing eastern sky graced the sunrise service.

The sudden throbbing of an airborne helicopter drowned out the invocation. Five more times during the service, the pounding engines of military helicopters overpowered the words. I wondered why so many church members around the world were supporting the evils of war instead of following the way of Jesus.

That afternoon I reflected on several recent experiences. In mid-March Max and I had eaten supper at the VNCS guesthouse with Duy, a soft-spoken student in medical school. In explaining Mennonite perspectives, I had emphasized pacificism. Duy approached Max and me immediately after supper. Concern lined his face. He spoke quietly so no one could eavesdrop. "Some of my friends have been jailed. I'm worried about them. I've heard that they are being sent to the northern provinces to be turned over to the North Vietnamese in a prisoner exchange, but my friends are not communists and they are not North Vietnamese. Please help me get in contact with my friends. I must find out about them. Will you help me?"

We learned that his friends were not shipped north. We learned about other political prisoners, too, even though President Thieu charged them with civil crimes so he could claim he held no political prisoners. Being neutral or advocating peace was illegal. Using spit and urine, beatings and electrical shocks, cramped cells and "tiger cages," the Saigon government tortured political prisoners. Don Luce and a delegation from the U.S. Congress had exposed the five-by-nine-foot "tiger cages" each of which held three prisoners inside.2

Could U.S. Christians claim innocence or ignorance? Income tax dollars from the U.S. sustained the Saigon government. Frances Fitzgerald, author of *Fire in the Lake,* wrote, "Created, financed, and defended by Americans, the Saigon regime was less a government than an act of the American will—an artificial military bureaucracy that ... represented no one except upon occasion the northern Catholics."3 To exist, the Saigon government depended on bullets, not ballots, and labeled neutralists as *communist* or *pro-communist.*

I celebrated Easter because Jesus said, "Blessed are those who mourn.... Blessed are those who hunger and thirst for righteousness.... Blessed are the peacemakers...." Happy Easter? No. Blessed, yes; but hardly happy. Although Jesus left his followers a legacy of suffering, he also left a legacy of deep joy that nothing could drown out. My pocket-size English-Vietnamese dictionary sensed a difference between *happiness* and *joy,* but unfortunately, it reversed their meanings in Vietnamese, rendering *joy* more superficial than *happiness.*

As my roommate Vinh and I sipped a glass of soybean "milk" one evening, he commented, "In English, when you meet somebody, you say, 'Hi. How are you?' But we don't ask that very often. Oh, maybe when we haven't seen somebody for a long time, we ask them, but not usually."

"So what do you say?"

" 'Are you happy?' or 'Do you have anything happy (to share)?' Life in Vietnam is too short. There is war, there is too much disease. It isn't so important how your health is, but it is important whether you are happy."

The language school pattern ("How are you?") had become spontaneous already, but I needed to supplement it with another option. Formal and informal education and reeducation enriched my life in Vietnam.

## In the Background

"Life in Kansas" demanded some attention as I prepared to address the Gia Dinh Mennonite Youth Group on the first Sunday in May.

What is Kansas? . . . animal, a flower . . . ? No, it's a state. . . .

Our farm was . . . one of the smaller ones. We usually had some chickens . . . sheep . . . hogs . . . milk cows . . . beef cattle . . . cats . . . a dog. . . .

Both of my parents grew up speaking German, and they remember thinking how lucky the children were who could speak English. . . . Even now when . . . uncles . . . (visit), part of the conversation may be in German.

My home church is the Alexanderwohl Mennonite Church. It is one of the few Mennonite Churches that came to the United States as an entire church. The church (congregation) migrated from Russia in the 1870s when Russia began compulsory military draft. My grandfather was only 12 years old when he came with his parents. Sometimes I wonder why the church didn't seriously consider migrating again when the United States began a compulsory military draft. . . . Of course, there is more than one way to witness to what a person believes, and so in the United States there were and are various ways for Mennonites to express their biblically based belief that military force is not really the way to solve . . . problems. For example, as my father was growing up in Kansas, World War I came along, and his oldest brother was drafted. Because my father's brother refused to participate in military activities, that brother was badly mistreated and was never very healthy after he was allowed to return home. . . . Right now I know a Mennonite young man whose home is 12 miles from where I grew up, and he is in prison for refusing to participate in the U.S. draft. . . .

Chin, who lived near the church building, invited me for a visit after the meeting adjourned. Easter Sunday her family had also invited me for a meal; this time I read a history lesson in English while she recorded it.

The next Sunday evening, Linh and I stood alone on the flat rooftop of the house where Max stayed. Linh, normally full of fun, looked serious.

"Jim, I've got to talk to you."

"Fine. I'm in no hurry."

"I'm sorry about what I have to tell you, but I hope you'll understand." He paused. "Do you know Chin?"

"Sure," I answered. "Just a week ago I did some recording for her in English after the youth group meeting was over."

"Stay away from her! One of my friends told me he would kill you if you ever went to her house again! He wants her as his girlfriend and is afraid you will steal her!"

I was shocked. "Okay! But I certainly am not trying to steal anyone's girlfriend! I didn't come to Vietnam to look for girlfriends. Please tell your friend that."

"But he's suspicious. Believe me, you must never go to her house again."

"Okay, I won't. But what if she talks to me at church or comes to the MCC office?"

"Don't worry about that," Linh reassured me. "But you must find some way to decline every invitation to go to her home. I'm sorry I have to ask you to do that. If you go to her house, there is no way I can protect you."

"I won't go to her house anymore, but I'm not asking anyone to protect me: not you, not anybody else, either. I never have asked anyone to protect me and never will."

"Let me tell you something else. Maybe you didn't know that I'm part of a People's Self-Defense Force and that I've got 20 guys under me. We all can kill. I will do anything for my friends. Please don't go to Chin's house because I do not want to choose sides between my friends."

"Listen, I will never go to her house again."

"It's strange," Linh reflected, "but up till two years ago I hated all Americans."

"If I were a Vietnamese," I responded, "I think I would be suspicious of every American."

"You know why I hated Americans?" He peered at me, squinting hard because he was not wearing his thick glasses, but he did not pause. "I saw a girl with a bottle crammed up her vagina by American soldiers. I'll never forgive them for that! I hate the VC, too. They killed my sister when she was pregnant and then killed my uncle by tearing him apart. I still keep a part of a bone from him as a symbol of my hatred for the VC. The VC have killed twenty of my relatives. What would you do if someone killed your youngest sister, and not only your sister but all the rest of your family except you? What would you do?"

"I don't know." I stared into the night. "I don't know."

"I'm a rascal," he muttered. "You have to be a rascal to survive here, but I'm not as bad as some of the guys under me. But, believe me, we would never do a beastly thing like the Americans did to that girl! My father taught me military tactics, taught me how to be a rascal. He wanted me to join the People's Self-Defense Force. There have been a lot of heroes in my father's family, and now the attention is focused on me—otherwise, I'd go anywhere— the U.S., Australia, anywhere—to get away from the hard life here."

He sighed. "The Vietnamese fought the Chinese for 1,000 years, the French for 100, each other for 20 years. Why does God allow Vietnam to go through such terrible experiences?"

"I don't know." I shook my head again.

"Every Vietnamese Christian prays to God for peace, and they ask God why they have to endure so much war." He continued, half in Vietnamese, half in English, "But there is no answer. Are Vietnamese less important than other people?"

"No, certainly that can't be right."

"I know I'm supposed to love everyone, but how can I? One of my friends downstairs has killed over a hundred people—by guns, by knives, by hands, by grenades. That's how he has survived. He is a good soldier!"

We chuckled gently at the irony and shook our heads.

Linh continued. "What does it mean to be a 'good' soldier? When I go to church, I try to forget the war, but I can't."

Although I summarized our discussion in my journal, I dared not record the reference to Chin. After Linh's rooftop warning to me, Chin came to the MCC office twice to invite me to her home, but I declined both times. Linh and I never discussed the issue again.

*Color-blind*

Duy, the soft-spoken medical student, visited the MCC office. "Two of my friends who are against the Saigon government have written to me. They say they will be sent to the front in an attempt to exchange them for some prisoners the communists hold. But my friends do not want to go because they are also anticommunist."

"Somehow the political leaders on both sides can't conceive of a person being neutral," I commented.

"For the political leaders, things are either black or white," Duy lamented. "They just don't recognize any other color."

That night, I led the Bible study for the Mennonite Mission Fellowship. Organized by the Mennonite missionaries and emphasizing the good news of reconciliation, the Fellowship had decided to review Ephesians, a book focused on overcoming barriers. In my closing prayer, I expressed gratitude because God was not limited to black and white, nor to red, white, and blue.

Bright yellow, gold, and orange banners welcomed the celebration of Buddha's birthday two days later. Following their tradition on this national holiday, Buddhists gathered in pagodas to pray for peace. The tradition still touched them poignantly: for the first time, I saw people pause to pray at a sidewalk shrine located diagonally across the block from our office. As protection from the weather, a special, temporary, pagodalike canopy sheltered the shrine and those who stopped, but it could not shelter them from the realities of life and death. There, at the corner of Phan Dinh Phung and Le Van Duyet streets, a Buddhist monk named Thich Quang Duc had immolated himself as a dramatic prayer for peace in 1963 to protest both the war and the cruelty of the Saigon government. After ten years, people still remembered him. The war still raged like a fire in their midst, consuming them. When would it end?

I flew to Pleiku. Maynard met me.

"Hi, Maynard! Happy Buddha's Birthday!"

"But it ain't so happy around here." He deliberately used poor grammar for emphasis. "Last night during the celebration here, someone threw some grenades into a pagoda."

The news I brought seemed painful, too. After weighing the options, MCC had decided to stop supplying foreign personnel to the Evangelical Clinic and to reassign the current Pleiku MCC medical staff. MCC agreed to continue providing other assistance, including medicines. Formalizing the transition fell to me. The hospital staff held a farewell for the foreign personnel before I left with them for Nhatrang to meet Max, who was serving as MCC director.

### Duck Eggs

Two days later, I drove to Pleiku on the route Maynard had taken to Nhatrang. Dr. Pradhan and I were returning to resolve leftover business.

A few miles north of the city of Qui Nhon, I turned west. One naked tree, without leaves or bark, lifted its bare branches skyward at the top of the long straight climb. Its lonely look struck me again. Then the highway swung north. We wound our way to Pleiku, inching across well-guarded, single-lane, makeshift bridges. Semi-camouflaged tanks, some with tents pitched beside them, lined sections of the road. Before reaching Pleiku, we passed a convoy of forty trucks that had stopped beside the highway. In the open crates, bald metal nose cones looked like rows of gigantic eggs: each of the trucks carried a load of bombs.

That evening, Pradhan and I visted Ursula, a VNCS worker from Germany. We heard a street vendor approach. Ursula's face brightened.

"Have you ever had half-hatched duck eggs?" she asked me.

"Nope. Not that I know of."

Pradhan chimed in, "You've got to try some!"

"Your experience in Vietnam would be incomplete without them. No visitor to Pleiku should ever leave without eating some," Ursula declared. "How many should we buy for you, Jim?"

"Two or three?" Pradhan prentended to be helpful.

"I think he should eat at least four," Ursula insisted.

"Help, help, help! I think I'll be doing good if I can get one down and keep it down!" I tried to sound as firm as possible.

Back inside the house, each of us squeezed lime juice into a little saucer that held a mixture of salt and pepper. Watching the others, I tapped a steaming hot egg on the table to crack the shell and then peeled back one side. I dipped the exposed corner into the lime-salt-pepper mixture and took a bite of the hot, chewy, crunchy mass. It tasted reasonably good. As I continued the peeling-dipping-eating process, I tried to avoid looking at the well-formed creature or thinking about what was in each bite.

"Here. Have another one."

"No, thanks," I replied. "I'm doing fine, but one will be quite sufficient."

"Oh, but they're so nutritious! You really should have another one to keep you healthy."

"Thanks, but I think I'll quit with one."

I enjoyed eating the foods in Vietnam and readily said so—with one exception. I never said I enjoyed eating half-hatched duck eggs.

*Safety in Numbers?*

After sorting and packing MCC things in Pleiku, I chauffeured Pradhan to Nhatrang again where he joined the staff of the Evangelical Clinic. Then I traveled to Dalat for a joint MCC-Mennonite Mission Conference which ended just a week before both Maynard and Titus left Vietnam. I planned to vacation with them on the first leg of their trip back to the United States. The day before leaving on vacation, I moved my belongings from the house where Max and I had been staying to the MCC office closet. I had roomed with Max because the Hieu family had found a family to rent the house where Vinh and I had stayed.

Maynard, Titus, and I all noticed the pock-marked landscape in Cambodia (Kampuchea) as the plane descended for our first stop. We read raised letters on the airport terminal: Phnom Penh. The stewardess requested that ongoing passengers remain on board, so we craned our necks to see as much as we could.

Maynard pointed. "See those old planes over there? They're called 'Puff, the Magic Dragon.' See where those windows are missing?" He paused while we scrutinized the "tail-dragger" planes parked on the other side of the runway. "That's where the guns are mounted: Gatling guns that can each fire 6,000 bullets in a minute."

"I'd heard of them," I said slowly, "but I'd never seen any before."

"It doesn't take long for them to shred an area the size of a football field." Maynard sounded as if he had seen them do it.

Less than twenty minutes later, we had a close-up view of the "Magic Dragons" sitting quietly beside the runway as our plane took off for Laos.

Laos, known as the land of a million elephants, required a special travel permit to visit Luang Prabang, an ancient imperial city. After having our passports stamped, we bargained for a ride to the Vientiane airport with a friendly taxi driver in Vietnamese, English, German, and our limited Lao.

The Luang Prabang airport, located out of town, used a transfer bus like the one I had missed in Dalat. The bus rumbled across a dilapidated bridge at the edge of town. We wondered where to find the youth hostel for lodging.

A brief walk brought us to the hostel. Sleeping space with a straw mat on the concrete floor cost less than fifty cents a night per person.

A few blocks away, we ordered our supper in Vietnamese at a simple restaurant with a dirt floor. While we ate, the Vietnamese owner of the restaurant shared his hopes with us.

"How I wish I could take my family back to Vietnam! My youngest two children have never even been there. Politically, though, it just wouldn't be good for us to go back now. When we go back, we want to visit the whole country—the North, the Central, and the South."

Wanting to visit the whole country sounded familiar. Many of my Vietnamese friends in Vietnam had expressed the same longing. I, too, cherished that hope for my friends even more than for myself. The folk songs of Trinh Cong Son verbalized the aspirations: "We Still Have Our Dreams," "I Shall Go Visiting," "Hue, Saigon, Hanoi." His music had become popular in the early 1960s, but it sounded dangerous to the Saigon government. "In 1968 . . . the Thieu regime banned his songs on the ground that they weakened the will of the people to resist."[4] Despite the ban, his music had become my favorite.

Stone buildings—the glory of a bygone era—sat on top of the highest hill in Luang Prabang. After Maynard, Titus, and I climbed to the top, they silently permitted us to photograph them. We also photographed an ornate Buddhist temple courtyard nearby. I had inspected the numbers on my film cartons without detecting any tampering in the expiration date. My film recorded the lush greens nicely. Unfortunately, the film also recorded the bright gold as a sick green. The red trim turned green, too, and so did all the other colors.

*Uncle Sam's Fingerprints*

Our flight from Luang Prabang back to Vientiane covered rugged countryside bordering the Plain of Jars. Secret U.S. bombing—hidden from people in the U.S., but certainly not hidden from the people where the bombs fell—began in the Plain of Jars in mid-1964 to support the CIA-financed Hmong tribal army of General Vang Pao against the nationalist Pathet Lao. In 1968 and continuing into the 1970s, the United States Air Force and Navy jets flew 300 bombing missions there every day. Finally, the U.S. planes had dropped approximately two tons of bombs for (or against!) every man, woman, and child in the area.[5]

In Vientiane, we saw Pathet Lao Headquarters next to the morning market. Before we left Vientiane, a Christian and Missionary Alliance missionary commented, "I think a coalition government (including the Pathet Lao) would be quite workable if the Lao people were left alone." If a coalition government could work in Laos, I wondered if a coalition government could work in Vietnam. Although a coalition government provided a logical solution to end the war in Vietnam, both the United States government and the Thieu government still sought a military victory after the Paris Agreement because they knew Thieu would lose at the ballot box.[6] Laos and Vietnam—suffering sister countries saturated with U.S. government and military involvement—were waiting for an end to the fighting.

Titus and Maynard continued their journey to the U.S. I flew back to Vietnam. My vacation was over. The war was not.

# Chapter 7

# OCCIDENTAL ACCIDENT

*Time-out*

Like an irregular skyline, my favorite books sprawled across my desk in the MCC office. Blocking some books from view, piles of paperwork flanked a sturdy, pale green typewriter and challenged its control of the desktop center. In July 1973, my friends usually found me at the desk, writing speeches or memos, doing bookkeeping, preparing materials for new MCC workers, or studying for the evangelism course. After my vacation, I had rented a studio apartment, but I ate no meals there, entertained no guests there, and seldom studied there. My long hours at the office matched Mr. Hieu's overtime in engineering and Mrs. Hieu's in teaching and still allowed me to eat suppers with them.

One afternoon in mid-July, I quit work early. I walked past the neat rows of parked bicycles which belonged to students studying upstairs in the Student Center where I had taught English. After starting the blue Lambretta scooter and nodding to the elderly, unarmed watchman whose presence discouraged theft, I merged my way into the horde of bicycles and 50 c.c. Hondas in the noisy traffic.

I pushed the Hieu's doorbell and waited beside the blank, blue gate. The tall gate, made from solid sheet metal, prevented anyone from peering into the house and yard. Designed without an outside latch, the undecorated gate required someone to be home at all times. Then from a miniature hatch, a pair of brown eyes quickly recognized my blond hair and bearded face. The hatch snapped shut, and the gate swung open into the narrow front yard.

A cheerful, contagious mood swept over the group celebrating the first birthday of the Hieu's son. Vietnamese tradition transposed birthdays—except for the first one—to coincide with the Lunar New Year celebrations. When Tet—the Lunar New Year—arrived, everyone turned a year older.

In the midst of the food and festivities, silence gripped our gathering. Dan, the birthday boy, with empty hands, sat on the floor in the living room, ready to choose an object. Would he choose the tiny toy, bringing a fun-loving future? Would he pick the pen, foreshadowing a writing career? Would his hand reach for the book, anticipating scholarly pursuits? Skeptical that his fate depended on his choice or on astrology, I also doubted that my destiny rested on the fortune cookie proverb in my pocket. I soon forgot what Dan picked.

*Problem-solving*

The scooter and MCC van needed repairing. Furniture waited to be shipped to Nhatrang. Refugees in a Binh Tuy camp needed food. I lent a hand.

Sunday mornings, the bilingual service at the Mennonite Student Center on Phan Thanh Gian Street provided an opportunity for students to sharpen their English skills and for me to strengthen my Vietnamese. If the speaker used English, a translator rendered it in Vietnamese, and vice versa.

One Sunday, I addressed the group.

> The world is full of hate, bitterness, and violence.... Many people apparently think that the easiest response is to hate in return. In fact, that's the usual military answer: if someone hates you, you should hate him; if someone threatens you, you should threaten him....
>
> But it doesn't stop there: if the other side violates the ceasefire, then you should violate it a little bit more in order to teach them a lesson. If one side had guns, then the other side thinks it must have bigger guns.... But it doesn't stop there: people are trained that if you want to be "safe" and "free," then you must hate and kill the other guy first—before he can kill you....
>
> There is another way.... There is a peaceful solution.
>
> And it's no secret. It's not glamorous. In fact, it's incredibly difficult. It's the way of love.
>
> I can't guarantee that it will work. But on the other hand, not even President Nixon can guarantee that bullets and bombs will work. Bullets and bombs can destroy ... things, but they can't

destroy ideas, and they certainly don't destroy hate. In fact, they increase hate. . . .

If there is any hope, then the way of love is the basis for that hope. Love is the only way of breaking out of the vicious cycle returning hate for hate. . . . Love is the only power that can really change people, but love doesn't force people to change. And that's why love is such a big risk. . . . Love . . . knows that most people aren't willing to follow it. . . .

My ultimate loyalty does not belong to the U.S. government or to any other political government. My loyalty is to love alone. . . .

That afternoon Max, Yoshihiro Ichikawa—Hiro, for short—and I practiced singing "They'll Know We Are Christians by Our Love." Max served as guitarist; I could not carry a tune; Hiro, an MCC worker from Japan, wavered somewhere in-between. In the evening, we sang the hymn as special music at a wedding.

Someone must have read my thoughts: I was a thousand times more willing to speak in public than to sing in public. The Mennonite Mission had asked me to address a Bible correspondence course graduation the following Sunday. Interrupting my preparations, four new MCC workers arrived on Wednesday.

I wished for an extra day in the week, but Sunday arrived on time. I turned to John 1:1-14 for "A Refreshing Pattern."

We are surrounded by patterns: clothing patterns, time patterns, family patterns, language patterns. . . .

But in this Scripture . . . we are told about a refreshing pattern. That pattern is Jesus. Jesus was the Son of God, but He also gave us the power to become the children of God.

Why is that refreshing? We understand that . . . (God) is like a loving Father. . . . It's refreshing because Jesus gives us the power to break out of . . . the handcuffs of years and cycles of years, the handcuffs of tradition and ritual, the handcuffs of hate and bitterness, the handcuffs of scepticism and meaninglessness. . . .

*Begging the Question*

When Max and I craved delicious sweet-and-sour pork, we generally ate at the reasonably priced Ngoc Huong Restaurant nestled near the heart of Saigon. Once, dining there after dark, Max and I had chosen a front table so we could watch our scooter parked on the sidewalk nearby. A man shuffled into the light by the scooter. We watched him. He watched us. He squatted to wait next to a tree. We kept eating. He stood, inched closer to us, then hunkered again.

Conscious of the man's presence, Max and I had kept talking and eating. Because of his squatting position, the bottom hem of his tasteless green slacks angled well above his bony ankles. The torn plastic straps of his dirty beige sandals showed the wear and tear of countless miles. His faded army-green shirt probably once belonged to a U.S. soldier twice his size. Having lost both sleeves and all the buttons, the baggy shirt acted like a makeshift vest, exposing his bare chest and skinny arms.

The nearer we came to finishing our meal, the closer he came to our table. We said nothing to him. He said nothing to us. We finished the sweet-and-sour pork and most of the stir-fried vegetables. A third of a rice serving sat beside the soup broth. We stood to leave. I expected the old man to reach out, hands cupped and begging for the loose change Max received from paying the bill. His hands did not reach toward us. He did not say a word.

Before we reached our scooter, he, with the waiter's silent nod, grabbed a set of our chopsticks, deftly poured the soup into the serving bowl of rice, and quickly scraped the sparse vegetable leftovers into the mixture. Then lifting the serving bowl to his lips, he began shoveling the mixture into his mouth. By the time Max pushed the scooter into the street and kick-started it, the man had finished wolfing the food, nodded his thanks to the waiter, and disappeared into the shadows outside. I had never seen anything like that before. I was glad the restaurant had obliged the man with our leftovers.

Next time, Max and I recognized a similar situation much sooner. Two street boys, as shabbily dressed as the old man, sauntered to our table. A waiter appeared as fast as they did and shooed them through the wide-open front to the sidewalk where they stood silently, watching us eat. My stomach suddenly felt uncomfortably full. Max felt the same message from his stomach. Consequently, the rest of our delicious sweet-and-sour pork sat untouched. We each ordered a banana for dessert, then divided one. We left the other banana. We stood. Like hungry vultures already in the landing pattern, the street boys slid past us in the aisle as we left the table. We did not look back.

I wondered whether our pale-skinned faces had attracted the beggars to our table. Later, when I saw another personified hunger pang hovering near Vietnamese at another table, I knew others faced the same agonizing experience.

I led the four new MCC workers into the restaurant and requested a balcony table so we could eat undisturbed while I continued painting a verbal picture of Vietnamese culture for them. No beggars came to the main floor.

During one block of free time in the intensive orientation schedule, the new workers ventured downtown by themselves. Later in the MCC office, Claire, a Canadian like her husband Wally, asked a gnawing question. "Why didn't you tell us about the beggars?"

I gazed at the floor. I shook my head. "I don't know." Then I sat silent again. They had been caught unprepared, just as I had been.

Linda, a nurse whose parents lived in Kansas, made a sick face. "It was awful!" The last word, pronounced from the abdomen, sounded nauseating.

Her husband, Murray, concurred. "The place was lousy with them!"

The beggars had overwhelmed Wally, too. "We ran into them everywhere we went. What do you do with them?"

Linda gave me no time to answer. She still looked sick. "We saw this guy with amputated legs, pulling himself down the street with his hands, dragging his stumps along on chunks of rubber tires." I knew. I had seen him, too.

Wally looked at me, talking fast. "I gave this one kid fifty piasters. You can charge it to me personally."

I looked over the topics yet to be covered in the remaining orientation sessions. "Beggars" stood near the bottom of the handwritten list.

"Well, I had it here on the list of things to talk about," I began, "but obviously we hadn't gotten to it. It's a hard thing to deal with. Some beggars are fakes: they can make more money off us rich foreigners begging than they could from a regular job. But that's no real excuse. The beggars are people, too, caught in this whole mess." The four new friends all focused on me. I felt hollow and transparent. I had no solutions. Maybe that was part of their orientation. I told them about the restaurant where we had eaten.

"Even those who aren't beggars," I continued, "are having a rough time. Members of the Mennonite Church in Gia Dinh who somehow had the resources to survive and rebuild after their houses were leveled in military fighting in 1968 and again in 1972 now are at the end of the rope economically. The watchman at the church has eight children and can barely afford enough rice."

Because the latest session at the Dalat Inter-mission Language School had already begun, the new MCC'ers could not enroll in those classes. When I represented the Mennonite Mission at the Language School Board of Director's annual meeting, I described my headaches in organizing a separate language study program for the four new arrivals.

"Why not send them to Dalat?" the Director of the Board asked. "Four students—that's enough to open a new class. No problem."

No problem? How I had sweat over the situation!

Before he had left for Bao Loc, Max had made me responsible for language study for the new MCC couples. Consequently, I felt authorized to shift gears and gladly took the two couples to Dalat for the regular program there. I wondered why I had not thought of requesting a new class for them initially.

*Pain in the Neck*

Wally and Claire, Linda and Murray, and I arrived in Dalat before noon on Friday, and by evening we had completed arrangements for housing and for orientation to the language school. On Saturday morning we strolled to the central market to buy a few household supplies. Everything seemed in order. "Let's go see Max," one of the four suggested. "How far is it?"

Max was at Bao Loc, leading a work camp which he had organized for university students. Max and the work campers were helping the refugees there build houses. Bao Loc, home of the best jackfruit I had found in Vietnam, lay eighty kilometers west. With ten months of experience in Vietnam, I translated the distance into Western terminology for the MCC greenhorns.

"About fifty miles," I replied. "Actually, the more I think

about the possibility of seeing Max, the more logical it seems. We should have plenty of time to spare." I had already confirmed my Air Vietnam plane reservation back to Saigon for noon the next day. I did not plan to be late this time.

"This trip can also be justified as a part of your orientation," I continued, "because you've never seen a refugee camp yet, have you?"

They shook their heads. I had visited the refugee camps at Bao Loc once. The cramped, messy conditions had etched themselves into my memory. Hieberts and Ewerts, the two couples, should visit the victims of an inhumane war, too.

I borrowed a dilapidated Landrover from a VNCS couple in Dalat for the trip to Bao Loc. After winding through the lush, rugged terrain for two hours, we arrived in Bao Loc, but Max was not in town. We bounced a few more miles to the refugee camps. The Landrover splashed through potholes.

Long tents, row after row, came into view. The surface of the unevenly packed ground, which served as a roadway between the tents, was slimy. The soggy, unpacked ground was even worse. Mud clung to our shoes. Something heavy also clung to my heart.

Ignoring the problems, the government forced six thousand refugees to call this their home. Max was not here. Four thousand more refugees across an even less accessible valley doubled the tragedy. Max was not there.

The Landrover lurched back to Bao Loc. Once again, we drove into the imposing, centrally located, Roman Catholic Church compound which served as Max's work camp headquarters, but Max and his work campers were not there. We waited. If Max followed his schedule, I knew he and his group planned to leave for Saigon the next day. We wanted to join their festivities on this final evening of the work camp. After eating supper, we returned to wait some more.

We sat in the chilly Landrover; 8:00 p.m. passed. Then the church bells chimed nine times, and finally ten. Padlocks prevented us from using the rooms for the work campers. Five people sleeping in the Landrover sounded unworkable.

"I don't think Max is coming back anymore." The verbalized skepticism represented all four of them.

"He's got to come back," I reassured them, "because there still is an MCC van here which has to go to Saigon, but let's go talk to those guys again."

Earlier in the evening we had asked two students who lived on the compound about Max, but they had not known his plans. This time, they served us tea.

"Please, you sleep here tonight." They offered us their flat, solid, wooden beds. "Tomorrow, after you meet your friends, you can go to Dalat."

"But where will you sleep?" I asked them.

"Oh, we can find somewhere else to sleep. Don't worry about us."

By 7:00 a.m., in a drizzle, our gray Landrover left the courtyard of the gray church. Under the canvas top in back, Murray and Wally, both over six feet tall, sat on the hard plank seats that ran the length of the flatbed. Because the highway improved at Di Linh where we stopped to fill the gas tank, Linda and Claire climbed in back so their husbands could ride in the cab.

I planned to stop at the famous Gougah Falls to offset the disappointment of missing Max. I slowed to 45 m.p.h., expecting to turn beyond one of the numerous curves to the right. The road curved right again, down the side of a hill. As we entered the curve I thought—as I had so many times before, ah, this could be the one: I'll bet we're getting close.

Suddenly, the back end of the Landrover swung toward the center line, as if to pass the front end! My heart pounded. A car sped toward us in the left lane. To avoid hitting it or sailing over the steep drop-off beyond it, I apparently cranked the front wheels to the right. In the next instant I thought, hmmmm, that's the wrong way to correct for the skid. Perhaps a mechanical failure complicated the situation, too.

The tail end of the Landrover somehow missed the oncoming car; perhaps the car dodged us. The Landrover hit something: perhaps just the soft shoulder of the road. Nevertheless, the impact threw me from the driver's seat. I do not know where I landed or how many microseconds I lay there.

I recall staggering to the back of the Landrover, which was lying on its side, to look for Claire and Linda. There! Oh, no! Beneath the Landrover! Who had enough muscles to lift the

Landrover high enough to get them out? Help! Other hands joined mine. We strained, but could not budge the heavy Landrover. Someone discovered that both Linda and Claire had miraculously landed in a narrow ditch and could be pulled out without lifting the vehicle.

Bouncing in the cab had given Wally and Murray minor bruises. Linda was conscious, but in pain. Because of the stabbing pain in my neck, I supported my head with both hands. Claire lay limp and quiet. Was she dead or alive? No one answered me, not even Vietnamese priests who stopped to help us.

"How is that girl who was hurt so bad?" I asked in Vietnamese on the way back to Di Linh.

"She will be all right," said the Vietnamese priests who were taking us.

"Is she dead?"

"Don't worry. She will be all right."

"But is she breathing? Is she alive?" I had to know.

"She will be all right."

Their evasive answers made me more nervous. I knew the theory: they wanted to protect an injured person from reality, so they still refused to tell me. I slouched in the front seat, using the back rest to support my head and neck. Nerve endings in my neck shot at each other like a video game.

"I drove too fast. I'm sorry. Oh, this neck hurts. I drove too fast. It's my fault." I thought of Claire again. "Tell me is she alive?"

A million times, more or less, after we left the accident site I silently prayed, "Lord, forgive me! Don't let her die!"

Then I addressed the priests again: "My neck hurts, it hurts!" We had to get Claire to a hospital as fast as possible: "Hurry up, hurry up!" I wanted to know about Claire: "Is she still alive?"

"Don't worry."

Don't worry! But I was responsible for her!

I heard an unexpected whimper from in back. Claire! Yes! Alive! What a relief! Perhaps not conscious yet, at least she was alive. "Thank you, Lord!"

*Patient*

Wally and Murray hovered by me in the emergency room.

"We better call somebody to let them know what happened," Murray said.

"Yeah," I agreed. "Better try calling the VNCS guesthouse in Saigon."

"But what should we tell them?"

"Just tell them it's my fault, that I was driving too fast," I said.

"But what are we planning to do?" Wally asked.

"I don't know. But tell them the Landrover went out of control because it was raining and the highway was slick." I lay on an examining table.

"Okay. But what do we tell them about the Landrover? How do we tell them where to find it?" Murray asked.

"Uhm, tell them it's about fifteen kilometers from Di Linh on the road to Dalat. Explain to them that it's in the ditch because it went out of control. Be sure and tell them it was my fault."

"Yeah, we'll tell them, but do you think we have to stay at this hospital?" Wally still wondered.

"I don't care," I replied. "Nhatrang would be nice and friendly because we know the people there, but there's no way I can handle a seven-hour car ride with these short circuits in my neck. And Claire's even worse off than I am."

"Okay. Well, we'll call Saigon and see what we can do."

The melody and some words of a prayer hymn drifted into my consciousness.

Dear Lord and Father of mankind, forgive our feverish ways,
Reclothe us in our rightful mind, hm-hm-hm-hm hmmmmm.

An invisible, ponderous record player needle tirelessly retraced the grooves. Since sitting brought most relief, I sat supporting my neck with both hands.

The automatic record changer in my mind unexpectedly found a chorus I had sung in children's choir. The well-worn grooves felt reassuring. I quietly hummed along with the inaudible music.

Children of the heavenly Father safely in his bosom gather;
Nestling bird nor star of heaven such a refuge ne'er was given.

Though he giveth and he taketh, God his children ne'er forsaketh;
Neither life or death shall ever from the Lord his children sever.

The chorus soared through my consciousness, soothing my spirit. God was good. We were all alive, but even death could not separate us from God's love.

Thinking I might have reversed some lines, I silently switched them and edited a word or two. It did not matter. The bright chorus started over.

Murray and Wally, with a Vietnamese vocabulary of 25 words or less, had contacted Mennonite missionaries in Saigon and also arranged for a helicopter to fly us to Nhatrang. The army helicopter landed a few yards from our Di Linh hospital beds, flew us cross-country over the rugged countryside separating Di Linh from the sea, and landed at the Nhatrang Evangelical Clinic.

I appreciated the Vietnamese pilots for flying the military helicopter on a humanitarian mission. I could never stereotype them easily again, but ironically, their kindness and the permission from their commander blurred the issues. Although geared to kill, the military forces had helped me in a special way. Of course, they considered me a "friend": what would they do to an "enemy"? That question remained. The helicopter ride, though awkward for me as a pacifist, did not change my basic philosophy: Jesus called his followers to love and forgive everyone—even soldiers . . . of both sides.

During the first days after the accident, sleep took priority. Not sick enough to be hospitalized, I stayed in an MCC unit house on the hospital compound and slept in a sitting position on a new cushioned rattan chair that I had helped ship to Nhatrang. Demerol and Phenergan shots helped me sleep.

Hearing of my whiplash injury, someone found a padded plastic neck brace. I wore it night and day. It held my head up and prevented me from turning my head. When I wanted look to the side, my shoulders had to turn, making my lower back pivot. My whole body had become a massive owl's head, constantly turning this way or that way to keep it visually informed.

Compared to Claire, I was fortunate. Claire suffered from a concussion and also from a broken clavicle. A major body cast held her bones in place while they healed. In the humid tropical climate, that cast turned into an inescapable itchy prison without relief for several weeks.

*Live and Learn*

I learned that, while I had been driving to Bao Loc with the new MCC'ers to meet Max, he was taking the work campers to Dalat as a reward for their hard work. We apparently just missed meeting each other en route. Then Max and the work campers had spent the night in Dalat. The next morning while driving back to Bao Loc, Max had seen the wrecked Landrover, but did not know whose it was.

By mid-September, some three weeks after the accident, the doctor granted Claire permission to travel from Nhatrang back to Dalat for language study, so she, her husband, and I flew to Dalat once again. Their small studio apartment was half a block from the villa where I had stayed when in language school.

Linda and Murray, who had arrived back in Dalat a couple of weeks earlier, rented the same room that I had rented. The elderly landlady there insisted that I spend the night across the hall from Linda and Murray instead of renting a hotel room. That frail grandmother and I visited while sipping tea; then she, her energetic nine-year-old granddaughter, and I climbed the stairs. As I sat on the edge of the bed, the granddaughter slipped off my sandals and washed my feet to make me feel welcome. Such simple, but moving, courtesy! As they left, the grandmother echoed the doctor: "Now you get some rest."

Seeing Linda and Murray again was as refreshing as the nap. Linda, an RN assigned to teach in the nursing school at the Evangelical Clinic in Nhatrang, had shed the crutch used for her bruised leg. Murray, too, was cheerfully facing the hard work of language study.

Early on Sunday morning, restlessness displaced my sleep. At 5:30 a.m., I penned a letter to Claire, Wally, Linda, and Murray to apologize for the accident. A recital of miracles came to mind. We had filled the Landrover gas tank at Di Linh just before the accident, but it did not explode. No fire broke out. Although a sheer drop-off gaped at the left edge of the highway, we neither dropped off the edge nor did we hit any oncoming traffic. Linda and Claire, though lying under the Landrover, were not caught because they landed in a narrow ditch. There were no fatalities, and we all were recuperating marvelously. I breathed another thank you prayer.

Later, I also learned that the Landrover I drove that tragic, rainy day had a faulty steering mechanism.

*Nhatrang*

An MCC doctor in Nhatrang had given me permission to accompany Wally and Claire Ewert to Dalat on one condition: I had to rest in Nhatrang again before returning to the hectic pace in Saigon. The compound of the Nhatrang Evangelical Clinic, which housed the MCC personnel as well, sat on a beautiful beach. High overhead, sea breezes played with the branches of the coconut palm trees while the ocean waves rolled in with a steady, therapeutic woosssh. I enjoyed Nhatrang as much as Pleiku. Nhatrang felt like home.

My ingrained work ethic pushed me to feel useful in spite of the neck brace that I still wore day and night. As I became more mobile, I sought small projects. Initially, I tackled only one project per day: tightening washlines, fixing a door lock, or helping a doctor's son with mathematics. Helping fry bananas and make peanut butter enabled me to befriend the Vietnamese cooks.

I enjoyed the kitchens since I had always enjoyed cooking and baking. Consequently, after the MCC'ers left for the morning, I usually spent some time "practicing Vietnamese" talking with the cooks. They knew surprisingly little about Mennonites and the Mennonite peace stance. The situation was less surprising when I realized that many of the MCC workers at Nhatrang carried heavy work loads. Furthermore, because their skills were needed from the first day they arrived, foreign medical personnel often lacked the opportunity for full-time language study. After supper, the cooks returned to their homes, while the MCC workers spent the evening maintaining unit life or relaxing.

Thu, perhaps my age or slightly younger, cooked for the household where I stayed. Mornings, when I went to the kitchen for water to swallow my pills, she was already hard at work. We talked about Mennonites and war and peace.

One morning while I leaned against the sink cabinet, Thu was chopping vegetables for lunch. "My husband was in the military, and then we got word that he had gotten killed in some heavy fighting. We had a funeral for the mangled body. I was terribly sad."

"That's too bad." I had not known.

"I was so sad. I adopted a son and named him Thuan—kinda like my name."

"That's really interesting."

"I'd like for you to meet Thuan sometime. He's a growing boy. It seems like his clothes are always too small for him." She smiled.

*Passing the Test?*

Although introduced to the staff on an earlier trip, I occasionally "toured" the clinic and the nursing school again during my recuperation. Ly (pronounced "Lee"), the petite translator from the nursing school, had jet black hair that reached halfway down her back in long gentle waves. I felt honored when she requested my help on September 27, 1973, my father's birthday. I did not know someday she would meet my parents and the rest of my family.

"I need some help translating a nursing test." She spoke softly. "Would you be willing to help me?"

"Sure, I'd be glad to, but I'm not sure how much help I can be. My Vietnamese is still pretty weak."

"Don't worry," she replied. "Sometimes I'm not sure how to make a smooth translation, so maybe you can help me polish the English."

"Yeah, I can do that. Please have a seat."

She opened her notebook and pointed. "This sentence, for example. Does it sound okay?"

That sentence was fine. Sometimes I suggested an alternative word. I often turned to my bilingual dictionaries to confirm my suggestions.

"What's 'duong trap'?" She looked at me.

"I don't know. Let me check." I flipped the dictionary pages. "Hmh. Incredible. It's not in here."

"Could it be translated 'chyme'?"

"I don't know. I never heard of that either. Let me try looking that one up." I grabbed my dictionary. "Hmmm. Nope. It's not here either. How about checking different tones?"

"No, the tones are right."

"Sometimes the Northern dialect doesn't distinguish between an initial 'tr' and 'ch'," I recalled. "Let's try checking 'duong chap.'

There it is. But it says 'chyle.' I never heard of that either. This is a headache. I give up." Eight years later she and I faced a far more serious headache.

In 1973, however, we tackled the next nursing test questions. Working in installments, we reviewed the entire test before I left for Saigon in October.

*Second Verse*

During supper that first evening in Saigon, the Hieu family asked about the past weeks. Because they had rented their other house, Vinh and I no longer roomed together, but I still ate suppers with him and the Hieu family.

Typing in the MCC office the next day strained my neck muscles, so I walked to Max's nearby apartment to rest. The rent had expired on my studio apartment while I was recuperating in Nhatrang. Rather than pay for an empty apartment, Max had collected my things and hauled them to his new location on Phan Thanh Gian. Consequently, his apartment served as my new home, too. I survived the week by massaging my sore neck and resting.

On Sunday afternoon, a different pain attacked me. My neck ached. My eyes ached. My whole body ached. I had a fever. Sleep? Impossible! Whenever my bones stopped aching, I noticed the intense pain in my neck, head, and eyes. After an unsuccessful fourteen-hour marathon of fighting the pain, I boarded an Air Vietnam flight for the friendly Nhatrang Evangelical Clinic.

The doctor diagnosed a virus. He prescribed sleep and rest with the medications. My relaxed schedule allowed visiting, including a short walk to Thu's home where I met Thuan.

October 17, the day completing my first year in Vietnam, seemed normal. I won a Rook card game. A Buddhist monk immolated himself in Nhatrang. Life and death, joy and sorrow, were woven side by side in the daily tapestry.

*To Push or Not To Push?*

Two days later I flew back to Saigon, and by the end of October, Vinh and I moved into a new room that the Hieu family had built for us on top of their three-story home. Khoa, a friend of Vinh's, climbed the outdoor stairway from the floor below and accepted me into his circle of friendship. Like Vinh's family, Khoa had come from the North.

Since the war dehumanized and stereotyped people, my contribution—perhaps infinitesimal—to peacemaking included asking people from the northern part of Vietnam about their family members still there. I had asked Khoa, too. This time, he brought pictures of Hanoi where he had posed with a younger brother.

In mid-November, I accompanied Wally and Claire to Pleiku where they would work. Claire had miraculously recovered from the accident. Having coordinated the shutdown of the former MCC unit in Pleiku, I helped open the new unit.

Hoa, the only Vietnamese nurse working with the Montagnard staff at the clinic, told me her concerns. We also discussed our views of following Christ.

"I like your perspective about inviting people to follow Jesus instead of pushing them, but I'm terribly sad about two Vietnamese evangelists who visited my parents," she lamented. "My parents are still Buddhists, and when these two men came to the door and asked to come in, my parents naturally invited them in. These evangelists looked around the room, saw the family altar, and made fun of it. They told my parents, 'You're stupid for believing in Buddha.' "

"That sure wasn't very tactful," I said.

"My parents put up with it for a while, but the two men just went on and on about how crazy it was to follow Buddha. My parents are very gentle people, but finally they got so angry that they asked the two men to leave. Is that what evangelism is all about?"

"No," I replied, "not in my thinking. Evangelism is supposed to be good news. But those two men probably figured they had done their duty in presenting the gospel to two hard-hearted unbelievers. I think God holds people more responsible after they have heard the good news, but I don't think your parents really heard the good news at all."

I thought of Phuong-Hang, the MCC secretary. Just a month earlier, she had told me she had decided to follow Jesus. That exciting news and her additional comments confirmed my philosophy. She had admitted, "My friends ask me, 'Did those Mennonites force you to become a Christian?' " Chuckling, she had added, "I tell them, 'They pushed by not pushing!' "

More discussions and hospital board meetings in Pleiku and medicine orders in Saigon, left only one day—Saturday—for me to prepare a message on freedom for a Sunday morning service at the Phan Thanh Gian Center.

> Freedom, as illustrated by Jesus is the ability to choose—
>    it's the ability to choose right instead of wrong,
>    it's the ability to choose love instead of hate,
>    and take the consequences for your choice.
> In fact, if you choose to go to jail rather than do something immoral that your government may ask you to do, then going to jail is an expression of your freedom to say "no" to the government. . . . The choices are not always easy ones. But, by the grace of God and with encouragement from your friends and family, I believe that you will be able to walk down the road of freedom as it was defined by the life of Jesus.

On separate days in January, my diary briefly recorded a special struggle. "No neck brace all day . . . 36 hours without neck brace . . . 48 hours without neck brace . . . one week without neck brace." After that, the pages never mentioned the neck brace again; the neck brace had become a souvenir.

# Chapter 8

# WHERE IS GOOD NEWS?

*Made in the U.S.A.*

On December 19, 1973, heartbroken, I wrote to the pastor of my home church in Kansas. *The Mennonite* published my letter.

Dear Ron,

I'm writing while the facts are still fresh in my mind and while my stomach still feels sick from the story. . . .

Directly across from our office here in Saigon there is a large hospital with crowded wards. On one of the beds is a girl about my age paralyzed from the waist down. She is handcuffed to the bed.

Last night Pat Martin (an MCC'er) served as the translator for an American reporter who wanted to interview the girl. Later in the evening at our weekly Mennonite Fellowship Meeting, Pat shared the . . . story.

Two months ago Chi Hien went to the market and after she arrived there, a strange lady came up to her and asked a simple question—something like, "How much are those flowers selling for now?" It was a trap. The police were waiting. They picked her up and whisked her off to a neighboring province (like transporting a person across state lines in the U.S.). . . . The lady was from an allegedly communist area . . . and Chi Hien was suspect because she had been talking to this "communist sympathizer." The actual reason given for picking Chi Hien up was that her papers weren't up to date, but that was a lie because both her ID card and her voting registration card were up to date.

She was taken to the interrogation center. They wanted her to talk, to confess. . . . Electrical charges were applied to electrodes under her fingernails. She was beaten from the chest down with a square club. . . . When she couldn't stand up any more and would fall to her knees, she would be jerked to her feet again by the hair of her head and then kicked in the groin. More beating. . . . Then a cloth was placed over her face and she was forced to swallow three or four buckets of soapy water, and every time her stomach looked bloated, it was kicked to empty it. Then she became unconscious. That all happened the first day. She has been paralyzed ever since. . . .

And the legal process? Yes, she received a court summons but was unable to go because she was paralyzed.

Chi Hien was arrested two months ago. . . . She arrived at the hospital one month ago, and it was only at that time that her parents and family learned of her whereabouts. . . . They are too frightened to visit her often.

A plainclothes policeman took Pat and the reporter into custody because they didn't have permission to enter the hospital and visit patients (but that kind of written permission really isn't needed). Before leaving with the policeman, Pat took a close look at the handcuffs binding Chi Hien to the bed, and there she read the words MADE IN . . . (USA). The policeman spoke English, and upon arrival in his office in the police station he proudly showed Pat and the reporter a graduation certificate he received for studying in the United States at a police academy. . . .

*How Long?*

"How long will you stay in Vietnam?" one of the Hieu children asked me after supper. Xuan, the youngest daughter, sat on my lap looking up at me. Her oldest sister, the fourth grader, perched sideways on the chair next to mine resting her feet on the spokes of my chair. Hanh, the in-between sister, stood leaning against me on the other side; I put my arm around her.

"I'll be in Vietnam for about two more years," I replied.

"But we want to know exactly." Oanh, the oldest, scooted closer.

"Well, this is almost the middle of January, so from now till the middle of October is nine months, and then it will be another year: altogether, a year and nine months." I was not like the U.S. soldiers who had anxiously counted each day until they could cross the Pacific back to "reality."

Xuan protested, "I don't want you to ever leave."

"Mr. Jim, will you come back to Vietnam?" Hanh's whine told me she hoped I would.

I turned to her. "I don't know," I answered. Sooner or later, each MCC worker needed to decide whether to return for another term.

Mrs. Hieu pursued the issue. "Is coming back the decision of your organization or is it your own decision?"

"The formal invitation must come from MCC," I explained, "but one of the important factors is how I feel about it."

"So on what will you base your decision?" she questioned logically.

"I don't know. I haven't thought about it too much, but I know one important thing is whether I feel comfortable with the language." My answer seemed unsatisfactory, even to me.

"Why don't you just stay? You don't even have to leave." Xuan's kindergarten logic impressed me.

"That would be nice, wouldn't it?" I responded.

"Yes!" the children chorused.

"We'll be terribly sad if you leave." Oanh already looked depressed.

"You're just like one of the family," Mrs. Hieu said.

"I really feel like I'm part of the family, too." The Hieu family had opened their hearts to me. They had personalized Saigon, a bustling city of more than three million people. I not only recognized faces: I had a home.

*Resigned*

Then the blizzard struck—not a blizzard of snow, but of paperwork. "We'd like for you to start teaching the evangelism course right after Tet," the head of the Mennonite Mission informed me on January 15. My heart sank: only one week remained before Tet.

As time had permitted, I had read background materials, but I still lacked sufficient preparation to start teaching. The Mission had assigned the topic, and I had not brought any books to Vietnam to teach such a course. Since no Vietnamese textbook existed for the course, I had to prepare a course outline, find resource materials, prepare class lectures, and plan homework. Anyone in the Giadinh church—high school age or older—could enroll. I felt overwhelmed.

Instead of relaxing during the Tet holidays, I crammed for the course, afraid that my other responsibilities would devour my time after Tet. My hunch was right: coordinating medicines for the clinics drained my time and energy.

At the end of January, Murray arrived in Saigon to investigate why the Nhatrang Clinic failed to receive the medicines it had requested. He brought a letter from an MCC doctor there:

> We at Nhatrang are beginning to feel that we are approaching a crisis involving the availability of medicines. . . . Let me give you a few examples. . . . We are completely out of aspirin, APC, all cough medicine, ampicillin (an important antibiotic), long acting penicillin, INH (cornerstone of TB treatment), and digoxin (basic heart medicine). That is only a partial list. Also we are very low and will be out of the following medicines within one month if no new supplies are received: Iron tablets and injection, Insulin, 3 or 4 of the basic eye medicines, all forms of penicillin, worm medicine, and Flagyl (medicine for amoeba).

Vietnam Christian Service, which had coordinated the medicines, next door to our office, had given the responsibility to MCC where it fell to me. Obtaining medicines began with a request from the clinics. Our Saigon MCC office stamped and signed the requisition forms before submitting them to the Saigon government's medicine warehouse located in Phu Tho on the outskirts of Saigon.

Theoretically, the warehouse sent us computer cards detailing which medicines were granted. Then I needed to pick up those medicines, pack, and ship them.

I had cataloged the computer cards the warehouse had sent MCC and the few cards that Vietnam Christian Service had given me, but the Nhatrang Clinic had submitted pages of requests with no word about their status. Murray and I drove to the Phu Tho warehouse to track the medicines. Again and again we heard, "That request was denied." Again and again we asked, "Why weren't we told, so we could submit another request?" No one answered that question.

Murray and I returned to the VNCS office. The friendly VNCS secretary who had handled the earlier medicine requests was vacationing. The VNCS director's wife, sensing our desperation, thought she might find some information at the secretary's desk. Indeed, she discovered a huge pile of unorganized, untabulated computer cards and related materials that covered the past six months! Working with Murray on medicines left me exactly one day—Saturday—to prepare for the first evangelism class on Sunday afternoon, February 3.

The clinic medicines devoured my time again the following week. A bureaucratic run-around at the Phu Tho warehouse absorbed one morning. That afternoon, working into the evening, I organized the scrambled computer cards from the previous six months and tabulated the information. Except for informing the Nhatrang Clinic, I finally completed my homework on the terrible backlog.

The next morning, Vietnam Christian Service received both more computer cards and a call from the medicine warehouse to pick up more medicines for Nhatrang. I drove to Phu Tho, but returned empty-handed.

Late that afternoon, I typed a memo to the Nhatrang Clinic, describing the accumulated information about the medicine requests. Then in my frustration, I typed a memo titled "Saigon Medicine Coordinator—Termination Report" to the Vietnam MCC Director and to the Vietnam Mennonite Mission director.

> The following items are submitted to substantiate the claim that it is simply physically impossible for me to be medicine coordinator and Bible teacher at the same time. It does not say one is more important than the other: it simply says I cannot be both. . . .
> And this is Friday afternoon! and tomorrow is Saturday! and then comes Sunday—and THE CLASS. How can I possibly get prepared in time?
> There are other people available—they are even qualified (one is a fourth-year medical student . . . and they want and need work. . . .

No one else was ever hired. Instead, the directors promised to have one of the office workers assist me with the medicines, but other, more pressing responsibilities soon called him away, leaving me as swamped as before.

In the evangelism course, I emphasized God's personal involvement with people as a pattern Christians should follow to spread the good news. During those weeks of teaching, however, my responsibilities forced me to reduce my relationships with others. The irony hurt. No electrocardiogram could record the cutting pain in my heart. My words rang in my ears like hollow propaganda.

I felt exhausted and exploited, but grown men are not supposed to cry. The piles of paperwork on top of my desk mushroomed higher and higher. I piled piles on top of each other, only to find that another pile soon filled space I had temporarily cleared.

My work in Saigon seemed like a hopeless swamp, and I felt it draining the joy from my life.

Three years, I thought to myself. I had signed a contract to work with MCC for three years. I'll grit my teeth and see it through. But not a day more than that. Fortunately, future events kept me from saying good-bye to MCC at the end of three years.

*Listen to the Heartbeat*

In mid-February, I listened as Jacqui Chagnon reported to an American church group visiting Saigon about her own recent visit to the North. Her comments included observations about the Thieu economy:

> Eighty percent of the finances for the Thieu government comes from the United States. You can not get 80 percent of your finances from outside and still be called free. Furthermore, only one percent of U.S. aid to Vietnam is nonmilitary. . . .
> Even Eisenhower finally admitted that if the people of Vietnam would have chosen their own leader in 1956, 80 percent would have chosen Ho Chi Minh.
> In North Vietnam, surprisingly, English is the number one foreign language taught in the schools. As foreign language choices, even French and German rank above Russian.
> At the close of our visit in the North, we cried as our host told us how his home had been bombed at Christmastime in 1972. His children had been killed. He wasn't against the American people, but he was against the system. Then . . . we smiled with him as he told us that the previous day his wife gave birth to a son. He was able to laugh, and we did, too.

Then a gaunt-faced Vietnamese lawyer in sandals addressed the group. I listened intently.

> At first I saw communists as a personal enemy. Gradually I came to see that they brought liberation from humiliation and consumerism, and that there is no real conflict with Christianity. Capitalism and consumerism are more anti-Christian than communism.
> The U.S. says it is here to save us. Save us from salvation! If the U.S. would pull out, then the "refugees" could go back to farm their lands. For real rehabilitation we need a moratorium on U.S. foreign aid.
> The church, too, first of all must learn humility. We need a moratorium on missions. Use your money to solve problems in the

U.S. Or if you are concerned about physical suffering around the world, send your money to Africa where the situation is worse than in Vietnam.
As far as suffering, we are moral victims of Nixon. Let me close with a few lines from a poem.
"Man is not our enemy.
If we kill man, with whom shall we live?
The enemy is fear."

The next day, Earl Martin invited me to a new network of relationships. I needed a break from the medicine requests and hoped the opportunity would ease my heartache.

I hopped onto the battered, once-white, Lambretta scooter behind Earl, heading for the jail. Through his MCC assignment in Quang Ngai, he learned that a friend's brother was in jail on the outskirts of Saigon in Bien Hoa.

Earl turned his head slightly so I could hear above the roar of wind and traffic. "I promised him I'd try to meet his brother since I was coming down to Saigon. They're relieved that he's off Con Son Island. He spent five years in the prison there."

I raised my voice. "Why'd they throw him in jail in the first place?"

"He was on vacation—legitimately—when his military unit was attacked by the other side. They accused him of leading the assault against his own unit."

"Wow, what a mess!"

"Now he's in a 'temporary jail' waiting to be turned over to the other side—maybe next week. He must have decided that anything was better than rotting in jail."

The waiting room reminded me of a windbreak for cattle. Poles supported the roof; the windbreak only had a north wall. The first visitors had squeezed together on the few, hard, wooden benches. After getting a number from the clerk, Earl and I eased between people sitting on the dirt floor and then sat beside them.

"Here," a woman beside us offered in Vietnamese, "you can sit on a corner of this blanket."

"No, thanks." Earl shook his head. "A little dust won't hurt our clothes any. Did you come to visit somebody from your family?"

The woman looked healthy. A large shopping bag of fruit and

vegetables rested against one leg. "My husband. I keep trying to see him. I haven't been able to see him a single time in three years. It's awful, I tell you."

Earl led the conversation. "Do you have any children?" he asked.

"Four of them. Sometimes I don't know what to do. I keep bringing fruit and vegetables for him, but I really would like to see him." Then she added, "What are you doing here?"

"A friend from Quang Ngai has a brother in there." Earl nodded toward the jail across the road.

"But you're Americans, aren't you? Why do you have to sit out here and wait? Can't you just go on in?" She popped the questions.

"Sure, we're Americans, but we aren't in the military and we don't work for the U.S. government," Earl explained. "We're with a church organization working for peace, so we have to wait out here like everyone else."

"You really speak Vietnamese fluently," commented an elderly woman sitting behind us on the bench.

Earl and I both smiled. "Oh, it's good enough to get around," he replied.

A smile broke across her wrinkled face, too. "I'll bet you've got a Vietnamese wife, huh?"

"Nope. My wife's an American, too, but we got married here in Vietnam, and we've got two children. What about you? Do you have a child here?"

"Me? No. I've kind of adopted a girl in jail here. She doesn't have any family to take care of her. Poor thing! She's only sixteen. Got a twenty-year sentence for talking back to a judge after a peace demonstration. I try to get out here as often as I can."

Earl turned to address the woman on the blanket again. "Does your husband get the food you bring?"

"Some of it gets through, but even then he doesn't eat it all. The prisoners share what they get from outside because the food inside is so bad."

Nearly two hours later, the clerk called our number. We crossed the street and entered the prison compound. A guard ushered us into a narrow room with two long benches and told us to wait. An official in a crisp uniform stalked into the room and into position behind a desk at the far end. His curt questions symbolized authority, although we did not know how much power he held. He left. We waited. Two more hours elapsed.

A guard appeared in the doorway. "We are very sorry," he began, "but you will not be able to visit the prisoner today. Here is a signed slip from him to indicate that he received the money you brought." Earl accepted the scrap of paper bearing the handwritten message. The guard gestured. "You may leave this way." Our "visit" was over.

Halfway across the road, Earl suddenly angled toward the waiting area instead of continuing toward the scooter. The woman on the blanket rose. "Did you get to see your man?" she asked.

"No," Earl answered, "but we did get a note from him saying he got the money we brought for him. You haven't been in to see your husband yet?"

"No, and visiting hours are about over." She sighed. "I'll still wait awhile. If I can't get this food in to him today, I'll try again tomorrow."

*Intermission 1*

Twice during the next months, I left gloomy, pressurized Saigon. My first opportunity came in March. I represented the Mennonite Mission in Dalat at a Bible Translators' Institute sponsored by the United Bible Societies. At the Dalat Institute, Protestants and Roman Catholics offically worked together on principles of Bible translation for the first time in the history of Vietnam.

The Institute asked me to lead devotions one morning at the beginning of the second week. To prepare, I reread *The Politics of Jesus* by John H. Yoder and chose the words of Jesus recorded in Luke 6:27-36 as my text.

> Mennonites have always emphasized religious toleration. In Europe, both Catholics and Protestants persecuted Mennonites....
> God wants the walls between people to come down.... But the Scripture we just read does not mean that we should only love each other at this Institute. It means much more than that....
> Jesus had political implications for his time. He spoke about a

kingdom, his baptism was like the ordination of a King, and the three distinct temptations were ways of becoming King. . . . Jesus was interested in visible, new relationships between people. . . . Our Scripture this morning said, "Be merciful just as your Father is merciful." God makes the sun shine and the rain fall on both North Vietnam and South Vietnam. . . .

Not only was Jesus relevant, he was the example. He said, "Follow me"—and his diciples saw the price. He told his disciples, "Love your enemies," and on the cross he lived it as he prayed, "Father, forgive them." Through the whole New Testament, whenever people are told to be like Christ, it is based on the example of the cross in two ways: 1) disciples are to be servants and 2) disciples are to love. . . .

I believe the way of evangelism is the way of peace. . . . If we look at 2 Corinthians 5:18-19, the good news is that God was making friends of all. . . . Peace is at the heart of the good news. The good news is that God is our King, our President, our Leader, and not Nixon or Heath or Wilson or Thieu or any person . . . our loyalty is to God. . . .

The church must lead Vietnam in reconciliation. Part of the excitement of this Institute is that the walls between Catholics and Protestants are coming down, but if we are to be faithful to what we translate, we cannot stop there. It will not be easy: Jesus promised us a cross. But he also promised us that he would never leave us.


During one supper at the Institute, I sat beside a Catholic priest who was a New Testament professor at a university in the southern delta of Vietnam.

"I believe that we need to use the Bible as our guide," I commented in our discussion of peace. "That means that it is possible to live under various political systems."

"I agree," he responded. "I myself lived in the North for ten years, so I know what it's like, but I think it's better here in the South—even with all the evils there are here."

"But do you think the differences are worth fighting a war over?" I asked.

"My students don't think so. They don't want to go to war. I personally think that poor people can legitimately defend themselves. Self-defense is justified, and that includes Vietnam's fighting the U.S. which is trying to steal what little Vietnam has."

"It makes me sad to think about all the U.S. has done in Vietnam." I chose simple words in Vietnamese because I could not recall more sophisticated ones, even though I could understand them in context when others used them. I expressed one other related concept. "I think the U.S. has had many bad schemes in Vietnam."

"Maybe you know that President Diem never wanted U.S. troops in Vietnam."

"Yes, I know." Hieu had told me.

The Vietnamese priest continued. "I think President Diem, who did work for peace, would have been better than President Thieu."

"But if the elections would have been held in 1956, I understand that 80 percent of the people in Vietnam would have voted for Ho Chi Minh. Do you think that is right?"

"Yes, I think so. In fact, Ho Chi Minh probably would have been the best leader for all of Vietnam. But the Saigon government was reprimanded—" (here he slapped the back of one hand with the other in a quick, dramatic gesture) "by the U.S. whenever we tried to talk peacefully to the other side," he continued.

Since 1954 the U.S. was the major roadblock to peace. The top levels of the U.S. administration neither wanted peace in Vietnam nor did they want U.S. citizens to discover that fact.

Senator Ted Kennedy raised questions about the U.S. involvement in Vietnam. On April 3, 1974, just a week after my discussion with the Catholic priest, *The New York Times* printed the text of a telegram from the U.S. ambassador in Vietnam to Secretary of State Henry Kissinger: "I think it would be the height of folly to permit Kennedy ... the tactical advantage of an honest and detailed answer to questions of substance raised in his letter."

# Chapter 9

# MIDTERM

*How Hard?*

The Friday after Easter, I sat behind my desk, reflecting on the week. I rolled a sheet of typing paper into the pale green, manual typewriter nestled between the piles of papers on my desk, set my fingers on the home position, and started typing a report to MCC for possible publication.

Today is Friday. A normal day. Exactly one week ago was Good Friday. On that day as I was traveling home, I met a convoy which was headed into Saigon ... fourteen army-green two-and-a-half ton trucks ... loaded with brand-new tightly wound barbed wire. Barbed wire. A contemporary crown of thorns. For Vietnam. Against Vietnam. On Good Friday. Made in ... (USA).
"Father, forgive them because they don't know what they are doing."
Jesus rose on the third day. How many days will it be till the Vietnamese (especially, Mennonite) church rises up and says NO to war? How many days will it be till the American (especially, Mennonite) church rises up and says NO to war? Three days? Three years? Three centuries?
"Father, forgive us for taking so long to say NO decisively. ..."
Today is Friday. A normal day. So was yesterday. And the day before yesterday ... the day before yesterday? Hmmm ... Wednesday ... hmmm ... April 17. Let's see ... November, December, January, February, March, April—yes, on April 17 I had been in Vietnam a year and a half. Exactly. Wednesday was such a normal day. ... The entire morning was spent tabulating computer cards related to medicine requests from the MCC-sponsored hospital in Nhatrang. The afternoon was spent studying ... (a book by David Augsburger) in preparation for the next session of the Bible class on evangelism that I am teaching at the Gia Dinh Mennonite Church. After supper with the Vietnamese family ... (where) I'm staying ... I played with the children for about an hour. ...

A normal day. A normal year and a half. What has been accomplished?

*Politically.* Not much. The war goes on.... Both sides have committed atrocities. You've probably heard plenty about the other side, so let me tell you about this side—the Saigon government. Every time I've been in Pleiku since the "cease-fire" I've seen loaded bombers fly out of the airport—and they return empty. Only one side has used bombers. This side. Made in America. News is still censored. Justice is a joke. Freedom is a farce. It's still illegal to be pacifist. Thieu's reelection in 1973 was rigged. But the U.S. Ambassador likes Thieu.

*Personally.* First of all, think back over how faithful you've been during the past year and a half, and then I'll share with you.... Okay, I've spent time playing with children, praying for peace, learning the language, listening to tears, sharing some humor, sensing people's despair, writing some poetry, welcoming new friends, talking about Mennonites, tackling balancing books, studying the Bible, shipping some medicines, running some errands, reading some books, helping "orient" MCC'ers, hurdling some "short-circuits," teaching some English, training some Christians, admiring the flowers, abhoring the barbed wire, wincing at gunshots, working at answers, asking some questions, doing little things.

On October 17, 1972, I arrived in Vietnam. Exactly one year later— on October 17, 1973—in Nhatrang a Buddhist monk immolated himself as a prayer for peace. On that day I, too, was in Nhatrang, but how hard was I praying for peace? How hard were you? And now it's six months later. The war goes on and on. Who is praying for peace now? One and a half years left in my three-year term: how hard will I work and pray? How hard will you? And how long?

*What the Bible Says*

The next day while I was typing in the MCC office, a friend stopped to visit. His stocky neck and his square shoulders matched his penname: Manh Tuong (literally, Strong Wall). His bulging arm muscles carried his weight on crutches because his legs had lost a childhood duel with polio. His wide, friendly smile made his measured lurches from side to side on the crutches seem less awkward. When Max held the screen door open for him, he saw me leaning back behind the typewriter.

"Is your work keeping you busy?" he asked me.

"Yeah, too busy," I replied. He muscled his way to the blue divan and lowered himself onto it. I continued, "Getting medicines and teaching the Bible classes out at Gia Dinh really keep me swamped."

Only a short section of his leg braces showed around his shoes below his trouser cuffs. His legs stuck straight out until he released a knee lock in the braces hidden by the trouser legs.

The three of us shared our concerns about the war and about the situation of political prisoners. The Thieu government had jailed Manh Tuong for helping translate a book documenting the involvement of politicians in the drug traffic in Southeast Asia. Consequently, his penname "Strong Wall" reflected a spirit much stronger than the muscles in his upper torso.

"Jim, I'd like to ask you for something." He spoke softly, like usual.

"Sure."

"I'm wondering if you've got an extra Bible you could let me have."

"Certainly!" I answered, surprised. I slid open one of my top desk drawers where I stored several paperback copies of the individual Gospels that the Bible Society in Vietnam produced. "Now these are just the first books of the New Testament." I pulled out one Gospel at a time. "This is a new translation into Vietnamese which I like much better than the old one."

"Thanks a lot." He smiled. "Do you think you would also have an extra Bible in English that I could have? That way I could compare them." Since his English was excellent, his request was natural, but I had not thought of that when he first asked.

"I've only got an extra copy of the New Testament in English, which is where you probably want to start reading anyhow." I slipped it from the row of books perched on my desk.

Max came to the rescue. "This Bible was running around the office and ended up on my desk. I don't think anybody claims it, so you can have it."

If Manh Tuong felt flooded with Bibles, he did not show it. "Thanks a lot, Max." He smiled and then explained, "You see, the first person who ever talked to me about Christianity was the interrogator who beat me up in jail. After beating me up he told me, 'You should become a Christian because Christians accept situations as they are and don't come into conflict with the goverment.' I'm interested in finding out if that's what the Bible really says."

"Well, that's sure not how I interpret what the Bible says or what Jesus taught," I declared. Touched by Manh Tuong's sharing and surprised that he was still interested in the way of Jesus, I searched for something relevant to say. "A lot of Christians use the Bible to justify going to war, but I think the words of Jesus are very clear against going to war. In fact, if that interrogator had really taken the words of Jesus seriously, he wouldn't have been beating you because Jesus emphasizes enduring suffering instead of inflicting it."

"I like your interpretation a lot better than his. We'll have to discuss this some more after I've done some reading." He straightened his legs by hand, clicked the locks on the braces, and swung himself into a standing position. "Thanks, again, to both of you."

# Chapter 10

# IT CAN'T HAPPEN HERE

*Alive!*

An MCC conference in Nhatrang at the beginning of May allowed me to "tour" the kitchens again. When Thu, the cook with the adopted son, noticed me approaching, she fairly flew to meet me at the screen door.

"My husband came back!"

"Your husband?" I was afraid I had misunderstood the Vietnamese words.

"Yes! I just spent a week with him in Quang Ngai. I'm so happy!"

"Wow! Congratulations!"

"Here, have a cookie. Careful, they're still hot."

"Thanks. How'd you know I was about ready to steal one?" I asked.

"Simple. I saw you eyeing them." She grinned.

"You're a good mind reader. Now tell me more about your husband. I thought you had said he was dead. You even had a funeral for him."

"Right. We'd been married about a year and a half when he was caught in some heavy fighting. The military told us he had been killed and sent us a body." She continued arranging cookie dough on the cookie sheet. "The body was in such terrible shape we couldn't recognize it, but we assumed it was his. We put up a nice gravestone, too. That was back in '68."

"Six years ago."

"Yep, six years already. He came back when prisoners were *trao doi*."

"Excuse me, what does *trao doi* mean?" I had followed the conversation in Vietnamese until that point.

"It means both sides give back their prisoners," she explained.

"Sure, I understand." I just remembered that it meant *exchange*. "It's almost as if a dead person has come back to life. I'm really happy to hear about your husband."

"Help yourself to the cookies. Why are you so bashful? I'm making plenty." She paused. "For me it's great, but we have no idea whose body we buried. The tombstone with my husband's name on it has been destroyed now."

"Yep, probably no one will ever know who was buried there. So, is your husband in Nhatrang now?"

"No, he's stationed in Quang Ngai, and after six months there, he'll be able to request a transfer to Nhatrang."

"That'll be great, but you mean he had to go right back into service?"

"Yeah, but I was able to spend a week with him in Quang Ngai. I'm so glad to have him back!"

"I'm sure! Thanks for sharing that good news. I'm going to take another cookie, and then I've got to get ready for an MCC conference."

Smiling, she said, "Go ahead—take two."

*Soaked*

May also brought the beginning of the rainy season. I had begun riding a bicycle to and from work, and the afternoon rains seemed to deliberately wait to dump their fury until I started my ride home to the Hieu house. To describe the situation to my niece, I wrote, "If you want to know how it feels . . . have your Dad climb up a stepladder and pour a bucket of water on your head. . . . "

My youngest sister and her fiancé had chosen July for their wedding. When MCC gave me permission to attend, I immediately began planning for the trip. At the central market in Saigon, I shopped for trinkets to give family members.

"How much is this?" I pointed to a dull brown, ceramic, elephant-shaped, toothpick holder.

"Two hundred and fifty piasters," the wrinkled, little, old woman replied.

Les and Cynthia stood through two sermonettes: one by my brother Don, one by me. Though Don and I shared many similarities, he was married, I was not.

What advice could I give the special couple on their wedding day? Several years earlier, I faced a similar question as officiating minister for my other sister Vernell and her husband Paul. For Les and Cynthia, I chose an extended analogy based on one of their Scripture texts and on my life overseas.

> The Scripture passage from Ruth mentions several commitments—
>  e.g., your people shall be my people,
>   your God shall be my God.
> But there is another commitment that is implied:
>  "your language will be my language"
>   because ... Hebrew ... and ... Moabite ... were different.
> In order for there to be real unity between people
> —in order for there to be real communication—
>   there must be a language in common.
> And after learning a language people can never be the same,
>  so I would like to suggest some parallels
>   between married life and learning a language.
> The challenge ... is to learn God's language—the language of love.
>  You committed yourself to this task at ... your baptism
>   so you have some idea of what it is like.
> Marriage isn't the only way to learn God's language,
>  but as you commit yourselves publicly to each other today
>   there is a ... rededication of yourselves to God.

The analogy touched the purpose and the setting of language study, the discipline and the patience, the humor and the pain, the repetition and the reward. My sermonette ended. The ceremony itself ended. Soon another Boeing 747 whisked me away from the refreshing days in Kansas and back across the Pacific to Vietnam without stopping overnight in Korea.

*Sunsets, Sunflowers, Sunburns*

In Saigon, separated from Kansas by only twenty-four hours of flying time, I tried straightening out my directions once more. In Kansas, the poets and the people saw the sun set in the west. Consequently I always felt uneasy when I saw the sun setting east of the MCC office in Saigon.

Just concentrate, I told myself. I pictured driving in Kansas to help me reorient my directions in Saigon. The attempt—so logical—failed. I knew that I traveled north to get downtown from Phan Thanh Gian Street and south to the Tan Son Nhat Airport, even though the map indicated just the opposite.

Several pounds of roasted sunflower seeds accompanied me from Kansas to Vietnam; I rationed those seeds among my friends. Eating roasted watermelon seeds was a traditonal pastime at Lunar New Year celebrations.

After supper at the Hieu home, I recounted my adventures on the trip.

"What are those things?" one of the children asked.

"Sunflower seeds!" I beamed.

"How do you eat 'em?"

"Well, you know at Tet we eat watermelon seeds, and you eat these the same way—only these are bigger and fatter." I showed the family how to use the front teeth to crack the seeds and expose the salty tidbit inside. Then I continued, "I brought them back with me from Kansas. The sunflower is the special state flower of Kansas."

Enthusiasm greeted one seed after another. The empty bag left just one question: "Mr. Jim, why are there three times more empty shells by you than by any of the rest of us?" We laughed. I had done most of the talking and still managed to amass the largest pile of empty shells.

The first Sunday in August, the Hieu family invited me to Vung Tau on a family outing. Five adults and four children squeezed into one light blue Volkswagen "bug." After a moderate amount of time in the ocean under the piercing sun, I relaxed under a huge umbrella on the beach because I sunburned easily. Unfortunately I was already sunburned: my legs turned vermillion. Vinh, my roommate, teased, "There are three kinds of meat: well done, medium, and rare. And I'd say your legs are rare!"

I had finished the evangelism course just before leaving for Kansas. The pastor of the Gia Dinh Mennonite Church, however, had told me earlier, "I think you won't need a translator for the next course because you can teach it in Vietnamese." Consequently, after the Kansas wedding, I stuffed seminary class notes and textbooks into my briefcase for my next teaching assignment.

Because the refugee problem escalated, Hiro, the MCC worker from Japan, and I investigated some resettlement camps near Binh Tuy. The Saigon government had promised land and money to the refugees. The promises rang hollow.

MCC had asked the two of us to visit the refugee resettlements to suggest a position for MCC's response to the situation. We made three recommendations.

> 1. We would counsel waiting . . . before committing ourselves to any program (of assistance).
> 2. Certainly MCC should not become involved in the distribution of relief goods—we encountered no requests for relief goods— the people want what has been promised to them: that's all they're asking for.
> 3. Because of our interest in peace and reconciliation we should keep alert to the political implications of the resettlement program.

By referring to political implications, Hiro and I implicitly opposed the Saigon government's use of the refugee resettlements (1) to control people, (2) to grab land which it did not formerly control, and (3) to continue appealing for U.S. government funds which never reached the intended people. Seeing people—refugees—used as pawns in a destructive political game saddened me.

*Splitting Image*

Back in Saigon, yellow propaganda banners with bold red letters stretched from one side of the street to the other and waved in the wind above the traffic. The Saigon government used billboards, too, in its campaign to influence people. One slogan attracted my attention and brightened my sermon at the Phan Thanh Gian Center the last Sunday in September.

> Today I want to talk to you about "Nothing." Let me start with an example. . . . This is a balloon (already inflated). It's just an ordinary balloon. (I let out the air.) How many of you saw anything come out of the balloon? Obviously no one saw anything come out of the balloon. Now I'm going to blow up the balloon again. . . . Now I'm going to let go of it. (We watched it sputter around.) Did you see anything come out of the balloon this time? No. But whatever was in the balloon was powerful enough to push it along. That's how it is with us.
> What really motivates us is quite unseen—for example, love or

hate. Can you . . . buy me three kilos of hate? Or what does seven liters of love cost? Even though we can't see them, they are still very powerful.

How many of you have personally seen President Thieu? If you've never seen him, how do you know he exists? Why trust what he says?

How can we know God exists? Why trust God?

Perhaps you have also never seen any communists. How do you know they exist? Why trust them?

The first point is this: we need to trust somebody. . . . Whom do we trust? and why?

Let's start with a slogan put up by the Saigon government. . . . Let's change it a bit and try to use it as a pattern:

Don't only listen to what the communists say,
But also look carefully at what the communists do.

So if the communists say one thing and do another . . . we won't follow them.

Now we need to substitute "the Saigon government". . . .

Don't only listen to what the Saigon government says,
But look carefully at what the Saigon government does.

And if the Saigon government says one thing but does another, then we won't follow it either.

For ex-president Nixon, the test would look like this:

Don't only listen to what Mr. Nixon says,
But also look carefully at what Mr. Nixon does.

Obviously, Mr. Nixon didn't measure up as president. . . . Now let's test Jesus:

Don't only listen to what Jesus said,
But look carefully at what Jesus did.

Jesus meant what he said. There was integrity in what he said and did. For example, he said, "Love your enemies and pray for those who persecute you." And Jesus did just that. . . . Perhaps the best example of this is at the cross: here we have a Man who loves his enemies, here we have a Man who prays for those who killed him. So Jesus passes the test. And that's why I've chosen Jesus to be my leader and not the communists, not the Saigon government, not Mr. Nixon, not President Ford.

The second point is the cost of following a leader.

It's quite clear what government leaders expect: you are to give your complete loyalty, you are not supposed to ask any questions, you are supposed to love their friends and hate their enemies.

What does Jesus expect? Simply stated, he expects us to live like he did. (I read the text: Luke 6:27-36.) In other words, he expects us to love everyone. . . . It's easy to worship Jesus, but it's hard to follow him. He himself said, "Why do you call me 'Lord, Lord,' and do not do what I tell you?" (Luke 6:46.)

I think that everyone has the feeling that life is sacred—at least human life, at least the life of family and friends. War seems radically wrong because it destroys human life.

The Bible has a beautiful poetic way of saying it: God breathed the breath of life into man. But what is that "breath of life"? No one can see it. No one can give it. But it's there, and it's real. And people can take it away: shoot a person—bang! (I punctured the balloon.) The pieces are still there. You can see the pieces, the bones, the body, the feet, but the spark of life is gone.

The military objective under the direction of government leaders is to destroy life. The objective of Jesus and his followers is to help people live and love. So you need to choose.

Various leaders and organizations may try to force you to choose their way. But Jesus won't force you. Mennonites won't force you. Love won't force you—because that's how love works: it doesn't force anyone. It's up to you to choose a leader and to make sure you know why you chose to follow that leader.

Sad news struck in September: the youngest brother of Trang, one of my language teachers in Dalat, was killed in action. He had been wounded in April when a mine exploded, but he recovered, returned to action, and now was dead.

The book *Confessions of a Workaholic,* by Wayne E. Oates, also touched me.

A ... dyed-in-the-wool workaholic ... usually is both talented to begin with and has acquired a set of highly marketable skills. He is much in demand. If he has no effective internal way of rating his priorities ... he collides with himself in the face of the many demands laid upon him: he is a perfectionist but he commits himself to so many people for the use of his skills that he cannot do his job well.[1]

That description came too close for comfort. Earlier in the year, I had an awful hunch about my impending work load. Then I felt the hunch turn to reality: I saw the work piling up. Instead of helping me say "no" to more work, Mennonite Mission and MCC gave me more responsibilities because the rest of their personnel in Saigon also had too much work to do.

I wondered how to change an oppressive system. I wondered how to change my priorities. Good news? Where? When? For whom?

# Chapter 11

# HAPPY NEW YEAR?

*Legacies of War*

I flew to the beautiful coastal city of Nhatrang to serve as the official MCC representative for the Nursing School Graduation Ceremony on October 2, 1974. Besides visiting with the MCC'ers and with Ly, the translator who hoped to participate in an MCC exchange program, I also strolled to the kitchens at each of the MCC unit houses. Visiting the cooks carried the fringe benefit of sampling their latest delicatessens.

Thu, the buoyant cook whose husband had returned, seemed reserved as she washed the dishes. "There's still some dessert left from last night."

"Guess a bite won't ruin my appetite for lunch." I found the dessert. "How's your husband doing? Is he getting ready to move to Nhatrang?"

"He won't be coming to Nhatrang," she mumbled.

"Seems like he should be able to request his transfer about now. You think the upper crust won't let him come?"

"No, that's not the problem. He doesn't want to come."

"Hmm. Strange. I figured he'd want to live close to his wife."

"At first things were fine." She stopped washing dishes. "But when I told him about my adopted son, he didn't believe that I had adopted him. He thought that I had been unfaithful and that the boy was mine, so he left me."

She gazed down silently, as if to study her hands dangling in the dishwater. She turned away. In a quick move, she raised her right shoulder, tilted her head to wipe an eye on the short sleeve, and resumed washing dishes.

"That makes me sad, too." I put my fork and empty plate on the counter. "Coming back was such happy news, but his not believing you is sure sad."

"I never expected that to happen. I told him the truth, but he didn't believe me, so now I've just got to keep going like before he came back."

"Yeah, there's no other way. I hope some day he'll accept the truth."

"Who knows? He said he was never coming back anymore." She paused. "Did you like the dessert?"

"Sure did. I always enjoy coming to Nhatrang because of the good food."

The next day I flew to Pleiku to help situate a new MCC family there. On vacation, Ly and another nurse arrived by bus from Nhatrang. For a one-day excursion, I took them to Kontum to visit the Minh Quy Hospital.

Accustomed to uneventful flights from Pleiku to Saigon, I was unprepared to find the conversation on one flight overwhelming. One of the Christian and Missionary Alliance (C. & M. A.) missionaries, who was translating the Bible for a Montagnard tribe in the Pleiku area, happened to be on my flight. He and I chatted while boarding the plane and sat together.

Soon after takeoff, the missionary peered out of the window and remarked flatly, "I used to like to go hunting in the jungle down there near Banmethuot, but then (after a while) there were too many animals in the forest—'two legged animals.' " His cool words sent a shiver through me and left me speechless.

*Mountains and Rivers*

When Max left for a four-month furlough at the end of October, many of his responsibilities fell to me. My longer hours at the office limited my time with the Hieu family. Getting home late at night also required waking someone—if not the whole family— with the noisy doorbell; the blank, blue gate could only be opened from the inside. Saving minutes by living closer to the MCC office looked promising. MCC emphasized personal relationships, and I, too, had stressed them. Yet at this time, I had to consciously cut back. Work finally forced me to move out of the Hieu home. The decision cut like a knife. Recalling enjoyable times with the family only increased the pain of leaving, but I needed quiet time alone, otherwise my work threatened to crush me.

Other reasons also entered the picture. The Hieu children were growing up. I had influenced them for a year and a half already. The time had come, I felt, for parents and children to have supper together without a foreign face.

I felt worst about telling my roomate Vinh, but almost paradoxically, I felt obligated to tell him first.

"Vinh, at the beginning of next month I'm going to be moving out."

"Why, Jim? What did we do to make you so sad?"

"No, no, it's not you or your family that's the main reason I'm leaving," I tried to explain. "It's all the work I've got to do, the late hours which bother the family, and the long distance from here to the office...."

Vinh was not satisfied. "If it's anything we've done, please, Jim, please forgive us. Don't worry about bothering us: you're a part of the family, we don't mind opening the gate for you. As for the drive to the office, there's a proverb which says, 'The road isn't difficult because of the mountains and the rivers, but it's only difficult if the heart isn't willing to travel it.' "

Exhausted, I had gotten home close to midnight again. I did not know what to say. I resented the distance from the house to the office, but he was right: the problem was not the miles, but my unwillingness to fight the heavy rush-hour traffic each morning. By working late, I at least avoided the evening rush hour. I felt guilty taking time to talk to friends because of the medicine orders that waited for me. I felt guilty writing letters home, even on Saturday or Sunday, because I could have done other work during that time. I hated punching the buzzer at the Hieu gate, bothering the family late at night. Things had mushroomed. My decision was final. I tried to explain.

"I'm sorry to see you leave," Vinh concluded. "My sister's family will be sad to see you go. Please don't forget us. Please come and see us."

"I'm certainly sad, too," I replied, "but I feel I've got to live closer to the office. I'll do my best to come back and visit, but I've got so much work to do, I don't know how often I'll be able to come."

"We really don't want you to leave." He intended to maintain our friendship. So did I. He turned off the light.

The next morning, by the time I hurriedly dressed for work, Vinh had already left. Perhaps the children heard my blurred stacatto descent on the three flights of stairs: zip, zip, zip. They waited for me at the bottom.

"Are you really moving out?"

"Don't go!"

"Why are you leaving?"

Their mother hushed the sad chorus and addressed me quietly, "Is it really true that you are leaving?"

I promised to consider moving back if my work decreased when Max returned.

*December Defeats*

December 1974 lunged at me like a blurred, grotesque nightmare. At the outset, packing, banding, and shipping medicines to Nhatrang and teaching English confronted me. Max had started buying nonprescription medicines for a few political prisoners and had begun assisting their families financially. Substituting for Max in that program opened a new side of Saigon to me.

Max had coordinated the Saigon side of an MCC people-to-people exchange program. In his absence, I completed the remaining details for both of the Vietnamese participants, Phuong-Hang, the former MCC office secretary, and Ly, the nursing translator from Nhatrang. Since government clearance for them looked imminent, they visited the office regularly. Consequently, I asked Ly to help me integrate medicine request lists from Nhatrang, Pleiku, and a one-room, MCC-sponsored clinic at the Mennonite Center in Gia Dinh.

I helped the MCC workers arriving for a mid-December conference with their multitude of business requests. During the midst of that beehive activity, a letter from Max arrived, asking me to determine the feasibility of a spring semester, short-term voluntary service program for a Kansas premed student.

On Monday, December 16, the Saigon government finally

granted the passports for Ly and Phuong-Hang, the two Vietnamese participants in the MCC exchange program. They still needed visas, plane tickets, and traveler's checks prior to their departure to the U.S. on Thursday, the 19th. At the airport, following Vietnamese etiquette, I requested permission to shake hands with Ly; Phuong-Hang shook hands with me without an additional request.

The last MCC workers who had come to Saigon for the conference left on the 20th. On Saturday, the 21st, Dr. Willms and his family—destined for Nhatrang—arrived in Vietnam, burdening me with their orientation.

Without having finished preparing my message, I stood before the audience at the Bible Correspondence Course Graduation Ceremony on Sunday, December 22. I turned to a favorite passage: the first chapter of John. The translator had never translated in front of an audience before. I felt tired and afraid my words would sound hollow. My stomach felt squeezed into a small hunk of lead.

> If I say "Christmas is a very happy time" but have a sad face, would you believe me? No! But if I smile when I say "Christmas is a very happy time," you will believe me. . . .

I lowered my voice and argued with the translator in Vietnamese. I did not like his translation. He tried another rendering. I did not like that one either and quietly told him. I turned to the audience, using English again.

> Christmas is God speaking sincerely to people. But God is invisible, so he needs to speak in a very special way.

I emphasized "the Word became Human," but I felt that the translator missed my point. I stopped to explain quietly in Vietnamese. We plunged ahead. I challenged the translator once more. I do not know how I concluded the message. When I stopped speaking, I headed for the door. I did not look back. I had been a failure. Everybody knew it. Stunned, I slumped into my chair in the MCC office downstairs—elbows on the desk, palms under my chin.

Orientation for the new doctor and his family began on Monday. Nhatrang still needed an ophthalmologist. On Tuesday,

December 24, a telegram announced the arrival of the new ophthalmologist in Saigon on December 26 or 27, but did not say from where he was coming, the flight number, or time of arrival!

*Snow Job*

Tin, the office assistant, also clamored for special help from me. He bargained as president of the Gia Dinh Mennonite Church Youth Fellowship. "Wednesday afternoon is the Christmas party for the young people in our church, and I'd like for you to be Santa Claus."

I disliked Santa Claus as much as I disliked Nixon. "No, I'm sorry," I explained, "there's really no way I could agree to that. Santa Claus symbolizes the worst of Christmas."

"Aw, come on," he pleaded. "It's just for fun. You'd be perfect."

"Look, Santa Claus is a Western symbol. There's no snow in Vietnam."

"Sure, I know there's no snow here," he argued. "Everybody knows that. So Santa Claus is just for fun. Won't you do it?"

"I really don't want to. Santa Claus is so superficial. I want to stay as far away from Santa at Christmas as I can."

"Please. This is just a fun party, so Santa would fit right in, see?"

Could Tin be right? Could Santa ever be "just for fun" without jeopardizing the light that Christ brought? Unconvinced, I finally succumbed to Tin's pleading. "Okay, I'll dress up as Santa on one condition: no one will tell the youth group who Santa is."

"If that's what you want, I won't tell them," Tin declared, relieved.

"There is one problem. How can I be Santa without saying a word?"

"Just use a different voice," Tin suggested.

"Nope. My Vietnamese would give me away." I paused. "I can't use English, either. Say, why can't I use German? Santa is a foreigner, right?"

Tin balked. "But if nobody can understand you, that won't be any fun."

"Wait a minute." Another brainstorm hit me. "Get some

brave person from your youth group to serve as translator."

"Nobody in our youth group knows German." Tin sighed.

"No, no, no. I myself only know a bit of German. I'll put together German words as if they were a sentence, and the 'translator' acts as if he is translating, but says whatever he wants to."

"That might work." He still sounded skeptical.

"Well, I'm sorry, but I will not speak Vietnamese or English, and this is the only way that I can think of to solve the problem."

"Okay, we'll do it that way," he quickly agreed.

No rain fell on December 25 as I slid into the knee-high boots that I had bought for the mud in Pleiku. The boots, nonfunctional for two years, just fit Santa. Tin had collected an oversize red stocking cap, assorted pillows for padding, and a brownish red housecoat with furry trim. Bright red lipstick clung like putty to my lips, cheeks, and the end of my nose. White flour softened the dark color of my beard and moustache.

A brave "translator"—a high school student—stood beside me on the outdoor platform. He was scared. So was I. I had one consolation: no one in the crowd knew German. I smiled and waved at the happy group.

I started by saying I had come from the Northland: *"Lieber Freunden, ich habe aus dem Nordland gekommen."* I looked at my young translator and nodded.

He cleared his throat and began in Vietnamese with a formal introduction. "Honored guests, ladies and gentlemen, brothers and sisters, and friends."

While he spoke, I planned my next sentence. Surely Santa had a long trip before arriving in Vietnam: *"Es war ein schreklich langsam Reise sein."*

The translator coughed once—a nervous, quick cough—and continued improvising valiantly in Vietnamese: "It is a great honor for me to be here."

I wished he would expand his "translation." I thought fast: snow—beautiful, but cold. *"Oh, das Schnee sieht shoen, aber es ist wirklich kalt."*

The translator suddenly caught the spirit of his task, gushing the words. "I just arrived from the North Pole, but my reindeer were too bashful to bring me the last block so I had to walk!"

The crowd laughed and clapped. I had nearly exhausted my German vocabulary. Why not admit that? *"Ich habe etwas vergessen sehen sein."*

The translator ignored my poor German grammar. "It was terribly cold when I left the North Pole," he said, "and it was just starting to snow."

Waving enthusiastically to end my speech, I said Merry Christmas and Happy New Year: *"Froeliche Weinachten und ein Glueckliches Neues Yahr!"*

The translator, warmed to his work, rendered my words: "I want to emphasize how honored I am to be able to share in your celebration today!"

Oh, no! How could I tell him I was done? I wanted off the platform. I pointed down and smoothly recited the German dative prepostions memorized in high school: out by with after since from to—*"Aus bei mit noch seit von zu."*

The translator, imitating me, pointed to the front rows of seated children. "There will be treats for everyone, and if you'll just stay in neat rows, everything will run even smoother."

Smiling, but desperate, I grabbed the translator by an arm and led him to the stairs. I paused to wave once more. The translator understood the direction: "And, now, I'd like to come down and meet you personally."

I pulled bags of candy from inside my bulging housecoat and distributed them, proclaiming, *"Froeliche Weinachten!"*

He imitated my sweeping style: "Merry Christmas!" For the first and last time, my German and his Vietnamese actually meant the same! Of course, no one in the audience would ever know, I thought.

I learned later that Mary Martin, one of the Mennonite missionaries, had observed quietly from a crowded corner of the courtyard. She knew German!

Thursday and Friday, December 26 and 27, I met every flight from Bangkok and Singapore, searching for a doctor I had never seen. I sandwiched those airport runs between orienting the Willms family and handling business details for them so we could fly to Nhatrang on Saturday, the 28th. Since the new ophthalmologist had also accepted the Nhatrang Clinic as his work location, I made

Saturday plane reservations for him as well so we could all fly together.

According to the passenger list for the last flight on Friday evening, the ophthalmologist had arrived on it. I had missed him! How could I find him in a city of three million people? He knew no Vietnamese. How could he leave with us the next day? I finally located him at a missionary guesthouse by phone. Saturday morning we all flew to Nhatrang as scheduled.

*What's New?*

January 1975 brought hardly any improvement. On February 7, diarrhea and vomiting struck me like lightning. And struck again. And again. A doctor diagnosed amoebic dysentery and ordered me hospitalized. Three days and seven bottles of IV fluid later—on the eve of Tet—the hospital released me.

On Tuesday, February 10, New Year's Day on the lunar calendar, Nhatrang called our MCC office: the new ophthalmologist wanted to leave on Friday morning for a conference in India. Fortunately for him, government offices—normally closed for three days at Tet—reopened on Wednesday. Meeting his deadlines, however, left me minimal time for recuperating or for visiting friends.

Wednesday morning, I completed the forms for the ophthalmologist's Vietnam exit visa and submitted them. Unfortunately, I submitted them to the wrong office and spent most of the afternoon retrieving the forms and his passport. Travel agencies waited until Thursday morning to open, so buying his ticket topped my agenda that morning. The travel agency only accepted dollars in cash, so I scurried back to our office without a ticket. My second trip produced his ticket. That afternoon I completed and submitted forms for his tourist visa to enter India. He arrived in Saigon that evening, expecting to leave the next morning. In the morning, I chauffeured him first to pick up his visa for India and then to the airport in time to meet his flight.

He expressed much gratitude for all my efforts. Deep inside, instead of feeling like a cheerful giver, I felt robbed. Feeling exploited, and then feeling guilty about feeling exploited trapped me in a vicious cycle.

The next week, 165 cartons of medicines from the Inter-church Medical Association (IMA) arrived for the three clinics. In spite of the huge shipment, IMA did not fill all of our requests, so I divided the shipment based on families of medicines and the packing lists. After the paperwork, I supervised the sorting, repacking, and shipping.

That Saturday, after four months of being buried under my work load, I felt that help had arrived when I met Max at the airport. Serving in Vietnam with the Mennonite Mission, Luke Martin had become MCC director. Although his work allowed him minimal time with his family, Luke had helped me at Christmas in 1974 and at Tet in 1975. I still have unanswered questions about those months, but life is too short and too fragile to harbor bitterness.

# Chapter 12

# TO STAY OR NOT TO STAY

*Another Moving Experience*

"I've been in Vietnam for eighteen years, and never before were things so disorganized here in Saigon," commented James Stauffer, head of the Mennonite Mission, as he shook his head. March was bringing a foretaste of April.

To pay debts, my landlady—a relative of the last king of Vietnam—unexpectedly sold the apartment complex where I was staying, forcing all renters to leave. I checked seventeen possible places to stay, none workable.

I had occasionaly chatted with an older man who worked for VNCS. He seemed uneasy about renting me a room, perhaps assuming I, as a foreigner, would want nicer accommodations. Finally, however, he agreed.

After turning off the main street just beyond a pagoda, I idled my scooter through the narrow space between two walls. Beyond a sharp jog, the pathway widened. Although his house was only two miles from the MCC office, motorized vehicles seemed rare on the tight alleyways in this section, so I turned off the ignition and coasted down the final, bumpy slope to his front door.

The walls of his house did not reach the roof, giving the structure an unfinished look even from the outside. He invited me into the sparsely furnished living room. The living room opened into the kitchen area where, next to a floor drain, two huge crocks stood half-hidden under the stairway landing. Overhead, a string stretching across the stairwell corner served as a makeshift rod for the plastic curtain which provided privacy for showering. A handy tin dipper lying on a ledge by the crocks provided the "running water."

The entire loft served as my bedroom. The low rafters provided convenient nails for hanging my mosquito net. Wide cracks in the single layer of flooring required caution: pencils could fall into the living room below, where the landlord and one of his young sons slept.

"I have one request." He glanced at me. "I'd appreciate it if you wouldn't tell too many people that you're staying with me."

"That's no problem." I, too, had a request. "What if an MCC'er like Hiro would like to stay here with me while he's in Saigon? Would that be okay?"

"Sure, but I just would prefer if your staying here didn't get around the VNCS office." Perhaps he wanted to avoid embarrassment about my stay in his unpretentious home. "You probably noticed how the neighborhood children gathered around when you arrived on your Lambretta. This is a pretty good neighborhood. The children here are curious, but you won't have to worry about losing anything. We haven't lost anything, and we usually go to Bien Hoa on the weekends to visit my wife and younger children."

"How many children do you have?" I asked.

"Lots of them! Fourteen children!" After he shared his concern for their education, we discussed other topics. When I did not understand his Vietnamese, he quickly switched to his extensive French vocabulary, testing whether I might find any similarity to an English word. His simple, open style impressed me. Our conversation included peace and war.

"What's this war doing to our country?" He immediately answered his own question. "It's destroying it. Pouring out all this blood—what's it accomplishing? Nothing. I sure hope it stops soon. We're all one people: why should we be fighting each other? I don't think it's God's will that people kill each other. What do you think?" He turned to check my response, perhaps wondering if he had said too much, though he knew a bit of my perspective from earlier conversations. His large, deeply wrinkled face looked tired.

I responded quickly, "I really agree with you. Unfortunately, the United States has been a complicating factor that's prevented reconciliation. And what really makes me sad is seeing Christians supporting the war and the killing. According to the words of Jesus, war certainly cannot be God's will."

"Both sides are people," he continued. In the midst of stifling propaganda, his words were like a breath of fresh air.

*What's Happening?*

The spring wind flipped the propaganda banners back and forth on every major street in Saigon. White words on a huge red banner proclaimed,

> The people are firmly determined
> —never to sell rice to the cruel communists,
> —never to talk to the brutal communists,
> —never to negotiate with the bloodthirsty communists,
> —never to lose to warmongering communists.

Red words on a yellow banner shouted at the people passing by, "We will never give up until the last communist is exterminated."

After a March MCC Conference, the Pleiku MCC workers temporarily could not return to Pleiku because the situation there had become unstable. They never returned to Pleiku. One sentence on the front page of the March 22 *Saigon Post,* an English newspaper, explained the instability: "President Thieu said he had ordered a strategic withdrawal from Pleiku ... because his forces were outnumbered four to one." Apparently only a few top military personnel in the Central Highlands had known of Thieu's decision at the time. When the rest of the people there suddenly guessed what Thieu had done, pandemonium threatened their sanity and their lives as many of them fled to Nhatrang.

The front page of that March 22 *Saigon Post* also carried an interesting headline in compact, newspaper style: "4 Religions Buck Draft." Among other changes, the new law drafted boys at 17 instead of 18 and canceled all deferments from military service for religious novices under the age of 21. The lead sentence in the article summarized the situation: "The four largest religious denominations in South Vietnam—Buddhism, Catholicism, Hoa Hao, and Cao Dai—declared Thursday their opposition to the new mobilization measures."

I sadly noted that the Hoi Thanh Tin Lanh Vietnam—the Evangelical Church of Vietnam—was not mentioned with the other four religious groups. In fact, the president of the Evangelical

Church traveled to the Bible Institute in Nhatrang with one message for the students: obey the government orders. Since the Evangelical Church held that view, then few people should have been surprised to find the same church counseling the Bible students the same way under a different kind of government after April 1975. I thought of Peter's message for church leaders: "We ought to obey God rather than men"(Acts 5:29).

"Communist Troops Open Fire on Refugees from Cheo Reo" headlined a UPI article by Joseph Galloway on that front page of the *Saigon Post*. Although dwarfed by the bold headline which fit the propaganda perfectly, one sentence in his article caught my attention. "Communist tanks in Quang Tri province on the North Vietnam border turned on their headlights after routing a contingent of South Vietnamese marines so the retreating troops could find their way at night, military sources said." Amazing! The so-called brutal, bloodthirsty, communist soldiers, instead of wiping out the retreating ARVN troops, not only allowed them to retreat, but helped them! Unfortunately, under other circumstances, the two sides were under orders to kill each other. Nevertheless, that humanitarian action by soldiers trained to kill enemies reassured me through the days ahead: a soldier—even a "communist" soldier—had a heart. I kept that front page.

In spite of the slanted headline and lead sentence about communists firing on refugees—troops and civilians—the article brought other surprises. "On other refugee routes Viet Cong and North Vietnamese troops waved at some refugees and troops that were . . . fleeing surrendered chunks of territory."

According to the article, "Communist troops tightened their grasp on eight abandoned provinces. . . . " "Abandoned provinces"? "Surrendered chunks?" What was happening? Why were the refugees—civilians and ARVN troops—running?

Murray Hiebert called from Nhatrang to describe the turmoil there. Several Nhatrang MCC workers flew to Saigon.

On March 25, we heard that Quang Ngai had been "taken over," that the other side—the "communists"—controlled it. Two MCC workers, Earl Martin and Yoshihiro "Hiro" Ichikawa, had voluntarily stayed in Quang Ngai through the changes, but we did not know their fate.

Earl's wife, Pat, and their children had come to Saigon earlier, but they held no advantage in knowing what happened in Quang Ngai after they left. In fact, a Quang Ngai acquaintance of theirs told them he had seen Earl being shot. An agonizing story, but reliable? We did not know. We tried to dismiss rumors, but we wondered how to handle purported eyewitness news of that kind.

Three foreign MCC workers still lived in Nhatrang, wondering whether to leave. Max flew to Nhatrang for discussions with them.

On the memorable morning of Sunday, March 30, at the student center on Phan Thanh Gian Street, the group celebrated more than Easter—a day when flowers bloomed in spite of barbed wire. The group also celebrated the public commitment of three new followers of Jesus. Prior to the water baptism service, each of the three students briefly recounted her own spiritual pilgrimage. Their sincerity and spontaneity moved me. Each of them had faced extreme family resistance to Christianity, necessitating secret Bible reading at home. The hostility in each family was gradually subsiding. Ngoc, one of the three, had participated in one of Max's work camps for university students. In her testimony, she credited both Max and me for influencing her to follow Jesus.

*Report from Nhatrang*

The next evening, the political upheaval in Vietnam tore at my heart again because it involved people close to me. The four MCC workers from Nhatrang, including Max, unexpectedly trudged into the MCC office where I was still working. They greeted me listlessly and slumped onto the furniture.

"Good night!" I exclaimed. "What happened?"

"We don't want to talk about it!" Linda snapped.

"We are literally drained," her husband, Murray, mumbled. Behind his glasses, dark shadows outlined his eye sockets.

Linda's eyelids drooped. "I'm sorry," she said, "but if I have to talk about what we went through in Nhatrang, I'll throw up."

Dr. Willms also appeared exhausted. His shoulders sagged. "I feel like I've betrayed my God," he murmured. Then he stared at the floor through the half-moon lenses in the glasses perched low on his nose. He slowly shook his head. "I don't know if God will ever be able to forgive me."

"That's enough!" Linda injected. "I don't want to hear another word!"

"We're all worn out." Max took command. "Where are Mrs. Willms and the boys? Is there any room at the VNCS guesthouse for Linda and Murray?"

After I answered those questions, Linda and Murray and Dr. Willms gathered their belongings and lumbered out the front door. I leaned back in my chair. Max rose sluggishly from behind his desk and hauled himself to the divan where he sat slouched with his feet resting on the coffee table. We sat silently. I refrained from asking the flood of questions inundating me.

"It was a mess," Max finally mumbled as he stared straight ahead.

"It must have been," I responded quietly.

"I never, never want to go through anything like that again." His words emerged slowly. "It was awful. We had a terrible time deciding whether to go or to stay. Just when we had made up our minds to leave, then someone would want to stay, and so we'd start all over again, and finally we'd decide to stay. And then it wouldn't take long, and we'd start talking again and decide to leave—except for Dr. Willms. He never wanted to leave.

"He said, 'I feel God is calling me to stay here, and besides I'm a Canadian so I wouldn't be in any danger.'

"So Murray decided he would stay, too, since he was also a Canadian.

"But then Linda said, 'If Murray stays, I stay!'

"So I said I was responsible for them and I was not going to leave them there by themselves. Since Linda and Murray weren't in terribly good health, I told them they should go to Saigon and that I would stay with Dr. Willms.

"At first they agreed, but then Murray had second thoughts. He told me that I was from Saigon, and that I didn't know my way around Nhatrang, and that since people in Nhatrang didn't know me, they wouldn't trust me. So he said Linda and I should go to Saigon and he would stay with Dr. Willms.

"But Linda said she would never agree to that. She said she was not going to go to Saigon without Murray and that that was final.

"So Murray said that he and Linda would stay and that Dr. Willms and I could go to Saigon.

"But Dr. Willms shook his head. He said, 'Not me! I believe God wants me to stay, and so I'm going to stay.' He said if I didn't want to stay, he would stay by himself.

"But Murray asked him how he could stay by himself when he couldn't even speak Vietnamese.

"Dr. Willms said he'd find somebody to translate for him and that nobody would want to hurt a doctor because he was there to help people.

"I asked him who was going to want to translate for him because the hospital had had too much help from the U.S.

"But Dr. Willms said he would simply tell the VC that he was Canadian.

"Murray about hit the ceiling when he heard that and told him that 'VC' was the worst thing he could call the other side. Then he asked Dr. Willms, 'How would you tell them you're Canadian when you don't speak any Vietnamese?'

"Dr. Willms said he didn't know and that this was a commitment between him and his God. He said he had to stay and face the consequences.

"So we all decided to stay, come what may. But then we got a call from the U.S. consulate saying the next flight would be the last one out of Nhatrang and that we needed to be at the airport in an hour. So we went through the whole thing again. That's how it was every day for the past several days. We just swung back and forth. If those crazy telephone calls wouldn't have come, the decisions would have been so much easier. We said the same things over and over. Finally we could hardly think any more. All of us were uptight. We couldn't relax any more."

"Man!" That was all I could say. I shook my head.

Max continued: "Nhatrang itself was a mess: all those people and those soldiers from Pleiku." He paused. "Those soldiers were bitter. They felt like they had been deserted in Pleiku. The top brass secretly left on their own planes and helicopters, but the rest had to find their own way out of Pleiku. So when those angry soldiers arrived in Nhatrang, they still had grenades, guns, and ammunition—which they used to take whatever they wanted. People were shot for putting up the slightest resistance."

How sad and ironic, I thought. The angry soldiers looted the very people they had been trained to protect.

Max was still unwinding. "Going to the bank was a nightmare. People got shot and robbed right in front of it. When we had to pick up money for hospital salaries, we went in a tight cluster. We tried to look nonchalant, but our hearts were pounding until we got the van unlocked and were on our way home.

"In all that chaos, though, I think the hardest thing was seeing Chi Nam, Wally and Claire's cook from Pleiku. When she first came onto the hospital grounds, we didn't even recognize her. Oh, she was in a terrible shape! You know how she always used to have a sparkle in her eyes and a big smile? She looked utterly defeated. We quickly put some food on the table for her and her children, but she was terribly listless. No, not listless, but she had kind of a dazed, frightened look. She didn't know where a couple of her kids were. Her clothes were torn, her hair was a mess. Man, I hated to see her that way. It looked as if she had cried so much that she couldn't cry any more. We wanted to give her some money, but she only took a little bit because she was afraid to be carrying too much money.

"Seeing her like that was almost too much for me to take. It was awful. We saw Chi Nam once more before we left. She didn't look much better. She said that she had panicked, and that the ARVN soldiers came around, demanding that people leave Pleiku and setting fire to the houses because they didn't want to leave any-thing for the communists. The soldiers also said the (Saigon) Air Force was going to bomb the city flat. Along the road, especially just before arriving in Nhatrang, the soldiers shot a lot of people who showed the smallest reluctance to turn over their money or valuables. She still hadn't found her other children, and she was worried about getting out of Nhatrang. We gave her some more money, but she still wouldn't take much."

Max stopped. I thought, Lord have mercy.

"Any word on Earl and Hiro yet?" Max swung his feet off the coffee table.

"Nope, not a word," I replied.

"I'm tired out. I'm gonna head for home."

I nodded. "Yep, you've obviously had a long day."

"Yeah, not just one day: the past several days—one day after another."

*Deciding to Stay*

In April, the exhaust fumes from the long years of war hung like thunder clouds over Saigon, threatening to explode and send the society into an unknown direction. The Saigon government clenched its teeth in fear: shortly after April Fool's Day, a new curfew in Saigon shut the city down every evening at 9:00 o'clock instead of midnight.

The Mennonite Missionaries and the MCC workers planning to leave Vietnam—including Dr. Willms—decided to use regular commercial flights rather than last-minute, U.S.-government, evacuation flights. On Monday, April 7, 1975, I bought the airline tickets for the entire James Stauffer family and for Luke Martin's wife, Mary, and their children.

That night I finished a long letter, begun the previous day, to my parents and other members of my immediate family in Kansas and South Dakota. Besides sharing my current activities, I also detailed my reasons for wanting to stay in Vietnam.

Sunday evening 6 April

At this point, Luke Martin and Max and I do not plan to evacuate from or be evacuated from Vietnam....

1. I think all three of us see our staying as part of our commitment to Christ and to His kingdom of peace and reconciliation. In some sense, the integrity of our years of witness is tied to our staying with our Vietnamese brothers and sisters through these days. The foreign Mennonites in Vietnam have always stood for peace and reconciliation ... and I have pushed the Vietnamese Mennonite Church as hard as I could to take these central issues of the Good News seriously in war-torn Vietnam. And now that Mennonite Church told the Mennonite missionaries that if all the missionaries leave ... because of the political-military situation, the church will be angry, sad, and lonely. Although recently I haven't participated in a lot of activities out at the Gia Dinh Mennonite Church, they still ... know who I am....

... new believers at our student center here on Phan Thanh Gian (Street) ... know my stance. I've preached ... the implications of Christ's lifestyle.... I've diagrammed the dichotomy between following Christ and following Caesar very clearly. I've let them know that our commitment to Christ does not depend on what kind of political system is in power . . . I need to stay for their sakes.

And outside the Mennonite community, there's a wide variety of Christians and non-Christians with whom I've shared . . . about peace. . . . (Now) I can stay and put my words into Jimshoes. Praise the Lord!

. . . leaving Vietnam at this time under the present circumstances has not been easy for any of the MCC'ers. . . . We have had such a unity of purpose that I could feel with them as they left. They left. I say that simply and uncritically. . . . Maybe in the near future or in the distant future some of them will return.

2. . . . we feel MCC should make its . . . resources available for Vietnam after any changes that may take place, and now it seems that the best way to do that is to retain a physical presence here in Vietnam throughout any changes. . . . Our staying should help make the seriousness of our commitment evident, and should be one way of trying to make clear that MCC is truly "a Christian resource for meeting human need" regardless of what kind of government is in power. Of course, we do not want to impose on anyone . . . but . . . we want to be able to respond immediately, and that is why some of our MCC'ers will be waiting temporarily in Bangkok.

3. Maybe a third response, suggested to us by one of our Vietnamese friends, would be simply to record the truth as we see it and experience it. I remember John Yoder's suggestion that perhaps

> only a Christian orientation permits a truly fair understanding of the facts of history. This is first of all the case because honest objectivity, respect for the truth apart from oneself, is possible only with the fundamental abandon of self-defense involved in Christian faith; second, the specifically Christian virtue of forgiveness should make it possible to see that even the apparent villain in historical conflicts is subject to causes not wholly his fault, and capable of some good; third, the virtue of repentance permits accepting for oneself or one's class or nation a part of the blame for what goes wrong in history; further the Christian hope makes it possible to approach the study of history in the deep faith that it will somehow make sense, that there will be signs of long-term purposiveness and of justice, and the Christian concern for human dignity, in the concrete form of the neighbor rather than in institutions or ideologies, enables the Christian historian to seek the meaning of history in personal and moral values, freed from the temptation to interpret primarily the story of regimes. . . .

Maybe the firsthand experience and the courage to share it could provide some alternative to the impressive propaganda systems which both sides and the United States are still using today.

I must say that I'm at peace with God and with myself in the decision to stay ... it currently has the approval of MCC Akron, the blessing of the Mennonite missionaries, and the support of the MCC'ers.

What will I be doing during the days ahead?

1. Clean off my desk—literally. In other words, finish up some MCC left-overs ... some memos.... And ... medicine orders.

2. For Mennonite Mission ... teach a Thursday evening Bible class for new believers (presently planning to focus on 1 Peter) and ... teach a Sunday morning English Bible class (continuing the study of the Gospel of John) ... teach some English classes here at our student center.... But in addition to teaching, I've agreed to serve as temporary head of the English teaching program here at the center.... I would like to start participating more regularly in ... the Gia Dinh Mennonite Church ... to lend them some support through these difficult days.

3 ... some personal things I'd like to do: Bible study ... meditation ... and study some Vietnamese history.

... Luke and Max and I plan to stay in the Mennonite Center on Phan Thanh Gian. And if there is a breakdown of public order in Saigon we would ... not go out on the streets at all. Maybe ... the best we can do is sympathetically "stand by": (like the) poem ... "God bless the friend who just stands by" ... and in that, too, there is courage and hope and peace. In the meantime we are working with several Vietnamese organizations in order to help displaced people and refugees....

... P.S. It's 11:30 p.m. Monday evening now.... The peppernuts that were shipped sea mail arrived today!

What did their letters say in response? An aerogramme from Paul and Vernell verbalized and summarized the wishes the whole family was sending.

Dear James,
We just received and read your April 6 letter.... We respect and admire your decision, and that of Max and Luke, to remain behind. It is your kind of faith and *agape* that Vietnam and the world needs, the kind that only God can give. You have our support and prayers in your decision and in your life in Vietnam....
(Then the handwriting switched from Paul's to Vernell's.) Yep. I knew you would, James! ... when someone asked what you were planning, I said, "Well, God sent him there, & he probably won't

leave until God tells him, too." I was secretly hoping you'd come home early, but after your letter today I feel that you did the right thing. . . .

Will mail continue to go in & out? Is yours censored?

This Thursday we're looking forward to meeting Ly (a participant from Vietnam in the MCC exchange program). . . . Mom & Dad have been keeping a close check on her schedule. . . .

If you can, keep writing & we will, too. . . . But there is power in prayer. . . . If communications ever do lag &/or I feel you're going through extra hard decisions again or in extra physical danger, I want to give that gift of fasting & prayer. . . . In other words, no matter where you are, you'll never be alone. May Jesus' love & power become more real & dear to you during this time, & may it help you to know that there are those who STAND BY THE ONE WHO "JUST STANDS BY"!

## Taking Charge

After I finished typing the letter to my family, James Stauffer, who directed the English program at the Center, and I discussed that program till past midnight. He planned to leave in the morning, so he and I also discussed the New Believers' Fellowship. Since the curfew prohibited travel on the streets, I slept on the divan in the MCC office.

While I was teaching a morning English class, several loud explosions suddenly thundered nearby. I dismissed class. A pilot from Thieu's own Air Force was bombing the Presidential Palace about ten blocks from the Mennonite Student Center. The bombs missed the Palace, and the late, but intense, antiaircraft fire also missed the plane.

After the violent racket ended, a new awareness of the unpredictable future lingered as I chauffeured the Stauffers to the Tan Son Nhat Airport. One by one, two by two, five by five, familiar faces left Vietnam. Since the building which housed the MCC Office and the Mennonite Student Center also had provided living quarters for the Stauffers, that evening I moved most of my belongings into a bedroom adjacent to the MCC office. Santa's boots, though, stayed in the unfinished loft I had rented just a month earlier.

The next day, as acting director of the English program, I revised the schedule and logged the income from recent book sales and student fees. That evening I taught an English class.

Studying 1 Peter confronted me Thursday because I had agreed to lead the Bible study for the New Believers' Fellowship that evening. Recalling that Clarence Jordan had referred to Peter as Rock Johnson, I began preparing an introduction to Peter. Vietnamese proper names included the word "Rock," so I transcended the awkward transliterations of the Greek and Hebrew by referring to Peter as *"Ong Thach"*—"Mr. Rock."

During my preparation, our office received a telegram bringing good news: Hiro and Earl were fine! As friends visited us, we shared the news with them.

Although I had attended the New Believer's Fellowship only once before, the group and I knew each other; we had regularly attended the Sunday morning services upstairs in the Student Center. The Fellowship met regularly on Thursdays in the Stauffer living room, which had just become the living room for Max and me. Grateful to be responsible only for the main Bible Study, I nervously sat through the opening prayer and hymns, worried that my material might take less than fifteen minutes to cover.

Together we checked the biblical references to Peter, first of all noting his names. Then we compiled a personal history of Mr. Rock like a job application and studied his role as a disciple of Jesus.

Exhausted, but pleased with the vigorous discussion, I laid the dwindling piece of chalk onto the chalkboard tray. Glancing at my watch, I realized that forty-five minutes had passed since I had begun! During the prayer time, I breathed an audible prayer in English. Afterwards, a handful of members asked about the Stauffers and asked if I was also planning to leave.

The Thieu government wanted to know who lived where, so on Friday Max and I registered the changes in the Phan Thanh Gian household with the local officials. With my bedroom less than ten steps from my desk in the MCC office, I finally had the most convenient housing arrangement possible.

On Saturday, I rang the buzzer outside the Hieu's blank, blue gate. The family had invited me for dinner. Visiting with the Hieu family felt like old times. Although months had passed, our friendship felt no gap. One question stood out: "Jim, when are you planning to leave Vietnam?"

I grinned. "In October at the end of my term with MCC!" Then I explained to the Hieu family why I planned to stay in Vietnam.

That evening, I climbed the wide, concrete stairway to browse through an art display on the rooftop of our Center. Although the refugee problems in and around Saigon confronted everyone, few people knew how to respond in productive ways. Art students, frustrated by the poor housing and shortages of food they had seen in the refugee camps, had asked MCC for permission to sell their paintings at the Mennonite Center to raise money for refugee relief.

With money my parents had sent me to use for a worthwhile project, I bought two paintings which appealed to me: a rain-blurred downtown scene, and a half-abstract portrait of legendary Kieu who dared to challenge fate. The tears of rainy skies seemed linked to Kieu's eyes.

## Two and a Half

Thursday morning, Luke and I walked next door to the VNCS office where a few friends had gathered to say farewell to a VNCS worker and his family. I edged in next to another VNCS worker who had helped me several times. The gaunt-faced Vietnamese man greeted me in Vietnamese. "Hello, Mr. Jim. When will you be leaving?"

In the context of those days, "leaving" meant joining the evacuation. "I'm planning not to leave," I replied.

His arms immediately swung around me in a quick bear hug. He said nothing. He did not have to.

Before long, he urged Luke, "You've lived with us, so now stay in Vietnam with us." If we stayed, he could bear the hardships of those days more easily. At last count, with the influx of refugees, 43 people lived in his house.

Later in the morning, Manh Tuong stopped to visit. He also supported our decision to stay, but for a different reason: "You really care for us, so you deserve to stay to see peace come to Vietnam."

For me, faithfulness to Jesus at that time meant staying in Vietnam, come what may. According to reports, some church members rejected their church membership since numerous church leaders, including foreign missionaries and Vietnamese pastors, had left Vietnam. I, however, had decided not to flee Vietnam like a refugee. Mennonite history, often the story of refugees and refugee relief, included other chapters, too. My staying seemed to lend integrity to my words emphasizing peace and love as the way of Jesus.

What about refugee relief? One university student from Central Vietnam was stranded in Saigon because the other side governed his home area. Unable to cross the boundary or to communicate with his family, he, like many other students, involuntarily became a refugee. Unlike many of the other refugees, he detested appealing to voluntary relief organizations and churches for help, even though Max had bought bags of rice for the students with MCC funds. "When you help out the hungry students," he told Max, "you are actually helping prolong the war because, if the students were hungry, then maybe they would make some demands on the (Thieu) government to let them communicate with their families in Central Vietnam. As it is, the students are fed, full, and quiet."

Answers to the dilemma of refugee relief were difficult. How could Mennonites do nothing in the face of such crying needs? On the other hand, how could we do relief work only to see our efforts thwart the call to end the war?

The two invitations to stay in Vietnam—one noting hardships, the other based on optimism—and the puzzle of responding to refugees lingered in my mind. That day, April 17, I had completed two and a half years in Vietnam.

As I was praying that evening, recent rumors flashed into my mind. "Lord," I prayed, "have mercy on Vietnam." A close relative of the Mennonite pastor had claimed to be an eyewitness to the massacre of the pastor's sister-in-law's entire family in Banmethuot in March, but a respected church leader who just arrived in Saigon reported that he himself rode with that sister-in-law and her family in a car from Dalat to Nhatrang. Who was telling the truth? This time, we believed the latter report. Contrary to rumors of cold-blooded killings by the communists, we heard stories that even overcrowded Danang was returning to normal under the control of the other side—"the communists."

Ironically, the outside world perhaps knew more about the

situation than we did in Saigon. The next day, Luke learned that the Thieu government banned all current *Time* and *Newsweek* magazines from areas of Vietnam still under its control. Maybe those magazines accurately described the situation. But who could be certain? Deep inside, I plead, "Lord, fill me with your integrity."

*Commitments*

That evening, Vinh invited me to a restaurant for dinner with his friends. After crossing the Saigon River, I parked my Lambretta scooter next to his 50 c.c. Honda at the edge of the dirt street.

"Hello, Jim. It's nice to see you." Built like a football player with a friendly smile, Trung spoke flawless English.

"Hi, Trung. I'm glad I could join you," I replied.

"Hello, Jim. When will you go?" Khoa was small-boned.

"Hi, Khoa. I'm not planning to leave."

"You aren't?" He looked surprised.

"No, I'm planning to stay. I haven't been working for the U.S. government or for the military, so I'm not planning to leave."

"He's a Protestant," Vinh explained to the ones who did not know me, "working for a social work organization." Several hungry customers who were not a part of our group arrived. "Why don't we pick out a table before they're all taken?" Vinh suggested. "Then we can sit and talk while the fish is frying." While we flocked toward a table on the makeshift front patio, Vinh told me, "This place has the best fried fish in Saigon."

The six of us sat around a battered metal table that rocked on the uneven ground where a sidewalk should have run. Vinh introduced me to his two friends that I had not met previously.

"We call him 'Mr. King.' " Trung chuckled as he referred to one of the guys that Vinh had just introduced. The smile vanished as he continued. "Tonight really isn't a very happy night for us, Jim. We're all good friends. You know why we are getting together? Some of us are planning to leave one way or another. We may never see each other again."

"That's right," Vinh agreed. "But—come on!—lets enjoy our time together. Now, how are we going to order? Each individually, or family style with one big fish in the center of the table?"

"We're all here to eat fish," someone said, "aren't we? So let's just get one big one." Others nodded their agreement.

"What are we going to drink?" asked Mr. King. "Shall we just order beer for everyone?"

Vinh responded immediately. "Jim doesn't drink alcoholic beverages." He turned to me. "What'll you have? A Coke?"

"Yeah, Coke is fine with me," I replied.

One of the guys teased, "Beer makes the fantastic fish at this restaurant taste even better, but you're going to drink Coke with it! What a pity!"

"That's no problem." I grinned. "They told me the same thing when I went to eat dog meat. 'The only way to eat dog meat is with beer.' Well, I had a Coke then, too, and the dog meat still tasted delicious."

"Dog meat? You ate dog meat?" They groaned.

"Sure, in a little restaurant in Thu Duc. It was really good. We had dog meat prepared five ways. Let's see: dog meat soup, fried dog meat, uhm, barbecued dog meat, dog meat sausage, and, uhm, there must have been one other way which I've forgotten. But I really liked it."

"I'm Vietnamese, and I haven't even ever eaten dog meat!" one guy declared. "The dogs will bark and bark when you're around. The smell never leaves you." We all laughed. He looked at me again. "What about half-hatched duck eggs? Ever eaten any of them?"

"Yeah, I can eat them all right, but I've never said that I enjoyed eating them. But I did enjoy that dog meat."

We stuffed ourselves on the fish. Finally, like a strange symbol of war and destruction, the fish skeleton—with unblinking eyes in its head—lay exposed on the platter. Our good-byes seemed awkward, too, in spite of the common theme: "Good-bye. Good luck." The unpredictability of the future limited our farewells to generalized well wishes. Perhaps our handshakes in the dim light appeared nonchalant to any observers, but to us they carried an air of finality. Whether individually determined to stay or to leave, we realized that the six of us would never sit around that table together again.

Monday evening, April 21, the radio carried President Thieu's lengthy, bitter resignation speech. The United States, he insisted, no longer supported him or his government. With his rigged elections, corrupt generals, and heavyhanded policies, I wondered whether his own people had supported him. My friends felt he had used politics and the war itself for his own gain. "I'm resigning tonight," he proclaimed, "but that simply means there will be one more soldier on the battlefield to fight the communists." Was his ringing declaration militant patriotism or was it mere propaganda? Time would tell.

The next morning I represented MCC at a meeting of humanitarian agencies discussing refugee problems. Just before adjournment, two Catholic Vietnamese nuns requested permission to speak. They fervently shared their commitment to stay in Viet Nam instead of evacuating. Together with a hundred of their sisters, they had also signed a declaration to stay, including a call to other citizens to stay, too. Their simple testimony carried an authenticity which the Thieu radio broadcast the night before had lacked.

*Rumors and Results*

The evacuation, and the rumors which precipitated it, tore through Saigon like a raging flood, uprooting families. Was history repeating itself? Some 20 years earlier, U.S. planes and ships had carried hundreds of thousands of frightened refugees from North to South in Vietnam.

In 1954, the CIA had launched vicious rumor campaigns to incite the evacuation.[1] U.S. Air Force planes had dropped leaflets warning, "Beware! The Virgin Mary Has Fled South. Follow Her Or Be Slaughtered by the Barbarian Communists."[2] Other leaflets predicted unity for the South and its U.S.-backed Catholic leader Diem on the one hand, but disasters for the North and its communist leaders on the other.[3] The subsequent "humanitarian" evacuation of Vietnamese by U.S. planes and the U.S. Seventh Fleet not only concealed covert U.S. operations in the North, but also provided propaganda for author Tom Dooley and others to "document" a massive "flight from communism."[4]

Although some 900,000 people had fled South, including approximately 700,000 Roman Catholics, no bloodbath of Catholics in the North ever occurred.[5] The refugees had brought what they could, stripping radio stations, libraries, laboratories, and factories in the North.[6] The U.S. government sent massive aid to the South:

$89 per refugee, which was more than the average yearly per capita income.[7]

The refugee plight also had drawn private agencies—including religious organizations—into the scene. Mennonite Central Committee joined that refugee relief work in 1954; 15 years later MCC began helping people on the other side.

One of the first MCC workers told me about his visits with refugees in 1954. Surprisingly, most of the refugees had esteemed Ho Chi Minh as a hero who had liberated Vietnam from French domination. "Well," Delbert had asked them, "why did you move South?"

"Oh, our priest said our church should move, so we did."

*New Rumors*

People used as pawns—the story was as old as war itself. Even with my limited knowledge about the history of U.S. involvement in Vietnam, the 1975 evacuation felt sinister. U.S. planes did not relocate the refugees in Vietnam, but this time the planes dropped the refugees like pebbles onto a foreign shore far from the familiar traditions and beautiful beaches of Vietnam.

Panic dominated the hearts and minds of many people who feared the rumors even more than the evacuation. "There will be a fierce battle over Saigon!" "Just before the end of the battle for Saigon, the (Saigon) Air Force will drop asphyxiation bombs over the city, so the communists will march into a city of dead people!" "Everyone who has ever worked for the Americans will automatically be shot!" "Anyone who knows English will be killed!" "All Americans will be killed!" "Everyone who has had a high position in the military will automatically be killed!" "All of the refugees who came from the North in 1954 will be killed!" "The bloodthirsty communists have no feelings!"

During those days, although I openly mentioned my decision to stay, I did not ask others if they were planning to go or stay. If people voluntarily told me, I listened. Asking them seemed too demanding: the fragile fabric of human dignity was wearing too thin to cover society effectively.

I knew some Vietnamese who were leaving. The pastor of the Gia Dinh Mennonite Church had gone to the United States for a conference earlier in the year, so his wife and children decided to join him there. They left Vietnam the same day I heard the nuns issue the call to stay in Vietnam.

That day, too, another member of the Gia Dinh Mennonite Church decided to stay: Tin, our office assistant who had become a close friend. He related his recent struggle. "When I finally decided to stay, it was as if a burden rolled off my shoulders." He glowed. In spite of his relief, his face and his voice darkened to convey the intensity of the wrestling. "It was getting hard to concentrate. In the back of my mind I was always wondering if I should go or if I should stay. If I was going, how should I go? Where should I go? But now I've decided to stay. I don't have nagging questions haunting me anymore."

Using the old black manual typewriter in our office because it had additional keys with Vietnamese diacritical markings, Tin typed a statement for himself and other Vietnamese Mennonites to sign. His commitment refreshed me like a cool breeze challenging a scorching desert of irrationality.

> 1. We will not leave our country regardless of what happens. . . .
> 2. We take the Word of God as the foundation for love and reconciliation between all people.
> 3. Because serving people is a beautiful thing, we must accept any difficulties or sacrifices.
> 4. Because of our strong faith in the eternal God, as Evangelical Christians we accept life as well as death.

The preface to the short declaration accepted responsibility for giving spiritual guidance in the midst of a confusing situation. The powerful conclusion, based on the four main points, used the same concise style:

> We sincerely issue this call to our Christian brothers and sisters as well as fellow citizens: let's stay in this homeland of ours with determination and courage in order to participate in mending the broken spirits and rebuilding the broken pieces of our homeland.
> We voluntarily will stay here in our homeland Vietnam.

*Take Us with You*

Just before noon the next day, a worried young man urged me to come to his house for a few minutes. Due to his persistence, I reluctantly agreed.

When I rang the buzzer beside the metal gate, the neatly dressed young man himself ushered me into the spacious home, half a block from the MCC office.

"Please have a seat." He gestured toward a divan with expensive-looking cushions and ornately carved armrests. After disappearing through an archway into the interior of the house, he quickly returned with two cups of tea which he set on the glass-topped coffee table and then disappeared again.

Almost immediately his mother swished into the room. I rose to greet her.

"Please be seated, sir." Her tone sounded artifically sweetened.

"Thank you, ma'm."

"It was so nice of you to accept my son's invitation to come." Formal and poised, she sat leaning forward in an oversized easy chair.

"It was no problem," I replied, also leaning forward formally.

"My, how well you speak Vietnamese!" Her sentences tumbled out.

"Thank you, but I really don't know very much yet."

"And your pronunciation is so clear." Like soap bubbles, her words floated between lips loaded with bright red lipstick.

"I try hard, but my vocabulary is still quite weak."

"Do have some tea," she gushed.

"Thanks."

"You work at the social work center just up the street from here, right?"

"Yes, ma'm, at the Mennonite Central Committee office," I answered.

"What kind of work do you do?"

"Well, I've been coordinating medicines for two hospitals. . . ."

"Isn't that wonderful!" she interrupted, then queried, "How long have you been in Vietnam?"

"Only two and a half years."

"Only two and a half years and you speak Vietnamese so well! I wish we would have had a chance to meet earlier so you could have helped my children with their English. It's too bad that you'll be leaving soon."

"I'm not planning to leave."

Her heavy makeup hid most of the wrinkles in her face, but no cosmetics could camouflage the surprise in her voice. "You're not planning to leave! But everyone wants out! We want you to take us with you when you go!"

"I haven't been working for the U.S. government or for the U.S. military, so why should I leave? I've also been teaching some Bible classes and have emphasized peace and reconciliation, so I'm planning to stay."

She lowered her voice, desperate. "You don't know the communists! They're terribly cruel! They'll kill you! You're an American. They're going to kill us, too, unless we get out of here! We're too rich. The communists hate rich people. They'll kill me and my entire family!"

"I've heard a lot of rumors, too," I admitted, "but I'm not sure they're true. But I'm still planning to stay, so I really don't know how to help you."

"Oh, but you've got to help us get out. All you have to do is sign a paper at the U.S. embassy saying you'll sponsor us. Please help us, sir."

"Well, as far as I know the only people they're letting on the evacuation flights are employees of the U.S. government and families of U.S. citizens."

"No, no," she challenged. "We know. It's very simple. You sign a sponsor sheet at the embassy. They'll stamp it and then we can get on the plane."

"I'm not sure just signing a sponsor sheet is enough, and I'm not even doing that for any of my close friends since I myself am planning to stay."

"Oh, sir, maybe you are planning to stay, but don't you believe in saving lives?" I nodded. She did not wait. "I think you're probably a Christian, and we're Buddhists, but I think Jesus taught that you should save lives. Please, sir, you've got to save us! The communists will kill us if we stay!"

I listened quietly.

She rushed on. "You'll be blessed by heaven if you help us leave Vietnam! You believe in doing good deeds. Here is an opportunity for you to save lives. Please help us! You are the only way for us to get out of Vietnam. We could pay you, but you don't believe in that, right?"

I nodded. Setting my tea cup on the table, I prepared to exit. "I'm sorry, but I don't think I can help you out."

"Oh, please, sir. It's so simple. Just sign that sponsorship paper at the embassy for us. Won't you do that for us? Please!"

Not wanting to hear another long speech, I thought fast. "I still don't think it is that simple, but I promise that I will go to the U.S. embassy and check." Understanding the process might enable me to help some of my friends.

"Thank you, sir! Thank you! Heaven will bless you! When will you go?"

"I'll try to check first thing this afternoon," I replied.

"Yes, good! I'll send my son to your office around three o'clock to pick up the paper."

"I'll go to the embassy, so your son may come and check, but I don't think I'll have any paper for you. And I might not be back by three o'clock."

"Yes, yes, okay, okay. My son will come to check with you at four o'clock. Thank you, sir. Thanks a lot."

"With your permission, ma'm, I'll be leaving now," I concluded politely.

"Yes, my son will meet you at four. Thanks. Good-bye, sir."

"Good-bye, ma'm." The air seemed much fresher outside.

After lunch, inside the huge U.S. embassy building, I picked up several sheets titled "AFFIDAVIT" and joined a long line on the main floor. People clutching passports and papers anxiously waited ahead of me. The line advanced sluggishly. A subtle tension permeated the quiet atmosphere. A chorus of eyes in drawn faces followed the official U.S. embassy stamp each time it landed with a dull thud. I finally reached the counter.

"Your passport, sir." The official's business-like voice remained level.

"I didn't bring my passport. I just came with a question," I responded.

"What's your question?"

"Is is possible for a U.S. citizen to sponsor anyone who wants to leave?"

"No, sir," he replied flatly. "Only you and your family can leave. You can't sponsor anyone else. Are you married?"

"No, sir, I'm not."

"Then you'll have to leave by yourself. Vietnamese employees of the U.S. government and their families can also leave. We're not making any exceptions." His voice carried an air of finality. He peered at the person in line behind me and reached for the passport and affidavits. As I had predicted, the rumors about simple sponsorship were false.

At the MCC office, a steady stream of petitioners ruined the remainder of my afternoon. When our office closed, the tally for my desk had reached seven people (not counting the rich woman's son), all persistent, each with a different reason to beg for my help to evacuate. I patiently explained my position to each one and repeated the story of my trip to the U.S. embassy.

*Foreigner*

In one hour the next morning, six more people—one at a time—begged me to help them evacuate. Six times I declined. Immediately after lunch, I refused two more evacuation requests. When I returned to the office from errands downtown, the depressing parade continued: I countered five more requests.

Similar requests flooded me like a photocopy machine gone berserk. Except one. The family called me to their home. I knew them well.

The mother, grim-faced, greeted me at the front door. The days of chaos had carved years of worry into her face. Her husband was at work. The children who were home pressed their bodies against hers, moving with her like awkward glued-on appendages. The youngest, a boy not yet three, clung to her.

"Please have some tea." She stared at me.

"Okay." I nodded and took a sip of tea.

"You've got to get out of here!"

"I'm not planning to leave," I replied calmly.

"Oh, you've got to leave, and we want you to take our young son with you as your adopted child."

Her unusual request and her abruptness surprised me.

"Please take him," begged one of the other children. Wide-eyed, almost fearfully, they studied me. Perhaps none of them believed I would stay.

"Do you know what the communists will do?" the mother questioned me. "When they come into Saigon, they'll take the girls who have long, polished fingernails, and pull their fingernails out!"

I shook my head in disbelief.

She threw the words at me. "Those communists have no feelings. They're going to take the people who worked for the Americans and skin them alive! And then they'll make shoes out of that human skin and wear the shoes with pride!"

I shook my head again. "I'm sorry," I said quietly, "but I simply can't believe all that."

"You're a foreigner," she snapped. "You don't understand."

There was nothing left for me to say. Rumors were sapping the life from these friends of mine, but I was helpless to stop the terrible, gnawing cancer. I felt hollow, saddened by their fear.

She resumed. "I come from the North. I know. We can't bear to see our son under a communist government. We've got to get him out of here! The rest of us will take our fate, but we've got to get him out. Please, put him on a planeload of orphans: say his parents are dead."

"I'm sorry," I insisted softly, "but I really can't do that either. Jesus wants his followers to tell the truth. In days like these, it's so hard to know what the truth is, so Christians have an additional responsibility to make every word they say be the truth. I couldn't say that your son is an orphan."

"Don't you understand? We'll do anything to get him out of here. We aren't asking for ourselves, but for him: isn't there anything you can do to help him?"

"No, I'm sorry. I don't think there's anything I can do." Silently I asked the Lord to bless them and remove the fear that was devouring them. I set the teacup, still nearly full, back onto the slatted coffee table.

Heavyhearted, I headed toward the MCC office. Dealing with strangers and with people who barely knew me proved hard enough, but seeing the lives of my friends shredded by vicious rumors left scars on my heart, too.

Another branding iron also seared me for life: "You're a

foreigner. You don't understand." Even though I was wearing Vietnamese sandals, I still was a foreigner and never would understand all the intricacies of the language and culture, but the basic problem lay much deeper. The problem lay in the rumors: I wondered if I was wrong. Would the communists really skin people alive? Although I could not disprove the ugly rumors, I discounted their validity.

Instead of eating supper, I prepared for the New Believer's Fellowship. Then in our meeting, we carefully studied the first two verses of 1 Peter, taking one phrase—sometimes one word—at a time. "Peter, an apostle of Jesus Christ, to the exiles. . . ." Exiles, strangers, refugees—the technical Greek word previously referred only to Jews living outside of Palestine, but Peter used the word to describe Christians.

"Why did Peter write it that way? Where is the Christian's homeland?" I asked the group. Many faces looked puzzled.

Suddenly one beaming member exclaimed, "In heaven!"

"That's right," I responded and then referred to a quotation from a commentary by William Barclay. "There is a famous unwritten saying which possibly comes from Jesus. 'The world is a bridge. The wise will cross over it instead of building a house on it.' It means that our life is a journey towards God, but does that mean we can escape responsibility in this world?"

After the meeting, I snacked on leftovers. "You're a foreigner." Yes, I was a foreigner. I had been a foreigner for a long time—even in my home church in Kansas when I had let my beard grow. "You wouldn't understand." No, perhaps I never would understand. Even if the awful rumors were true, I believed God's love would sustain me in life and in death.

*Friday, Saturday, Sunday*

Friday, April 25, more than twenty individuals confronted me with requests to help get them and their families onto an evacuation plane. Each time, I explained my commitment to stay and my inability to help them. Late in the afternoon I finally escaped the office pressures by driving in the hectic traffic to cable my parents from the post office. "AM FINE SITUATION UNSTABLE BUT QUIET BUT NO MORE DIRECT US MAIL LOVE JAMES."

Saturday, I chauffeured Luke to the airport. The Vietnam MCC workers waiting in Bangkok faced uncertainties regarding their future, so a representative from the MCC office in Pennsylvania had flown to Bangkok and asked Luke to join the discussions there.

"So I'll see you after your conference," I said, convinced that I would be back at the airport to pick him up in a couple of days. He was less certain.

"Once I've left, there would be good reasons for not coming back."

"Yeah, I can see that: your family's all in Bangkok," I replied.

"Of course," he added, "there would also be good reasons for coming back, but even then, the situation here might have changed so much that I can't get back. There might not be any more flights bringing passengers to Saigon."

I nodded slowly. "Maybe so." That can't happen, I thought to myself, he's got to come back.

That night, Saigon suddenly found its protective shield pierced by an incoming rocket. During the recent decades of death-dealing war, Saigon had never been threatened by bombers, giving it the illusion of saftey. The great city, which had bought the blood of so many innocent lives with foreign dollars, realized it was vulnerable, too. The magic had evaporated. The "Achilles' heel" lay exposed.

The incoming rocket, like the bombs and artillery made in the U.S, had not distinguished between men, women, and children. This rocket, perhaps made in the U.S. but launched by the other side, indiscriminately caught young and old in its blast and in the raging fire that followed. Corruption in the Saigon regime had produced a cruel irony: munitions which the U.S. sent to the Saigon government, instead of protecting it, were used against it. Max had been in Quang Ngai when one of Thieu's generals had been caught selling truckloads of military supplies to the other side in that area. Of course, Thieu removed the general from his post, but then sent him to the southern delta where Thieu raised his rank and gave him greater responsibilities. Thieu knew that without the corrupt generals on his side, he had no power. The explosives also lacked morality: they dealt an impartial blow wherever they landed, regardless whose hands had launched them.

The rocket had landed in a shantytown near the heart of Saigon. People who praised the good life in Saigon compared to the drab existence of Hanoi ignored the reality of areas like this. If the glitter of U.S. gold touched the people living in these shacks at all, it was a negative touch of exploitation by those at the top of the hierarchy.

Saigon was no longer safe. Max and I surveyed the disarray. As if trying to cover a hot secret, twisted sheets of tin roofing lay awkwardly over the collapsed, burnt wooden frames. A ring of spectators stared silently as victims poked into ashes at the edge of the smoldering ruins. Although I had my camera, taking pictures seemed inappropriate: the wound was too fresh.

Sick at heart, I rode back to the MCC Center with Max. Over the years, the United States had sent not twice as much, not ten, not twenty times as much, but thirty times as much military aid to Vietnam as the Soviet Union and the People's Republic of China had sent.[8]

Only one side—only the Saigon government with U.S. support—had been using bombs, bombs made in the U.S. Yet, in spite of the tremendous responsibility the U.S. carried for the destruction in Vietnam, destruction was destruction. I would never approve any destruction inherent in war.

I could not picture Jesus piloting a bomber. I could not visualize the Man from Galilee firing artillery, throwing grenades, or aiming a gun. The suffering servant I knew taught his followers not to lord it over others (Matthew 20:25-26). God's Anointed showed how to absorb suffering instead of inflicting it. The risen Lord called his followers to let the light shine by being reconciled. The Prince of Peace was my pattern, good news my message.

*Telling the Truth*

During office hours on Monday morning, 17 more Vietnamese begged me to help them evacuate. One university student met me on the front porch in midmorning.

"Perhaps you don't remember me." He smiled, speaking flawless English. "I'm Tan, and I want you to take me with you when you leave." He seemed vaguely familiar. Maybe we had met.

"But I'm not planning to leave."

His jaw dropped. Then he spewed statistics. "But don't you know (such-and-such) division of the NVA is on the northern outskirts of Saigon and the (such-and-such) division of the NVA is circling to the east of Saigon?" By the time he finished his question, I had already forgotten the division numbers he had cited for troops allegedly from the North.

"No, I really didn't know they were there," I conceded, "but I don't think it makes any difference to me because I'm determined to stay."

"But you can't stay! You've got to leave and take me along! There isn't much time left before the communists take over!" His smile had vanished.

"I honestly don't know what's going to happen. There might even be a negotiated settlement—who knows? I have to admit it looks like time is running out, though."

"Look, you've got to be realistic," he argued. "There are more North Vietnamese troops on the way. There's no hope left. We've got to get out of here now while we still have a chance."

"You can go ahead and leave, but I'm staying."

"That's easy for you to say, but I have no way out unless you leave and take me with you," he persisted.

"I'm sorry, but I'm not leaving, so I'm not taking anybody with me.

He shook his head. "I don't believe it. I think you're planning to leave, but you just don't want to take me along with you. All the other Americans I know have already left, so you were my last hope, and now you won't help me." He sounded exasperated and desperate. "I speak English, and I promise I will not give you any problems if you take me along with you."

"Whether you speak English or not doesn't make any difference to me." His aggressiveness, however, disgusted me.

"But you could at least sign the papers for me so I can get on the plane."

I answered like a tired tape-recorder.

"But you could say I'm a relative—like a brother-in-law."

"No, I'm sorry, I can't. I believe in telling the truth. Now I've got some business downtown, so if you'll excuse me, I'll be on my way."

"I'm going to get out of here somehow even if you don't help me!"

Relieved when lunchtime finally came, I cycled to Gia Dinh; Vinh had invited me for lunch. As we tackled the simple meal with our chopsticks, we discussed my decision to stay.

"There's a Vietnamese saying, 'like a duck hears thunder,' " he teased.

"I can understand those words but I don't know what the phrase means."

He grinned. "It's like this: the duck isn't afraid because it doesn't know what's going on."

"Actually, just this morning a guy stopped by our office and tried to explain all the troop movements around Saigon. He used all kinds of numbers, but I really didn't pay attention to them." I grinned, too. "Maybe I really am like a deaf duck that doesn't hear the thunder."

"There's another expression like that, too: 'like water poured on a duck's head.' "

I chuckled. "In English I'd probably use the expression, 'It went in one ear and out the other.' "

Vinh always seemed to capture the essence of a situation with a neat expression. I recalled his response to my pacifism: "A deaf person doesn't tremble at the sound of gunfire."

As we finished lunch, he confided, "My sister and the children have left."

"I noticed the house seemed pretty quiet." I did not ask about the grandparents who lived upstairs.

"We really need your help. Her husband is still stuck here. It's terribly unfortunate. Can you help him get out?"

"I doubt it, but at least I can check." Other close friends of mine had decided to stay—including the ones in the Mennonite Fellowship who had signed the declaration to stay in Vietnam. Consequently, turning down other evacuation requests had been relatively simple. Vinh's request, however, was the only one that I was willing to take seriously. "I'll go out to the airport to see if there's been any change in the policy."

The sun glared at the multitude waiting for the makeshift evacuation office at the airport to open. Like the tip of an iceberg, almost every person in the long line represented a clan hoping to evacuate. Some women, children, and the elderly sat waiting on blankets which covered part of the scrawny lawn. Here and there, people held newspapers to shield themselves from the sun.

I wondered whether to believe the posted office hours. When the door at the top of the steps finally opened after lunch break, the line surged forward. The U.S. guards muscled the door shut again. One guard hollered, "Look! We're only going to let a few of you in at a time. If you can't do this orderly, we're just going to shut down the whole operation!"

The line continued to push in one direction: toward the door. Caught in the human tide, pushed from behind, I braced myself against the pressure to avoid pushing those in front of me. I soon was too drained to resist. Since the door opened to the outside, the pressure involuntarily reversed itself at irregular intervals to allow the next people to enter.

At last, I stood next to the door. Once inside the beehive, I filled out duplicate copies of the simple affidavit for Vinh's brother-in-law. Under the column heading "Relationship," I wrote "close friend."

The official at the head of the shortest line frowned. His hulk resembled an all-American football hero rather than a clerk. I wondered whether someone had pulled him from some other job, given him a U.S. embassy stamp, and ordered him to start processing papers. Other than a glimspe to confirm a similarity between the passport in his hand and the person in front of him, he hunched over the tiny desk as if to hide his rugged, clean-cut, face.

"Okay, next." He clipped the words efficiently, almost gruffly.

I handed him my passport and the affidavits.

"Is this a male or female?" He pointed to Vinh's brother-in-law's name.

"Male."

"Is he related to you?"

"Well, he's a close friend—like I wrote in there," I responded.

As if waiting for me to change my mind and revise the affidavit, he asked again, "But no relation?"

"No, I guess not in the sense that you are using the word." I chose my words carefully. He apparently stamped his approval if affidavits listed relatives, even if the affidavits were lying.

His ballpoint swooped across the page, through the name, relationship, and nationality of Vinh's brother-in-law, then angled back across the blank space and swung across the bottom of the sheet, leaving a large "Z."

"I'm stamping your passport to show that you went through the line," he growled, "so you won't be able to come through here again." His tone of voice automatically overruled all challenges. He followed the letter of the law, just doing his job. "You won't be able to take anyone along when you leave."

He would not bend; neither would I. He refused to let my friend evacuate. I refused to falsify the affidavit. In light of his last statement, I wanted him to know one more thing about this bearded Kansas lad who faced him. Although my heart was pounding, I tried to keep my voice steady. "But I myself am not planning to leave."

His words sizzled like sparks from a raging fire. "If you know what's good for you, you'll get out of this damn place as fast as you can!" He shoved the worthless affidavits and my passport at me, probably wishing that he himself could leave Vietnam on the next evacuation flight.

For myself, however, Vietnam felt like home. Staying seemed natural. I knew the language well enough so that, if given the opportunity, I could explain in Vietnamese who I was.

Exiting the evacuation office brought immediate relief. Having braved the storm to no avail on behalf of a close friend, I resolved to keep as far away from it as possible. Enough was enough. After handing the worthless affidavits to Vinh as a symbol of my efforts, I cycled back to the MCC office.

*Back to Basics*

Bold, front page headlines announced that the Republic of Vietnam had installed a new president: Duong Van Minh—"Big Minh." As Max and I listened to radio broadcasts in Vietnamese that evening, we felt the impact of his leadership. Instead of the bitter anticommunist slogans that had poisoned the airwaves, we heard references to "brothers on the other side" and to "the Provisional Revolutionary Government."

The changes in vocabulary preceded other changes. To implement the Paris Peace Accords, Big Minh immediately released political prisoners, restored freedom of the press, and asked the U.S. Defense Attache Office and all its employees to leave Vietnam within 24 hours. Since President Minh did not demand that all U.S. citizens leave, I felt reassured about my decision, but I wondered whether his impressive contributions could produce a coalition government, and thus avert a major battle over Saigon.

After supper, I climbed the stairs to the flat rooftop of the Mennonite Center, my home. Muted by the miles, the irregular sounds of bombing and gunfire wafted from the outskirts of the city. I looked toward the airport. A thin line of involuntary bonfires on the horizon produced an eerie red glow.

How strange, I thought, to watch the war like a spectator watching competitive sports! Would the fire and the fighting reach our home? How long, Lord, until the insanity of the war would end? What would happen to Max and to me?

As a pacifist, I had decided long ago if any one demanded my belongings during a breakdown of public order, I would promptly comply. For example, a looter could have my camera: it would not be worth risking my life to protect.

Another potential danger at our doorstep, perhaps related to looting, came from angry soldiers of the Saigon regime who might seek revenge on any white-faced foreigner. In frustration, bitter ARVN soldiers—armed to the teeth and full of Thieu's propaganda—might turn their guns on a citizen of a former ally just as they had turned their guns on their Vietnamese compatriots in Nhatrang. For what and for whom had the soldiers been asked to risk their lives? Thieu, I heard, had left Vietnam with crates of gold and a hefty Swiss bank account. He was unwilling to risk his life for his country. Even without wearing a soldier's uniform in the ARVN, I sympathized with the soldiers' despair. Consequently, I knew that my blond hair and blue eyes were a liability.

Of course, another inherent danger, perhaps more remote, loomed on the horizon just beyond the shrinking perimeter of the area controlled by the Saigon government: soldiers of the other side—the "communists." In spite of the rumors, even the front page of the *Saigon Post* acknowledged that those soldiers remained more disciplined than the soldiers of the Saigon regime. Nevertheless, after fighting the United States for more than 20 years, a soldier might relish eliminating one more U.S. citizen when confronted with a live specimen face to face. Even without wearing a soldier's uniform for the PRG, I sympathized with the soldiers' hatred. Consequently, I knew my U.S. passport was a liability. Mennonite Central Committee had contacted the Provisional Revolutionary Government at various times and had shipped medical supplies to it, but how could every PRG soldier have heard of the Mennonites? One well-placed, tiny bullet might short-circuit my chance to speak Vietnamese, to share my Mennonite perspective, or to note my European background.

My thoughts swept on. Events beyond my control had shredded the psychological padding between life and death. Forced to face the options, I reaffirmed my pacifist commitment. If my life were threatened, I would not reach for a bayonet or gun because I would not have any.

I remembered an illustration from one of my seminary professors: anyone with a gun has to worry whether it is loaded, whether the bullets will fire, whether the gun mechanism will work, besides worrying about an accurate aim and firing in time. I avoided all those worries by not having a gun, and I prayed for God's grace to respond like Jesus. On the rooftop I consciously laid my life into God's hands once more. Then no other hands held any fear for me.

Without knowing the exact words of my family and friends halfway around the world, I knew they supported my stay. The reports later confirmed my gut-level feeling. One neighbor in Kansas, for example, had asked my mother, "Aren't you worried about James?"

"No," my mother answered, "like for all our other children, when he walked down the aisle wearing cap and gown at his high school graduation, I put him into the Lord's hands and said, 'Thank you, Lord, for letting us have him for 18 years.' Why should I take him back? I have given him to the Lord."

"But if you aren't worried about James," the neighbor lady retorted, "it makes me even more worried for him."

"But you shouldn't be," my mother replied. "If something

happens to him, it's no farther to heaven from Vietnam than it is from Goessel, Kansas."

Shortly after arriving in Vietnam, I had learned of the MCC policy which encouraged MCC workers to formulate and file their own funeral and burial arrangements with the Saigon MCC office. On a stub of paper barely half an inch wide and three inches long, I had jotted miniature notes. The bare outline included Romans 8:38-39 as a New Testament reading and "Amazing Grace!" as a hymn. Even though the scrap of paper lay buried somewhere in my unorganized desk, on the rooftop I easily recalled the reason for picking that hymn some two years earlier: " 'Tis grace has brought me safe thus far, and grace will lead me home." The Scripture passage from Romans expressed the same idea: nothing could separate citizens of the heavenly kingdom from God's love.

*Expectations*

Max had heard a radio announcement declaring a 24-hour curfew for the next day, so I expected a leisurely day. I had already suspended English classes. Exhausted by 8:30 p.m., I switched off my bedroom light and fell asleep.

The next morning—Tuesday, April 29—I slid into a pair of faded blue jeans. MCC workers in other parts of Vietnam had worn jeans regularly, but I never felt comfortable dressing that informally in Saigon. With the 24-hour curfew, however, I expected no visitors.

Nevertheless, a neatly dressed student dropped in, begging me to help him evacuate. He dared to violate the curfew; I did not. Several years earlier, a Vietnam Christian Service worker had been shot and killed when violating a curfew at night. He reluctantly left. Perhaps my bare feet and flying shirt tail convinced him that I was relaxed and planning to stay.

In the living room, I scrunched down on a cushioned rattan easy chair and propped my feet up on the coffee table. In that comfortable position, I finished reading a book on the Lord's Prayer and then closed my eyes for a nap.

Max answered a ring from the front gate just before noon and ushered the new believer into the living room. Surprised by the visit and embarrassed by my appearance, I greeted Lieu, a faithful member of our fellowship.

"Jim! I thought you had left! But you're still here!" she chirped.

"Yes, I'm still here, and I'm planning to stay." Maybe my extraordinarily informal outfit served a special purpose after all.

"I'm so glad to hear that! I don't know what our Fellowship would do if you would have left, too!"

"Well," I replied, "I'm not sure how much of a contribution I'll be able to make, but at least I wanted to stay. The Lord certainly will not be evacuating, either. But don't you know there's a 24-hour curfew?"

"Oh, sure, I know. But there are a lot of people out on the streets anyhow, and I didn't have too far to go. What did you do this morning?"

"I just finished this book on the Lord's Prayer. It's a good book." I reached for the book on the coffee table. "The thing that impressed me the most was the story at the end. The writer says that when Jesus went back to heaven maybe something like this happened." I flipped to the end of the text and translated the gist for her.

"Maybe the angels asked him, 'Did you build any buildings on earth?'

" 'No,' Jesus replied, 'I didn't build any buildings.'

" 'Did you write any books?'

" 'No, I didn't write any books.'

"The angels really were puzzled. 'Well, what did you leave behind?'

" 'A little band of men and women who love me,' Jesus replied.

"The angels were surprised. 'Wasn't there anything else?'

" 'No, nothing else,' Jesus said.

" 'But what if they fail you?' the angels asked.

"Jesus replied softly, but firmly, 'They will not fail me.' "

"What a neat story!" Lieu exclaimed. "You'll have to share that with our Fellowship!"

Tin, our office assistant, stopped to visit after lunch. When we asked him about violating the curfew, he smiled. "I just had to come see how you were getting along."

How could Max and I feel lonely with good friends like that?

Then a member of the Gia Dinh Mennonite Church Youth Fellowship dropped in to visit. Just after she left, two university students who had gone on a work camp with Max arrived to check on our well-being. The librarian-receptionist for the English program also braved the curfew.

Then two desperate people insisted that I must help them evacuate. I stood facing them in the yard. Although we heard helicopters throbbing overhead, I lacked the power to help anyone board them.

"Actually, I'm glad to see the U.S. military finally leave Vietnam," I remarked to the two would-be evacuees.

"But who is going to protect you?" one of them asked me.

"I don't believe in using violence," I responded, "and I've never asked anyone to protect me. I follow Jesus and have put my life into his hands."

"But what if the communists kill you?"

"That's their problem, not mine. At least I don't want to be guilty of killing anyone," I explained.

"But you wouldn't have to worry about that if you would get out of here."

"But I'm not worried," I explained. "I'm determined to stay."

"Why are you so determined to stay?"

"Jesus taught his followers to follow the way of peace and reconciliation. I'm following Jesus, not the U.S. government."

"But lots of missionaries have left, so why should you stay?"

"I know lots of missionaries have left, but I also know one missionary who wanted to stay, went to Bangkok for a meeting, and now can't get back." I was thinking of Luke Martin. "Besides even if all the missionaries would leave, it still doesn't mean that the Lord is evacuating."

Contrasted to those in Vietnam wanting to evacuate but lacking a way out, Luke—who had been planning to stay in Vietnam—was stuck outside without a way in. When he was ready to return to Vietnam after the Bangkok conference, no more commercial flights flew to Saigon. His words of farewell at the airport had proved accurate. He was among the people who wished to be in Vietnam to witness the changes, one of the few who passionately longed to stay in Vietnam, but whose dreams were unfulfilled.

*Nothing New*

At 1:00 p.m., in the middle of the 24-hour curfew on April 29, I listened to the news. Just before 3:00 p.m., between visiting with guests, I stepped to the kitchen again. Our only radio sat on a kitchen cabinet. While I listened to the news, I ate a banana. The United States Armed Forces maintained an English radio station in Vietnam, and although I generally detested both the style and content of the broadcasts, the English broadcasts allowed me to be a lazy listener. The banana tasted delicious; the news was dull.

At four o'clock, I listened to the radio again, hearing the usual mediocre mix of national and international news with a couple of stories about Vietnam.

All of our visitors had left by suppertime; Max and I listened to the six o'clock news. The news sounded vaguely familiar. The announcer stumbled again, on the same word. The news was not new! I chuckled. No humans were at the radio station any longer: the progress of science. The equipment in the radio station was simply rebroadcasting the same old news every hour.

Another aspect of the U.S. Armed Forces radio broadcast surprised me. A special booklet issued to U.S. citizens arriving in Vietnam had explained evacuation procedures introduced by a confidential radio announcement: "The temperature is 104 degrees and rising." Immediately after that message, the radio would broadcast the Christmas carol "I'm Dreaming of a White Christmas."

Curiosity had prompted me to listen to the radio, but I never heard the message. I never heard the carol. Perhaps too many unauthorized people knew about them, thwarting their use. Perhaps too much chaos would have resulted.

That night I did not dream of a white Christmas that was kept pure by ugly army green uniforms, seasick navy blue ships, or fuzzy air force vapor trails. I only prayed that the war would end and that God's will would be done on earth as in heaven. Sleeping soundly, I crossed the border separating Tuesday from Wednesday, April 30, 1975.

*Tired and Relieved*

Like a sixth sense when I awoke, I knew the fighting had moved closer overnight. The undisputed sounds of war on the outskirts of Saigon rekindled my yearning for an end to the destruction. Too much blood had already been shed, but what can pacifists say when the guns are firing? Is it enough to be a "friend who just stands by"?

Although the day had just begun, I was already tired. Tired of the war. Tired of thinking about the war. Tired of pleas for help to evacuate. Tired of hearing rumors. Tired of being tired.

One, two, three more people came to beg me for assistance in evacuating. Finally they left, obviously disappointed.

Rockets occasionally were landing in Saigon. When a small rocket landed a couple of blocks from us, Max and I began taking elementary measures to prepare the house in case heavy military action came our way. Although we had discussed sandbags, we had never purchased any, so we figured the best structural protection in the house against incoming rockets was a cramped, centrally located closet which we had nicknamed "MCC Conference Room."

A friend of Vinh's, a former work camper of Max's, and the MCC secretary came to see us. Instead of asking for help evacuating, the three helped Max dump the odds and ends from the closet onto the office furniture. I drew water into pots in the kitchen because the fighting could destroy the water lines.

At 10:15 a.m., the Vietnamese radio announcer asked everyone to stand by for an important announcement. As we gathered around the radio which sat in the middle of the assorted junk from the half-empty closet, we speculated about the approaching news flash.

"Do you think it means the end of the fighting?"

"I don't know. I hope so."

"What else could be so important?"

At 10:30 we heard the announcement: Big Minh ordered the "brothers" under his command to stop shooting and asked the "brothers" on the other side to do the same. The rocketing stopped immediately. The cease-fire worked! What a relief! It seemed like an answer to prayer.

"Well, it looks like the fighting is over."

"Yeah, I guess so."

We smiled tiredly. As far as we could tell, the war was over. I wished I would have tape-recorded the historic announcement. Since an orderly transfer of governmental power looked imminent, we did not bother emptying the rest of the closet. The MCC secretary prepared a simple lunch for all of us.

None of us knew what to expect next. Gunshots! On our street! The shooting quickly switched from the opening random shots to a steady stream of automatic gunfire. Was it house-to-house fighting after all? What had happened to the cease-fire? Was this a resistance movement disobeying Big Minh's orders? Was it the beginning of the rumored bloodbath?

Strangely, though, no flood of refugees poured down the street to escape the fighting. Shots suddenly rang out next to our house! Bang, bang, bang! Resounding bangs, quieter bangs, medium-sized bangs, bangs without number! Still, no one was running on the streets. We peeked through the curtains. Forced to be innovative in a land impoverished by war, the children had just improvised a new game.

Many ARVN soldiers under Big Minh's command, filled with panic at the news of the cease-fire, had abandoned their weapons and ammunition. Some shed their helmets and telltale uniforms. As if attracted by a gigantic magnet, helmets, uniforms, guns, and ammo belts piled up across the street from our center.

Without understanding the grim realities, Vietnamese children—like children in other lands—played war games with toys of war. No longer limited to toys, the children we saw had just discovered the stockpile of deserted guns. Gleefully grabbing the loaded guns, they aimed them straight up and pulled the triggers. Oblivious to the dangers of their play, the youngsters staggered under the weight of the guns and struggled to keep the muzzles aimed up.

Once we understood the situation, we stayed out of the front rooms and off the roof. Fortunately, nearly no traffic traveled the street. We heard later that stray bullets from the children's war games had caused a few casualties.

By midafternoon, the one-way street in front of our house buzzed with traffic going both directions, reminding me of a carnival. Occasionally a truckload of soldiers for the Provisional Revolutionary Government (PRG) cruised past. Some of the "communist" soldiers, wearing helmets different from the ones we were accustomed to seeing, waved to people on the street.

We noticed that a number of happy people in the bustling sidewalk traffic carried things looking vaguely familiar. We finally realized that some of the office furniture in the unorganized "parade" belonged to the VNCS office next door to us. Apparently, without staff members keeping an eye on the office, looting it became a pastime for children and adults. Sometimes the sidewalk in front of the MCC office turned into a rest stop for heavy loads. Stuffed under arms or precariously balanced on sagging shoulders, lamps, desks, roller chairs, even ceiling fans appeared to float past our front yard wall.

Was our house next for the looters? No. No one came to our gate demanding to be let in. No one jumped our fence to rob us. No one threatened us. Maybe the looters only ransacked abandoned houses and buildings. Perhaps our openness about staying spared us from the looters.

A Japanese pickup suddenly pulled up to our front gate. Did we know the people inside? Yes! Paul and Sophie Quinn-Judge from the American Friends Service Committee brought Manh Tuong to visit us. He had obtained press passes for Max and for me. The passes, issued by a group of students helping with administrative details for the Provisional Revolutionary Government, allowed us to travel around the city without complications, but Max and I were still too timid to leave the house that afternoon.

After they left, Ngoc, who had just been baptized at the Mennonite Center on Easter Sunday, bicycled to ask if we were all right. Then, one by one, the trio who had spent the day with Max and me left. Ngoc, reassured, also left.

After making supper, munching it leisurely, and washing the dishes, Max and I sat in the living room reflecting on the events of the day. The bell at the front gate rang once more. A friend of Max's from the days when Max had taught English in Quang Ngai, came to visit us. Looking older than a student his age should have, he shared his story.

"I was in Danang during the evacuation panic. My parents thought my younger brother and I should leave. With my own eyes, I saw people trampled under foot while trying to get into boats. It was terribly dangerous if the boats weren't close enough to the dock. But people kept trying—and not making it—until there was a human 'carpet' high enough for people to walk on to board the boats.

"I lost track of my brother. I don't know what happened to him. What will I ever tell my parents?"

He stopped. Sitting quietly in a corner of the divan, he stared down at the tile flooring. He did not cry. Max and I also stared silently.

Max's friend continued. "Even after getting into a boat, people weren't safe. The (ARVN) soldiers demanded gold, money, and watches at gun point. The soldiers shot reluctant people and threw them overboard. Our boat lost its engine, so we came ashore short of Nhatrang, and then I walked the rest of the way. I always stayed close to shore, hoping to avoid the fighting. I got terribly hungry and thirsty, but I didn't dare quit. I'm lucky to be alive.

"The worst thing was seeing the dead bodies that washed up onto the beaches. At one place there was a whole pile of children. It was sickening. Sometimes I wondered if I would see my brother among the dead bodies." He never found his brother.

Max's friend accepted our invitation to stay overnight. The day had drained my energy. Too many questions and too many unknowns remained, preventing me from feeling exuberant.

# Chapter 13

# THE MORNING AFTER

*Disproving Rumors*

THE WAR WAS OVER! What a relief! I had just begun typing reflections about recent events when the librarian-receptionist of the Student Center arrived. He had always appeared nervous. The last time we had met, he shared his deep worries about the impending, foreboding, perhaps inevitable changes in Vietnam. This time, however, I noticed an enthusiastic bounce in his steps as he parked his bicycle in our front yard.

After the usual polite greetings, he blurted, "You'll never guess what!" His words seemed as buoyant as a helium-filled balloon with only a pair of sandals holding it down to earth. "I met a Christian soldier! A Christian soldier from North Vietnam!"

"How did you know he was a Christian?" I asked.

"Well, I talked to him! I was terribly scared because I didn't know what might happen when the communists would arrive. And yesterday when they came into the city, I didn't dare to go out of the house. I kept all the doors locked. But this morning I decided to go downtown to see what was happening. Naturally, there were lots of soldiers, but then I suddenly saw one with a cross painted on his canteen! Incredible! So I just got up all my courage and asked him about it. Of course, I had to be careful, so I just said, 'Excuse me, I just noticed that thing painted on your canteen—the, uhm, cross.' "

" 'That?' he said. 'Oh, sure, that's a cross. I'm a Christian, so I decided to paint a cross on my canteen.'

"So I told him I was a Christian, too, and we gave each other a big hug right there! Christian brothers! And then I came here to tell you about it!"

I was glad for him—glad to see the burden lifted from his shoulders and to hear of reconciliation taking place. I cherished his experience, but the irony in a cross on a soldier's canteen also tainted my joy.

The Prince of Peace never wore a military uniform: He loved his enemies instead of attempting to kill them. Clearly, "Christian soldiers" on both sides of the line in Vietnam had felt obligated to point guns at each other and pull the triggers. How could the call of patriotism from their respective governments have overridden loyalty to Christ's call to live in love?

Surely, if Christians were more faithful to Jesus and declined all military service, then the light of the worldwide Christian fellowship would shine brighter, and both God and humanity would be spared countless heartaches.

The librarian had just left when another member of the Gia Dinh Mennonite Church came into our yard beaming. Khai, a draft dodger under the Thieu regime, had seldom dared to venture a few alleyways beyond the church building. I had often observed the Thieu military police park their jeeps across from our office and stop young men driving past to check their draft papers.

For Khai, that threat had evaporated. "Isn't this great? Now I don't have to worry any more! I'm free! I can go where I want to go!"

One word summarized his feelings: liberation! Members of the MCC staff and some former work campers, perhaps because they had not shared his cramped lifestyle, assessed the government changeover more cautiously when they visited us later that morning. Nevertheless, everyone we met, whether enthusiastic or cautious, breathed a sigh of relief because the war was over.

Then curiosity propelled Max and me out of the house. We pedaled our bicycles downtown. We blended into the familiar disarray of traffic which seemed immune to the radical socio-political changes. We chained our bicycles next to the sidewalk benches which faced the the National Parliament building of the former government. Two street urchins promised to watch our bicycles for mere pennies: neither they nor their price had changed.

The flags had changed. On our way downtown, we had seen a pile of bright yellow flags, each with three characteristic red stripes, lying in the gutter on Le Van Duyet Street. They had represented the previous government, and now they, like the Saigon regime, lay discarded.

New flags fluttered from flagpoles, car radio antennas, and improvised flag holders on three-wheel motorized rickshaws. Nearly all of the new flags looked official: a bright yellow star centered in a half-red, half-blue background. Here and there, though, we saw a background of green cloth instead of blue!

Apparently, in hurried whispers at the change of government, people who had not been close to the revolution asked about the flag of "the other side." The answer came just as quickly, but in Vietnamese, the word *xanh,* without qualifiers meant either *blue* or *green.* Then, in backrooms, in secrecy, in fear and trembling, each green and red background soon bore a golden star. Those who waved the homemade flags thought they could join the revolution and pass the test of loyalty with flying colors.

Perhaps, though, the best patriotism is color-blind. I knew God did not wear red, white, and blue. God had broader horizons than three red stripes across golden yellow. A yellow-gold star on red and blue—or green—could not limit God's perspective, either. Long before I went to Vietnam as a Christian pacifist, waiving—not waving—flags appealed to me. The prophet Micah had asked a simple question: "What does the Lord require of you but to do justice, and to love kindness, and to walk humbly with your God?" (Micah 6:8).

A so-called "Christian nation"—the United States—had failed: its bloodbath of B-52 bombs, napalm bombs, daisy-cutter bombs, and CBU bombs had not brought justice, kindness, or humility to Vietnam. Would a so-called "communist" government relate to its own people any better? Max and I, like most of our close Vietnamese friends, adopted a wait-and-see perspective about the revolution, but we saw no bloodbath in the streets of Saigon. After the change of government, we did not even hear rumors of any communist bloodbath. I was thankful that all of the previous rumors proved false. No fingernails were pulled out. No one was skinned alive. No one who spoke English was shot. No one who worked for the Americans was shot. No massacre occurred at the Bible School in Nhatrang. None of the ugly rumors were true.

*Meeting Soldiers*

Before we picked up our bicycles, we hunkered alongside a soldier wearing a uniform as unfamiliar as the new flags. To avoid straining the tendons in my heels which were unaccustomed to hunkering, I set my sandaled heels on the curb and angled my toes down to the paved street. Max bravely initiated a conversation in Vietnamese with him: "Hello."

The soldier responded unenthusiastically. "Hello. Are you French?"

"No, not French," Max replied.

"So what nationality are you?"

"American."

"I don't believe it. All the Americans left, didn't they?"

"The U.S. military left," Max explained, "but we're working with a social service organization—not with the military—so we didn't leave."

"Missed your evacuation flight, eh?"

"No, we didn't want to leave. Why should we leave?" Max asked.

"What do you want here now?" the soldier countered.

"Well, we want to try to understand what is going on and to see if we can contribute something."

Confident of himself and his country, the soldier bragged, "Look around, try to understand, but we don't need any more American aid."

Then, as if just realizing who we were, he asked, "Has anyone been hassling you?"

"No," Max replied, "no problems."

"Do you have enough food to eat?"

"Yes, enough."

"Does your family know you're all right?"

Surprised and impressed, I wondered why the soldier asked. Of course, the official government policy respected all foreigners who had stayed in Vietnam, but why should he be concerned? Possibly he wondered if we had special communication with the outside world, but more probably he knew the agony of cut communications, experiencing times when he was unable to contact his family.

Still a bearded foreigner, but no longer a stranger, Klassen donned a traditional Vietnamese *ao dai* to celebrate Lunar New Year 1975.

Klassen a few months after his arrival in Vietnam in 1972.

Klassen, wearing sandals and a conical hat, ready for the ride home after work during the rainy season in Saigon.

These two boys in Dalat taught Klassen the art of paper folding in November 1972 before he could speak Vietnamese.

En route to language school, Klassen caught the city bus near the Dalat Central Market.

In 1973 Klassen lost control of this Landrover in a drizzle, but there were no fatalities.

A visit to Gougah Falls, though near the scene of the accident, had to wait for another day.

MCC/Mennonite Mission conference in Dalat in 1973. Klassen is third from the right in the back row.

Giving Klassen a brass friendship bracelet in 1973, Pastor Sau said, "All I ask is that you remember to pray for me and for my people."

"Auto mechanic" Klassen replaced a Landrover U-joint in Pleiku.

TOP (left to right): The new MCC secretary poses with the two MCC exchanges—Phuong-Hang (the former MCC secretary) and Ly (the nursing translator from Nhatrang). BOTTOM: These new Christians in the Phan Thanh Gian Fellowship weathered the 1975 socio-political changes with Klassen (at far right in the front row).

TOP: Murray Hiebert and Yoshihiro Ichikawa visit with two former political prisoners, Chi Hien and Manh Tuong, and with Earl Martin. BOTTOM: MCC-fostered friends. (Ly is at the far left in the front row; Klassen is next to Luke Martin who is on the right in the middle row.)

Barbed wire—a constant reminder of the war—surrounded the
Pleiku Evangelical Clinic (visible in the background).

Transition time for MCC co-workers and friends. Left to right: the new MCC secretary; Phuong-Hang (the former MCC secretary); Tin (MCC/Mennonite Mission office assistant); and Klassen.

Klassen taught an evangelism course at the Gia Dinh Mennonite Church which met in this building.

A legacy of war allowed Klassen to look through the walls of the boyhood home of Pham Van Dong in Central Vietnam.

Klassen met the artist of this piece, who had been held as a political prisoner under Thieu.

Day of departure in December 1974 for the first and last MCC exchangees from Vietnam. Ly is third from right, Phuong-Hang second from left.

Quang, the first new Christian to ask Klassen to baptize him. Klassen performed the ceremony on June 29, 1975.

Klassen leading a Bible study in Vietnamese during the summer of
1975 with his outline of 1 Peter 1:13-25 on the chalkboard.

On the outskirts of Saigon, as elsewhere, war builds barriers. Who will tear them down?

Christian and Buddhist soldiers lie buried side by side in a Vietnamese military cemetery. Why did they die? How many have no tombstones?

Klassen (left) poses with Max and two active members of the Phan Thanh Gian Fellowship in 1975.

The baptism of Lieu's sister in January 1976.

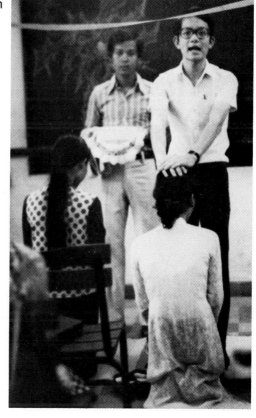

A new day at Nhatrang, a new opportunity to make friends.

Jim and Ly, husband and wife, still seeking God's will together.

"What do you think of Vietnam, of the Vietnamese people?" he asked.

"The Vietnamese really have a strong spirit. . . . " Max began.

"Naturally, we've got a strong spirit!" he interrupted enthusiastically. "How else do you think we defeated the Americans and liberated Vietnam?"

I wondered about defeat and liberation. Of course, I rejoiced that the fighting was over. I was relieved that we could sit on our haunches visiting each other. I, too, admired the courageous spirit of the Vietnamese people, but I felt no pride in any military defeat or any military victory. Military actions had destroyed too much. Theoretically, if one side "won," the other side "lost," but warmongers had turned defeats as well as victories into rallying cries for more killing and destruction. I saw no winners in war: war turned everyone into losers.

The war was finally over. That reality gradually penetrated my consciousness. Max and I were visiting with a soldier from "the other side." In fact, "this side" had collapsed: Thieu and his gold had evacuated. Politically, "the other side" had become "this side" with no other side to fight it. The war was over!

Besides Max and me, others gingerly queried the people wearing rubber tire sandals and strange army helmets. Curious individuals clustered here and there to visit with the newly arrived soldiers. A helmet or two near the center in each group confirmed the major attraction: soldiers from the People's Liberation Army (PLA) which had been organized by the Provisional Revolutionary Government. Perhaps as a deliberate strategy to allay fears and disprove rumors, most soldiers carried no weapons. I saw reconciliation taking place.

I had not known what to expect during the preceding days, but I had braced myself to face rough water. The final test, though, of facing a gun pointed at me never came. Nevertheless, the political, social, and economic transformations exhausted me, as if I remained fully conscious during surgery using only local anesthesia. Perhaps I never would understand: I was a foreigner. The roots of the revolutionary changes had been established long before my arrival in Vietnam: now I was a guest, sleeping through the revolution with my eyes open. During my nap, I also slept with my eyes closed.

*Meeting Friends*

Just before supper, Lieu, who had braved the 24-hour curfew on April 29, rang the buzzer at the gate. This time her younger sister Lan bicycled along.

"Jim! You didn't leave! Are you okay?" Lieu's characteristic enthusiasm pitched the sentences as rapidly as ever.

"No. No problems at all."

"Praise the Lord!"

"I've thanked the Lord a lot, too," I replied. "The war is finally over, and the transition between the governments was quite smooth. Oh, we saw things from empty houses go by on the street yesterday afternoon, but nobody tried to take anything from us. What about you and your family?"

"We're all okay, too. We're rather worried, though, because we don't know what's going to happen now." Her words still tumbled toward me, but an invisible cloud dulled the sparkle in her eyes.

"I really don't know either. At least there hasn't been any bloodbath," I said. "We've trusted the Lord this far, and the future is in his hands, too."

Though I had been exhausted during the previous pressure-packed days, the Lord had granted me serenity like the calm in the eye of a hurricane.

"You're right. But we're still scared. Please pray for us, would you?"

"Sure I'm willing to do that. And I need your prayers, too." Maybe they wanted me to pray in their presence. "Do you want me to pray right now?"

"Yes." They both nodded instantly. Then Lieu hesitated, "Is that okay?"

"Certainly!" I offered a short prayer, thanking the Lord for his love and placing our lives into his hands. I also thanked the Lord for Lieu's shining witness and for her sister and asked the Lord to bless them in a special way.

After Max and I had supper, the gate buzzer rang again. Max answered it. Voices—excited voices—reached my ears. Friendly voices. Familiar voices. Whose? Ah, ha! It had to be! Earl and Hiro! Bear hugs and greetings!

"Earl! Man, it's good to see you! Did you know you're supposed to be dead? Eyewitness report!" My heart beat fast.

"Yeah, that's what Max just said. I look pretty dead, don't I?" We all laughed.

"And, Hiro!" I exclaimed. "I couldn't figure out why you were so determined to get to Quang Ngai! Man, I had a mess getting that ticket for you! I think yours must have been almost the last flight!"

Hiro's eyes twinkled. "You don't think I wanted to miss all the excitement, do you?" We laughed again.

Our stories flowed continuously throughout the evening. The truth—stranger than fiction—often prompted laughter. Earl and Hiro described their trek to Saigon and events in Quang Ngai. I had another story to tell.

"Say, you've got to hear about our latest MCC money-raising project. Once when I went out to the airport in the middle of all the evacuation mess, a guy offered me a thousand dollars in green U.S. bills if I would say his sister was my wife! I told him I was sorry, but I wouldn't sign any papers like that because I had to be as honest as I could. Then I told him I didn't care how much money he offered me because I wouldn't be able to keep the money anyhow since MCC didn't allow independent money-raising projects. When I got back to the office, Max and I decided we could make MCC Vietnam self-supporting: we'd just go into business selling our signatures for a thousand dollars apiece to pretty girls who wanted to evacuate!" We chuckled.

Max sobered. "You guys should have heard the rumors. They were tearing people up. One Sunday, one of my work campers was here telling us the communists were going to shoot us and that we had to leave and take her and her family along. The next week, she was back asking if she and her family could stay here with us because the communists would only respect foreigners!"

Hiro and Earl had spent the entire day hitchhiking the last leg of their trip to Saigon. At 1:30 a.m., our adrenaline levels finally dropped to normal. Max, Hiro, and Earl headed for sleeping quarters; I headed for the office. An inner drive compelled me to chronicle the April flood of rumors and the events of the past several days before I could sleep. I rolled a sheet of paper into the typewriter and began with April 28. At 3:30 a.m., I quit.

*The Next Day*

Friday morning, May 2, when the MCC secretary and several work campers dropped by for a visit, we chased the helter-skelter piles of stuff in the MCC office back into the closet. The sidewalk in front of the office, however, remained hopelessly messy. Without permission from us, the public had informally allocated the sidewalk linking the MCC office to the VNCS office as a trash-dumping site. I had often seen a lone figure or two combing through the smelly, unsightly garbage to rescue valuables—pieces of cardboard, or empty cans and bottles—before the trash collectors made their rounds. The former official trash collectors, perhaps uncertain who would pay them, suspended their services. The garbage pile mushroomed into the street.

When the Provisional Revolutionary Government had moved into the city, I had heard its appeal over the radio: all civil servants should keep working. Saigon never lost its electricity or its water service: minor blessings perhaps, but in a city bulging toward a population of four million, a blackout or severe water shortage could have produced incredible chaos. The new administration also resolved the trash problem before it became a major health hazard.

Friday afternoon, feeling braver than the day before, I took my camera downtown. After all, the temporary passes for Max and me indicated we were reporters. We photographed a U.S. army tank which rested against a huge tree on the sidewalk behind the former Presidential Palace. Perhaps the tank had been abandoned while still moving and then smashed into the tree. Three blocks away from our home, a runaway tank had bowled over a traffic signal-light pole.

I photographed the post office with the new flag. I snapped a photo of the abandoned U.S. embassy building with its hundreds of sunken, undersized windows designed to resist attack by "the communists" who ironically were now guarding it. The formidable fortress still dwarfed the buildings around it. Like a dinosaur skeleton from a previous era, the lifeless building silently guarded its secrets about earlier days when it had crushed human life beneath its feet. Years later, in a book written by Frank Snepp, I learned that some of the vicious rumors prior to the collapse of the Saigon regime had originated in the CIA offices in this building. The poi-

sonous rumors had given birth to ungodly twins—fear and panic—
that wrecked and maimed society as deliberately as the deadly
minefields the U.S. military had left behind. Agent Orange fathered
cancer and birth defects. The U.S. military and political involvement in Vietnam caused deformities which will last for generations.

A truckload of PLA soldiers unexpectedly drove by as I took
the photo. Unsure of their reaction to my camera, I froze. They
waved. I relaxed. My film caught the juxtaposition: home rule had
replaced foreign rule. Like the uncertainties facing people in a
fledgling United States of America in 1776,[1] countless questions lay
beneath the appearance of normalcy in Saigon. Downtown, Max
and I met several PLA soldiers and visited briefly with them. Then I
snapped a photo of a group of curious onlookers surrounding a
PLA soldier.

Barbed wire barriers in Saigon tumbled. At one corner along
Phan Thanh Gian Street, the pillbox guardhouse stood empty, the
barricades lay toppled, the barbed wire lay pushed back, opening
the formerly closed street.

A steady stream of guests visited us after our photo spree. One
man, some ten years older than I, parked his bicycle in our front
yard. Since he preferred to visit outside, we sat on a concrete bench
in the shade. He and I had once visited his family in the southern
delta where I learned he belonged to the Hoa Hao sect, a strongly
anticommunist religious group with roots in Buddhism. He
removed his light green nylon hat, perhaps the same nondescript
one he had worn on that weekend trip two years earlier.

He glanced around and lowered his voice. "How soon are you
leaving?"

"When will I be going?" I echoed. "Where? What do you
mean?"

He leaned toward me. "Will they be sending a helicopter to
pick you up?"

His question struck like a bolt of lightning: he thought I still
would evacuate! "No," I explained, "I'm not planning to leave."

"You aren't!" His mouth stayed open. Perhaps a lightning
bolt just struck him, too. He glanced around again. "But the communists—they're all around. What'll they do when they find out
you're here?"

"No problem. Why should I be afraid?"

"You're an American."

"That's right. But I've already been downtown and met some soldiers."

"You better be careful," he warned. "They hate Americans."

"Probably so, but they didn't do anything to us."

"Did they know you were American?"

"We told them if they asked."

He cross-examined me: "Then you really aren't planning to leave?"

"That's right. Besides, the evacuation flights ended several days ago."

He glanced around again and thrust his face at mine. "Do you think the United States would send my people guns or money to fight the communists?"

I could not believe it! "No, I don't. The U.S. Congress cut off funds for Vietnam. The United States is tired of sending guns to Vietnam. Vietnam has seen enough war. There's a new government in power here, and you and your people should accept it rather than fight it."

"But we hate the communists!" he growled. "Could your organization give us money to fight them?"

Incredible! I thought he knew me better than that. Perhaps he doubted me. I knew I must try again. "No," I began, "our organization would never give anyone money for fighting."

*History and Current Affairs*

After breakfast on Saturday, my fingers resumed speed. Like an irregular roller coaster, experiences coursed through my mind, demanding to be typed.

> . . . a member of the Mennonite Church (in Gia Dinh) . . . had been primed to take over the Sunday morning Bible Study Class for new Christians at the (Phan Thanh Gian) Mennonite student center. But unknown to us, in order to help support the family, his wife had been working for the CIA. So they felt they had to leave. And now they are gone. Evacuated. I felt disappointed. And betrayed.

My stomach felt hollow, yet heavy, as I tried to comprehend the inconsistency of Christians working for the CIA. When I had visited Pleiku, I learned that some non-Mennonite missionaries freely shared information with U.S. government contacts. Their actions, though saddening me, had not surprised me because I had seen photos of a world-famous U.S. evangelist standing beside Richard Nixon with hands raised as if to bless the bullets and bombs being sent to Vietnam. That fundamental distortion of the good news agonized me, paralyzing my fingers at the keyboard.

Painting a cross on a canteen started long ago: wooing Christians in A.D. 312, Emperor Constantine turned the cross of Jesus into a tool of the military, ignoring the clear teachings of Jesus about love. In exchange for the emperor's favor, many Christians forsook their Master's teachings and left the pacifist pattern which had been characteristic of all Christians up till then.

Since that time, rather than praying for their enemies, many Christians have preferred the popularity of the cross on the canteen. Ignoring the biblical mandate to feed their enemies and give them a drink, those Christians have followed seductive government orders to kill people designated as "enemies." Peace and love, instead of being the hallmark of a new community living under Christ's leadership, have been diluted to a lukewarm inner swamp unrelated to Christian ethics. Yet even in Vietnam, some Christians had not succumbed to the pressure of narrow patriotism.

Ngoc, baptized at the Phan Thanh Gian Center less than a month earlier, had signed the Mennonite declaration in April, determined to stay in Vietnam. Now she, together with another enthusiastic participant in the Center's Bible study program, arrived for a visit. They shared their hopes and fears.

"Oh, I was scared, Jim! Before Saigon was liberated, I was really worried. Yeah, not so much scared as worried. There were so many rumors. I know MCC and the Mennonites talked about reconciliation, but I hated the 'communists' and even had the chance to evacuate. Even though I hated them, somehow I wasn't afraid. If I would have gone, I would have just gone to study at some U.S. university, but I didn't even know my own homeland, so how could I go abroad for study? I first wanted to learn about Vietnam and really wanted to know what they were like. You guys were staying, so I thought I would stay, too, but my parents wanted me to go— that was their dream ever since I was small. I didn't know what to do—every day I cried so hard my eyes got all swollen. But I decided to stay, and I'm glad I did. Now—would you believe it?—I've been downtown all by myself, and I've even talked to some of them. So I really am a brave person, right? Some of them have cute faces."

That afternoon a teacher who was a member of the Gia Dinh Mennonite Church shared his perspective. Although he faced uncertainties for himself and his family, pragmatism characterised his perspective.

"We're going to make it," he said matter-of-factly. "We'll just need some time to adjust. I don't think the new government will force socialism. It will maybe take five years, and probably six or seven till things level off. We'd been taught how to do things another way for so long already, and people had a lot of imported luxuries which they really didn't need. Under the new system, people may be poor but not hungry. The new system is actually more biblical—everybody living at the same level."

His conclusion astounded me, but I replied, "I know in Acts chapter two, it's clear that the early church shared everything they had with each other."

"Our church should have been training people for a situation like this, but it really hadn't. I'm concerned about the future of our church. I think the preacher had too much power in the past. Before Luke (Martin) left, he said anybody could baptize: he said I could or you could."

"That's interesting." I tried not to show my surprise at Luke's suggestion that I could perform water baptism. My Anabaptist-Mennonite understanding of Scripture, however, allowed any sincere believer to baptize others. Hearing that Luke shared a similar perspective excited me.

The teacher continued. "The Bible says we are all equal before God, but people seem to like being baptized by someone important. But the important people in the church needed God's salvation and mercy as much as anyone else."

Then, shifting the focus slightly, he observed, "Everybody does some meditating about his or her own life—some more, some less, but everybody thinks about it. Even the government cadre who is director of my school now said he needed faith in order to live. Of all the propaganda that had been going around, the thing I thought about the most was that they don't have feelings. But they do! They laugh and cry like anyone else. And the rumor about the blood-bath—that they would kill a million people—there was no way they could kill a million people and still administer the country."

"I couldn't believe all the rumors, either, but I didn't know how to argue with people who were so frightened by them," I admitted.

"A close friend of mine," he said, "was caught in 1969 and jailed on Con Son Island. I fled just in time, so I wasn't picked up. He was a schoolmate of mine and from my village, and now he is head of the largest high school in Saigon—Petrus Ky."

Suddenly, everybody seemed to have at least one link to what had been "the other side." The change, perhaps, was not so much in the links themselves as in a readiness to acknowledge relationships which had previously been hidden or disclaimed for survival under the Thieu government.

As Christians wrestled with the new situation, they discovered new meanings in familiar biblical passages. I agreed that the concept of everyone living at the same level lies closer to the heart of Jesus' teaching than capitalism does. Although I had been a strong critic of the greed and exploitation inherent in capitalism, I had never studied the economic theory of communism. Nevertheless, I had been trying to follow a simple lifestyle, willing to work as an unsalaried MCC volunteer.

Some Mennonites had followed a communal lifestyle for centuries as part of their faithfulness to the teachings of Jesus. Some seminary friends of mine in Indiana had formed a house church, contributing all their earnings to it and drawing funds from it to meet their needs. Their lifestyle had challenged me, but just as I refused to give any government my full endorsement, I had reservations about economic systems, too.

*What Kind of Liberation?*

On a bicycle trip, Hiro and Earl heard that the Japanese Embassy might have permission to send telegrams to Japan. They raced to tell Max and me the news. Since Hiro was Japanese, this was the first possibility of communicating directly with our families. We excitedly drafted a brief telegram and then dashed to the

Japanese Embassy to send it even though we did not know whether the message would reach our families.

Sunday morning, as usual, I led the English Bible study in the book of John. Max played guitar for singing. My conversation with the students and friends lasted long past noon. A Gia Dinh Mennonite Church leader requested my presence at a staff meeting the next morning—implying I was responsible for maintaining the relationship to that congregation in Luke's absence.

That evening I challenged Max, Earl, and Hiro during our discussion. I was more reserved in my use of the word *liberation* than they were.

"Everybody is using this word *liberation*—even you guys. I'd like to know how it really applies here. When I use the word, I have to think theologically: Jesus is the real liberator. But that's not what people are talking about when they use the word now. And even militarily, it was a collapse of the Thieu government more than a liberation. So I'm ready for some insights." I was pushing them hard, and I knew it.

"Look at all the families being reunited. Isn't that fantastic? Isn't that a liberation?" Earl's rhetorical questions started turning the wheels.

"And just look at the political prisoners who are out of jail," Max added. "I'd say that's liberation."

"It's also the end of a false economy." Hiro was direct. "Vietnam is liberated from a puppet government that was held up by U.S. dollars."

"Okay," I replied, "I can't really argue with all that. I think family reunification is great. I'm glad to see the political prisoners free, and I'm glad that the U.S. is out. But why can't I simply refer to *the change in government* instead of talking about *liberation?*"

"What if Thieu and his boys would have won?" Earl asked. "Do you think *liberation* would have described that? If he would have won, maybe there really would have been a bloodbath. Maybe that's why people were so scared."

"What you're seeing is a revolution," Hiro emphasized. "This society is being turned upside down. People have to adjust to new ways. Your friends in the Bible study group are going to have to do things differently, too."

"Like what?" I asked, puzzled.

"Like—don't make them too dependent on you."

Max suggested another facet. "Look at the involvement of students. They're liberated from their books and their narrow perspective. It's more of a community spirit, rather than such intense individualism. Now they're involved in practical things. I'll bet most of them never swept streets before. Would something like that have happened under Thieu? Nope. I bet they would have snubbed their noses at manual labor like that."

Earl agreed. "Right. Now self-less, public-serving actions are encouraged. The heroes are those who sacrifice for society. In this new social order, the poor are the beneficiaries, and the rich are the disenfranchised. Now the poor will be able to enter the 'elite' professions because privilege isn't based on wealth. It's a liberation from material success as the model for emulation. But the initial phase is going to be terribly hard—it's no picnic. Sweeping social changes are difficult for both the rich and the poor—and this revolution will be emotionally more difficult for the rich."

Needing quiet time to process the discussion, I went to the rooftop to meditate. I set two chairs face-to-face, using one to prop my feet. A cool breeze whispered in the trees. The street noise, muffled by the height, was less distracting than in the office on first floor. This evening, as usual when I meditated on the rooftop, my first thoughts expressed gratitude to God.

*Awe*

By midweek, I had cleared several piles from my office desk, attended a meeting at the Gia Dinh Mennonite Church, found the deed to the church building to prove who owned it, and participated in several discussions on the relationship between the church and government. Two events turned Wednesday into a special day—one week after the change in governments.

That morning, a friend brought a former political prisoner named B.C. to visit. What had made him such a terrible menace to the Thieu government? As an artist who concentrated on the struggle for peace, B.C. had painted doves, mothers crying, rocks with tears, broken guns, and gaunt prisoners. The Thieu government had felt endangered: his pictures had undermined zeal for the war.

B.C. spoke softly, with a ready smile. His loose-fitting, black outfit accented his skinny body. We invited him to stay for lunch, but while we ate and talked, I fumbled for words, unable to concentrate. He had endured too much pain. His vast experiences and poignant art overwhelmed me. I felt more awe for him and his gentle ways than for any president.

That evening, Quang and I discussed religion and politics. He had stayed with the Luke Martin family while attending high school. Then when the Martin's had left, he had joined us in the two-story Mennonite center.

"I'd like to be baptized," he told me, "and I'd like for you to do it. Would you?"

His question took my breath away. What should I answer? Although I had graduated from seminary, I was not ordained, feeling the ceremony conferred illegitimate status. Nevertheless, I had accepted licensing for one year with the authorization to perform marriages and had officiated at the wedding ceremony for my sister Vernell and her husband, Paul. Now my license had expired.

Like a flash of lightning, I also remembered my commission from Kansas to spread the Gospel of Peace in Vietnam. A baptismal service surely symbolized peace and reconciliation that transcended barriers. I felt certain that the Lord would accept the baptismal pledge, even though I lacked ecclesiastical titles. Obviously, Quang agreed, but what would other people think? Specifically, what would the Mennonite missionaries think?

Luke! Yes! I recalled that the teacher had told me, "Before Luke left, he said anybody could baptize: he said I could or you could." When I had heard that statement, I did not imagine I would need the reassurance so soon.

On the other hand, Hiro's warning also rang in my ears: "Don't make them [your friends] too dependent on you." The days of U.S. domination in Vietnam had ended. A new era had begun. How was I helping Christians to adjust?

Those thoughts sparked across the "circuit boards" in my brains in miliseconds. They provided a background for the issue without resolving it.

I took a deep breath. "Well," I answered slowly, "I probably could do it. I've known you long enough, and I believe you are sincere. I'm willing to do it, but I think it might be better if you'd ask one of the elders from the Gia Dinh Church to do it, rather than having me, a foreigner, do it."

"But you've always said that Christians don't emphasize nationality. And I really want you to do it, rather than anyone else."

How could I argue with his logic? How could I decline his heartfelt desire? "Okay. Actually, I feel honored that you asked me."

A smile broke across his face. "That'll be a day I'll remember for the rest of my life. Thanks, brother, thanks a lot!"

I smiled at him. "I'll certainly remember it, too!"

*Shepherds*
The next afternoon, I led the New Believers' Fellowship in studying 1 Peter for the first time we met after the change of government. The vigorous discussion—ranging far beyond the text—stretched late into the evening.

"Do you think we should sign up for student work projects or not?"

"Why should we? It's not required."

"Yes, but why not participate in good projects?"

"If we do one thing, then soon we'll do another, and another, and who knows where we'll end up?"

"Wait a minute, if we participate now, in something we approve of, then they'll have to listen to us if there's something we don't agree with."

"Right, I think it's a good idea to get involved."

"Not me. I'm going to wait and see."

"Wait for what? Look at all the work that needs to be done. Besides, isn't service to others what Jesus taught?"

"That's right. Mennonites always emphasize that Jesus came to serve, not to be served. You could even call Mark 10:44-45 the 'Mennonite motto.' "("For the Son of man himself did not come to be served, but to serve....")

Neat, I thought. I wished I would have thought of calling it the "Mennonite motto." I listened intently, trying to catch each person's comments in the rapid discussion. Suddenly, someone noticed my silence.

"Jim, what do you think?"

"I've enjoyed listening to your energetic discussion. Actually, I can't tell you what to do. You're the ones who will have to work that out. In general, my perspective is that we need to try to support the good projects of any government and always be willing to ask questions or suggest alternatives for things we don't agree with."

The next evening, Tin and another Gia Dinh Church member described their recent trip to the southern delta city of Can Tho. While there, they met an evangelist from northern Vietnam who succinctly analyzed the impact of recent events on the Protestant Church in southern Vietnam: "Even before the 'wolves' came, the shepherds ran away and abandoned their sheep."

That observation appeared well founded. Not only U.S. Embassy and military personnel had evacuated: uncertainty and panic had filled church leaders, too. Some foreign missionaries had drawn parallels to China, some took early furloughs, some thought of family, some evacuated in the final helicopters. Consequently, by April 30, 1975, only one independent foreign Protestant missionary—whom I later met—had voluntarily remained in southern Vietnam. A few other missionaries had involuntarily stayed in Banmethuot. For one reason or another, all the other foreign Protestant missionaries from every denomination had left.

Technically speaking, I was not a missionary: I was part of the MCC relief and social work team. According to my theology, however, every Christian bears a responsibility for letting the light shine and sharing the good news, not just with words, but also with actions. In Vietnam, actions spoke louder than words. The earlier solidarity of personnel and programs of the foreign Mennonites in Vietnam had transcended the traditional distinction between service-oriented MCC and evangelism-oriented Vietnam Mennonite Mission. By teaching Bible, I had become a de facto missionary.

All the official foreign Protestant missionaries had left, partly due to a truncated gospel. Those missionaries, except for a few, had ignored the teaching of Jesus to love all people—even so-called "enemies." When the missionaries left, many Vietnamese pastors and evangelists also felt an overwhelming magnetic pull and left Vietnam. Since most Protestant churches in Vietnam had concentrated power in the preacher, many congregations faced a crisis, groping for new leadership as well as for new theological understandings.

*Involved in Politics?*

In mid-May, a formal, front-page newspaper announcement asked all individuals, including foreigners, to register with the government. Max, Hiro, Earl, and I also hoped to register the programs of Mennonite Central Committee. We each received a mimeographed registration sheet in Vietnamese. An official completed the data blanks in our presence.

> The Internal Security Committee of Saigon Gia Dinh certifies:
> Mr. James Klassen (Nam Hai) . . .
>     Of American Nationality,
> A worker for Mennonite Central Committee . . .
> Has registered with the security organization
> on May 17, 1975 . . .

The next week, Ngoc asked, "Are the Mennonites involved in politics?"

"Not in the sense that I think you are using the word," I said. "Can you explain what you mean by *politics?*"

She lowered her voice and shifted uncomfortably. "Well, some people think you guys work for the CIA." Once past the terrible three-letter abbreviation, she resumed a normal conversational tone. "I've argued with them and said you don't. Finally, I decided to ask you directly."

"I thought that's what you meant when you used the word *politics.* I can assure you that none of us are involved with the CIA. We don't believe in their secret style and dirty tricks. We believe that Christ taught us to live open lives based on peace and love. So we try to be as open as we can, but unless the skeptics would come live with us 24 hours a day, there isn't any way we can prove to them that we aren't working for the CIA."

"It's such a relief to hear that! This really started to bother me. They say you only wanted to stay in Vietnam because you work for the CIA."

"I guess I can understand why they would think that. They probably aren't Christians and really don't understand that the real reason we stayed was based on our concern for peace and reconciliation."

"That's what I told them, but they don't believe it."

"I'm glad that you and our other close friends believe it. Perhaps we can't hope for more than that, although we'll keep trying to make our witness as clear as possible. I also need to add one thing about politics: in a sense, everything we do has political implications. For example, I got a visa to come to Vietnam under the old government so I could work in the MCC program here—and that was a very political act. At the same time, Mennonites were talking to the Provisional Revolutionary Government representatives in Paris—and that was also a very political act. Perhaps the best we can ever do is to try to be balanced and not regard anyone as our enemies."

"But what do you mean 'working here was political'?" she asked.

"Let me try to explain. I was helping to get medicines to Vietnam for two, uhm, three clinics—Nhatrang, Plieku, and Gia Dinh. Those medicines were really just helping people under the government of one side, right?"

She nodded.

"Okay, at that same time, MCC was also shipping medicines to help people under the PRG—and people would say that was a very political act. But I would contend that both were political, not just the shipments for people under the PRG. Does that make sense?"

"But why didn't you ever tell us about those shipments to the PRG?"

"I don't know." I searched for answers. "I tried to stress peace and love and reconciliation as being the Jesus way. I guess maybe we didn't want to complicate life for our friends here. Maybe we should have been more open. I remember that the Mennonite missionaries did circulate one article about church life in the North to the leaders of the Gia Dinh Church."

"Yes, I think that would have helped us to see things more clearly."

"You might also be interested to know that MCC had a small program to assist families of political prisoners under the Thieu government," I added. "It was a small program, and not something we wanted to publicize. Still, we felt that we had to do something here in Saigon specifically related to our peace concerns. So now, is MCC involved in politics or not?" Not waiting for her answer to the rhetorical question, I continued. "Since the change of government, lots of people have told me, 'Oh, you could stay because you weren't involved in politics'—which, according to them, means I didn't work for the U.S. goverment, for the CIA, or for the U.S. military—so I usually just smile and nod my head. I wasn't involved in politics the way they are using the word, and they haven't got time for me to explain."

"I'm still concerned about the people who say you work for the CIA," she lamented, almost crying. "It hurts when they accuse you of that."

"Don't worry about it," I reassured her. "We can't expect that everyone will understand us."

Halfway around the world, people in my home community in Kansas were accusing me of the very opposite political activity. One member of my home church strolled into the backyard where my mother was gardening.

"Do you know what people are saying about James?" He asked assertively. "Do you know they say he is a communist?"

"Why, that's impossible!" my mother exclaimed. "He stayed voluntarily."

"Yes, I know. That's exactly why they say he's a communist. Why else would he want to stay?"

"He stayed to share the love of Jesus. That's why."

"But do you know for sure he's not a communist?"

"Well," my mother declared, "he still believes that the shed blood of Jesus washed away his sins, and that's good enough for me."

My stay in Vietnam under the Provisional Revolutionary Government carried obvious political implications. My time in Vietnam under the former Republic of Vietnam, however, had carried just as many political implications and just as many questions—implications and questions which many Christians chose to ignore because that regime had been supported by the U.S. government.

*Crossing Borders*

In the middle of the week, several Vietnamese government representatives paid us an unexpected visit. They asked about our well-being as well as about our former programs. Their choice of words, following all the social graces for politeness, conveyed one underlying message: this government carried the responsibility for its own people and for its guests. Times had changed.

In fact, the dream of reunifying the entire country was becoming a reality. Letters and telegrams crossed the former boundary lines that no one had openly defied for nearly 20 years. People began traveling across the once-forbidden ground, reuniting families and loved ones. Formal reunification at the governmental level still looked distant. One nagging question stung my excitement: what or who had prevented the reconciliation from coming earlier—20 years earlier? U.S. government actions in Vietnam pained me.

When international telegram service resumed on Friday, May 23, 1975, Max and I carefully chose our words. Perhaps all words are important, but the words of our first telegram seemed to carry a special significance. We wanted them to convey our feelings, summarize what had happened, and describe the current situation—all in 20 words or less, including the address!

Max and I decided that one joint telegram to Kansas would temporarily suffice for both of us because my parents could contact Max's parents in Oklahoma. "RA KLASSEN RR2 BOX 102A NEWTON KANSAS USA ALL FINE NEVER ENDANGERED STILL TEACHING BIBLE CALL EDIGER (signed) LOVE JAMES MAX."

Invigorated by such direct contact, Earl, Max, Hiro, and I formulated a telegram to MCC headquarters in Akron, Pennsylvania. With all four of our names on the signature line in the telegram, we hoped the Akron MCC office would understand that Hiro and Earl had arrived safely in Saigon.

*Believing Whom?*

To understand changes in the society, I relied on my friends more than on newspaper accounts. During a discussion in our living room, Ngoc commented, "We were really caught in an ugly system: schoolmates might be close friends, but then when they got into jobs they would become fierce antagonists. I'm glad I won't have to struggle against all that. Under the old government people were free—free to be corrupt, free to be selfish, free to exploit others."

The church, I thought, has a responsibility to call the citizens of God's kingdom to a higher way. Sometimes, though, the call was muted, as I learned when a member of our new believers' group came for pastoral counseling.

"I'm confused," she complained. "Before the revolution some Catholic priests were saying one thing and now they're saying another. Before they were saying, 'We've got to fight the communists!' Now they're saying, 'We've got to support the revolution!' What's going on? How can they switch like that?"

"Some Protestant preachers are that way, too," I observed. "Perhaps they felt they had to say that to survive under the old system, and now they feel like they have to say something else to survive under the new government. For myself, I can say the same things both before and after the change of government, since Christ is my leader, and I won't carry a gun for anyone."

"Okay, so you won't fight anyone, but do you support whoever is in power?"

"No, no." The words popped from my mouth. "I've never encouraged blind obedience to any government. No matter what government we're under, we have a responsibility to ask questions because we have a higher loyalty. So just like I'm not going to try to overthrow any government, I'm also not going to just close my eyes and follow whatever it says."

Again and again I asked God to grant the church courage for a more prophetic witness to the new government than it ever dared to have with the old one. The end of May refreshed the ecstasy and the agony of being a Christian.

To prepare for the baptism service, I studied every New Testament reference to *baptism* and *baptizing,* including derived references. New believers wanting to be baptized shared their pilgrimages, exciting me and humbling me.

Lan, one of the candidates, told me, "I would like to be baptized, but I have so many bad things inside of me."

"Baptism doesn't mean you're perfect," I responded, "but it means you will try to follow Jesus—it means you promise to try to follow his way."

The next day her older sister Lieu confirmed an amazing transformation. "My younger sister just told me you are going to baptize her. Wow! I never expected that. I'm really happy. She always used to be critical of everything. In the [Bible study] meetings, she would come and never say anything. She would just sit there silently. But she must have been listening to what you and the Stauffers were saying." The Stauffers had previously been leaders at the Center. Lieu continued: "That must have been the way God worked. And since she decided to be baptized, she's been so kind. It's so unexpected. She'd normally pick apart anything anybody said, but not anymore!"

Later in the day, Ngoc told me, "I signed up for social work and really am putting my heart into it because Jesus wants us to help others."

Those glimpses of faithfulness, although my contribution to them had been meager, rewarded my staying in Vietnam. God's Spirit was at work.

The next day, Hoa, one of the nurses from Pleiku, shared a depressing experience she had just before the change of government.

"In April," she recounted, "the pastor-administrator told the hospital staff that whoever wanted to stay could stay and whoever didn't have the spirit to stay could go—but he himself left three days earlier than he said he would.

"You know the nurse named Phi?" Hoa barely paused. "Well, when everybody was evacuating to Nhatrang, her husband suggested that two other nurses and I should not go in the hospital pickup because it was too crowded, so he dumped us off with our bags. But then he piled his soldier friends into the truck. I'll bet when he got to Saigon he probably had the nerve to ask you to reimburse him for the trip. Did he?"

"Yeah, he did," I admitted. "He said the pickup was too crowded for you."

"That's a lie! We were already in the pickup when he dumped us off. We managed to get a ride near the end of the string of vehicles. He was near the front and made it to Tuyhoa. We couldn't make it when the fighting broke out."

She talked on and on, describing the twelve tough days she spent in the forest before finally returning to Pleiku. In Pleiku itself, she saw huge sections which had been looted and burned by the ARVN soldiers and unhappy Montagnards. She concluded: "An experience like this makes it clear who was truthful and who was not. I will never believe a preacher again."

Though not referring to me, her words rang in my ears. I was "preacher pro tem" at the Phan Thanh Gian Center, currently preparing a catechetical study and a baptismal service. I knew Scripture declared, "Teachers will be judged with greater strictness than others" (James 3:1).

As I wrestled to develop a concise, balanced theological statement for my friends in the June catechism class, I appreciated my former studies in seminary. The "Foundations of Mennonite Life and Thought," which I prepared for the class, dealt with the role of the Bible, Jesus, Grace, Discipleship, the Individual, the Christian Community, Suffering, Nonviolence, and Evangelism.

*Study-Work*

Not wanting to impose ourselves on anyone in the new situation, we MCCers let friends come visit us rather than going to visit them. Consequently, we cherished each friend who was willing to reestablish ties with us foreigners.

Early in June, a graduate of the nursing program in Nhatrang also stopped for a visit. A huge smile lit up the nurse's face as she gave me a package. "This is for your niece," she explained. "You remember when her Bible school class sent some money a year ago to help my sisters go to school?"

I had nearly forgotten. At that time, I had written five anecdotes, one for each day, for the teachers in the summer Bible school in South Dakota to share with the pupils. The brief narratives described this nurse's family and mentioned customs, geography, church life, and the impact of the war. After the Bible school ended, I again had served as the link, forwarding the children's offering from South Dakota to the nurse's family in Vietnam.

"Wow!" I turned the pages of the stamp collection. "I know

my niece will be impressed. That's really thoughtful of you. Thank you very much!"

"It's my personal stamp collection. I won't be collecting any-more, so I wanted to give it to your niece."

"It's an outstanding collection. There are lots of stamps in here that I never even knew existed—like these triangular ones." I pointed to a prominent set distinguished from the familiar rectan-gular pattern. "On behalf of my niece, I want to say a sincere thank you."

"You're welcome, but the album isn't much."

"But it really is special. Thank you. And how is your family?"

"We're fine," she replied. "We've got a little orchard and garden. Dad and my brothers go fishing, and when they catch more than what we need, we sell them for a bit of additional income."

"What about your oldest brother? Did he have to go to *hoc-tap* sessions?"

We were conversing in Vietnamese, so I said *"hoc-tap"* without needing to translate it. Although *hoc-tap* literally means *study-work,* it is often translated into English by the derogatory word *reeduca-tion.* Life itself is an ongoing educational process, and alert minds around the world—including those of scientists—often must revise their understandings. Consequently, I prefer to translate *hoc-tap* as *study-work,* avoiding the word *reeducation,* just as I avoid the word *enemy* to describe people.

"Yes, he went for three days," she noted, "and then they told him to go home and do something productive."

Others, too, had reported similar experiences. Because the local governing bodies carried substantial responsibilities, many policies under the "new" government lacked standardization. Nevertheless, draftees from the former regime generally returned home after a three-day study-work program which oriented them to the new situation.

*Two Responses*

That evening, the contrasts of the new situation struck me through two visitors. The first was a new, sincere Christian who often attended the Fellowship meetings at our center. She arrived at dusk with a heavy heart.

"I was selected to teach at the model school for the whole city."

"That sounds like quite an honor," I responded enthusiastically.

"Perhaps you didn't know that I'm a graduate of the National Conservatory of Music. That plus a college education gave me quite an advantage over a lot of other elementary school teachers. The problem is that now I'm expected to teach the children—youngsters, ten and under—the songs of the revolution, including songs about killing, and I don't like it. It doesn't feel right."

"What about teaching them other little songs and choruses?" I asked.

"Oh, I've tried. I like to teach them fun songs, but I've been so bold that I've been accused of being antirevolutionary. I don't want to teach them songs about war. I want to teach them about how to love everybody in order to build a strong society in my homeland."

"It sounds like you have a good perspective. I don't know why they would accuse you of being antirevolutionary."

"You see, this school is supposed to be a model school," she said. "That means everybody is watching me with an eagle eye. Maybe somewhere else they wouldn't be so strict. For days now, I've been telling myself every day, 'Today is absolutely my last day,' but it wasn't."

I nodded. "You're really confronting a tough problem. I don't know if it's helpful to know or not, but every government likes to have people's loyalty starting at an early age. Governments glorify war and killing and honor military heroes. I agree with you, though. It doesn't seem right."

"I don't know what to do. How can I teach there with a happy heart?"

I listened sympathetically, but without having any easy answers.

Soon after she left, the buzzer from the gate rang again, and a slender, young man introduced himself. Max, Hiro, and Earl had left earlier.

"I was in prison for seven years under the old system—including three years on Con Son. My final days were in Kontum after the Paris Agreements."

"I think I was aware of that. There was a block of time when your parents didn't know where you were, isn't that right?" I asked. His father was a renowned author.

"That's right. I just wanted to stop by and say thanks to all of you for your concern during that time. When those prison doors finally opened up and I was free, it felt great!"

"That's for sure!" I nodded.

"I just got back to Saigon on the first of May and have really been busy since then. For me," he continued, "the revolution is a dream come true. Under the old government, I had been a student, but I got upset at the university teachers. Listen, I'm sorry I'm so long-winded. I really don't even know you very well, and here I've taken up so much of your time."

"Oh, that's no problem at all," I reassured him. "I'm really pleased to have met you and I am really glad that you are out of jail."

"I'm honored to have met you, too." He stood to leave. "Please give my greetings to the others. I'm sorry I can't stay till they get back, but I'm on [civil defense] guard duty and promised that I wouldn't be gone long. Actually, it's illegal for me to be alone without a gun at night like this, but I just wanted to stop by for a quick visit."

The unusually dark night quickly swallowed him with his dark outfit.

*What Will You Do?*

Several weeks earlier, another former political prisoner had stopped at our Center to visit. Phuong Que, as she called herself in writing, was a petite young woman who had been a high school philosophy teacher. In 1970, shortly after she married, the Thieu government had arrested her and her husband and tortured them in each other's presence because they had participated in a peace demonstration. Phuong Que's husband died in prison.

Max and Earl asked her a difficult question. "What will you do when you meet the man who tortured you and your husband in prison?"

She leaned forward. "To be honest with you, there will be a little flame of anger inside of me which will want to flare up, but I've got to control it, because if I would kill him, at least ten members of his extended family would be after me and my life. But the cycle of hatred must stop."

Later she told Max, "I met my interrogator, but I only felt malice for half a second before I remembered it was time to build a new society."

Another former political prisoner, imprisoned as a high school student for protesting the war, had survived the tiger cages on Con Son Island. Max asked him, "What will you do when you meet the man who tortured you in prison?"

"Oh," the survivor said, "I've already met him, and I told him not to worry. We're in a new era now, and—who knows?—he may be one of the most productive members of our society."

Churches, too, struggled to deal redemptively with awkward situations. On Sunday, June 15, the Gia Dinh Mennonite Church held a congregregational meeting. In the vigorous discussion, several conclusions surfaced: the pastor—because of his absence— no longer served as pastor of the congregation nor as head of the Mennonite Leadership Team nor as the director of the Gia Dinh Center which included a reading room, elementary school, and clinic. In spite of that, the congregation neither excommunicated their pastor nor revoked his ordination.

From their new vantage point, the members also discussed two handicaps in the Mennonite Mission legacy. The Gia Dinh Mennonite Center, which had depended on funds from U.S. Mennonites instead of being self-supporting, suddenly placed an unbearable financial burden on the congregation. The other headache, perhaps ironic, surfaced when attempting to register the English program of the Mennonite Center on Phan Thanh Gian Street with the new government: that program had never been registered under the old government and consequently no official documents existed to substantiate that Center as a school.

Since the congregation's former liaison to the Phan Thanh Gian Fellowship had evacuated with his wife and family, formal action designated a new representative named Trung. He promptly reported the congregation's decisions to me. Since he and I were responsible for the approaching baptisms, we outlined the service and agreed to keep the ceremony simple.

## Laugh, Cry, Look Ahead

Mai, a university friend of ours from Central Vietnam, had told us about a study-work session he attended in Danang while he was traveling around the country trying to find his parents.

"One evening there was an old woman," Mai had related, "a refugee from Hue, in this jam-packed room, and she had something she wanted to say: 'If we had known you *bo-doi* [PLA soldiers] were coming, we wouldn't have run. Evacuation was terribly difficult—a lot of people died. We ran because we thought the communists were coming, and you know how terribly cruel and vicious they are.' " The woman had not realized that she was speaking to the very people she was calling "communists."

Obviously, all the bloodbath rumors proved false, but the society torn by war for so many years still bled internally. Mai never found his elderly parents. He traveled up and down the coast of Vietnam looking for them, worried that they might have been crushed in the evacuation stampede, yet hoping for some word about them. Even when he thought they might have been lost at sea, he kept searching for them, hoping they might still be somewhere just out of touch. The lines in his young forehead seemed deeper each time he visited us as he passed through Saigon, the newly named Ho Chi Minh City.

As he lost weight, a large mole on his right cheek became more prominent. After several months on his relentless quest, he stopped at our office, finally defeated by a fateful magnet that had drawn his parents beyond his reach.

"I can't spend all of my life looking for them. I've tried—how I've tried! I've done my best. But I'm quitting now. I've got to look toward the future. I've got to start taking care of myself now and not worry about finding my parents. I've got a job as a translator for an export-import company, and it looks like I can handle the work."

We invited him to stay for lunch to celebrate his new work.

## Baptism

Teachers in Vietnam traditionally received immense respect, and as a Bible teacher, I was elevated even higher. The honor, however, disturbed me; my theology recognized different functions in the Christian community, but not different ranks. Nevertheless, whether I liked it or not, I exerted a sizable influence in the Fellowship, particularly for the newest believers. They understood the biblical foundations of Mennonite life and thought through the filter of my perspective. In looking for independent resources in Vietnamese, I recalled an article the former MCC secretary had translated.

Max and I had encouraged the Vietnam Mennonite Mission to translate several of the "classic" Anabaptist-Mennonite documents into Vietnamese. Finally, the MCC secretary translated Harold Bender's "The Anabaptist Vision." Bender had found that the Mennonite forebears—nicknamed "Anabaptists"—held three primary emphases: first, the essence of Christianity was discipleship rather than doctrine or subjective experience; second, the Church was based on voluntary membership by adults; and third, the ethic of love and nonresistance applied to all human relationships. I shared copies of the translation not only with the catechism class but also with the entire Fellowship.

In the baptismal service on Sunday, June 29, 1975, my reflections on the biblical meaning of baptism followed the opening. I had penciled Vietnamese words and phrases into my English outline at many points and hoped that my spontaneous translation of the rest would sound reasonably fluent.

> ... The word *baptize,* or *baptism,* has a broad meaning.
> First ... a ritual washing of hands before a meal ... Luke 11:38....
> Second, it refers to John's baptism of repentance....
> Third, the baptism of Jesus. In His life, He had two baptisms ... a water baptism by John.... *Baptism* is also used to refer to Jesus' suffering and death in Luke 12:50....
> The fourth use of the word *baptism* in the New Testament refers to the water baptism of believers. It is a symbol of entry into the Church.... It is also a symbol of the believer's response to the Good News and of an inner baptism by the Holy Spirit which has broken the power of sin. Water baptism is a symbol of unity with other believers ... this is also called being united in the Spirit ... being united in Christ.... So we can say baptism is a symbol of taking the first step on a new road, of walking in the light as well as a symbol of a clean conscience, 1 Peter 3:21.
> Another way of saying it is ... baptism is covenant: between God and us, between ourselves and God, and between each other....

Fifth ... the voluntary suffering and death of believers for following Jesus—for being obedient to God's will.... Mark 10:38-39.

And sixth, there are two figurative uses of the word *baptism*....

So the word *baptism* has a variety of meanings.... Christians do not always agree about the mode of water baptism, but we need to remember three things.

First, the Bible does not describe the mode and it does not prescribe the mode....

Second, nearly every ancient pictorial representation of baptism shows the believer standing in the water and the baptizer scooping up water and pouring it on the believer's head. The baptism of Jesus is also shown in this way: Jesus stands in the Jordan, and John scoops up water and pours it on the head of Jesus....

Third, we need to remember that water baptism is only a symbol. Of course, it is an important symbol, but neither the water nor the ceremony have any magic power.

Mennonites accept any method of water baptism....

I pray that the candidates ... will find the baptism of the Holy Spirit a reality in their lives as we use water as an outer symbol today.

A duet sang. Then Trung read a statement on the rights and responsibilities of baptized members. Quang and three others each shared a testimony, followed by the Fellowship's unanimous vote to accept them. In keeping the ceremony as simple as possible, I addressed only three questions to each candidate.

"Are you willing to be baptized now?"

"Do you accept Jesus as the Savior from your sins and Lord of your life?"

"Are you willing to join the church to serve God as long as you live?"

Without hesitation, each candidate answered all the questions affirmatively. I felt an awesome responsibility resting in my hands. With less than three years of experience in the Vietnamese language, I wondered how my memory would serve me as I nervously dipped water with my cupped hands from the basin that Trung held. I invited the candidates, two at a time, to kneel. Then, sweating as I squeezed the words from some remote wrinkle of my brain, I laid my hands on each head. My voice quivered. *"Vang theo loi Chua Gie-xu day"* ("Following the teaching of Jesus and upon your public confession of Jesus as Savior and Lord")—and scooping some water, I continued, "I baptize you in the name of the Father, the Son, and the Holy Spirit. Amen."

After inviting the newly baptized members to stand in the name of Jesus and the church, I commissioned them.

> Now you are members of Christ's church . . . remember that Jesus summarized the Old Testament Law with two simple statements. The first: "You shall love the Lord your God with your whole heart, and soul, and mind." The second: "You shall love others as you love yourself" (Matthew 22:37-39). Consequently, we are reconciled with God, with ourselves, with the Christian Community, and with all those outside that community. May God grant us the strength to follow Jesus faithfully until the very end. Amen.

The president of the Gia Dinh Youth Fellowship shared his reflections. Following a prayer and a hymn, the Fellowship closed the worship service by singing the chorus, "Hallelujah! Thine the glory, Hallelujah! Amen!"

*Reminders*

Early in July, I chauffeured two of the American Friends Service Committee workers to the airport. We MCCers felt akin to them because they also emphasized peace and reconciliation. Ready to be reunited with his wife and family, Earl had also requested an exit visa, but he did not leave until later in July.

One afternoon, the horrifying sounds of active combat shattered the lazy atmosphere. I thought of movie scenes of house-to-house fighting. But no one was fleeing. Why not? Creeping to the rooftop and then crawling to its back wall, we MCC guys peeked over the top. Smoke billowed into the sky. Quick glimspes at the street parallel to ours also revealed no fleeing refugees.

A fire, raging through the ammunition warehouses on Tran Quoc Toan Street, was detonating the explosives. Since the wind was blowing toward us, our neighbors started evacuating. We, too, grabbed our passports and registration papers. My briefcase bulged with my other essentials: seminary study notes, my Bible, diary, books on Vietnam and on theology, and a folder of writings for my spiritual pilgrimage.

The fire confined itself to the military compound, so we did not have to flee. The bangs and booms, however, provided a grim reminder: the impartial power of military hardware could easily hurt and destroy innocent people.

*New Horizons*

Even though the MCC secretary came from a non-Christian. home, she helped polish my translations for the Thursday afternoon Bible studies in 1 Peter. Her voluntary attendence at the Bible study delighted me.

A member of the Fellowship asked me, "Why don't you pray in Vietnamese? You lead the Bible study in Vietnamese, so why do you always pray in English?"

"Well, I never thought about it much," I admitted. "Nearly everyone in the group is interested in learning English, and it's easier for me to pray in English. I guess that's why."

"We'd really like it if you'd pray in Vietnamese. Would you?"

"Sure, I'll try."

In mid-July, I tackled a pet peeve of mine: I disliked huge, cold, blank, closed, metal front gates. I enlarged a picture of a dove and then penciled the result onto the inside of our blank metal gate. Using white paint, I carefully filled in the form of a dove and then freehanded a sunflower. Off to the side, I painted the first words to a popular Vietnamese song: "If I were a bird, I would be a dove. If I were a flower, I would be a sunflower." Only a select few—namely, those for whom we opened the gate—ever saw my handiwork because I lacked the courage to paint anything on the outside of it.

After glancing at the gate, one friend asked skeptically, "Why did you paint the sunflower with a missing petal and another one drooping? Is that supposed to have some profound significance?"

"No, that's just for looks," I replied. "It just seemed like it was too boring to look at if I put every petal in, so I deliberately left one out to lead the eye upwards toward the dove. Is that okay?"

I never touched the paintbrush again. Perhaps I had stumbled onto a more profound representation of reality than I had originally planned. No human government is perfect, neither is any revolution: if the gate conveyed that inadvertent political commentary or if the painting simply cheered the atmosphere surrounding the locked gate—either way rewarded my effort.

Near the end of July, my birthday precipitated a flury of telegrams from family members in the U.S. On the appointed day, Max, Hiro, and Earl presented me with some "official" rubber tire sandals. In his simple lifestyle, Ho Chi Minh had worn sandals like that; consequently people affectionately dubbed them "Ho Chi Minh sandals." In spite of their ungainly looks, the sandals cradled my feet comfortably, and the tire soles carried an unwritten lifetime guarantee! The adjustable straps, made from tire tubes, slipped through slits in the soles and could be readily replaced. In fact, the ends of the straps dangling underneath the soles led to another nickname: "bearded sandals." If anyone challenged my political affiliation, I dispelled all worries: "A bearded guy has to wear bearded sandals." Two years earlier, another birthday gift might have also carried political overtones: the MCC secretary had given me an elephant, and that had not turned me into a Republican!

*Registration*

The days just prior to my birthday had brought a special concern to our Fellowship. Citing security reasons, a new PRG policy statement required registering all meetings. Framed with solid lines on the front page of the newspapers, the announcement specifically mentioned church meetings. Some of my Vietnamese Christian friends saw sinister implications in the announcement, and several friends shared discouraging predictions with me.

"Did you read the announcement about church meetings?"

"Yeah, but it wasn't only about church meetings," I noted.

"But church meetings were included. Sure, it was a general announcement, but, really, it's just a way for the government to hassle the churches."

"You've got to remember that just a few months ago many Catholics and Protestants were enthusiastically anticommunist," I commented. "So the government is probably suspicious that they might want to sabotage it."

"You know what's going to happen? The registration process will be long and drawn out. Naturally, the government will finally accept the registration, but by the time permission to meet is granted, the enthusiasm for meeting will be all gone. No one will be interested in coming to church anymore."

Their predictions were wrong. Within three days, Trung, the acting director of the Phan Thanh Gian Center, completed the registration process for us. Apparently a formality, the process never broke the continuity of our meetings.

Sunday morning, the day after my birthday, Trung reported to our Fellowship. "I'm happy to announce that the meetings here at the Phan Thanh Gian Center have been registered. We were concerned, but our worries are over: permission has been granted for religious activities here. But we should remember that when we get together, it's to study the Bible and not to talk about politics."

His definition of politics was different than mine, but I did not challenge him. For me, simply proclaiming Jesus as Lord carried direct political implications by affirming a higher loyalty than any human government could demand. I could not separate life neatly into mutually exclusive spheres, one religious and one political.

*Remembering the Impact*

During the next weeks, I spent time with Quang, who had just been baptized a month earlier. At his request, the two of us studied the book of Ruth. One evening as we visited in Vietnamese, he shared several glimpses into his past.

"I remember the first time I ever saw Americans. Our family was busy cutting up bananas for our hogs. The Americans were huge and said things in a strange language which no one in our family could understand. All we knew how to do was shake our heads and say, 'No VC. No VC.' The Americans offered us some candy, but we declined."

"That's interesting." I nodded. "But now you're even living with Americans and studying English!" We chuckled.

He continued. "Homes out in the countryside were often made of bamboo timbers. When the American soldiers would burn one of these huts, the timbers would crackle and pop. The soldiers thought they were burning a hut used to store ammunition, so they'd throw in a grenade to destroy it more completely."

"Hmmm, I didn't know bamboo made noises like that when it burned. I'll bet those soldiers were really proud when they thought they were destroying some big ammunition warehouse even though it was just bamboo burning. I think a lot of the U.S. soldiers didn't understand much of what was going on. They didn't understand the Vietnamese language. They didn't eat Vietnamese food. They didn't know who their friends were or who their enemies were. I think most of them were terribly frightened when they were in Vietnam."

Quang glanced at me. "Have you heard about My Lai?"

"Yeah. Once when I visited Quang Ngai, Max took me out to 'Buddha Mountain'—I don't know what it's called in Vietnamese—and we looked out over that area. The killing that took place there was really awful."

"My family originally comes from Quang Ngai, but we had to move." His shoulders drooped; his voice softened. "My Lai was not the only situation like that. There were lots of others. Usually mostly women and children and old people were massacred because the young men could escape in time. There would be lots of shooting and crying and blood. Relatives returning and seeing the sight would sometimes go crazy."

"My Lai made big headlines," I recalled, "but we really didn't hear about the others. I remember Max telling about how, shortly after he arrived in Quang Ngai, he talked to the handful of survivors from one village. They told him there had been a terrible plague. Later, when they knew him better and trusted him, they told him that the Americans had wiped out nearly everyone in their village. I'm sure glad that's all over now."

Quang still remembered. His keen adolescent mind wrought poetry from his insights. I helped translate one of his poems.

"Please Let Me Refuse."

I would like to refuse one ready-made heaven. . . .
Because that heaven parallels hell,
But hell is actually my home:
It's a long weary war,
It's a hundred years of slavery,
      a thousand years of oppression.

I would like to refuse that heaven
      displaying its merchandise
On the city street of Freedom,
With all the "Freedoms" listed
On bills of lading from England, America, and France.

I would like to refuse
The heaven and the god
      of cold glittering church buildings
And of cold air-conditioned restaurants
Belonging to coffin contractors
      for those killed in combat.

Slogans promising full stomaches and warm clothes
   by tricky traitors
Hang on barbed wire fences around schools
And on iron bars and shackels of beastly prisons.

I would only like to be the smallest gentle lamb
In the flock which the Lord leads.
. . . and I will go together with Him.


Quang's poem portrayed the foreign architects and their pup-
pets who had initially trumpeted the war as a solution to political
problems and then abandoned the little land of Vietnam. In 1935
and 1936, however, Vietnam had been the second largest exporter
of rice in the world.[2] Then in the 1960s and 70s, the U.S. and the
former Saigon government had deliberately created refugees, driving farm families into refugee camps or into cities so that both the
farmland and the people could be controlled more easily. That
situation, along with bombing and shelling the land, plus herbicidal
sprays and the destruction of half the draft animals, soon turned
Vietnam into a rice importer. By 1975, the United States had been
supplying over half a million metric tons of rice to Vietnam per
year,[3] but when the United States withdrew in April 1975, the U.S.
also abruptly terminated the food shipments. The U.S. also ended
all financial assistance to Vietnam. Vietnam was still facing
overwhelming difficulties. One of Quang's sisters from Binh Tuy
explained the impact of the food shortage and economic crisis.
   "There was a family of a soldier from the former regime who
was really out of money. For two days they had gone completely
without eating anything. Husband, wife, and six children. The husband wanted to commit suicide but didn't have the nerve, so he decided to go steal something and get shot as a thief in the process. He
went to the market and grabbed a woman's purse, and just stood
there. Of course, the woman hollered, and the soldiers came. The
man just knelt, holding the purse and crying. They questioned him
and checked to see if his story was true. Then they gave his family a
fifty kilo bag of rice, and sent him off to *hoc-tap* (study-work)."
   Quang requested the prayers of the Fellowship on his behalf
for two problems he himself faced. One problem related to his future studies: should he stay in the impressive city of opportunity or

return to the countryside to live with his parents and accept the
limited educational opportunities there?

A second, more immediate problem confronted him. He had
moved to our Center on April 29 and had submitted his papers to
the local People's Self-Defense Office for formal approval. On April
30, however, the government changed, and his paperwork disappeared in the shuffle. As a result, he was living in Ho Chi Minh City
without any residence papers.

Quang returned to the house the Martin family had rented and
asked the owner for help. The worried owner, however, refused to
cooperate, angrily insisting that the old family register, which confirmed Quang's living there with the Luke Martin family, had been
burned. Trung, the head of the Gia Dinh congregation, also refused
to help. A friend of ours, Chi Hien—who had been shackled to the
hospital bed across the street from the MCC office—finally agreed
to vouch for Quang. Although she was a non-Christian and a new
member of the Workers' Party, she eased the complicated process
for him—a Christian.

Then after agonizing over the decision, Quang decided to join
the Labor Union, hoping to find work in Ho Chi Minh City. His
parting words early in September affirmed and admonished me.

"Jim, you have made a great contribution to the church group
here at Phan Thanh Gian during these months, but I can see that
the whole program here is still much too dependent on foreigners."

"I know I still have too much power. I plan to stop leading the
Thursday afternoon Bible study soon. I will always remember your
baptism. Thank you."

Even though an Executive Committee had been elected for the
Fellowship at the Phan Thanh Gian Center, I carried too much of
the leadership. In addition to my other responsibilities, the Fellowship asked me to lead the Vietnamese Bible study one Sunday
morning in mid-August. That Sunday, for a change from the
exegetical study of 1 Peter on Thursday afternoons, I explained the
radically different principles involved in paraphrasing Scripture.

*Like a Family*

Besides devoting time to Quang and other members of the
Fellowship, I visited with our household assistant, Tuyet. Perhaps

244 JIMSHOES IN VIETNAM

more as a courtesy to the Stauffers—whom she highly respected—than as job security, she had agreed to help Earl, Hiro, Max, and me with cooking, laundry, and housecleaning. We quickly recognized her outstanding cooking skills, neat laundry work, and efficient housekeeping efforts. Nevertheless, she remained aloof, quietly taking care of her tasks and then retiring to her separate quarters each evening. Her hard work deserved praise, but the relationship was very formal, and like the typical person in her role, she never ate meals with us.

We MCCers, however, detested such strict roles. Because she was puzzled and perhaps intimidated when we helped wash the dishes after eating, we reassured her that her job was not in jeopardy and that she had washed the dishes clean enough. Earl insisted that she start eating her meals with us. She reluctantly complied. Even though we MCCers conversed in Vietnamese, barely a word passed between her lips when she initially joined us at mealtime. Gradually, however, she became a real sister in our MCC "family" and freely shared her homespun philosophy as well as her strong Christian convictions.

"There is a big difference whether you try to raise the North to the living standards of the South or whether you try to equalize the two by lowering the living standard of the South," she commented, apparently hoping for the former.

"But you have to remember," Hiro admonished, "that the South had a false economy with all those U.S. dollars pouring in. I'm surprised the government hasn't taken harsher measures to lower the standard here in the South."

"Even moving back to the countryside," noted Max, "has been a voluntary program as far as we've heard."

"They've been talking to people in the area of the city where my dad lives," she added, "but they've mostly just been encouraging the unemployed people to go to the countryside and do something productive. Of course, they're pretty smart because they tell the unemployed that their rice allotment in Saigon will be cut off, but if they move out to the coutryside, they'll get a simple house, some tools, seeds, and six months of rice."

A few days later when she and I visited after lunch, I mentioned the traditional Vietnamese garb. Worn with slacks, the tight-fitting bodice with flowing tails had traditionally graced both men and women, but most men, except for the elderly, had abandoned the *ao dai* in favor of Western styles. "Did you know that I have an *ao dai*—" I asked.

"You do?" She sounded astonished. "Would you believe I still remember when all the ladies wore *ao dai*'s? Even out in the countryside. When you went out of your house, you wore an *ao dai*. It's really too bad we lost that custom, isn't it?"

I nodded. "During the past years of war, Vietnam has lost a lot more than just that custom."

"I wonder," she mused, "has there been any other country in the world which has had to endure the hardships of war like Vietnam? Do you think any other country will dare to try to fight us now?"

During the months following the change of government, Tuyet, more than any other person, deserved the credit for the health, appearance, education, happiness, insights, discipline, and stability of the foreign MCC team in Vietnam. She shared her perspective about the Fellowship and also critiqued my Vietnamese paraphrase for the Sunday morning service.

On the last Thursday afternoon in August, just before I lead the Bible study on 1 Peter, a member of the Fellowship briefly shared an experience. "When I became a Christian a year ago, an enthusiastic girl told me, 'We're sisters because we have the same Father!' At the time it sounded really strange because we were of different nationalities, but now I understand. And now even Jim doesn't seem like a stranger."

I glowed happily inside, even though I still remembered an earlier judgment from the evacuation days: "You're a foreigner." Foreigner? Yes. Stranger? No. That apparent contradiction paralleled the paradox of friendship itself: making friends took time and effort, yet I cherished each friend as a gift from God.

*Crossing Boundaries*

The former librarian of our Center, who had met the soldier with a cross on his canteen, shared another experience. He excitedly related his experience in the study-work program.

"Our cadre teacher today said that before entering the discipline of jungle life, he wasn't sure if he could tackle it, but after he committed himself to it, it was no problem. In fact, they were prepared to endure the hardships for another twenty to thirty years, if necessary, in order to wear out and defeat the U.S."

"Yeah, that sounds right." I nodded, adding, "One guy told Max that as he was bouncing around inside bomb shelters during B-52 bombing raids, it only made him more resolved to try to defeat the U.S."

The librarian resumed speed. "Our teacher was one who 'told it like it is.' It's absolutely not the policy of the revolution to make everyone wear black outfits. It was simply that in the jungle, black was a protective camouflage and easier to wash because they didn't have soap. And *ao dai's*—he said that of course, they're beautiful, and everybody recognizes that, and even the female government workers in town are wearing them. He himself has put on shoes—rubber sandals are practical for some things but not for others."

"Oh, no," I groaned in fake anguish, "I just got a pair of 'bearded sandals' for my birthday!"

Smiling, but not distracted by my interjection, he forged ahead. "He said that as far as their life in the jungle went, sometimes it was tough—real tough—but sometimes they were living a pretty easy life because people would share food like chicken and duck with them. Then when they came to Saigon they really had to tighten their belts because these days everybody in Saigon is in the same boat. Of course, there were times down in the tunnels—sometimes the air got cut off. He voluntarily admitted that the lifestyle of the South is higher than the North and that some PLA soldiers are profiteering off the economic difference between North and South."

Although both North and South acknowledged complications in building bridges across the former boundaries, I was often amazed. Because the Southerners were unaccustomed to meager rations like the North had endured, the North even sent commodities South—including rice. Communication through the post office also excited Phuong, a former work camper of Max's. Though dressed like usual in a gray *ao dai,* Phuong abandoned her reserved style as she handed me a photograph.

"We just got this picture of my grandmother who lives in the North! She was already old when communications were cut between the North and the South. We hadn't heard from her for so many years that we thought she was dead. But she isn't! She's eighty-six years old now and doing fine. Isn't that great!"

The mail service linking the different regions of Vietnam brought joy far out of proportion to the slim stamps on the envelopes. Then, on September 1, the *Tin Sang* newspaper, having a Roman Catholic as chief editor, announced the resumption of international mail service.

*Contrasts*

One day, Ngoc, a member of the Fellowship who readily shed tears, told me about buying medicines for her sick mother.

"Yesterday morning I went all over trying to find medicine for her and finally found some. The price was 1,500 piasters per bottle. When I got home I found out that my dad had bought some for 625 piasters per bottle. When I took mine back, I was very polite. They refunded the money, but then they were scared that I was an undercover agent for the revolution, which I am not. All that made me very sad, especially to think that they were charging three times the proper price to people who were even poorer than my family. So you know what I did?" she asked.

"No, I don't," I said.

"This morning I reported all that to the proper district office. They were friendly, and there I met Tuan who had already known Hiro and Earl from Kontum and now knows the rest of us Mennonites." He was the one I had met in the late evening visit early in June. Ngoc bubbled on. "Although I wasn't officially part of the revolution, they said that we're all part of the same family and thanked me for sharing. They were doing a study on pharmacies."

The next day Ty, another enthusiastic, but younger, member of the Fellowship, shared a similar story about positive changes.

"Before, I couldn't afford to study at the National Conservatory of Music, but now I will be able to study there, so that is really exciting. Even public schooling under the old system was extremely unjust: you had to put your parents' occupation on the application form, and if they were 'big shots,' then you could get in real easily, but if they weren't then it was nearly impossible to get into public schools."

"Into public schools?" I echoed in disbelief.

"That's right. Public schools. In the test to pass from fifth to sixth grade, I myself placed second among the pupils from thirteen schools, but I wasn't accepted by the public schools. And the public schools looked down on private schools. But now things are based on your skills, and the revolution pays a lot of attention to children. Before, because of family connections, I was invited to sing on TV and was paid for it, but if some of my friends wanted to perform, they had to pay the TV in order to get on the air. But now lots of children's groups—some really talented—are performing on TV to get experience, and then the good ones will be selected for more training."

Khanh, a university student who had participated in one of Max's work camps, reflected a darker picture in the thirdhand story she told me. She wore a well-laundered yellow T-shirt and red jeans which were as faded as her hopes for studying abroad.

"If, in the new society, everybody is supposed to be equal, then why is so much stress placed on one person—Ho Chi Minh? Let me tell you one incident, okay? My friend's family is Buddhist, and they had an altar in their home with Buddha above the picture of 'Uncle Ho.' When some officials stopped in at the house they noticed that and said it was not acceptable. My friend's parents said that he was a great man, but he was not Buddha, and then that night her parents were taken away."

I shook my head. "That's hard to believe."

"You just read the papers and believe everything they say!" she retorted. "You're far too gullible. You MCCers are much too enthusiastic about the revolution. You really don't know what is going on out there."

"Of course, we aren't Vietnamese even though we can speak the Vietnamese language," I acknowledged. "But I certainly don't believe everything I read in the newspaper regardless what government is in power. Actually, I think the best way to try to understand the situation is through good friends like you."

She seemed to soften. "My brother from the North is visiting us. He stayed there in 1954 when the rest of our family moved South. He's married now and has a family. Of course, it's great to see him again, but we argue terribly much. He says I wear hippy clothes and listen to immoral American music, and I tell him he's far behind the times—that he's from 'out in the sticks' and doesn't know anything. You MCCers talk about reconciliation all the time, but it's hard. It's terribly hard." She turned away.

"I don't think I've ever claimed that it would be easy," I responded quickly, perhaps defensively. "But I think it's fantastic that you and your brother can actually get together. I really do hope that things will smooth out for you as you talk things over."

"Yeah, I sure do, too. I've got to be going. Greetings to Max and Hiro." She flipped her long hair over her shoulders, slipped her oversized sunglasses down from their perch on top of her head, and slowly bicycled away.

The next day, after the Sunday morning services, Al Knoles visited the MCC office. He was the only foreign Protestant missionary who voluntarily stayed in Vietnam through the change of government. Although repulsed by his booming voice, I was interested in his experiences and listened to his stories.

After Al left, Hiro, Max, and I bicycled downtown to see the film, *Little Girl of Hanoi*. The heart-rending film included documentary sections from the Christmas of 1972 when the U.S. bombed Hanoi, including the Bach Mai hospital, eight embassies, and residential sections. In those twelve days, the North endured six times as much explosive violence as the atomic bomb which the U.S. dropped on Hiroshima in World War II. Exiting the theater, I felt as if all eyes were focused on me as a U.S. citizen and I could not hide from them.

How could I be proud to be a U.S. citizen? But, like the history books of all other nations, Vietnamese history also bore the names of its own military heroes written in blood, so how could I be proud of them? As a Christian pacifist, I realized that no nation on earth could feel like home. I concluded that militarists would never understand my latest pun: "The test of a Christian is always a cross-examination."

After I relived that pain of my first Christmas in Vietnam, the agony of being a citizen of the U.S. lingered for several days. When had Vietnamese bombs ever fallen over downtown Chicago or over Capitol Hill in Washington, D.C.? Hearing that the U.S. president had proclaimed "self-determination for all peoples," Ho Chi Minh wrote to the U.S. president at least eight times in 1945 requesting U.S. assistance to throw off the chains of French colonialism. Instead of helping Ho Chi Minh, the U.S. answered him by first supporting the French and then by finally fighting him directly.[4] Why, I wondered, why?

*Respect Responsibilities*

In the Thursday afternoon Bible studies on 1 Peter, after five months of detailed study, we finally reached the crucial section in chapter two on church-government relations. Consciously stepping down from the leadership role, I had already switched from a lecture format to a discussion format which used study questions I prepared weekly. Nevertheless, laying the groundwork for the discussion questions on 1 Peter 2:13-17 required solid input from me.

> . . . the previous two verses about being pilgrims and aliens form the general introduction for the next section. . . . Today we are going to study verse thirteen which is the specific introduction.
>
> The opening word . . . in the Greek . . . does not mean *obey.* A better word perhaps would be *recognize,* which would include *accept.* . . . Its primary meaning is *respect.*
>
> . . . this word of Peter's is not a call to blind obedience. . . . In Acts 5:29, Peter clearly says, "We ought to obey God rather than people." Both Peter and Paul died at the hands of government authorities.
>
> The second word we need to study carefully (Mark 16:15, Colossians 1:23) . . . refers to people, as part of God's creation, even though in those two verses the adjective *anthropine* (human) is missing. In 1 Peter the adjective is there, so the meaning clearly refers to "the human sector of God's creation" or, more simply, to "human beings."
>
> If we understand it like this. . . . We are to respect the king or the people in power, not because of their high office, but because they are people like everybody else. . . . Christians are not anarchists. In fact, Christians . . . in general, will want to follow the government, but sometimes Christians will not follow but suggest other alternatives.
>
> . . . Why respect every human being? "For the Lord's sake," not in order to gain any advantage or privilege or for any other reason. . . .
>
> Then, following "Respect every human being for the Lord's sake," we should have a colon because that is the introduction for the examples in the rest of the chapter.

Discussion on the passage waited till the following week. In the meantime, since I had told the Leadership Committee that I planned to stop leading the Thursday Bible study at the end of September the Committee convened a special meeting of the Phan Thanh Gian believers after the worship service on Sunday morning. Ty opened the session with a brief history and evaluation.

> Our Fellowship here is quite special in a number of ways. We're a young group. The first members were baptized just this past spring. We're also a small group, so sometimes there are more guests than members. There's also a distinct style or atmosphere about our group which is more informal and more personal than lots of regular church groups.
> After Stauffers left, Luc was in charge, and then Trung. A committee of representatives was elected which was supposed to meet regularly, which hasn't happened. And two of the members haven't been attending the meetings regularly, and another one is now a member of the Saigon Labor Union.
> It's understandable why there is a turnover of guests, but it's hard to understand why baptized members don't attend regularly when possible. That might be related to another characteristic of our Fellowship: members are individual Christians without having Christian families. That means we have to work extra hard to get our "homework" done in order to get permission from our parents to attend.
> One other distinctive thing about our group is that it's trying to follow Mennonite ideals rather than mainstream Protestantism.

She concluded, "Jim doesn't know when he will leave, and we also don't know when we will be leaving to participate in activities to build our society and help our people."

"That means each one of us will be a leader with a responsibility to share and contribute—not just Jim. Of course, he will still be one of us and will be expected to contribute just like everybody else," commented Ngoc.

*Money*

The government took a major step toward eliminating inflation and corruption the next day, September 22. The Provisional Revolutionary Government had expected to exchange all the currency from the former government for new money within eighteen hours. Because the local authorities did not know how to handle us MCCers, three days lapsed before we could exchange our worthless bills for new cash. Our friends had offered to loan us new money till our own transaction was completed, but we simply curtailed our spending.

The exchange rate returned one new piaster bill for five hundred of the old ones. Everyone received some cash in the exchange, but depending on individual and family circumstances, money beyond a graduated maximum automatically turned into a personal, but government-controlled, savings account, instead of cash, thereby reducing the gap between rich and poor. That fundamental reorientation revived the storytellers.

"Were you able to get your money exchanged okay?" a friend asked us.

"Yeah, finally, after three days of running around. What about yourself?"

"Our family didn't have any problems. Of course, we didn't have much to exchange. But did you hear about this rich, old woman? She had ninety million piasters! Imagine that! They hauled it to the bank in huge sacks, and then when she got just a little handful of new money back in exchange, she fainted!"

Ngoc, too, shared a story with me—her own true story.

"When American soldiers were in Vietnam, anyone associated with them generally tried to soak them for all they were worth. And that gave the Americans the wrong impression of the Vietnamese. Usually the people who hung around with Americans weren't very ethical."

"I'm aware that a lot of unhealthy relationships developed when the U.S. soldiers were here. Naturally, though, a war environment is never a healthy one," I commented.

"Would you believe it? A respectable girl, even though she might know English fluently, would stay away from Americans. In fact, my own father worked in an American military office, and my sister wanted a job there. She studied English hard, but in the end, my father wouldn't give her permission to work there because the atmosphere was terrible." Then she quickly added, "Of course, not all Americans were like that, but far too many were."

*Walking Together*

Grateful that friendship transcended barriers of nationalism, I cherished each of my friends. They demonstrated the friendship in creative, thoughtful, moving ways. The MCC secretary, for example, had selected poetry and quotations, hand-copied them into a blue notebook, and then gave me the personalized book the last Thursday in September. The flyleaf in Vietnamese simply read, "Presented to Jim so that you'll remember Vietnam and one of your friends."

As I leafed through the pages, I found poetry by Khalil Gibran, Trinh Cong Son, Langston Huges, Christina Rossetti, and St. Francis of Assisi. Several of the secretary's own poems graced the pages, too. She had also neatly copied poems by Max and by me. I felt humbled by her gift. A short selection by Camus caught my attention.

> Do not walk in front of me
> I may not follow
> Do not walk behind me
> I may not lead
> Walk beside me
> And just be my friend.

A few pages farther, like a quiet premonition, another quotation captured the heartbeat of the Fellowship's sharing time that Thursday afternoon. Schopenhauer had penned the unforgettable words: "Every parting gives a foretaste of death; every coming together again a foretaste of the resurrection."

Two members opened the sharing time with a farewell letter they had just composed to a friend who had evacuated in April. Like a cry from their heart, the letter closed with the question: "Do you—will you—remember us?"

"I think you should send the letter to your friend," Ty encouraged them.

Ngoc added, "It seems like the feelings—the spirit—of Orientals is much deeper than other parts of the world. Maybe it's a special gift from God, but it also makes life difficult. Life for me would have been so much easier if I never would have met the Mennonites. Try as hard as I can, though, I can't hate them. It's strange that I should love them so much."

"That sure must be a gift from God," Ty agreed. "It's natural to love your own kind, but when love can cross boundaries, then it truly is from God."

Then Yen shared a burden from her heart. "Some of my

friends used to talk to me about the Lord, but I just shrugged them off because I was too superficial to think seriously. Then they went to study abroad. Now, since the revolution here, I've become a believer in God, but how can I let my friends know?"

"If your friends really were concerned about you," Ty responded, "then somehow now they should feel at peace about you even though there may not have been any direct verbal communication. I think God can do that."

That night, as I thought about my friends, my journal entry included a series of unanswered questions related to them. How can I let them know I will never forget? How can I say "thank you" for all they have given me? How can I let them know that leaving Vietnam will tear a chunk out of my heart, too?

# Chapter 14

# THREE YEARS

*Summary*

October 1975 formally ended my three-year contract with MCC. Terminating my leadership of the Thursday afternoon Bible study allowed me time to document and summarize my experiences from the past years as the basis for personal reflections and for recommendations to MCC.

There was only one way to start, namely, with gratitude.

> Perhaps one way of expressing my sincere appreciation is by sharing a feeling I have: prior to coming as well as throughout the years of service here, I know of no other organization in Vietnam with which I would have rather worked. I highly respect MCC and consequently have made a sincere effort to do my best.

The painful memories of an excessive work load, however, sat beside that feeling of gratefulness like a Siamese twin.

> More than once it seemed that . . . responding to that (work) demand left me numb . . . and without joy. . . . My understanding of Christian community suggests that alongside of my affirmation . . . there should be some constructive criticism . . . (like) the 4-H motto . . . 'To make the best better.'

April 30, 1975, had liberated me from more than half of my work load. In my report, fifteen single-spaced pages documented the difference I experienced between being overloaded before April 30, 1975, and simply being busy after that. I also shared my recommendations regarding language study, personal relationships, translation projects, medical programs, nursing education, personnel recruitment, and peace witness. I summarized the report:

... I have learned a lot about sunshine and rain, about shepherds and ranchers, about satisfaction and frustration, about success and failure, about peace and war, about discipleship and propaganda, about life and death, about highlights and disappointments, about liberation and bondage, about Good News and bad news, about flowers and barbed wire, about smiles and tears. I have learned a lot about memos and Mennonites, medicines and administration, Mennonite Central Committee and Mennonite Mission, myself and others, the Orient and orientation, the Occident and accidents, office hours and work loads, errands and second miles, English and Vietnamese, Bible and baptism, teaching and learning.... I have learned a lot about little things and big things ... about Ping Pong and paperfolding, about poetry and prayer, about Tet and Christmas, about children and adults, about questions and answers ... about words and deeds, about friends and family, about dreams and reality, about hope and joy.

Few people, if any, could have predicted that the past three years would have been such dramatic ones for me ... so I want to express my gratitude to MCC for the ... unique experiences I've had in Vietnam as a result of my work here with MCC....

In some sense, however, the end of my three years in Vietnam is just a beginning.... I am prepared to leave or to stay longer....

Back in the "old" days, when thinking about this report, I jotted the following note, "I have found MCC to be extremely hard of hearing sometimes...." But (fortunately) the situation has changed.... Again let me express my appreciation to MCC for letting a little Kansas sunflower do some growing in the beautiful tropical land of Vietnam. May God give us all the grace to always stand straight and tall facing Him and thereby bringing a bit of sunshine into the lives of those around us. Amen.

I felt the need to thoroughly document my statements. When Max critiqued the rough draft, he felt it was too long-winded. Perhaps he was right: the final copy, including appendixes, stretched 34 pages.

More importantly, Max thought that I was minimizing the work of others and that I should have said "no" to some of the work. I typed my response to Max.

... precisely when I was able to think about others, then I really was stuck. E.g., VILS (Vietnam Inter-mission Language School)—in my opinion Luke already was overloaded, but I was assuming he would be the board member to represent MCC.... But with three foreign personnel in Saigon, when Luke said "no" and you said "no," then I sure didn't see too many other options for a VILS board respresentative.

... especially when you were gone, saying an absolute "no" was impossible. In December 1974, for example, whose request should I have turned down? Where should I have drawn the line? . . . should I have refused to work on that brainstorm for voluntary service which you suggested? Should I have refused to push on your request for political prisoner materials and MCCers articles with a January deadline? Should I have refused to attend the joint MCC-Mennonite Mission conference with Krauses? Should I have refused to do the final stuff for Hang and Ly? Should I have refused to orient the Willms family? Should I have refused to give the Christmas sermon? To be very frank with you, I still am wondering to what and to whom I should have said "no"—to you? to Luke Martin? to James Stauffer? God knows I tried to say "no" to the medicines, and I didn't get anything but a brick wall. . . .

Your last statement, "MCC is hard of hearing, not deaf," is a classic. If I wouldn't believe that, then I wouldn't have bothered to write a single page. . . .

Like the revolution in Vietnam would say: it's part of our history and we can't ignore it, but let's go on to build a better future.

*Coping*

In October, the pendulum of joy and sorrow swung back and forth for the Gia Dinh Mennonite Church. Trung and Khai reported the latest developments.

"How's the Fellowship doing here?" Khai asked me in the MCC office.

"Fine," I said. "I'm in the process of reducing my responsibilities in the group. The goal is to try to make the group more independent so that when I leave they'll be able to handle things by themselves."

"Who'll be taking over?"

"The responsibility will be shared. This week Vuong will be in charge."

"We hope you'll be willing to stay actively involved with the group."

"Yes. Sure," I said. "I plan to keep meeting with them until I leave."

"Good." "That's great." They echoed each other. Then, as if to gather courage for plunging ahead, they glanced at each other.

"Jim," Trung paused. His broad shoulders sagged. "Uhm, we've been having some difficulty out at our Church Center in Gia Dinh. The congregation had put Lam in charge of the church compound, but then he invited the head of the district government in

258 JIMSHOES IN VIETNAM

our area to move in there with him. One person was even killed at our Center."

"Excuse me, did you say, 'killed'?" I blurted.

Khai responded. "Yes, that's right. It was accidental, but still, it makes our congregation uneasy. Other people have also been held at the Center, making it like a jail." He shook his head. "All because of Lam. If he just wouldn't have invited the district official to live there...."

"We had to do something," Trung interrupted. "We couldn't let that go on. Here are the signatures of the church members saying that they are willing to join the United Evangelical Church of Vietnam under the leadership of Long. Even Lam signed. Long promised to move the district officials out of the (Gia Dinh) Center so we won't be bothered by them any more."

"What do you think about that?" Khai popped the question.

"Yes," Trung echoed the question on their minds, "what do you think if our congregation joins the United Evangelical Church?"

"If that's what the church wants to do," I replied, "then that's fine. That's really up to the church. History shows that the (Mennonite) missionaries have not wanted to force you or the church to follow their wishes, so I'm sure that now, too, a decision by the congregation to join together with the other congregations in the United Church would not raise any problems in the minds of the Mennonite missionaries."

"Good. Thanks."

"We're glad to hear you say that."

At noon, Lam himself appeared at our Center.

"What do you think about joining the United Evangelical Church?" I asked.

His slender frame straightened. "I think it's okay, but I don't agree with all the tricky things Trung pulled in order to do it, like not announcing it at any Sunday service, but just going around from house to house. And signing his name as the chairman of the congregation. He called the paper with the signatures *'Bien Ban.'*"

"I'm sorry, but I don't know what *bien ban* is," I admitted. Our conversation, like the one earlier, was in Vietnamese. I generally could infer the meaning of a new word from the context, but this seemed to be a crucial point. I reached for my dictionary while he tried to explain.

"It's like when there's a meeting and a secretary writes down what is said and all the decisions that are made."

"Oh, okay. I can understand that." The dictionary confirmed my understanding: *minutes.* "So, everybody signed the 'Minutes.' "

"Yeah, 'Minutes.' Really strange: how can you have 'minutes' if there's never been a meeting? And he never came out here to ask the opinion of the Phan Thanh Gian Mennonite Fellowship, did he?"

"No, not as far as I know," I replied.

"So, can you see why I'm discouraged?"

"Yeah, but you signed the paper, right?"

"Sure, why not sign? I really would like to see the district officials move out. When the church first asked me to stay at the Gia Dinh Center, I was willing to, but it's such a big place. I was really lonely staying there by myself, so I invited the head of the district government to come live there, too. I thought that would help keep it safe, but I never expected so many problems. I really hope Long can help us out. What do you think the missionaries will think when they hear that we're joining the United Church?"

"Like I told Trung and Khai this morning," I confirmed, "I don't think that's a problem. I don't think any of them would oppose that."

A week later, I visited with Mrs. Trung. "We've really been concerned about you MCCers," she said. "Have you had enough to eat?"

"Yes, we're doing okay. For a while, around the time when Earl left, we were running out of money, but then Mennonite Central Committee was finally able to send us some through a bank in Hong Kong that could transfer it to a bank here. That got here just before we ran out."

"That's good to hear. Have you been having any difficulties?" she asked.

"No, not really. Things seem pretty stable. Oh, once in a while I break a pedal off my bicycle." I grinned. "It wasn't designed for a big American like me. But, no, we haven't been having any problems. What about you?"

"Our real concern is for the church," she replied. "Some members will come to visit us at home, but they won't step inside the church building with the way things are there right now. It's so hard to know what to do. And things are desperate economically, too. Families who had been helped with loans from the church to build their homes have sold the beams and roofing because they were out of work and needed money. It doesn't seem quite right, but they're really caught in a bind."

"Yes, that's why I said we guys don't have any problems."

"Perhaps you didn't know," she continued, "that my husband had been held briefly because of his association with the church, but then they released him. Long has promised to help us to get the district officials to leave, but we haven't seen any results yet. We're praying that God will lead us in helping the church to stand firm."

"That's right. We've really got to depend on the Lord."

Three days later her husband, Trung, brought us a variety of news. Typical of the changes buzzing through society, the city government had just changed the name of our street from Phan Thanh Gian to Dien Bien Phu. Trung explained developments dealing with the Mennonite Center where we stayed.

"There won't be any more private schools. They're all public. That means that the English program here won't be reopening."

"That's no problem for me," I said. "I'm not a very good English teacher anyhow. Of course, we had thought if it would reopen, it would give us a formal program in the eyes of the government. Although Mennonite Central Committee would like for us to serve as official MCC representatives here, the government seems to be reluctant to see us in that role. The Ministry of Foreign Affairs says that we are guests, just like any other visitors to Vietnam."

"Does that mean you'll be leaving soon?"

"I doubt it. We don't have any plans for leaving. Of course, the government could ask us to leave at any time."

"We sure hope you'll be able to stay a while longer. And I do have some good news about our situation in Gia Dinh."

"Good. What kind of good news?" I asked.

"Our church—that is, the Church Board—unanimously decided to let our Gia Dinh Center school facilities be used as a public school at both the elementary and secondary levels. So the Ministry of Education looked at the school and has approved it. The approval includes using all the former workers and teachers who have completed the study-work program, and they also approved use of the church building for religious activities. We're really happy for that."

"Great! That really does sound good. Now, what does that mean in terms of the district officials?" I asked.

"Well, that was one of the reasons we went to the Ministry of Education. With Long we just never got any results. But now the district officials have to clear out of the Center so classes can be taught there."

"So, how soon will all that be happening?"

"Registration for school starts on the thirteenth. Let's see, today's Friday, the tenth, right?"

"Right." I glanced at the calendar. "That would mean registration starts on Monday already. That's fast. That's great."

"The school will open formally on the nineteenth, just like all the rest of the schools in the South. All the workers will be paid 30 piasters per month plus rice."

The church had always believed that the primary Christian impact of the school depended on the staff rather than on compulsory religious education for the students. The staff, with a few exceptions, remained the same, but under the new arrangements, the government paid the salaries! How ironic, I thought. That certainly did not sound like government repression of the church. In fact, that cooperation raised questions similar to the ones that my alma mater, a Mennonite college in Kansas, faced with funds from the U.S. government for loans and work-study programs. What is the impact of receiving government funds? Does the money stifle the conscience and silence the witness?

Two days later, Trung spoke on behalf of the entire Gia Dinh Church Board which met with me at our Phan Thanh Gian Center. "We have several things we would like to share with you and thought it best if we were all here. Unfortunately, though, one of the board members couldn't make it, but I can assure you that we've discussed these matters carefully and have reached agreement on them.

"First of all, in light of our decision to join the United Church, the sign out in front of this Center will be repainted to read 'United Church' rather than 'Mennonite Protestant Center' as it now is.

"Second, there will not be any English program here since we could not get permission from the government for any private educational program like that.

"Third, we would like for you brothers to continue living here. It's spacious and should be adequate to accommodate you." They all nodded.

"Thank you for coming to share your decisions with me," I began. "We have enjoyed staying here at the Center and appreciate your willingness to let us continue to do so. I have one question, though, which I would like to share with you: what are you thinking about the Youth Fellowship here? They really need a long-term leader. Can a representative from Gia Dinh come regularly?"

"The young people are free to organize their own activities," Trung asserted. "We'll try to help them out with getting guest speakers for Sunday mornings, but you should just go ahead and be their leader."

"I feel I've been carrying too much of the leadership," I countered, "and so I've been trying to reduce my responsibilities. One problem is that I don't have any idea how soon I'll be leaving."

"Well, you just keep right on. When you have to leave, let us know, and then we'll discuss the situation again. Does anyone have anything else for the agenda?" Trung paused. "If not, that concludes our meeting."

In the informal discussion that followed, one of the board members asked me, "Did you know Na's father?"

"Uhm, I'm not sure. Could you describe him for me?"

The description jogged my memory. The board member continued.

"He and his family moved back to their farmland out West, and we just heard that he was killed while clearing some land. It seems like he accidentally hit a buried mine."

That danger of death, triggered by an unsuspecting hoe or scythe, faced farmers every day. The legacy of war still stalked the land. Over 300,000 tons of unexploded ordnance still lay buried in Vietnam, and the U.S. government refused to release maps of known minefields.[1]

*What's Normal?*

A couple days later, Tin, a former office assistant for MCC, explained his work in the countryside to us. "I used to think I was working hard for MCC," he said with a twinkle in his eye, "but I'm working twice as hard now." His bronzed skin and rippling muscles confirmed his words. "Sometimes we're down on our hands and knees all day pulling weeds, but then when we get together for worship, we can really praise the Lord. I think the best basis for real Christian fellowship is when everybody is working hard, like out in the countryside. Compared to that, worship services here in Saigon feel empty."

"Yeah, I'm sure that's true." I nodded. "Everybody in your group is working hard: they all have to pull together, and they all have the same kind of experience. Sure, that would make for a strong sense of unity."

"When I look at churches now since the revolution," he observed, "I think there are three kinds, like the parable of the sower. There are some churches that have simply closed down."

"Maybe those are the ones where the pastors evacuated," I suggested.

"It could be," he granted. "Then there are the weak ones: they've lost members, and the preachers just preach the slogans of the revolution."

"That's too bad, but I think you're right. Lots of people are unsure of themselves, so it's probably not surprising that some of them are Christians. Actually, I know some," I admitted.

"But, you know, there's another kind." His face beamed. "There are churches that are even stronger than they were before, and they're growing. They've got active leaders that talk straight. Where I'm working, we've got that kind of fellowship. It's great!"

A week later, he returned, mourning an older brother of his. Tin's eyes, puffy and red, hinted at the tears he had shed. He spoke slowly, deliberately, as if trying to control his voice. "It's my brother Thong. He passed away."

In a flash, Hiro moved to Tin's side, slipped his arm across Tin's back to rest a hand on Tin's shoulder. We slowly sat down on the back steps. I had been cleaning the storage room. That work could wait.

"When did he pass away?" Max asked.

"Yesterday afternoon, about four o'clock."

We sat in silence. We had known that Thong had been seriously wounded in action in January. Tin added, "The funeral's tomorrow morning at nine."

Terrible war, I thought. Why couldn't it have ended sooner? Why couldn't it have ended last year? Why did Thong have to die? Stupid war. Why couldn't it have even ended before the Christmas bombing in '72? In fact, why weren't the elections held in 1956? Crazy war. Why did soldiers have to die? If the presidents and generals were so excited about fighting, let them fight each other instead of sitting in padded, air-conditioned offices playing war games.

The war had torn life apart. Phuoc, another brother of Tin's had been missing in action at An Loc in 1972. Surviving that incident, while on patrol in 1974, Phuoc's unit decided to relax in the shade of a huge tree. Two members of the unit were killed when one of them accidentally sat on a mine hidden there. Phuoc caught shrapnel in his wrist. Even though he needed immediate medical attention, rescue personnel refused to pick him up because it was dark. A helicopter finally flew to evacuate him because he was due for a promotion. He reached a hospital five hours after being wounded. He considered himself lucky: two days later, combat wiped out the rest of his unit.

When our MCC office team had visited Phuoc at home to wish him a speedy recovery, his father spoke on behalf of the family. "We are hoping that the hand will not function like normal, so he can only do office work."

I had been stunned by his statement. Never before had I heard anyone wish for less than a complete recovery. War warped the meaning of wholeness.

Ordered to the battlefront early in 1975, Thong was seriously wounded. Even though the war ended, he remained bedfast, never recovering. Nearly six months after the guns were silenced, the war claimed his life.

The next Sunday, another one of Thong's brothers shared his own radiant testimony at the worship service in our Center. The group, numbering nearly 30, listened intently as he concluded, "We often asked the Lord why we had to carry such a heavy burden. But in the end, there always was a way."

Just a month before Thong's death, Max, Hiro, and I had visited a display which documented U.S. war crimes in Vietnam. The exhibit included tiny, grotesque human fetuses genetically deformed in the aftermath of napalm and defoliants. No eraser could magically erase the effect of the war physically, psychologically, socially, economically, agriculturally, or politically in Vietnam. Nevertheless, Vietnam was still willing to establish diplomatic relations with the United States after April 1975.

"That's not so strange," one of my friends explained. "When you look at the pages of Vietnam's history, we had to drive the Chinese out repeatedly, but each time after we drove them out, we'd send a delegation up to China and say, 'Look, we're sorry we had to drive you out, but we really would like to have diplomatic relations with you and be your friends.' So why should it be any different with the U.S.? We didn't want the U.S. in here dominating us, but we'd like to have diplomatic relations with the U.S. and be friends. In fact, China is big and close, and if we want to be independent, we really need ties with the U.S. so China won't run over us again."

*Trying*

Ty had a link to center stage: her own sister, with a round face like Ty's, had become well-known as a member of a traditional opera troupe. We MCCers pedaled our bicycles to the theater where Ty's sister was performing. Although the script far outstripped my vocabulary, the stylized makeup and the choreographed movements of the ornately costumed performers allowed me to catch the basic plot.

Ty, who sometimes played drums in the orchestra for her sister's opera, recounted a recent experience. "Some soldiers without guns stormed the theater. They blew whistles and forced their way in. They claimed that they didn't have to pay because if it weren't for them, the troupe wouldn't be there to do their tradtional opera.

"People in the theater were scared, but several of the performers spoke directly about the problem. One of them told the soldiers, 'You're right: if it weren't for you we wouldn't be here, and we sincerely appreciate your efforts in liberating our country. But when you act the way you did, people are scared. You acted just like the soldiers of the old system. Plus, you see, we have to make a living, too, and the revolution gave us permission to charge you admission—but it is a special low price and you should respect that.' The soldiers sheepishly paid their admission, and the show went on."

The next morning we three MCC "representatives" had an appointment with Dr. Le Van Loc at the Ministry of Foreign Affairs. MCC had imported several inexpensive metal dectectors for farmers in the Quang Ngai area to use to clear their land of unexploded munitions. Since MCC no longer had any representatives there, we decided to let the government distribute the detectors. Loc, who had met Mennonite representatives in Paris during the peace negotiations, gave us a warm reception.

"We sincerely appreciate MCC's understanding of the programs to rebuild our country. We can distinguish between the different kinds of Americans," he assured us.

After leaving his office, we stopped to visit Frances Starner, a U.S. reporter, who had also stayed in Vietnam. Her investigative reporting in Laos had brought her renown, and she enthusiastically described her research, pointing out parallels to Vietnam.

"In 1967 and '68," she began, "official figures showed that the U.S. was giving 63 million dollars in direct economic assistance to Laos. Now these figures did not include any gold. You see, the U.S. was also shipping 27 million dollars' worth of gold to Laos per year at that time, but that fact was hidden away. Oh, and the official line from the U.S. was that the U.S. was so proud of the Laos's industriousness in bringing in revenue from excise tax on gold sales—but never saying that the U.S. itself was supplying the gold. Nor were they reporting that anyone in Laos could go to the bank, exchange five hundred kip for one U.S. dollar, and then start trading gold. You had to have U.S. dollars, see, to buy and sell gold. It was rumored that the U.S. embassy burned huge quantities of kip that had been exchanged for green dollars."

We shook our heads. "That really is an amazing story. It's incredible how the U.S. was managing things so the economic picture would look good."

"Yes," she continued, "that's where my research paid off. But, you know, Vietnam really wasn't that much different. Here in Saigon, lots of people long for 'the good old days,' not realizing that the Thieu regime was importing between six and seven hundred million dollars' worth of goods per year while only exporting about twenty million dollars' worth."

"But on the surface it looked so rosy," Max agreed. "And most people bought the propaganda. I can't believe how many people have no idea what was going on economically under the Thieu government, and they don't believe me when I tell them. And then they blame all the economic problems now on 'the communists,' not realizing the impact of the sudden cutoff of U.S. aid to Vietnam. It's disgusting."

"Ah," said Hiro grinning, "whenever people don't believe you, just send them to *hoc-tap!*"

Frances chuckled as she added, "Whenever the U.S. had any economic assistance project, where did they go? Down to the rich delta where people were already well off. They didn't go to the really needy farming and fishing areas of Central Vietnam because they couldn't get spectacular results there."

Late that afternoon, the wife of the former librarian for the English program at the Phan Thanh Gian Center requested a copy of my residence papers which had been certified by the head of our city ward. "I'm sorry to have to bother you like this," she said, "but the authorities down in Ben Tre who are holding my husband have requested something to prove that you're still here."

"Well, I'm still here, and I'm glad to do what I can," I replied.

"We told the authorities there that Mennonites were progressive Americans, but they just told us, 'Americans are Americans and they're all alike.' " She imitated the skeptical tone.

"That's interesting because just this morning at the Ministry of Foreign Affairs, Dr. Loc told us they could distinguish the different kinds of Americans. So, if that photocopy of my papers is not good enough, maybe you'll have to take your story to higher levels of government," I suggested. "Finally, somebody somewhere—like Dr. Loc—surely will have heard of Mennonites."

"Well, we're certainly going to keep trying," she declared. "I've already been pretty brave. I told them if they had some legitimate charge, then they should let us know, and if not, then they should let him go."

"That's right." I nodded.

"You want to know how brave I was? At first they demanded that I bring rice for my husband, but I stopped when we started running low at home. Finally, I told them that if they needed to hold someone, then they should hold me instead and let my husband make a living for the family because I don't have any professional skills and we are running out of money."

"I think you're right. I'd encourage you to keep trying. The local authorities do have a lot of power, but finally they have to listen to the ones who are above them, too. So I think you shouldn't be afraid to go to the higher-ups. If there's anything else we can do, please let us know."

"Yes, I certainly will. First of all, we'll see if these certified residence papers are enough. I hope so because it's what they asked for. Thank you so much."

The librarian was released in mid-November. We never heard any reports—nor even any rumors—of torture at detention centers or at study-work camps, and that situation reflected a significant change from the previous regime.

*Friend or Foe?*

News of the U.S. trade embargo against Vietnam arrived in early November. Like an immature youngster pulling a prank on a crippled neighbor, the U.S. President had applied the Trading-with-the-Enemy Act to Vietnam, stopping shipments since the end of April. In spite of having signed the Paris Peace Accords in 1973, the United States had suddenly regarded all of Vietnam as an enemy rather than recognizing that the end of the war had finally come.

At a snap of the U.S. president's fingers in February 1972, mainland China had turned from foe to friend. Just over three years later, in April 1975, another presidential snap turned all of Vietnam into an enemy. As a Christian pacifist, I had never regarded China as my enemy. I was also unwilling to begin viewing Vietnam as my enemy.

My friends and I continued to be friends, transcending the irrational whims of political leaders. In fact, one of my friends was an ethnic Chinese high school student. Her thick large glasses accentuated her full, round face.

"I'll bet you don't know why I have to wear such thick glasses, do you?"

"No, I sure don't," I replied.

"I love to read, and when I was small, after I was supposed to be asleep at night, I would read under the covers with a flashlight. But it was too hard on my eyes."

"I really enjoy reading, too, and always have. But I've never done that."

"What do you enjoy reading?" she asked.

"Right now it's mostly religious books—books about Christian life or about Jesus or about the Bible—and books about Vietnam."

"You know, one thing just recently struck me: Jesus was born to a poor family, not to an emperor. I think that's really important."

"Sure. I do, too," I agreed. "It's interesting how some people are rereading their Bibles now and suddenly discovering that the Bible talks about equality and sharing material goods. But those concepts were there all along. In fact, Marx himself didn't see Christian people living according to what Jesus had taught, so he became critical of the church."

"Did you know I was just baptized last month?"

"No. Congratulations! That's great!"

"Well," she explained, "I had considered myself a believer for three or four years already, but never wanted to get baptized because I simply hadn't seen church people living the way they should."

"Sometimes it's a discouraging picture." I nodded.

"I'm a member of the Church of Christ, and there's a high attendence the first Sunday of the month because that's when we have communion. But then attendance tapers off until the beginning of the next month. I went to visit Dalat and it's the same way at the Evangelical Church there. Say, by the way, what's the difference between the Evangelical Church of Vietnam and the United Evangelical Church of Vietnam?"

"That's a good question," I replied. "I'm not real sure myself, but as I understand it, some of the smaller, independent churches have felt like it would be an advantage to join together with each other, so that's where the name 'United Church' comes from. Some people also feel reassured because its leader, Mr. Long, has had connections with the revolution for a long time."

On Thursday, Lap, the newly elected leader of the Fellowship, led a discussion on baptism.

"Who can baptize others?" he asked.

The first two answers popped forward: "preachers," "deacons."

"Anybody else?" the leader asked.

"Evangelists."

"Okay. Can anybody else perform baptisms?" the leader persisted.

"Pastors!" someone exclaimed. We chuckled.

"I think 'pastors' were probably included in 'preachers.' Where does the Bible say only preachers can baptize?" He paused. Silence reigned. He glanced from person to person around the circle. Like others, I shook my head. His conclusion caught me by surprise. "Following the great commission at the end of Matthew 28 is the responsibility of every Christian, not just the preachers or deacons or evangelists."

He impressed me. He sounded very Anabaptist—like the founders of the Mennonites—except for one thing: when I visited his home, I learned that he kept a knife next to his pillow for self-defense!

*Solving Puzzles*

On November 10, we heard the special announcement that the Democratic Republic of Vietnam with headquarters in Hanoi and the Provisional Revolutionary Government of South Vietnam with headquarters in Ho Chi Minh City had just taken the first formal steps to reunify the country. The delegation from the South that was helping resolve the reunification details included Father Chan Tin, whom I had met when working on political prisoner concerns under the Thieu government, and Ni Su Huynh Lien, an active Buddhist nun.

Since the Fellowship asked me to lead another catechism class,

I spent nearly all day researching the words of Jesus in the Sermon on the Mount. The church in New Testament times probably used the Sermon on the Mount for catechetical instruction, and I decided to follow that pattern since the class members already had a copy of H. S. Bender's the *Anabaptist Vision* as well as my paper "The Foundations of Mennonite Life and Thought."

Late in the afternoon, a telegram for me arrived at our door. Telegrams always prompted mini-celebrations. Although the telegram clearly brought news of family activities in South Dakota where my brother and his family lived, it was signed "SHALOM AND NIEBROSIS." *Shalom*—a Hebrew word for *peace*—sounded typical enough, but what was *niebrosis?*

I racked my brain. *Shalom* and *niebrosis.* Since the first word was Hebrew, then the second could be Hebrew, Greek, German, or a medical term. No.

Who sent the telegram? Don, Roine, and Rachel. Maybe that was the clue: donroinerachel or lehcareniornod. No. Our relationship! That was it!

Take *nie* from *niece,* *bro* from *brother,* *sis* from *sister.* Then mash the abbreviations together, and what have you got? "NIEBROSIS"!

If they could do that, so could I. Years later, they recounted a subsequent conversation. Mother had called to South Dakota to share my telegram.

"And then James signed off," Mother concluded. "But they don't even have his name, and they didn't even get the last word spelled right, *love unbroken.*"

After hearing Mother complain about the misspelling of *unbroken* again, Don asked, "How did they spell it?"

"Well, it's supposed to be *love unbroken,* but they've got *love unbroson.*"

Don burst into laughter. "No, Mom, that's no error! That's exactly the way he wrote it. That stands for *uncle-brother-son.*" He was still chuckling. "See, we sent him a telegram signed *'niebrosis'* for *'niece-brother-sister.'* So he just followed the same idea."

"Oh, you guys! I can't believe it! You read each others' minds from halfway around the world!"

A poster, which "niebrosis" had sent to Vietnam as my

Christmas gift in 1974, also proved interesting. In November 1975, the College of Pedagogy sponsored a contest for those majoring in foreign languages. Since Ngoc was majoring in English, she asked Max and me to help her with an English display, focusing on peace. I loaned her the "neibrosis" poster which, quoting Corinthians, proclaimed "LIVE IN PEACE" in radiant colors.

Someone in the MCC office found a miniature replica of the well-known antiwar poster, "War is not healthy for children and other living things." After enlarging it, Ngoc painted a replica for the display and selected several poems that Max and I had written. In mid-November, she beamed with the results: the unique display won first place.

*In Touch*

Leading the new catechism class which started in mid-November filled me with excitement and awe. Another November highlight came when front page headlines in a Vietnamese newspaper announced a Mennonite-Quaker delegation's visit to Vietnam. Friends of ours had enthusiastically read the news, too. The delegation's visit and related newspaper reports provided additional validation for the message which we had shared: the good news of reconciliation transcends the barriers that otherwise divide humanity into antagonistic groups.

We MCCers hoped to meet the delegation after it arrived in Ho Chi Minh City. We knew two members of the delegation: Bob Miller, former Asia Secretary at the MCC headquarters in Akron, Pennsylvania, and Luke Martin, former MCC director in Vietnam and former Mennonite missionary in Vietnam. Both Bob and Luke stayed in a hotel just blocks from our office. Because their tightly packed itinerary might only allow time for a phone call to us, we pedaled our bicycles to the hotel for an unscheduled visit with Bob Miller. Authorities terminated the visit after ten minutes.

Three days later, the highest levels of Vietnamese government overruled the "security restrictions" that had prevented us from formally meeting the delegation. Our appointed hour flew by as we discussed home life, church life, Bible teaching, and news about mutual friends. In our discussion of MCC plans for future assistance to Vietnam, we three MCCers stressed that the delegation's visit and the formal continuing relationship between MCC and Vietnam reassured our Vietnamese friends.

Our visit with the delegation ended when the guests for the evening banquet with the delegation began arriving. I was glad to learn that the delegation met religious leaders, including Mr. Long, the head of the United Evangelical Church of Vietnam.

That evening Hiro, Max, and I reviewed our discussion with the delegation. The delegation's tightly packed, government-supervised schedule had surprised us by its contrast to our own liberty to travel around town.

The next morning Ngoc and two of her friends found me alone on the rooftop of our Center. Slouched in an armchair in the shade, I had propped my bare feet on a sad-looking folding chair in front of me. I grabbed several more folding chairs, snapped them open, and invited the three guests to sit down.

"Thanks, but we'd rather stand." Leaning against the wall which rimmed the roof and resting their elbows comfortably on top of it, they watched traffic on the street below.

"Did you know we got to meet the Mennonite delegation?" I asked.

"No! Tell us about it!"

After sketching the details, I concluded. "They were wondering whether it was time for us guys to think about leaving since we aren't the official representatives for MCC in the eyes of the government anyway."

"Well, what did you tell them?"

"I'm not ready to leave, but I think maybe Max and Hiro are," I said.

"Do you think you're going to be leaving soon?"

"No. I doubt it."

"What do you think about Vietnamese girls?" Ngoc asked me, abruptly changing the conversation.

"Well, I think they're very beautiful, and the *ao dai* is prettier than any other national costume in the world."

"Have you ever thought about marrying a Vietnamese girl?" Ngoc persisted.

"No, not really. I didn't come to Vietnam to find myself a wife."

"Other Americans probably didn't either, but then they've married Vietnamese girls. Don't you think you'd like to marry a Vietnamese?"

"I don't know. I'm pretty stubborn. I haven't been interested in marriage at all, so how can I be interested in marrying a Vietnamese?"

"If you aren't interested in marrying a Vietnamese, then you're racially prejudiced," Ngoc asserted bluntly.

"Wait a minute! I said I wasn't interested in getting married, and that was the reason I said I wasn't interested in marrying a Vietnamese. So how can you call that 'racial prejudice'?" I asked defensively.

"So, would you marry a Vietnamese or not?" Ngoc repeated.

"Good night! I don't know. I suppose that's an option. When that time comes, if I ever do get married, I'm going to have to ask the good Lord for some guidance in choosing someone to be my wife. And listen: just because I might not marry a Vietnamese, you can't say I'm prejudiced against Vietnamese. For instance, say I would marry a Vietnamese: oh, then the blacks could say to me, 'You're prejudiced against blacks because you didn't marry a black'; and the American Indians could say to me, 'You're prejudiced against us because you didn't marry an American Indian.' See? It's irrational to think that just because I don't marry someone that I'm automatically prejudiced against her people. Jesus' idea of loving people is certainly broader than marriage. Say, besides, Jesus himself never married anyone." I decided my impromtu sermon was long enough, except for a final question: "And you wouldn't say Jesus was prejudiced against Vietnamese, would you?"

"Of course not," Ngoc retorted. "But take it as a theoretical question then. 'Would you be willing to marry a Vietnamese?' "

Her persistence exasperated me. "Okay," I agreed reluctantly. "If it's a theoretical question, then I can give you a clear theoretical answer. Yes, I would be willing to marry a Vietnamese, just like I would be willing to marry a Chinese, a German, a Russian, a black, or a member of any other racial group. I believe that God's love is big enough to transcend racial differences even in marriage. But I would certainly have to do some careful thinking about it because marriage is not easy, and marrying across cultural lines complicates an already complicated situation. I have some good friends who have married across cultural lines, and I truly wish them well, but I'm not sure that's for me. But good grief! How do I know? I'm not even interested in marriage. In college and seminary I had to study hard, and in MCC I've been working hard, and up to this point in my life I've felt it's been a real advantage to be single. Maybe some day way down the road in the future, I'll have to ask the Lord about whether I should get married or not, but not yet."

"Please, don't be sad. I was just wondering. Okay?" She waited.

"Yeah"—I managed to smile weakly—"but you sure made me think fast about stuff I'd never thought of before." One day, however, questions about cross-cultural marriage would confront me again.

The next afternoon, Mrs. Bay, the former cook at the Vietnam Christian Service guesthouse, dropped by to see us. "I heard you guys were still here."

"Yeah, we're still around."

"How are you doing?" she asked.

"Sometimes I get fed up with being 'unemployed,'" Max admitted.

I refused to let his answer represent me by implication. Researching the Sermon on the Mount and leading the catechism classes demanded hard work and gave me a perspective different from his. "I've been busy leading Bible classes here, so I haven't had time to get bored."

"How are you and your family doing?" Hiro asked her.

"We're okay. The children are in school," she responded.

"What kind of work are you yourself doing?" Hiro inquired.

"I'm selling vegetables now. It's a difficult life. I have to get up at 4:00 a.m. to get the vegetables ready. Sometimes the wholesaler only sells in lots of 50 or 100 kilos, so then sometimes I have to sell perishable vegetables at a loss to get rid of them in time. Many people come to look but don't buy anything. We're just trying to scrape along from one day to the next."

"Yeah," Hiro said, "the U.S. sure left the economy here in a mess, and unfortunately, things like that don't get cleared up overnight. It's going to take a while till things get better."

*Love or Justice*

In one of the MCC late-night discussions at the beginning of December, Hiro asked me, "Why do you always emphasize 'love, love, love'?"

"I guess it's because I think it's so basic. God is love, and we're supposed to be loving, too," I answered.

"But love is so abstract," he persisted. "Love sounds so simplistic. What do you mean by *love?*"

"Well, *love* would include respect, and caring, and being involved, and listening, and helping. How's that for starters?"

"That still sounds so mushy."

"Okay, what about *justice?*" I took the offensive. "You like the word *justice*. What does that mean?"

"*Justice,*" Hiro asserted, "is a good, solid word compared to *love. Justice* means equality, and people can understand that."

"Wait a minute! Let's take an example: Vietnam is in a new situation now, so let's say two guys go to the local rice distribution center and each picks up a bag of rice. Justice, right?"

"It looks like it."

"Yeah, but what if one of the guys is single and the other one has a wife and children?" I asked. "So if each guy took home the same amount of rice, that sure wouldn't be justice would it? No way. But at first it looked like justice. So now take two men, each with a wife and eight kids"—under pressure I forgot to use a more dignified word for children—"and each man gets the same amount of rice. Justice, pure and simple, right? Baloney! The children in one family are all below the age of twelve, and in the other family, five of the eight are teenage boys. Now try and tell me that teenage boys don't eat any more food than preschool kids."

"Well, then all you have to do is say the boys are adults and should get an adult's allotment of rice." Hiro stood firm.

"So we define them to be adults. At what age? Seventeen? Fifteen? Thirteen? Pick any age you want to, and I'll say it's arbitrary. And if justice comes down to a set of arbitrary definitions, then I'll say it's just as abstract as love. And if I can take my choice, I'll take love."

Max, agreeing with Hiro more than with me, joined the dialogue. "But love without justice is hollow."

"Sure, I can't argue with that." I nodded. "That's good theology. Love includes a lot of things, and I'll gladly include justice in the list. But justice without love is also pretty cold."

I had explained my position; they had explained theirs. The discussion enlightened us all. I quietly resolved to reduce my use of the word *love*. Hiro, ready for more action, declared, "I'll tell you something that really bugs me: everybody says, 'Sorry, sorry.' As if it's that simple: do whatever you please, and then say, 'Sorry, sorry.' " He had launched us into "solving" another of the world's great problems, or more accurately, into sharing our perspectives with each other as a small-scale Christian community.

# Chapter 15

# MERRY CHRISTMAS

*It Depends*

When should Max, Hiro, and I leave Vietnam? On December 1, a telegram from Bob Miller at the MCC headquarters in Pennsylvania suggested that we three should consider leaving. The telegram prompted a lively discussion for us.

I explained my position to Max and Hiro: if I had a choice, I preferred to stay through Christmas because I was leading a catechism class and helping prepare the Christmas program for our Center. Leaving immediately after Christmas also seemed illogical. Tet, the Lunar New Year, arrived a few weeks after Christmas, and I felt that leaving just before Tet would ruin the celebration for my friends. Besides, I wanted to celebrate this Tet—the first Tet since the war had ended—with them, and I felt that MCC owed me one last, more relaxed Tet. I was willing to leave after Tet.

In the meantime, our friends continued to visit us.

"I've been an active participant in school activities and am class president," Ty remarked. "My teacher was surprised because I wasn't a member of the (government-sponsored) student organization. She had just assumed that everyone in leadership positions was a member of the student organization. Yesterday, though, I did join. It's got organized activities on Sunday morning—I think intentionally so. But I made my position clear. I told them that if it was something important, I would attend; if it's not important, I will attend worship services like usual."

"That sounds like a healthy perspective. I'm glad that you were open with them about your priorities," I responded.

"So many of the meetings are just meetings, and I can't stand

*279*

them. If there's something important or productive, I'll be there to help; but if not, then I sure won't be there."

"If our Fellowship meeting on Sunday mornings is going to cause problems, then sometime maybe our group should talk about meeting at a different time," I suggested. "After all, there's nothing extra special about Sunday morning."

"Don't worry about it. It's no problem right now anyhow. And I really enjoy practicing those carols for Christmas. I like Christmas. Christmas this year is going to be a huge celebration because it's the first one since liberation, and the government isn't uptight. I also think it's going to be big because people still have money. Maybe in the future, life will get tougher, but at least they're determined to celebrate this Christmas."

A few days later, the former MCC bookkeeper surprised me when he described a government concession for Christmas. "Civil servants who said they were Christians on their personal history form can take off December 25 as a holiday. The rest of the government workers will have to work like usual."

Friends also shared news from different churches. About 50 percent as many people were attending the Evangelical Church of Phu Lam as before, whereas the Mennonite Church still had about two thirds as many as before. The most exciting report came from Tin's older brother.

"Out in Honai, where my folks have moved—you know, where Tin was working—the church was just started two months after the revolution. It's got about ten families now and is really dynamic. Evangelist Trung Tin is pastor there, and he is outstanding."

Another telegram from the MCC office in Akron arrived on Saturday, December 13. This time, the message was specific: it recommended that we MCCers should leave Vietnam in January. Several days later when Ty asked Max to play the portable electric organ for the Christmas program at our Center, he declined, perhaps influenced by the telegram.

"It has the appearance of foreigners running the show—of dependence on foreigners," he asserted. "And furthermore, it's an escape for some who are trying to recreate 'the good old days' or who just come for the fun of it."

The evening before the Christmas program at our Center,

Ngoc rang the buzzer at our front gate. Something bothered her. She, Max, Hiro, and I sat on the cushioned rattan furniture which circled the living room. The furniture felt more comfortable than the discussion topic.

"As far as dependency goes, we certainly don't have a material dependency on you or on Jim." Ngoc addressed Max. Hiro had avoided formal involvement with the Fellowship.

Ngoc continued. "If you want to talk about a kind of 'spiritual' dependency on Jim, maybe you are more correct—but even then it's not because he's an American." Glancing around the circle, she added, "I respect all three of you—not because of your nationality—but because you're you."

Ngoc looked at Max. "Everyone in the Fellowship was sad to hear that you thought we come here just for the fun of it. If it weren't for God, we would not be coming here at all. There are a lot of other places which are a lot more fun. And don't think that we don't know about the risks involved—that was clear to us before you even thought about it—and we are still prepared to accept that risk because of God's love. If we didn't have God's love, we would have stopped coming long ago. People who just come for the fun of it may come for a couple of weeks and then stop."

"Maybe I was thinking too much about those who have stopped coming, but I'm concerned about the future," Max stressed. "Will there be any changes?"

"Sure there'll be changes," Ngoc acknowledged. "Big changes. For one thing, there'll probably be fewer people, but exactly what kind of changes—I don't know. It will depend on the situation."

Then Hiro joined the conversation. "I just can't keep quiet any longer. Based on my experience and what I've seen in Vietnam, many groups haven't been able to survive after the missionaries have left. Maybe now you don't see the dependency of your group, but maybe after a year you will."

"In fact," Max agreed, "sometimes love for missionaries turned into hate after they left."

*Celebrate*

Music opened the Fellowship's Christmas Program on Sunday afternoon, December 21. The celebration packed the second floor of the Phan Thanh Gian Center to capacity. Besides duets and a meditation on "Gifts and Giving," the program included a play, "The Birth of Jesus," written by the leader of the Fellowship. The Youth Fellowship from the Gia Dinh Mennonite Church sang, followed by a harmonica duet. Although Max refused to play the organ, he still directed our Fellowship in singing two songs in English: "The Little Drummer Boy" and "The Star of Bethlehem." Our Fellowship invited everyone to the rooftop for refreshments after the program. As my contribution, I had baked refrigerator cookies, molasses cookies, and ginger snaps.

The Fellowship called a special meeting on Monday afternoon and invited Max, Hiro and me to attend.

"Seems like there's been quite a bit of talk recently about your leaving. Is there anything to that?" someone asked us.

"Ever since the MCC delegation visit last month, the MCC head office in the U.S. has been putting on increasing pressure for us to leave," Max explained. "In fact, just this morning we got a letter from the MCC office in the U.S. telling us that we should plan to leave."

"Did it say why?"

"The main reason is because we aren't able to serve as official MCC representatives in the eyes of the government," Max replied.

"So how soon will you be leaving?"

"We haven't decided, and even after we submit our request for exit visas it might take a while. But regardless how long we stay, this group will have to think about the future. Maybe this group has been too dependent on foreigners," Max asserted.

Hiro pushed the idea. "I don't know exactly why I was invited since I haven't participated in the Fellowship activities. But since I'm here, I would like to ask one question: there's been a revolution in Vietnam, but has this group changed any?"

Ngoc answered immediately, "The basic revolution in our lives occurred when we decided to follow Jesus. That was the change."

Lap, the president of the Fellowship, added, "We didn't follow the old government, so now why should we suddenly decide to follow the new government? If we would change and follow the new government, some outsiders would say we were scared and wishy-washy."

The next day, Tuyet, who cooked for us, and I visited after supper.

"Well, Sunday afternoon you finally saw why I needed to 'practice' the 'rum-pa-pum-pum' so much while helping with the dishes," I commented wryly, referring to my part in "Drummer Boy."

"I nearly laughed out loud when I heard that song." She grinned. "I couldn't help thinking of your 'practice sessions.' "

"Now that I've memorized the 'rum-pa-pum-pum,' don't you think I should keep on practicing just in case I'll have another opportunity to use it?"

"No, no, I wouldn't say that!" she exclaimed, feigning horror.

"I'm sure enjoying this Christmas a lot more than my first Christmas here. That was the year when the U.S. bombed the North so terribly at Christmas."

"But when you look at the Bible," she observed, "politics really isn't doing anything strange. The Bible says that grass withers, flowers fade, but only the Word of God lasts forever."

"Yeah, you're right," I agreed, "but sometimes I still wish politicians wouldn't be so irrational."

"There have been some improvements by the new government," she noted, as if to cheer me up. "And one thing is clear: everybody is going to have to work hard. Back in the old days down in the southern delta, life wasn't too difficult because one growing season would produce enough rice so that farm families could take off during the dry season, but the new government probably won't allow that. Everybody will have to do their share all year round."

"I think you're right. Since the U.S. cut off its food shipments and with all the unemployment now, Vietnam needs all the food production it can get. Too bad some people are afraid of hard work. You sure aren't one of them! I've been impressed with how much work you do and how fast you get it done, and I've appreciated your willingness to review my input for the Fellowship."

"I've had a sad feeling the past several days—a kind of premonition about that letter from your director asking you guys to leave," she said.

"Is that right? We always knew that sooner or later we'd be leaving, but when it comes right down to it, leaving is hard. This will be my last Christmas in Vietnam," I acknowledged quietly.

"So this Christmas is happy, but sad. Since we probably won't ever meet again, during these last days together we'll have to laugh so we won't cry."

Surprised, I smiled. "Some day I hope to come back to Vietnam to visit, maybe with an MCC delegation, but we probably wouldn't have a chance to meet."

"Yeah, and who knows where I'll be? I'd like to keep working here in Saigon and also do some tailoring at home," she said.

Christmas Eve, I sat near the back of the crowded sanctuary of the Gia Dinh Mennonite Church so I could take photographs. Khai, the relieved draft resister, led both the children's choir and the youth choir. Their enthusiatic singing radiated festivity. The children's charming recitations reached the farthest corners of the sanctuary.

An older member of the Gia Dinh Youth Fellowship shared a Christmas meditation. She concluded, "This is the first Christmas with peace in Vietnam. Now we need to find peace with God through Christ who brought salvation." While the ceiling fans whirred to counteract the hot, humid weather, Trung read a letter bringing Christmas greetings from an Evangelical Church in Hanoi.

Besides Pastor Sang and the precinct chairman, special guests included Long, who was head of the United Evangelical Church, and his wife. Long led closing prayer, and I noted that twice in his prayer he mentioned loving God and country. He used the unity for which Jesus had prayed in the garden to refer to the reunification of Vietnam. I felt more comfortable when he asked God to grant Christians a heart willing to serve the people.

Several members of the congregation who had moved to the countryside exerted a special effort to attend the Gia Dinh Christmas service and asked me to convey their best wishes to all of the Mennonite missionaries who had formerly served in Vietnam. The program ended at 9:30 p.m., but I only stayed briefly to socialize before leaving to attend another Christmas program.

Since the government had lifted the curfew for Christmas Eve, a special service began at 10:00 p.m. in the large Tran Cao Van Church that had formerly been known as the International Protestant Church. I had never seen people pack that sanctuary so tightly before: besides those sitting on jammed pews and on three rows of chairs behind the last pews, other people stood squeezed into the outer aisles of the sanctuary and behind the chairs. The program itself, organized by the Christian University Students of Saigon, consisted primarily of singing. Pastor Cuong, the guest speaker, had recently completed doctoral studies in the U.S.

> The birth of Christ divides history into two parts—before Christ and after Christ. Christ made a profound impact on history. Our lives, too, are divided into two parts: before and after deciding to follow Christ. Deciding to follow Christ changes history.

The program ended at 1:00 a.m. I had to awaken early, however, to make final preparations for the baptismal service at the Phan Thanh Gian Center. For our Fellowship, celebrating the birth of the Prince of Peace included celebrating the spiritual birth of five candidates ready for water baptism.

A student who had participated in Max's work camp shared his testimony first. Seriously following Christ for a while already, he explained how he had seen God at work in recent events in his life. After reading a passage from chapter four in 1 John, he concluded, "God is love and demonstrated that love by sending Jesus to serve. I promise to love God and to serve the people. I will always remember this baptism and this Christmas."

Speaking so quietly that we had to strain to hear, Yen reviewed her pilgrimage. "My parents are Buddhist, so when I grew up, they gave me a Buddhist religious name without even asking me. I just started coming here after liberation. Finally, I tried praying, and my prayer was answered. I really don't know exactly when I became a true believer, but I had always believed there is a God.

"My uncle doesn't like it when I come here," she continued, "and he has not given me permission to meet foreigners any more. But how can you prevent someone from following a religion?" she asked rhetorically. "I believe Jesus really lived, died on a cross, was resurrected, and is coming again. One verse that has meant a lot to me comes from Matthew 7, where Jesus says, 'Only the ones who do my Father's will, will enter the kingdom of heaven.'"

Nhung, the next to share, smiled as she began. "I always believed there was a God, but, you know, it was the kind of belief that didn't influence my life. It just went in one ear and out the other. I really loved Mrs. Stauffer and studied English under her here in 1972, but I was always carefree."

She sobered. "My mother died a week before liberation. That got me thinking, and then I started coming back to the Center, determined to give religion a try. But I was careful, you know, still testing things out. I said a trial prayer on June 27 and found happiness, and then I suddenly realized that I better start following Jesus seriously or else the words of my prayer wouldn't mean anything. So I sat down and wrote a letter to my brother telling him that I had decided to follow Jesus."

Her face brightened. "Right at that time I was wishing for something, but I didn't want to bother God with it. You know how it is. I wanted a bicycle so bad, but I didn't even dare pray about it, but God knew! My brother bought me a bicycle."

Smiles lit our faces, too. She continued. "But then it got stolen! Well, I thought, 'The Lord gives, and the Lord takes away!' " We chuckled.

"I was able to get another one," she added. "But there's something even more impressive. Before I decided to follow Jesus, I loved those who loved me and hated those who hated me. But I've changed now to loving everybody."

Wearing glasses with huge, round lenses, Thuy recounted her pilgrimage. Her usual pace was fast. When she was nervous, it was faster. "I've believed in God for a long time. Exactly what, I wasn't sure. Initially, I really didn't care about religion—I just wanted to enjoy life. Churches? I've attended them all: Christian, Mennonite, Catholic, Evangelical, Jehovah Witness. You name it, I've been there. But it felt best to come back here.

"As some of you know," she continued, "I'm studing at the university in the English section, which is the most reactionary. Believe me, that makes life tough. How can I go on studying there? With God's grace, I've accepted it. I'd like to be baptized because I believe that will help me stand firm."

Wearing bright red overalls with a white blouse, the fifth and final candidate stood shyly behind the podium. "I'm not a Vietnamese," she began quietly. Although she did not say so, perhaps she came to our Fellowship having already absorbed the brunt of cruel racial discrimination. The carefully chosen words in her brief testimony conveyed her sincerity. "Actually, I'm Chinese. I had a good friend who left the country some time ago because he wouldn't join the military. That made a big impression on me. I've been attending the Center here for quite a while now. The peace emphasis fits what I believe, and baptism feels right."

I appreciated those five simple, yet profound, testimonies about God at work. I wondered how patriotic fervor and nationalism could trick some Christians in North America into thinking that God's Spirit only thrived under western-style "democracy." The leader of the Fellowship asked each candidate three questions to confirm the commitment first to Jesus as Lord and Savior, then to lifelong service through the church as the body of Christ, and finally to water baptism as a public symbol of that commitment. After the Fellowship voted to unanimously accept the candidates, I held the basin of water and the towel as he administered the rite.

The moving baptismal service had hardly ended when the telephone in the MCC office rang. Loc, from the Ministry of Foreign Affairs, called to report that tractors from MCC and a bill of lading for clothes and milk had arrived. He concluded, "And best wishes for a Merry Christmas."

What could I say in return to this diplomat who probably held no allegiance to Jesus? I groped for words.

The Christmas buffet that Frances Starner, a U.S. reporter, hosted that afternoon gave me more insight into the revolution. The star of the get-together, Colonel Thao, as talkative as the hostess, had worked with Ho Chi Minh.

"He lived a very simple life," Thao observed. "One time for National Independence day he was planning to wear his old conical hat. Well, finally his chauffeur bought a new hat and requested the old one to give to his sick son as a momento and as a boost to getting well. It worked."

Thao, a media man for the new government in Saigon, also reflected on the current economic situation. "The situation in Vietnam is not due just to the revolution. Even if the old government had won, there would have been a mighty tough road ahead because the U.S. was still cutting off its massive aid to the South. So either way, Vietnam was going to have to face hard times."

A letter of greeting from a church in the Soviet Union and Christmas music opened the program at the Hong Bang Church that evening. The program featured a drama of the legend of the fourth wise man. Sidetracked to help unfortunate people along the way, giving them the jewels he had intended to give Jesus, the fourth wise man arrived too late to meet Jesus with the other three wise men. The fourth wise man was comforted, though, when he heard that Jesus had said: "Inasmuch as you have helped the least of these, you have helped me."

Thus, my first Christmas in Vietnam and my last Christmas in Vietnam became superimposed, like the juxtapostion of barbed wire and flowers.

The aches and pains of planning and transitions in the Fellowship lasted until the end of December. On the last day of the year, Ngoc shared her reflections. I, too, looked back.

"I've been trying to prepare the group for my leaving," I said. "Granted, right after liberation maybe the group was too dependent on me. For example, my lecturing on Thursdays, but that ended at the end of June, and my preparing discussion questions ended at the end of September. And then the group was fully on it's own. I had told Max that if we had a choice about our leaving, to give me till the end of October before leaving."

"So were you planning to leave at the end of October?" Ngoc asked.

"No, not really. But I was trying to tell him I would have fulfilled my basic obligations to MCC and to the missionaries by the end of October. In November the Fellowship elected a good Executive Committee, and I tried to emphasize that they were to take responsibility. Obviously, we didn't leave at the end of October, so I accepted some other responsibilities. Maybe my role in the Christmas program was a step backward, but maybe not."

"You mean by playing the part of a wise man in the Christmas drama?"

I nodded.

"No, certainly not! You were perfect for the part in your *ao dai,*" Ngoc insisted, referring to the traditional Vietnamese outfit I had worn.

"I don't know. Maybe playing that part was taking too much

of an active role." I remembered hearing a parable someone on the Clinic Board at Nhatrang had used, so I continued. "Like the Evangelical Clinic at Nhatrang: when it was built, the beach stretched a long ways in front of it before reaching the ocean, but over the years the ocean gradually ate away at the beach, until finally a retaining wall had to be built. A latecomer would wonder why the hospital was built so close to the ocean. After we leave, the situation will change, but I hope that during the past months the right decisions were made."

"Over the past months." Ngoc paused. "Why, our group hasn't even existed a whole year yet!"

"That's right. It's clear that the Fellowship here is a 'young' group, and in my opinion, it has matured quickly: there is no 'missionary' on the Executive Committee, which is quite a contrast to other churches which had missionaries in leadership positions for years. For a couple of days in November I was uneasy about the future of the Fellowship, but not any longer."

Unschooled in the piles of books and theories about mission-church transitions, our Fellowship had been thrust into the midst of the great debate. One basic belief, however, sustained us: the Good Shepherd would never desert his flock, regardless where the sheep might be scattered. Church tradition celebrated his birth in December, and the wave of that mighty tradition had swept us high above most of the hidden perils of transition.

## On What Basis?

The celebrations of Christmas ended; the work of Christmas continued. Sharing time during our worship service on the first Sunday in January illustrated the magnitude of the task.

Ty began, her energy as concentrated as her petite form.

"Since liberation, I've studied a lot about the revolution. But whenever I participate in the revolution, it has to be on my conditions. I'm taking a firm stand, so I'm not afraid to participate in the revolutionary groups. I think some preachers shudder at my involvement, and they're sure I'm on the way to becoming a party member. I'm participating, but I'm making it clear that my religious commitment comes first. Following Christ means service, not just prayer and Bible reading. And let me share something else with you. Last fall I was terribly busy, and I was sharing my testimony with others, but it seemed too automatic, too much of a burden, too much like a routine. And then I saw I was lacking the motive of love—and since that time things have really perked up."

Kha's words, though few, revealed deep insight. Her low-pitched voice contributed to their impact. "We are to witness and serve in whatever situation we are, and with the change of governments, now God is expecting us to witness to the communists, too."

Huong shared a longer story. Her intensity scarcely allowed her time to breathe. "Just last night at the regular weekly meeting for Christian students at the Church on Thong Nhat Street we learned some history about the Protestant Church in the North. Before, all we heard about were the Christians who had come south (in 1954). There were 13 pastors who stayed as well as a few sturdy Christians who understood that God wasn't abandoning them. Until 1959, they were regarded with some suspicion because so many of their number had left, but because none of them were involved in a scandal that was uncovered that year, they were respected. From 1970 to 1972, the young people organized themselves, and 40 attended a conference. At the annual general conference in 1975, there were 600 delegates. They hope to open a seminary soon and have 10 candidates to study there. With that history in the North—including the fact that there is open acceptance of Sunday and Thursday church meetings—it is clear that the church can't blame the government if the church collapses. If the church dies, we are the ones who have killed it."

*Serving*

Just after our morning services ended, Trung and another member of the Executive Committee gave me an informal report from the Gia Dinh Center.

"Each member of the staff at the school in our Center is now getting 30 piasters," Trung noted, referring to the new currency. "Each staff member also gets 10 kilos of rice per month as part of the salary."

I nodded. "That sounds quite reasonable. Very interesting—same people working, only now the government is paying their salary, so it sounds like things are stable out in Gia Dinh. There's one thing about this Center, though, that your Executive Committee probably should discuss, and that's the library upstairs here." I referred to the Phan Thanh Gian Center. "Since the English program won't continue here and since we MCCers are getting ready to leave, you might want to make some plans for the books."

"Sure, we'll put it on the agenda for our Executive meeting this week."

That afternoon, having noticed the blanket of leaves which covered the concrete parking space in our front yard, Ngoc, a member of the Fellowship, picked up a broom, demonstrating voluntary service. Not to be outdone, I grabbed another broom and began sweeping vigorously, too. After dumping the leaves into the trash bin, we sat on a concrete bench to rest.

"Those leaves really needed to be swept up," I acknowledged. "Thanks."

"The idea of service has really become part of my life," she replied. "Even at school people have noticed that I've been motivated by the ideals of love and service like you MCCers always emphasize, so I'm now vice-president of a unit of 30 students at my university."

"Is that right? I hadn't known."

"I haven't said much about it," she responded. "The leadership interpreted my involvement as being very 'progressive,' so the unit leader and I have to evaluate unit members, and our evaluation will be part of determining their eligibility for further study. It's terribly hard, Jim. It's such an awesome responsibility." She almost broke into tears.

"I'm sure it's tough, but I'm also sure that in the whole school there's nobody more fair than you are."

"Well, I never thought of it that way," she replied soberly. Although a cheery mood still evaded her, at least tears had been averted.

In the middle of the week Max, Hiro, and I all happened to be in the MCC office when Tin, our former office assistant dropped in for a visit. His skin was even darker than when he had visited us in October. He laid his dark blue corduroy golf-style cap on the desk beside him.

"You wouldn't believe how busy I am these days. It's as if

when I was working for MCC, I was only working with one hand, but now I'm working with two hands. Yep, working twice as hard, eating three times as much, sleeping half as much. I haven't even had much time to study the revolution."

We chuckled. "Not studying the revolution doesn't look like it has hurt you any," I said. "Your muscles look like a champion muscleman. If Uncle Ho (Chi Minh) could see your muscles, I'm sure he'd forgive you for not sitting around to study the revolution." I grinned.

"But besides all the regular work," Tin remarked, "it's really strange—I've got this automatic response: when someone needs help or something needs to be done, I'm immediately in there pitching away while others are just standing around wondering what to do."

Hiro affirmed him. "When I need a concrete example of the revolutionary lifestyle, I can say that it does exist—in you."

Tin smiled. "That lifestyle, at least in part, is due to the influence of MCC. I'm glad that my girl friend also recognizes the importance of Christian service. I never want to lose the spirit of service."

*Christian or Non-Christian*

The next day the MCC secretary confided in me. "Being baptized is easy, but it's hard to live the way Christians should. Under other circumstances, I might ask to be baptized, but right now I don't know if I could be faithful to that commitment. If I make a commitment, I want to keep my word."

As I listened, I prayed briefly, silently for her. I had helped to plant and water the seeds of her Christian faith. The next step was hers at the Spirit's bidding.

A week later, on my way back from downtown, I stopped to browse at a Liberation Bookstore half a block from home. In the cramped quarters a few steps below ground level, I found several copies of a mimeographed Catholic Christmas songbook for sale, much to my surprise. While roaming the aisles in the spacious official Liberation Bookstore on Le Loi Street downtown, Max unexpectedly discovered a supply of Ken Taylor's paraphrased Living Bible in English for sale there. If the government was trying to stamp out the influence of Christianity, then why grant Christmas holidays to Christians and allow government bookstores to sell Bibles and Christmas songbooks?

A "Christian nation," however, had left an undesirable legacy in Vietnam. My Vietnamese friends who followed Christ constantly wrestled with the negative impact of U.S. involvement in Vietnam. During the sharing time at the Phan Thanh Gian Center on Sunday morning, Phung stumbled over her words.

"At the movies, a friend of mine saw a political cartoon against religion. It showed President Nixon as an airplane, with his nose as the nose of the plane, his arms out at the side as the front wings, and his shoes turned up as the tail of the plane. While pulling a banner saying 'Merry Christmas,' the smirking plane dropped bombs on Hanoi. My friend didn't know how to respond."

Our Fellowship sat hushed by her report of the attempt to wrap the Christmas of 1972 into one package with Christianity and the bombing. I shook my head. Then from across our circle, the worship leader responded.

"First, we must recognize that what Nixon did is terribly ugly and that, second, what he did is even worse because he did it under the guise of religion. I can't remain silent in the face of that. But it's clear that Jesus is not like Nixon: Jesus wants to save Vietnam, not destroy it."

Such insight! Unforgettable words! We nodded. Ty, the vice-president of the Executive Committee for our Fellowship, shared a similar conclusion based on a different experience.

"I've seen films of American soldiers reading the Bible and then going to the battlefield. It's sad but true. I have to admit that it makes me very ashamed. But we must show by the way we live that that is not the Jesus way."

That powerful discussion provided the setting for the next hour when I led the baptismal candidates in a study of the Sermon on the Mount. I reminded the candidates of the mini-sermon we had just heard, "Jesus is not like Nixon: Jesus wants to save Vietnam, not destroy it, and that is good news."

The next Sunday, I saw the fulfillment of a dream that had begun six months earlier. Then Lieu had been excited because her sister Lan wanted to be baptized. On Sunday morning, January 25,

Lan and two other candidates formally committed themselves to Christ and joined the Fellowship through water baptism. Lieu herself was absent: at the end of October she had died from heart problems. At that time, I silently adopted her vision of seeing her sister baptized and committed myself to turning it into reality if possible. Consequently, the baptismal ceremony completed that unspoken pledge. A simple celebration of the Lord's Supper closed our worship service. I felt as awed as if my friends and I had stood on top of Mount Sinai.

*Moving*

I felt that mountaintop experience concluded all of my responsibilities to MCC and to Mennonite Mission. I also felt I essentially achieved the formal and informal goals I had set for myself. Having done my best, I was ready to leave Vietnam—after Tet, of course. And Tet was less than a week away.

Preparing to leave brought complications. In the eyes of the Gia Dinh Church, Max, Hiro, and I were responsible for the "United Evangelical Church Center." What would happen to the Center after we three left? No one seemed to know. Because Long had preempted vehicles from the Gia Dinh Center, we wondered whether he would preempt the Phan Thanh Gian Center, too.

Max, Hiro, and I had hunted for an apartment so the Center could avoid undergoing a transition during the final days before our leaving. Those days would be hectic enough without worrying about the Center. We wondered why the Gia Dinh Church seemed reluctant to plan ahead or to share plans already made.

"Ngoc and Lap from the Fellowship came to talk to us," Trung had reported to me. "But we told them not to worry about the Center as long as you are here. We'll wait until your leaving date is set."

"But," I had responded, "those last days can be quite frantic. It seems like it would be better to plan ahead."

Several days later, when he realized that we actually intended to move, Trung told Max, "I'm going to be in the countryside for Tet and won't be back to accept the Center keys until February fifth, even if you do move before that. So just turn off the electricity, and be sure to lock things up tight."

The next day, Tuesday, January 27, we MCCers moved from the Center into a third floor apartment on Dong Khoi Street. On Wednesday morning, several members of the Fellowship and I returned to clean the second floor of the Center, arrange the chairs for our Tet gathering on Sunday, and sweep the yard. Trung happened to stop at the Center while it buzzed with activity. He noted that Max, Hiro, and I had already moved.

"After Tet, the Gia Dinh Church will send someone to take care of this Center," Trung told members of the Fellowship and myself. "Until then the young people—the Fellowship—can take care of it. The Gia Dinh Church will also discuss the possibility of Long using it as an office."

Two hours later, when I was alone at the Center taking care of final details, Trung returned with Long.

"I just heard that you have moved out of the Center here."

"Yes, that's right." I nodded. "We moved yesterday, and this morning several members of the Fellowship and I were getting things set up for Sunday. The first Sunday of the New Year always seems special. We're ready to turn the keys over to Trung, but he suggested that the Fellowship should take responsibility for the Center until after Tet. I'm wondering what you see as the future of the Center?"

Without hesitating, Long announced, "It will be the office for the United Evangelical Church of Vietnam. Forty churches have now joined. Perhaps the main reason they've joined is that Pastor Mieng is too conservative in his leadership of the Evangelical Church of Vietnam—he hasn't enthusiastically endorsed the revolution."

"Will the Gia Dinh Executive Committee also be meeting soon to discuss the future of this Center?" I asked, puzzled.

"This Center belongs to the United Evangelical Church of Vietnam," Long declared, "which means it belongs to me. I accept responsibility for it before God until the day when the Mennonites return to Vietnam and need an office."

"It's quite unlikely that foreign Mennonites will be coming back to work in Vietnam like they were doing before," I commented.

"The Mennonite delegation, however, was the first one to visit liberated Vietnam, so it might happen," he asserted.

"It might, but it's highly unlikely." I shook my head. Still confused about Long's other presuppositions, I asked, "What is the responsibility of the Gia Dinh Executive Committee in deciding the future of this Center?"

"The Gia Dinh Church is part of the United Evangelical Church, of which I am the head," Long explained. "And Trung is my representative."

"Yes, Long is the head of the United Evangelical Church, and I am the Gia Dinh representative," Trung echoed.

Their words numbed me. "Yes, I understand," I said flatly. "Thank you."

"I will introduce myself to the group here this coming Sunday morning," Long promised. "I personally will lead the Sunday morning services here, and I'll have the books in the library inventoried and organized. Where two or three are gathered together, Christ is in the midst, so he hears the promise I'm making to you today. And the important thing is how we live, not just the words we say. I've served as a Steering Committee member of the National Liberation Front, but the revolution is not communist. Jesus himself was a revolutionary emphasizing love and equality. He wants everyone to be united."

Astonished by Long's sudden display of power, I shared my new knowledge with members of the Fellowship who came to visit the new apartment. The next day, the head of the Fellowship related his discouraging experience to me: "I went to talk to Long about the Fellowship helping to pay for water and electricity at the Center. He said that the United Church will take care of it all—which means that the Center is totally under its control."

I tried to brighten the gloomy situation. I had bought some of my favorite fruit, jackfruit, to celebrate the imminent arrival of the New Year. Comparing the jackfruit flavor to bubble-gum, Max claimed that I must have been addicted to bubble-gum in my adolescent years. The unique fruit, in its tough casing which resembled alligator skin, brought strong reactions: people either loved it or hated it. No one remained neutral. In spite of the teasing, I loved the fruit and shared the cripsy, dark yellow chunks with my friends.

Tuyet, our former cook who had just recently returned from a trip to the countryside, also came to visit. Like an older sister, she had brought groceries for us. I helped unpack the food and snip a few stems while we talked.

"People in the countryside are rich compared to a lot of people in Saigon now, including myself," she observed. "Lots of prices there are cheaper."

"In a way, that makes sense," I responded. "After all, if they are producing the food, why shouldn't the prices be cheaper there?"

"But I'm not just talking about food prices. And when I say they're rich, I mean they've got enough money to buy whatever they want. Of course, the people who participated in the Back-to-the-Countryside Program don't have quite so many advantages yet." She was referring to people—especially those previously unemployed in Saigon—who voluntarily participated in the government-sponsored resettlement plan to open new areas of the countryside for cultivation. She paused, shifting the focus. "Something else has sure been strange, too."

"Oh, what's that?" I looked at her.

"I've never been so open with any of my other friends as I've been with you guys. It's strange, isn't it?"

"Well, we sure were glad when you were willing to start eating with us." She broke into a smile as I continued. "I really think of you as an older sister. You've helped us so much during these past months—and I don't mean just cooking and that kind of stuff, but I mean helping us grow spiritually and understand what's going on."

"In spite of knowing you all pretty well, it's hard for me to admit that I'm poor," Tuyet confided while washing lettuce. "My family wanted me to do anything but be a servant, but after I told them my good experiences working for missionaries, they accepted it and were happy. I worked longest for the Stauffers. I liked working for them. Originally, I spent a lot of time with them, even doing some relief work which I really enjoyed. After their children came along, then things naturally changed somewhat." She paused.

"When I was staying with the Hieu family," I noted, "they had a cook and a baby-sitter, and I always tried to be polite to them. But when Mr. and Mrs. Hieu were home, it was obvious that my primary relationship was supposed to be to them and their family and not the cook and the baby-sitter. When Mr. and Mrs. Hieu weren't home, I'd talk to the cook and baby-sitter, but even then the Hieu children still wanted priority. The children were good language teachers, though. When I didn't understand something, they would explain or repeat it until I did understand. Knowing the language has really helped make my stay in Vietnam enjoyable, even though I still feel my ability is quite inadequate."

"You're doing pretty good already. You could study as long as you live and still not know everything there is to know about the Vietnamese language, so you shouldn't feel bad," she reassured me. "Over the years I've picked up a few English words, but not many. And as far as hard work goes, it really isn't a problem if you enjoy the work and the people you are working for."

"I'm not so sure about that," I challenged her. "Before liberation, sometimes when I was working at top speed day and night for MCC and the Mennonite Mission, I really got fed up with it and couldn't find any joy in it because there was too much to do."

"But even after liberation," she commented, "it looked like you were studying pretty hard to put out all those Bible lessons for the Fellowship."

"Yeah, I've been busy, but not half as busy as I was before," I replied. "What about your plans for the future?"

"I haven't decided yet exactly what I will do. What about yourself?"

"Well, I enjoy Bible study and would enjoy teaching Bible, but before I'd teach, I'd probably do some more formal Bible study at a seminary first. First of all, though, I want to spend some time in Kansas with my parents." The Lord's agenda for the next decade of my life would surprise me.

*Tet*

Friday morning, January 30, 1975, Lunar New Year's Eve, I snapped photographs of Tet festivities: firecrackers, flowers, banners, and crowded streets. Firecrackers sparked mixed emotions for me. Many children enjoyed the noise since this Tet was the first Tet in several years which allowed firecrackers. Maybe making children happy was legitimate, but firecrackers carried overtones of warfare, bringing grim memories to some people. I knew a Montagnard woman who had been close to intense fighting and bombing at Banmethuot the previous spring. Consequently, she refused to venture onto the streets because the exploding firecrackers involuntarily resurrected the vivid, terror-stricken experiences.

Sunday dawned bright and clear—a perfect day for worshiping God at the beginning of a New Year. Wearing my dark turquoise *ao dai,* I pedaled to the Phan Thanh Gian Center. Arriving early at the Center, I punched the plastic buzzer button outside the locked gate. The front doors of the Center stood open, but no one responded. I waited. Not expecting any problems, I rang the buzzer again. Still no response. I pushed the button for a hefty, long ring. A short, frail man appeared in the doorway and then limped to the gate.

"Good morning, sir," I greeted him cheerily. "Happy New Year! I'm here for the worship service."

"There won't be any worship service here this morning," he replied flatly.

"No service," I echoed. "But Long told me that our Fellowship could continue meeting here."

"Long hasn't had time to get things set up yet."

"What needs to be set up? Several friends and I got everything set up on the second floor earlier this week. Even if it was rearranged since then, it wouldn't take long to set it up again."

"I'm sorry, but there will be no meeting here today. Long instructed me not to let anyone in," he insisted.

"But Long told me that he himself would be here to introduce himself and lead the service today."

"Long is out for the day. So it's impossible for him to lead any service here. Do you understand?" He used the same flat voice.

"Yes, I understand," I acknowledged slowly, "but I don't understand why."

"Do you have any more questions?" He sounded irritated.

"No, sir, I don't," I replied weakly. "Thank you, sir. Goodbye, sir."

"Good-bye." He turned away from me toward the open front doors—doors which suddenly seemed to have invisible bars across them.

I felt numb. My stomach felt hollow. A heavy hand had smashed the Tet celebration for our Fellowship, and although I knew the fingerprints, I felt helpless. Frustrated by Long's broken promises, I decided to attend the Gia Dinh worship services; God was bigger than Long's padlock on the front gate.

Although many members of the congregation had gone to celebrate Tet in their native areas of Vietnam, about 35 people participated in the New Year service in Gia Dinh. A young man, who had been headed for military service a year earlier, served as worship leader. He asked me to lead a prayer.

That afternoon I pedaled my bicycle to the imposing Tran Cao Van Church for festivities sponsored by the Su Van Hanh Youth. Members of the Phan Thanh Gian Fellowship were waiting for me there.

"We were locked out of the Center this morning." "We couldn't believe it!" Their voices quivered.

"I know," I replied. "I got there early. Had to ring the buzzer three times before an elderly man—maybe a caretaker—came to the gate."

"You mean somebody came to the gate?" Their eyes widened in surprise. "We stood and waited and waited and rang and rang. The front doors were open, but nobody ever even came to the gate for us."

"You know what? Today is the anniversary of my baptism." Ty had lost the usual sparkle in her eyes. "And it really is a strong psychological blow to have the doors close on the very first Sunday of the New Year."

"It's cruel," Ngoc declared. The situation had brought tears to her eyes, but now she had no tears, only anger. "And it's destroying our witness. Today, Tet, the first Sunday in the New Year, I had finally talked my sister and my brother-in-law into coming for the first time—and that was important. We waited and waited. No one answered the bell. To be treated so rudely doesn't line up with God's way. I worked so hard to get my sister to come. We were all dressed up for Tet, too. I don't know if she'll ever come again."

In the afternoon worship service, Pastor Mieng's sermon stressed discipline. A young Vietnamese medical doctor, however, climaxed the worship service with his challenge. As if cherishing the words like water sprinkled on a thirsty flower garden, a hush fell across the packed sanctuary as he spoke.

Christians don't have to be ashamed when talking to revolutionaries. The higher levels of the administration admit that there are problems, but that's natural: "When you plant rice, you're going to sweat." This past Christmas in the delta, there were churches where cadre apologized for slandering the Christians.

But we also need to recognize that the revolutionaries have made great sacrifices—for ten years, for twenty years. Christians must be ready to make even greater sacrifices. Christians must also love their country and must go beyond that to emphasize people. Christians need to support and participate in the worthwhile programs of the government—including building a new society, rebuilding our country, helping our people. And not only participate, but participate positively and wholeheartedly. If the church doesn't follow the road of service, then where is the church headed? The church is not just for worship.

## Farewells

The next day, February 2, 1976, the formal and informal farewells to Max, Hiro, and me began with students from summer work camps Max had organized. Hiro and I had adopted the students as part of our extended family, too. While cracking and eating roasted watermelon seeds, a traditional Tet pastime, Max asked a serious question: "You've been around us for a while, and now we're getting ready to leave. What do you think of us and the philosophy of MCC?"

Awkward silence followed. Only one student was brave enough to address the question directly. Khanh, whose brother had come to visit from the North in September, asked, "You really want to know what I think?"

"Yes." "Really." "Certainly." We gave her our full attention.

"You won't be angry with me?" she asked.

"No, we really need to reflect on what we've been doing here."

"Well," she began, "you've got to understand I'm just speaking for myself; the others can speak for themselves. You three could think about social work because you have enough and don't have to worry about the rest of your family. For myself, I like the idea, but I'm never going to be able to spend years at it like you have because I've got to work to help support my family."

I had never considered MCC service a luxury, but I was unable to argue with her logic. Later, as the work campers left, I raced down the long hall after them. I had forgotten to give Khanh and

Phuong each a copy of the New English Bible that I had promised them. Fortunately, I reached them and handed them each a Bible just before the elevator arrived. Tears glistened in their eyes. They glanced away, perhaps hoping I would not notice. The elevator arrived promptly, eliminating the need for drawn-out, awkward farewells.

"Best wishes to you all for a blessed New Year." I raised my voice so they could hear while entering the elevator. Then a slight, polite nod of my head accompanied my final, quieter words: "Good-bye, friends."

"Good-bye, Jim." "Happy New Year." "Good-bye."

The elevator doors seemed to slap shut with finality, like giant ram-driven shears, chopping off our relationships. That evening, the Fellowship organized a farewell meal in our apartment for us MCCers. I said my good-byes inside the apartment to avoid accompanying anyone to the cruel elevator.

The guest sitting beside me at the farewell left a deep impression. "Tell the church in America what it's really like here. Tell them that our activities continue, and that it's not like they imagine (a Marxist country to be)."

A similar message came from Pastor Cuong, who had received his doctorate in theology in the United States and was currently directing Christian youth work in Saigon while teaching at the Evangelical Bible Institute in Nhatrang. Unable to attend the farewell, he had jotted me a note in English.

Give people a true picture of the church in Vietnam as far as you know, and the freedom we still have in the country. Many are concerned and want to know the truth. They might not believe what we write from Saigon due to their suspicions that we are obliged to give them an optimistic picture! They'll believe you more than what we write from Saigon.

One member of the Fellowship brought her elderly uncle whose appearance resembled Ho Chi Minh and who had just arrived from Hanoi. Although he had made no commitment to Christ, he also shared his reflections before he left.

"You now have a responsibility to share with your people in order to help them understand us. You have experienced Vietnam."

A steady stream of friends came to visit us during the week, including a former nurse from the Evangelical Clinic at Nhatrang and her husband.

"Heard you are getting ready to leave," she began.

"Yeah," Max said, "we plan to submit our application for exit visas this week, but we really don't know exactly how long it will take after that before we leave. What about yourself? What are you doing now?"

"I'm doing fine—working in a food production plant as a nurse for the hundred and thirty employees," she replied.

"Good. What about the clinic?"

"Perhaps you know that it was turned into a convalescent center."

"Yeah, we had heard that."

"Well, they've done some painting and repair and fixed it up real nice," she explained. "And at the Province Hospital now there are three doctors, including an excellent one from the North."

"How's Thu doing?" I asked, referring to a former cook for the MCC unit.

"Fine. She's married and is cooking for the Health Office."

"Very interesting," I nodded. "What about the other cooks— Hai and Sau?"

"Hai went out to the countryside. Sau has a small business, but is not doing well financially."

"That's too bad. Please give them my greetings if you have the chance." I stayed in the apartment to avoid seeing the elevator doors snap shut again.

I walked to the photo shop where I had taken my latest film for developing. In a talkative mood, the friendly proprietor asked about me and my work. I obliged him.

"You have been in Vietnam during historic days," he declared. "People would give millions of dollars to have experienced what you have experienced, but you can't buy it with money—yet you were here and saw it with your own eyes." His next sentence sounded like a short poem.

"Excuse me, sir, but I didn't understand that last sentence of yours."

He explained it phrase by phrase.

"So it's a proverb which means 'a grasshopper can upset a wagon.' "

"Yes, you've got the basic idea," he responded. "And that's Vietnam and the United States—nobody thought a tiny country like Vietnam could upset a big country like the United States. Isn't that right?" he asked.

Friday, February 6, Max, Hiro, and I completed our applications for exit visas. Since none of us had ever been to the Hanoi area, our curiosity prompted us to request leaving from there for Bangkok.

Saturday afternoon, Trinh, another former nurse from the Evangelical Clinic in Nhatrang, came to visit.

"Because my brother was a major in the military under the old system, I can't get a job as a nurse anymore, so I'm selling fruit now. Actually, I was scheduled to go to Long Khanh today, but Kha's older sister encouraged me to come say farewell to you guys," she noted.

"We do appreciate your coming. Too bad about nursing, but at least you aren't unemployed."

"I long for the old days at Nhatrang," she lamented. "Now I'm like a fish out of water. You probably never knew that I went past the Center on Phan Thanh Gian many times, but I never dared to stop there because people thought you were working for the CIA."

We sighed. "Yeah, we know some people think that. We're glad that our friends understand us, and, of course, we wish everybody else would, too, but that's impossible."

Vinh, my former roommate, also stopped to visit.

"Yesterday we filled out our exit visa applications," I told him. "We were brave enough to ask to leave through Hanoi."

"You may get a chance to see Hanoi before many of us Vietnamese do, who knows?" he responded. "In my opinion, the North has nothing so bad that it was worth 30 years of fighting by the South, and on the other hand, the South wasn't so bad that it was worth 30 years of fighting by the North, either."

"I agree." I nodded. "If you really examine any situation carefully, there aren't any good reasons for going to war."

"There are injustices either way," he added. "Since liberation, more than 3,000 Party members in the North have been jailed for corruption."

"Is that right? I hadn't heard."

"And there are some questions which need to be answered, too—like what's the difference between nine months of 'study' in a camp under the present government and the political prisoners under the old government?" His question was concrete: his brother-in-law was currently in one of the camps.

"There isn't any perfect government," I replied, "but in my opinion, one important difference between the old government and the new one is that people aren't tortured at the camps. And the camps are part of an overall educational thrust. Under the old government, the political prisoners were hidden away and really tortured."

"The theory of communism is above criticism," he commented, surprising me. He continued, "But the way it is now, it isn't working."

"What do you mean by that?" I asked.

"Vietnam needs industrial development, and capitalism could bring that much faster," he asserted.

"Maybe so," I admitted, "but isn't Vietnam's real strength in agriculture? I think industrial development and agricultural development should go together, rather than having industrial development take the lead, because it takes too much imported raw material." I accompanied him to the elevator, this time daring the sliding doors to sever our relationship.

I awakened at five o'clock Sunday morning to finish writing my farewell for the Fellowship. At 7:00 that morning, our Fellowship worshiped together with the congregation on Su Van Hanh Street. Their regular worship service was early to avoid schedule conflicts with other activities.

Elderly Pastor Sang used Matthew 17:8 as his text. Moved by his sermon, I underlined the verse and wrote his name in the margin of my Bible. "The disciples looked up and saw no one but Jesus," he concluded. "They saw only Jesus. We, too, must learn to look to Jesus in every circumstance of life."

After the service, our Fellowship met separately to plan for the future. The members invited me to give a formal farewell. As a public speaker, I had learned to perform under pressure, but this time my voice sounded unusually weak. After reviewing my reasons for coming to Vietnam and for staying, I shared my reasons for leaving and added a few words of encouragement.

> Why am I leaving? I always planned to go back to my family in Kansas sooner or later anyhow. MCC's continuing assistance to Vietnam does not require foreign personnel in Vietnam any longer, so I've submitted my application for an exit visa, requesting February 16 as the date of departure. The United States, though, is not heaven: many people there, too, need to hear the good news about Jesus, just like here in Vietnam . . . .
> What about coming back to Vietnam? I certainly would like to! . . . but I don't know if it would be possible for us to meet each other. . . .
> You really know my basic beliefs. Nevertheless, I would like to take this opportunity to share a few things that might be relevant.
> Sometimes the church has no place to lay her head. . . . Sometimes the church stands outside the door ringing the doorbell, but that's how it is with Jesus, too.
> As far as nonviolence is concerned, it isn't easy, and it isn't an escape. Love can sometimes mean confronting people with the truth. In following Jesus, you should remember that good deeds are never prohibited . . . like last Sunday . . . Dr. Son emphasized service. Following Jesus is not easy because our Savior is also the example for our life. Baptism is the first step, not to be taken lightly, because it is a baptism until death.
> Different members have different responsibilities, but "the ground is level at the cross." No one stands taller than anyone else there. One of my favorite authors, Khalil Gibran, has written, "To be close to God, be close to people." Perhaps that is one way of summarizing one of my favorite passages from the Bible. Turn with me to 1 John, chapter four. . . .
> "Dear friends, let us love one another, because love comes from God. Whoever loves is a child of God and knows God. . . . If someone says he loves God, but hates his brother, he is a liar."
> Finally . . . I would like to ask your forgiveness for the times that I've said or done things insensitively, incorrectly, or made you sad. I'm not perfect. I, too, am weak and need your admonition. . . . Remember me, and pray for me. . . .
> I also want to express my appreciation to you. . . . Many times I have been moved by the sharing you have done with me—you've been so sincere, so open. Sometimes I have felt my spiritual life waning, but you have helped resurrect it. How can I ever repay you? I can't, but I will do my best to pass on what you have given me. . . . I will never forget. . . . Whether we are happy or sad, we are still blessed because—like the end of Romans, chapter eight, says so well—we know that nothing can separate us from God's love.

*Unfinished Business*

That afternoon the talkative driver of a three-wheel, pedaled rickshaw gave me his perspective. "It isn't even a year since liberation yet. Vietnam is like a baby taking its first steps, it isn't so sure on its feet. Give Vietnam a few years, and it will be a strong country. We've got the natural resources. And we've all got to work together. But right now Saigon is still pretty much the same as it was before—it's not very progressive. People are still just interested in making money for themselves, not in the common good."

Max, Hiro, and I visited the Ministry of Foreign Affairs twice during the week to see if our exit visas had been processed. Unfortunately, we had submitted the applications to the wrong department, so they were not ready.

Max and Hiro had packed their belongings by the middle of January and were ready to leave. I, however, appreciated the delay because I needed to organize and inventory all my books, photographs, negatives, miscellaneous papers, handful of souvenirs, and files of Bible study materials before submitting them to the Ministry of Cultural Affairs. Since untold valuable, historical artifacts had slipped out of Vietnam in the April 1975 evacuation, the Ministry of Cultural Affairs checked all luggage to prevent any further loss. A steady stream of friends provided temporary relief from my tedious inventorying.

Ngoc visited on Saturday. "The leaders at my school called me in and asked me to give up my religion. We had a long discussion, and finally they had to admit that both my religion and I are positive assets for the revolution's goal of serving people. But they still encouraged me to get rid of my religion so I could fit in even better. But I'll never do that."

The next day, I attended the Gia Dinh worship service because Khai had asked me to share a few farewell reflections with the congregation. Then the Phan Thanh Gian Fellowship met with Trung in Gia Dinh.

"It is clear," Trung asserted, "that the churches must be united into one large organization under the revolution."

"Has the revolution ever said that?" I asked.

"No, it hasn't," he admitted. "But we decided it was best. I showed Jim the minutes of our meeting. There really was no need for us to consult the Phan Thanh Gian group because Gia Dinh is like a father and Phan Thanh Gian is like a child—so Phan Thanh Gian simply had to go along. When the Central Committee of the United Church which Long heads decided to use the Phan Thanh Gian Center as headquarters, our own Executive Committee agreed."

"We can accept all that even though we would have liked to contribute our ideas, too," one member of the Fellowship commented. "But what really puzzles us is why Long didn't allow us to meet there for Tet."

"I was out of town for Tet," responded Trung, "so I really don't know why he didn't allow you to meet there. But let me remind you: don't put your faith in people—no one is perfect."

That week a motorized rickshaw driver seemed to echo the same conclusion: "You have to believe in the religion, not in the people."

But if I could not trust Christians, whom could I trust? The Marxist government also wondered whether it could trust Christians in Saigon.

On Friday the 13th, the government had discovered guns, ammunition, radio broadcasting equipment, and a printing press at the Vinh Son Church. The press for counterfeit money had possibly printed as much as ten million piasters.

Although some people thought the government itself had planted the evidence, many Christians felt that the government would use the situation to restrict religious activities. The expected suppression never came.

I scribbled a few notes as the FM radio station reiterated the offical government policy on Tuesday, February 17. The government had a lenient policy toward religion, but denounced the activities of those who misused it. According to the broadcast, in a U.S. Congressional investigation, the CIA acknowledged using missionaries and preachers as employees, but promised to discontinue that practice. I doubted that the untruthful CIA would keep its promise.

The U.S. public and the rest of the world were learning what Vietnam already had experienced: the good news could be blurred by the narrow political vision of missionaries and preachers employed by the CIA. I wondered how Christians—"ambassadors for Christ"—thought the devious CIA could help spread good news. Jesus brought truth that transcended political systems.

Two days after the radio announcement, Ngoc arrived at a conclusion which might have surprised many of those missionaries and preachers when she said, "The theory and policy of communism is really excellent." She continued, "Putting it to practice, though, is terribly difficult. Actually, the best way to make it work would be if everybody were Christian—unselfish and loving. Or, in terms the revolution understands, Vietnam only has one Ho Chi Minh."

*Countryside*

Trang, one of my former language schoolteachers, knocked on our apartment door. Her visit surprised me, since I had not seen her for several years.

"You're speaking Vietnamese very well," she observed, smiling.

"I've tried hard and made some progress since I left the language school in Dalat. Actually, though, my vocabulary is still quite weak," I replied.

"You're doing great," she countered. "I've known some Americans who were here a lot longer than you've been here, but they knew just a handful of words—and that was all."

"The language school gave me a good foundation, and you were certainly one of my best teachers. What are you doing now?" I asked.

"My whole family is out in a New Economic Zone. Our area is called Cu Chi and has 10,000 families. Everyone in our family has gained weight. We've got good land: the things we plant grow, and we feel productive. Now we can see the results of our labor, thanks to the Revolution," she said, beaming.

"That's good." I nodded. "I grew up on a farm, and I know what a good feeling it is to see things grow. I liked raising sheep best of all."

"Before (the change in government), my father was mentally ill," she confided, "but now, since we've moved out to the New Economic Zone, he's doing fine. He never did like the city life very much, so now, even when he has a chance to come to Saigon, he doesn't take it. He loves it out there."

"Great. I'm still a country boy at heart," I confessed. "Living in a big city is okay, but I like living in the country or a small town a lot better."

"I myself am here in Saigon because I got sick and needed to come for medical treatment."

Her round face and friendly smile appeared normal. "I hope you'll have a speedy recovery," I said.

"I'm doing quite well. And I've been feeling God's leading in my life through it all."

"Yes, that's the most important thing," I agreed. "What kind of church activities have you been involved in? I've always enjoyed your singing."

"I'm currently leading a children's group in a church in Gia Dinh. They're so much fun to work with." She glowed. Perhaps referring to new opportunities to use her talents, she added, "After so many leaders evacuated, the church has become more like the New Testament church."

"I'm glad to hear that about the church." I nodded. "Of course, I'm saddened that so many leaders left, but I hope that the church will continue to be faithful and stand strong."

"Although there are changes, the changes are very slow," she added, qualifying her earlier statement. "The younger leaders want change, but the older ones resist it. The hierarchical system of church leadership was inherited from the Christian and Missionary Alliance missionaries who were the first ones in Vietnam, so it's been around a long time."

"But if you can see signs of becoming more like a New Testament church, that's great," I reassured her. "If responsibilities can be shared instead of emphasizing status or office, that looks like the right road to me."

The same day, my first language tutor also came to visit. Though shy, she had drilled me on the Vietnamese tones before I went to study in Dalat.

"The situation in Saigon is really tough," she commented. "Unemployment is still such a big headache. It's 97 percent in Saigon."

"Ninety-seven percent!" I echoed. "Whew! No wonder the government is encouraging people to move to the New Economic Zones."

Later in the conversation, I asked about her own activities. "I heard you had joined the Student Organization. How are things going for you?"

"I've requested to get out, but no one has responded yet," the language tutor explained. "I joined because I wanted to work with children. At first, it was okay, but now their original enthusiasm is pretty well gone, and I'm tired of trying to lead them when they don't respond. I don't like them, and they don't like me anymore. That's the way it is now."

A contrasting view came from a boy who was a former next-door neighbor. Insatiable curiosity had regularly propelled him through the gate or over the fence into the courtyard at the Center where nothing had escaped his big brown eyes. Barely a fourth-grader, if that old, he seemed more mature now.

"You'll never guess where I've been," he said, straightening his shoulders. "Go ahead, try."

"Nope, can't guess." "I don't know." "I give up." Max, Hiro, and I conceded in rapid succession.

"I've been in the countryside," he bragged. "Spent a whole week there."

"What did you do out there?"

"Went fishing at nighttime. Oh, man, was it fun! We caught fat crabs, and were they ever huge!" His hands demonstrated the size to impress us.

"What about your schoolwork?" Hiro asked. "Played hookey, huh?"

"Not me." He shot Hiro a sideways scowl. "I'm a serious student. All caught up with my lessons already."

"That's great." Hiro patted him on the back.

*Tough Plowing*

As February turned to March, I read *Listen, Yankee,* a book describing the revolution in Cuba. Fidel Castro had wanted to maintain diplomatic relations with the United States. The United States, however, threatened his life and tried to isolate Cuba, forcing Castro to turn to the Soviet Union for help. U.S. relations with Vietnam seemed to follow a similar pattern.

The Fellowship scheduled a meeting with Long for the first week in March.

"We were interested in coming to meet with you," Lap, the leader of the Excecutive Committee for the Fellowship, began, "so we could discuss things openly to try to arrive at an understanding of each other in Christian love."

"I am responsible for services here every Sunday," Long crowed. Then he asserted condescendingly, "Obviously, many things had to be changed. One of the members of your group told me that you had been meeting just to have a lot of fun. Now we meet on Sunday morning for worship, and on Thursday evening for prayer meeting. That person also said you don't want to listen to any adults."

"I don't know who that was, but obviously that person didn't know us very well," a member of the Fellowship countered immediately. "For example, we do want to have a certain amount of time for sharing with each other, and we are willing to listen to anyone—young or old."

"One of the problems we would like to discuss with you," Lap added, "is why we couldn't meet here on the first Sunday of the Lunar New Year."

"Like I said," Long replied, "the whole program needed to be revamped, and I didn't have time to do it, and I had other commitments for that Sunday. Besides, church holidays should be more important to Christians than Tet."

The vigorous discussion finally slowed, allowing me to squeeze in a comment. "As Christians, I think we can understand and forgive each other, but what answer I should give to the non-Christian guests who came that Sunday at Tet and found only a locked gate. Tet is pretty important for 'outsiders.' "

"You MCCers are really to blame for moving out so fast," Long declared. "If you would have let us know at least a Sunday in advance, the transition could have been made much smoother."

"But Trung never told us what would happen to the Center after we would move out, so how could we let you know in advance?" I asked.

"Well, the sign out in front has read 'United Church' for a long time already. But it's time to let bygones be bygones. You are welcome back here."

His fast, smooth style left me unconvinced. Although I felt his "welcome back" lacked credibility, too few Sundays remained to test it before I left.

Reports, though, from other members of the Fellowship who sporadically attended there confirmed my suspicion: he berated the Mennonites in their presence. Lacking a genuine welcome back to the Phan Thanh Gian Center, the Fellowship met for worship with the congregation at the Tran Cao Van Church and then met separately there for a time of sharing and Bible study each Sunday.

Early in March, Hiro and Max decided to visit Frances Starner, the unique reporter. When they knocked on the door to her apartment, they found a government investigation in progress there. The next day, the doorman at the apartment complex where we lived began logging the names and addresses of visitors. Without knowing the purpose of the log, some of our friends complied, some declined. The new procedures made us cherish each visit even more.

When Tin, our former office assistant, came to visit us, he shared encouraging as well as discouraging aspects of his life in the countryside.

"At the end of this month it will be time to start planting rice, but there isn't enough time to get our plowing done by hand any more," he lamented. "Hiring a tractor to do it would cost 35,000 piasters per hectare. Even hiring a team of oxen to plow would cost 20,000 piasters per hectare. Those are the only two options for us to get the plowing done in time."

He obviously calculated the cost using the old currency, not the new. By any standard, though, the price was prohibitive.

"That's awesome," I said, shaking my head.

"So what are you planning to do?" Max asked.

"I'm working out now for 800 piasters per day," Tin noted, "but rice costs 400 piasters per kilo, so we don't have enough to pay for plowing." He paused and shook his head, still figuring by the outdated currency which had been exchanged at the rate of 500 to one.

"But life also has its bright spots," he added. "My girlfriend is writing her mother in Hue, and if it's okay, then we'll probably get engaged in June and plan for a wedding in December."

"Congratulations!" "Sounds great!" "Blessings to you!" Max, Hiro, and I chimed in.

"As you know, my parents are very old already, so we're planning to get married sooner than we might have otherwise," Tin explained.

"But I still remember how impressed I was with that poem your dad worked out and recited from memory at Tet a year ago," I recalled. "So how are your parents doing?"

"Pretty good," Tin replied, "except that my mom's eyes are very weak."

"Oh." I shook my head. "What about that dynamic church you're part of?"

"It's fine. Got about eleven families now. Really a strong fellowship. Our pastor is finishing his last year at the Bible Institute, so that makes it rather hard for us, but we're doing fine."

Before Tin left, Hiro, Max, and I held a quick mini-conference. Although Tin had not asked for it, we agreed to give him some financial assistance.

During the sharing time the next Sunday, Ty described her answer to challenges. "Whenever anyone starts downgrading religion in general or pushing me real hard about my own religious beliefs, I say, 'Just remember: some of the most progressive people around the world who supported the revolution were Protestants and Catholics.' "

Two days later, the former MCC secretary explained an unusual aspect of the revolution. "I got paid ten piasters for helping take the census."

"That's pretty good," I replied.

"But the most impressive thing was that the supervisors—who really didn't do much—only got six piasters. Imagine that!"

"That's the way it should be," I affirmed. "The people who got out and did the hard work should be paid better than the upper levels. And that's quite a change from the old system."

Later that day, Tuyet, our former cook, described problems in some of the New Economic Zones. "Not all of the New Economic Zones are the same. Generally, the areas in the delta are better," she observed. "But I heard about one area where the people went for two days without water until a really concerned female government worker got on the ball and told the higher-ups, 'How can I be responsible for all these people if they're dead!' So she got water. The people later told her that two more days was the maximum they would have waited before marching on Ho Chi Minh City to protest the situation. The people aren't afraid any more."

"The Vietnamese people have always had a strong spirit," I remarked. "In my opinion, any government in Vietnam will have to look out if it isn't doing what the people want."

*Volunteering*

Two members of the Fellowship visited me. "The Mennonite emphasis (on service) has had a big influence," Ngoc commented. "I think that a movement with the Mennonite spirit—without being called that—is getting started among Christian young people. In my university group, the first volunteers for work in the New Economic Zone called Le Minh Xuan were all Christians. I myself was first, and Hai was second. Christian young people are realizing that they have to participate more enthusiastically and work harder than the rest, because that's the Jesus way and because then they have a place to stand. Otherwise, the revolution will say that they just stand and talk but don't do anything."

Christians at work in productive ways—the theme echoed through conversations. The next Sunday evening, a member of the Fellowship and former neighbor of ours explained her involvement with the work projects for students. "I went to a New Economic Zone today and helped dig canals!" she related enthusiastically. "There were two thousand of us! Can you imagine two thousand high school students all working together? It was a big project. Terribly exciting! I really wasn't well-prepared," she admitted. "It was my first experience. How could I know what it would be like? I wore white jeans!"

*Going, Going, Almost Gone*

Two days later, on Tuesday, March 30, I learned that I would be leaving Vietnam in one week. Hiro and Max received no word about their visas. But I was leaving. Leaving. The countdown had

316 JIMSHOES IN VIETNAM

begun in earnest. The days, the hours, the minutes, the seconds were numbered.

One week. One week to reinventory my possessions and to pack. One week to get my visa processed and to have my belongings cleared for exit. One week to translate a poem and to say good-bye.

As friends came one by one, I told them the departure date. One by one, we said good-bye. Each time the elevator doors snapped shut at the end of the hall, they sounded more intense—so final.

Saturday. The Ministry of Foreign Affairs handed me my exit visa, but Hanoi had denied my request to leave from there. Two weeks earlier, Max, Hiro, and I had seen a bus from Hanoi parked on the street less than two blocks from the Phan Thanh Gian Center. Hanoi, however, was not on my itinerary.

The Ministry of Cultural Affairs scrutinized all luggage leaving Vietnam, but the officials there needed my exit visa before checking my belongings. By the time I finished packing the boxes of books and other items, the doors to offices inside the Ministry had closed for the day as well as for the weekend. According to rumors, the Ministry took at least a week to inspect everything. Even if I arrived at the Ministry when it opened Monday morning, the Ministry would have only two days to check through my volumes. With no option other than the regular procedures, I hoped my favorite books, photographs, and souvenirs could be approved in time.

Sunday. My last Sunday in Vietnam. During sharing time, Ty contributed good news.

"My class was cited as the best class in the whole school." She beamed. "And that means that the work of the class executive committee was responsible for that praise coming, and I'm the class president. I was quite surprised because I hadn't joined the Student Organization. It seems like some students who are so interested in joining the Student Organization just do it for personal gain. I myself have been willing to volunteer for work projects because I'm a Christian, and I understand that the life of Jesus is a pattern for service."

"But I won't volunteer for some simple stuff like cleaning the streets!" a visitor from the Tran Cao Van Youth Fellowship exclaimed. "But give me some worthwhile job, and I'll do that."

"But maybe you have to volunteer for some simple work, too," Ngoc countered, "so that you have a basis for speaking. For example, sweeping sidewalks: I volunteered to help—not many did—yet we were expected to sweep the whole ward, starting at 4:00 a.m. while the people were still asleep. After we were done, I told the leadership straight out that it was ridiculous for us to have done all that because in a socialist society each one is supposed to pull one's own share of the load. And I said that if each family would keep things clean in front of their own house, then the problem would be solved."

Between other topics, I announced that I had my exit visa and was scheduled for a midweek flight to Bangkok.

*Greetings and Good-byes*

Monday. To pay my respect to Pastor Mieng and to ask for his analysis of the situation facing the Evangelical Church, I visited him in his office on Tran Hung Dao Street. He was serving as the head of the Evangelical Church of Vietnam, the largest Protestant church association in the southern part of Vietnam. The elderly pastor seemed to know who I was.

"Hello, Mr. Reverend Mieng," I greeted him politely. "How are you?"

"I've been extremely busy, but basically in good health." He spoke slowly, thoughtfully.

"And how's your family?" I asked.

"Fine, thanks," he replied. "My son Tin is at the Bible Institute. His church at Honai is growing."

"I'm happy to hear that. I think I know one of the families that's attending his church. And as far as the Bible Institute at Nhatrang is concerned, how is it doing?" I asked.

"The enrollment has been good again this year," he responded. "The school is having a tough time financially, but it still keeps going. Next year may be even harder, though, because there may be a problem with rice if students can't bring it from their home area to Nhatrang. Buying rice on the open market in Nhatrang could be very expensive, and it might not even be available."

"Seems like there isn't any place in Vietnam that has too much rice." Then I shifted the subject slightly. "I'm personally interested in house churches and am wondering if you have any news about the ones in Quang Ngai."

"No," he replied, "I really don't have any recent information about them. But I do know that the pastors of the Evangelical churches in that area are quite willing to let them use church buildings if their meetings need to be more official. I'll know more after our General Conference. Perhaps you know that our General Conference is normally held the first week in April."

"I think I may have heard that, but I had forgotten," I admitted.

"This year, however, because of the upcoming, nationwide elections, the government prefers that people wait until after the elections to travel, so the conference will be in May."

"Yes, I see." I nodded. "I'm getting ready to leave Vietnam now. My exit visa is for the day after tomorrow, and I was wondering if you would like for me to take along any message for Christians outside of Vietnam."

"Yes, yes, I would," he replied immediately. "First of all, I have a message for the missionaries. Give them our greetings and our appreciation for their past contribution. The church in Vietnam exists because of them.

"And to church leaders and Christians," he continued, "give them our greetings and tell them to pray for us, just as we are praying for them."

"When I meet Vietnamese, is there anything special I should tell them?"

Pastor Mieng paused. "It is not possible for me to call them back to Vietnam because that is a political thing—that is the responsibility of the government. Even during the evacuation, it was very individualized: I couldn't advise people to go or to stay because if they followed my advice and then would be dissatisfied, they would blame me. I assume they were following Christ even in their leaving, and I pray that they will continue to do so.

"The church has not been involved in politics," he emphasized. "The church has been interested in saving souls."

I remembered hearing of his trip to Nhatrang when Thieu revoked the military deferment for ministerial students. He had encouraged the students at the Bible Institute to follow the law, and in my opinion, that was a highly political act. Of course, encouraging the students to disobey the law would have been a very political act, too. I remained silent.

"I'm not sorry I stayed," he continued. "I feel like the Lord has been able to use me during these days." He paused longer than usual.

"You have a busy schedule, but you have taken precious time to share with me. Thank you very much, Mr. Reverend. And as I have the opportunity, I will share your message with the missionaries and Christians. Thank you, again. I pray that God will continue to bless you and the church in Vietnam."

"Thank you for coming to see me." He shook my hand. "I pray that the Lord will bless you and grant you a safe trip."

Tuesday. The Ministry of Foreign Affairs invited Hiro, Max, and me to a farewell luncheon, even though I was the only one with an exit visa. Although the Provisional Revolutionary Government refused to grant Hiro, Max, and me status as official MCC representatives, perhaps the luncheon expressed appreciation to MCC, anyhow. Anh from the Ministry of Foreign Affairs and Thao from public relations hosted the meal. They seemed more optimistic about the outcome of the elections in the United States than we three did.

During the meal, Anh observed, "Building a new society in Vietnam is hard work. There are still many problems to be solved. Unemployment is a big problem, and the economic difficulties are very real. All our gasoline, for example, has to be purchased outside of Vietnam. Getting rid of the decadent society is also hard work: getting prostitutes into legitimate, productive work isn't easy. And there are still lots of coffeehouses which are also unproductive. Yet there is tolerance: out of respect for his efforts last April, General Duong Van Minh was given voting rights though he was a general."

The Ministry of Cultural Affairs cleared my assortment of boxed goods without exception. Each box bore an official wax seal to ensure that it would carry neither more nor less than the approved contents. Since the procedures required that luggage be at the Air Vietnam Office a day prior to departure, I hurried directly from the Ministry to the Air Vietnam Office.

That evening I grabbed three hours of sleep. I awoke just after midnight: Wednesday had arrived. No more time for sleep.

## Day of Departure

Wednesday. April 7, 1976. The day of my departure. I hurriedly sorted the final odds and ends for my blue-gray suitcase and my shoulder bags. Max, Hiro, and a couple other friends of mine accompanied me to the Air Vietnam Office downtown. My suitcase passed inspection.

We made small talk while waiting. Someone ordered a cold drink for me from a street-side vendor.

The driver boarded the transfer bus. I shook hands with each one who had come to say good-bye to me. Following polite Vietnamese custom, I requested permission from the females before shaking hands with them.

I boarded the bus and took the backseat. I waved good-bye to those good friends once more as the bus pulled onto the street. I was tired and numb.

As the bus jogged to the airport, I soaked in one last view of the familiar streets. At the airport, I was the last passenger to leave the bus.

Inside the terminal, all the passengers stood in line again to have their passport, ticket, visa, and vaccination papers checked once more. Around the corner, at the security desk, I emptied all my pockets. I had no guns, no contraband. I had nothing to hide.

"You won't be able to take these with you," an official declared, pointing to two letters, a notebook, and my two address books. "The rest is okay."

Incredible! Ngoc had handed me one of the letters just before I boarded the bus; I had read it on the way to the airport. I had received the other letter earlier from another friend. The little notebook, recently purchased, had few notes in it. The address books, however, contained the addresses of all of my friends around the world! My heart pounded.

"Excuse me, sir, what's the problem?" I asked.

"You won't be able to take these with you," he repeated. Then, as if to soften the blow, he asked, "Did someone bring you to the airport that you could give them to?"

"No, sir," I answered. "I came on the Air Vietnam bus."

"Could we send them to your office?" he asked.

I had mentioned that I worked for Mennonite Central Committee. "Yes, thank you, sir. But we just recently moved. Let me give you the new address of the other Mennonite Central Committee workers." I printed the address on a slip of paper. "Excuse me, sir, those are my address books with the addresses of my friends, including the address where I'm supposed to go in Bangkok when I get there. Could I at least look at that address once more?"

I carefully copied the Bangkok address of Bruce and Karen Harvey and then handed the book back.

"Right through there." He pointed. "You pick up your hand-carried luggage on the other side."

I found my luggage and hauled it upstairs to the waiting room. I felt like I had just endured an amputation without anesthesia. Questions zigzagged through my head. Why had I been so naive and emptied all my pockets? Why hadn't I put those address books in the boxes submitted to the Ministry of Cultural Affairs? How could I communicate with my friends without having their addresses? I sat motionless.

The loudspeakers finally blasted the boarding call. The passengers lined up to have all their papers checked once more as they left the waiting room. An official met me at the top of the stairs.

"Seems like this is yours." He handed me a faded blue address book.

"Yes, it is." I nodded numbly. "Thank you, sir. That helps a lot."

Anh, from the Ministry of Foreign Affairs, greeted me just outside the door at the bottom of the stairs. Oh, no! What now?

"I just wanted to report that the tractors from Mennonite Central Committee are being used in the delta," he said.

"Thank you," I replied. "I'll let the MCC office know."

"Best wishes for a safe trip," he added and shook my hand.

I scurried across the hot asphalt to the plane. A stewardess stood at the bottom of the boarding ramp, checking plane tickets and visas. I handed her my passport and ticket.

She looked puzzled and handed them back. "You don't have a visa, sir."

My heart sank. I desperately paged through the passport. She was right: no exit visa. It had been stamped onto a separate card. Although I had clutched the passport tightly, the visa must have slipped out as I cruised from the terminal building to the plane. I turned back, searching the pavement with each slow step.

"No, no, don't worry. It's okay," insisted another airport official who had just arrived on the scene and analyzed the situation in a flash. He escorted me to the boarding ramp and addressed the stewardess. "This man's visa was on a separate card and they kept it in the terminal."

The puzzled stewardess tore my boarding pass on the dotted line and allowed me to board. I eased into a seat halfway back in the plane, hoping no one would sit beside me. I had preferred sitting even farther back so I could be more alone, but others had already taken those seats. I overheard conversations in Vietnamese and in French, but I ignored them.

No one sat beside me. Although I tried to focus on the future, my thoughts—like a fly trying unsuccessfully to break out of smooth molasses—kept reviewing the past few hours as well as the major changes that Vietnam had experienced during my stay.

As the jet taxied to the runway, I noticed junked helicopters still bearing U.S. symbols. The rusting helicopter carcasses apparently had lain crippled and awkward for nearly a year already. Helicopters in working condition bore red flags.

During the climb after take-off, I saw strange, straight rows extending for miles on the ground. I had never noticed them before. They reminded me of an aerial view of the hedge-tree boundaries in Kansas, but these looked like mirrors. Why, yes, then I knew: these were the irrigation canals some of my friends had helped build. My friends. God bless them. When would I ever see them again? The higher the plane climbed, the lower my spirits sank. Good-bye, Vietnam. Good-bye.

# Chapter 16

# TELL IT LIKE IT IS

*Bangkok and Beyond*

Countless questions probed the wrinkles in my brain unsuccessfully. Would Thailand accept me without an exit visa from Vietnam in my passport? Would the U.S. government hassle me because I came from an "enemy" country? What questions would news reporters ask? How soon could I call my parents in Kansas? How long should I wait in Bangkok for Max so we could travel to the U.S. together? Exhausted, I dozed fitfully a couple times during the flight.

I waited for the other passengers to disembark in Bangkok. I had no deadline, and I faced passport problems. Besides, juggling my two shoulder bags and briefcase down the narrow aisle in the plane took extra caution.

Inside the terminal, the line crept around a corner to the official desk. Balanced on a strong shoulder, a massive portable camera towered above people ahead of me. The cameraman, loaded with film cartridges and battery packs, appeared linked to another man who inched toward me. Finally, I overheard him.

"Are you James Klasser?" he asked.

Blank looks or a shake of the head answered him. A sinking feeling hit me. He, his lagging cameraman, and the bulky equipment hunched closer.

"Are you James Klasser?" His voice sounded tired. The people in front of me shook their heads. He glanced toward the end of the line. His eyes conveyed his despair: only a handful of candidates remained. He persisted.

"Are you James Klasser?" he asked me directly.

I shook my head. "No," I replied sluggishly. "I'm James Klassen."

"Yes! Klassen!" His eyes danced. "James Klassen, you're the one we're looking for! You just came from Vietnam, right?"

"Right," I answered flatly. My heart pounded.

"We're from ABC Television, and I'd like to interview you right now."

The cameraman backed away and adjusted the camera lens. The interviewer frowned at the line of people and shook his head.

"Let's go outside and use the plane as a background," he suggested.

"Okay, it's not going to make any difference if I lose my place in line."

On the way outside, I wondered why they seemed so rushed. Fortunately, the deafening roar of planes taking off and landing drowned our words, so I suggested filming the interview after I finished the official airport immigration procedures. They agreed. I lugged my shoulder bags and briefcase inside, relieved because I did not need to answer their questions just yet.

As I neared the offical desk, I suddenly noticed Linda and Murray Hiebert waving to me from the other side of the glass wall. Wow! I grinned and waved.

I wondered how ABC knew about my arrival because I knew Murray and Linda had not publicized my telegram to them. I also wondered how the ABC film crew obtained permission to enter the inner sanctum of the terminal for an interview with me even before my passport held the offical stamps. They filmed me as I filled out the visa request card at the desk.

The floodlight glared, the film rolled, but while I began completing the form, my ballpoint pen ran dry. Aware that the unblinking camera recorded every move I made and that the media could blow minor incidents out of proportion, I envisioned a distorted headline: "Vietnam Desperate: All Ballpoints Running Dry." Someone handed me another ballpoint so I could finish the form.

After receiving my tourist visa, I swept through the doors to meet Linda and Murray. The television crew followed like a shadow.

"You don't have to be interviewed right now if you don't want to," Murray said after we greeted each other.

"But we'd like to do the interview right now," the ABC newsman insisted.

"But they have to accommodate you," Linda explained to me. "If you'd like to drop off your luggage in your hotel room and take a shower to freshen up a bit, they should give you that much time."

"Yeah. Wow." I nodded. "I'd really like that. It's been a long day."

"But we've got to have the film of the interview on its way by 5:30 this afternoon, or else it's old news," the ABC interviewer claimed.

"Okay." Murray looked at his watch. "There's plenty of time."

"At which hotel are you staying? Can we meet you there?" The ABC man stood poised to write, pad and pencil in his hands.

"No," Murray objected. "We'll come to your hotel."

A Swedish newspaper reporter also clamored for an interview. After I declined, Murray, Linda, and I left for our hotel.

"Don't tell the reporters where you're staying," Murray advised, "or they'll be on your tail day and night. They want your story, so make them fit your plans. Don't let them twist your arm to do things you don't want to do."

We met the ABC team in their hotel lobby just after 4:00 p.m.

"Would you like something to drink?" The newsman seemed relaxed.

"Well, maybe we should do the interview first," I suggested.

"Aw, don't worry, we've got plenty of time."

"Well, if you say so." I shrugged my shoulders.

I kept glancing at an ornate wall clock. The news team seemed oblivious to the vanishing minutes. "I'd be ready for the interview," I finally said.

"Okay, let's go do it," the interviewer agreed.

He dillydallied in choosing an acceptable corner of the hotel courtyard for the backdrop. Then the cameraman leisurely arranged his equipment. By the time we completed the interview, my wristwatch showed nearly 5:15. I expected someone to yank the film out of the camera, scribble an address on the shipping container, and race into the traffic to beat the 5:30 deadline. No one rushed.

The interviewer asked several more questions after the camera stopped rolling. The cameraman methodically packed the equipment. At 5:30, mystified, I still saw the container of film sitting serenely on top of the camera cases.

The crew had demanded an interview at the airport, claiming a 5:30 deadline. I saw 5:30 come and go without any attempt to meet or beat the so-called deadline. Other reporters would also puzzle me.

Linda, Murray, and I telephoned the MCC headquarters in Pennsylvania. Darkness fell. International calls required an elaborate procedure and a considerable wait. Hoping for clear connections, we called from the post office.

I anticipated much-needed sleep. A hotel boy, however, met us on the dimly lit lane into the hotel parking lot.

"Some reporters are waiting for you in the hotel lobby," he explained in hushed tones. "They've been waiting for you all evening. I thought maybe you wouldn't want to meet them."

Linda and Murray handled the conversation. "Yeah. Thanks. Is there any other way into the hotel?"

"Only an unlocked back window to the kitchen," the boy said.

"Do you think you could take us that way?"

"No problem. Follow me."

We skirted the swimming pool, staying in the shadows, and then ducked below the lobby window level. We crawled through the unlocked window into the kitchen. An open hallway led directly from the main lobby to the outside patio next to the back stairway. One by one, we slipped unnoticed past the archway, like characters in a novel of oriental intrigue.

We climbed the stairs. Room keys! Oh, no! When we had left the hotel, we surrendered our room keys at the front desk like usual. The alert reporters sat facing the front desk, unofficially guarding the bulky key ring in our pigeonhole. The resourceful hotel boy remained cool.

"I'll get the master key." He smiled and scurried away.

Murray, Linda, and I avoided the reporters because we had not yet planned our schedule, and I felt dead tired.

"We should at least tell the reporters you won't talk to them anymore tonight," Murray said.

"Fine," I replied. They knew more about reporters than I did. "I'm going to sleep. I've been up nearly 24 hours. Thanks for all your help and for taking care of the reporters. See you in the morning. Good night."

I had just opened my suitcase and started unpacking the minimum daily requirments when I heard a knock at my door. Murray stood there.

"Sorry, Jim, I hate to bother you, but the news team downstairs is from CBS, and they said they have to leave by 6:00 tomorrow morning and will be gone all day to do a story near the Cambodian border. They really would like to interview you yet tonight. Do you think you can do it?"

"Yeah, why not?" I looked at my watch: 11:00 p.m. "After all, I'm still dressed. Just give me a minute and thirty seconds to splash some water into my face and put my tie back on."

Peter Collins, the interviewer from CBS, asked questions similar to the ones ABC had asked. What about unemployment in Vietnam? What about resistance movements? What about the New Economic Zones? How'd they treat Americans? What kind of MCC programs were there? What about medicines?

After the filming, the questions became more personal. What about my friends? What about reprisals? What about letters? What about Vietnamese who wanted to return? One crew member had married a Vietnamese. I treated all questions seriously, even when the cameras were not rolling. In fact, I enjoyed the informal discussion more than the recorded one. Two hours after I had retied my tie, I bid the CBS team not "Good night," but "Good morning!"

In my room, I reached for the telephone. Tired or not, I wanted to call home. I lay on the bed while waiting for the operator to make the appropriate connections and call back. I must have dozed. The ringing telephone jarred me awake. Bangkok. The operator must have gotten Mom and Dad. Mom and Dad!

From 10,000 miles away, their voices floated into my ears like music! Since 1974, our contact with each other had never been this direct.

We talked about big things and little things. My compass oscillated no longer. It pointed in only one direction: Kansas.

328 JIMSHOES IN VIETNAM

Naturally, the other end of the compass needle still pointed to Vietnam. Kansas and Vietnam—the two remained inseparably linked in my soul.

I had waved good-bye to Vietnam. I knew the welcome mat waited for me in Kansas. Those family ties had stretched around the world, and they were pulling me back. I thought of a poem in my briefcase which Dad had composed. He had given it to me just before I returned to Vietnam in 1974.

Love

Love is like a rubber band
    That binds our hearts together;
Though it be stretched from land to land
    By distance, time, or weather—...
Its potent force cannot be broken.
    Its voice is clear though oft' unspoken.

This band that stretched to earth from heaven
    Still works great things as bread with leaven.

When that great trump of God shall sound,
    This cord that comes from God of love
Will fetch us from the barren ground
    And snap us back to our home above.
The bowstring drawn so tight through life
    Then sets us free from pain and strife.
As swift as an arrow we shall fly
    To meet our Savior in the sky.

May this cohesion never wane
    Till it effects a *Wiederseh'n* (a reuniting).

*Believe It or Not*

Knocks on my door aroused me before 7:00 the next morning. The CBS team!

"Excuse me," I began, "but I thought you were leaving early this morning for the Cambodian border."

"Yes, we were, but when our head office in the States heard about the story on you, they canceled our trip and told us to get pictures of your pictures to go with the story. You did bring along some photos, right?"

"Yes, I did," I admitted slowly.

"Well, we would just like to have you lay them out, and then we would run our camera over them." He spoke rapidly with sweeping hand gestures.

"I don't think I'm willing to do that."

"Why not? It would really be simple."

"No," I countered, "it would not be simple—first of all, because they aren't organized at all, and second, because they are primarily pictures of my friends, and I don't want to create problems for any of them."

"Don't worry," he reassured me. "You pick out whatever pictures you want, and then we'll pan our camera across them. We won't even take any close-ups."

"Look," I insisted, "I'm telling you the truth: I packed my pictures in a hurry, and they are all mumbo-jumbo."

"We'll give you time to sort them."

"No, it would take way too long, and I've got other stuff on my agenda. And besides, I'm not willing to risk jeopardizing any of my friends."

"But it would really strengthen your story."

"I'm sorry, but there is no way that I will let you film my pictures."

He looked defeated. In spite of the late night interview with me, perhaps he had not realized how stubborn a pacifist could be.

To soften the blow, I added, "I felt like we had a good interview last night—and early this morning—and I hope that your head office in the States will accept it without the film of my pictures."

"I do, too," he mumbled.

"Better put your pictures in our room for safe-keeping," Murray advised later. "They know your name, but I don't think they know ours."

"You're famous," Linda teased. "Look." She pointed to the back page of *The Bangkok Post*. "Bet you didn't expect to make the headlines that fast."

My amazement grew with every word I read. No UPI reporter had interviewed me, yet the article included "direct quotes" attributed to me. Neither the vocabulary nor the syntax in the so-called quotations sounded familiar: I had not referred to the revolution in those terms. I remembered seeing the Swedish reporter at the airport, but I had declined to let him interview me. I also recalled a fellow circling the courtyard where ABC had interviewed me, but I assumed he had been too far away from the TV camera to hear what I had said.

"If any reporter asks you about the article," Murray explained, "don't say that you didn't say that, because if you deny having said that, then they'll blow that up into a big story, and you'll be even worse off."

"Oh, good night!" I sighed. "What a mess."

"If a reporter asks, just say, 'No comment,' " he added.

"Okay," I agreed. "After all, if they're making up words to put in my mouth, the article could have been a lot worse. But how could they dare to use quotation marks if they didn't even talk to me?"

Murray shrugged.

"You're learning, Jim. You're learning fast," Linda replied.

"What about the CBS trip to the Cambodian border? Do you think they really had one planned?" I asked.

Murray shrugged again.

"Getting the news is a highly competitive, cutthroat business," Linda answered again.

"Well, I'm sure glad you're here to help see me through these days. What about the guy from *The Washington Post* who's coming this afternoon?" I referred to an interview that Linda and Murray had arranged for me.

"He's one of the best there is in Bangkok," Murray assured me. "Now that doesn't mean that he'll necessarily agree with you, but at least he'll do a fair job of reporting what you say."

"Sounds good enough to me," I replied.

"By the way, what about Pastor Mieng? There was a rumor that he was in jail for months."

"Incredible! Not as far as I know. Why, I talked to him just before I left. Let's see, today is Thursday; I talked to him Monday—four days ago."

Murray and Linda had arranged formal and informal interviews for me, including one with the Fund for Reconstruction and Rebuilding Indochina. The representative said, "The situation in

Vietnam is so different from what was expected, it's almost as if people are disappointed there wasn't a bloodbath!"

At Linda and Murray's invitation, Vietnamese—mostly refugees—interested in returning to Vietnam clustered in the hotel lobby the next morning. Surprised by my fluency in Vietnamese when I introduced myself, they pelted me with questions.

"Are there still cars in Vietnam?"

"What about Hondas (50 c.c. motorcycles)?"

"What's the rice situation like?"

"Do people still eat *pho* (a popular Vietnamese noodle soup)?"

As a U.S. citizen, I felt I owed the U.S. embassy in Bangkok the elementary courtesy of informing them that I was in Thailand en route to the United States. An embassy official apparently maintained a list of U.S. citizens who remained in Vietnam after the end of April 1975. As a result of my call, I hoped he would delete my name from the list. Wanting to stay as far away from the U.S. government as possible, I hoped to avoid his interrogating me in person. I survived his handful of questions over the phone.

"What happened to you when the communists from the North took over?"

"First of all," I challenged him, "I don't regard the changeover of governments in Vietnam as a takeover by communists from the North. The bulk of the resistance to the Saigon government always was in the South, and certainly not all of the resistance was communist."

"Well," he admitted, "I worked for the U.S. government in Dalat in the mid-60s, and we knew then that most of the resistance in the area was local."

"That's very interesting," I commented. "That's not what the U.S. was saying at the time, though. Just like now, the U.S. government keeps talking about a takeover by communists from the North. Nearly all of the officials in the Provisional Revolutionary Government that we had any contact with were Southerners." I wondered what he had done in Dalat for the U.S. government.

He was silent.

"As far as the change of governments at the end of April a year ago, the transition was amazingly smooth," I added, in order to answer the thrust of his original question. "I was never threatened with a gun pointed at me. We never lost our electricty or our water service. And, as you surely know by now, there never was any bloodbath."

Although he had conceded one major point to me, I doubted that my words would bring any changes in U.S. propaganda about Vietnam. At least I had done what I could: I had told the truth as I had experienced it.

A couple days later, Linda and Murray returned to Laos where they served as country directors for the MCC program. Relieved to leave the ringing telephones at the YMCA Hotel, I moved into a hotel next to the Baptist Youth Hostel. Nevertheless, FEBC radio found me and tape-recorded a three-hour interview with me. NBC television and radio followed suit.

"Forty years from now," the NBC interviewer told me off the record, "we'll see that Vietnam really was the defeat of American arrogance and American neocolonialism. The Vietnamese are quite capable of handling their own affairs. Thailand needs some basic reforms, but I'm not sure that any of the current leadership can do it. Revolutions aren't easy."

*Where Is Vietnam?*

Without word on Max's departure from Vietnam, I left Bangkok alone. While the Boeing 747 was still climbing after takeoff, the pilot announced, "We're at 15,000 feet now and will be climbing up to 33,000 feet. Then we'll be circumventing Vietnam—staying about 30 miles off the coast."

Yes, I thought, that is how many people would like to respond to Vietnam—staying just far enough away so they don't have to feel the hurts or share the joys of the Vietnamese. Christians serious about following Jesus, however, could not circumvent Vietnam.

Although MCC had proposed that I begin a speaking tour before meeting my family, I declined; traveling in the U.S. without first meeting my family seemed like a crime. The closer I came to Kansas, the more excited I became.

Plane connections from Thailand required an overnight stay in Los Angeles. I wondered how people would respond to me and to my experience. The taxi driver taking me from the airport to my hotel appeared friendly.

"I'm on my way to Kansas," I commented. "Just getting home from Vietnam where I spent three and a half years working with a small, church-sponsored, relief and social work organization."

The driver looked straight ahead. "Nam, huh? My brother was killed there. I myself was there with the Air Force. My being there turned me against the U.S. government. I'm really bitter about the whole thing."

"When I think of all the destruction the U.S. caused there and all the dirty tricks it pulled, it makes me sad, but I don't think I'm bitter," I said.

"My experience really made me cynical." He studied the traffic. "There are so many problems here in the U.S., I can't figure out what it was trying to do over there."

"Since I'm a pacifist," I responded, "I wasn't there with the military, so what the U.S. did in Vietnam really looks irrational to me. The war didn't solve anything—it just caused a lot of destruction and hatred so now there's that mess to clean up besides the attitudes which hardened."

He glanced at me. His voice softened. "I've got a nine-month-old son." The dashboard lights lit up the smile on his face. "It's fun to watch him grow, and I want to teach him the way of peace." The smile vanished. His voice hardened. "I never want him to go through what I've experienced."

We shook hands at the end of the ride. Ironic, I thought, that an ex-G.I. gave me such a warm welcome back to the U.S. I wondered whether he had told many others what he shared with me.

Early the next morning, April 21, another taxi took me to the airport. Again, I briefly explained where I was headed and from where I had come.

"I was in Nam two years," the stocky young man remarked.

"Oh, really. Where were you stationed?" I asked.

"Well, actually, I was in the navy offshore," he replied.

"Did you ever get onshore to try some good Vietnamese cooking?" I asked.

"Nope, never did. Went ashore in Bangkok once, but never in Nam."

He had been "in Nam," but never actually in Vietnam to see

the havoc his ship hurled onshore. Under orders, he had circum-
vented Vietnam, never leaving his floating, metal haven to
experience the smiles or tears of the Vietnamese.

*Welcome Home*

Airborne again, the anticipation of arriving in Kansas
prevented me from sleeping even though my night had been short.
Mom and Dad, and three other family members—all beaming—
threw their arms around me when I arrived in Wichita. What a
warm welcome! Then they grabbed my jam-packed shoulder bags
and briefcase, marveling how heavy they were.

My schedule allowed one full day in Kansas. I collected im-
pressions, like a bag of mosaic tile, to organize later. The pastor's
wife shared one "piece."

"Jamie prayed for you every day." She referred to their youngest son.

"Wow! Although I couldn't know the specifics," I responded,
"I knew that my family and friends had been praying for me. I
could feel it. I wasn't standing alone in Vietnam."

Then my family members and I spent a day driving to South
Dakota where the temperatures stayed cool. Rachel, Roine, and
Don—neibrosis! (neice, brother, sister)—had warm welcome for
me there. The conversation lasted till 5:00 a.m.

*Election Day*

That evening in South Dakota, we viewed my slides from
Vietnam. Midnight passed. April 25 arrived. As I packed my luggage for a month-long MCC itineration, my Vietnamese friends
halfway around the world were voting in nationwide elections to
select representatives for a new national assembly that would formally reunite Vietnam.

I wished my friends well, even though I had lost my zest for national elections in the United States in 1972. That year, ironically
perhaps, I voted by absentee ballot from Vietnam for a World War
II bomber pilot named McGovern, the leading peace candidate.
The other candidate, Richard Nixon, won through Kissinger's de-
ceptive claim that "peace is at hand." Then at Christmas, "Tricky
Dick" Nixon had ordered the heaviest bombing campaign in his-

tory. After that, I decided that voting in national elections, like registering for the draft, required too much compromise. A U.S. presidential election, said someone in Vietnam, was like choosing between malaria and yellow fever.

Was the election in Vietnam any different? One aspect had surprised me: the election campaigns publicized the candidates' past, rather than campaign promises. Before I left Vietnam, though, one skeptic told me, "The elections will be rigged." He had seen no hope for his favorite candidates—a Buddhist nun and two Roman Catholic priests[1]—who if elected, might have a moderating effect in the national assembly. Disproving the skeptic's awful expectations, one of the Catholic priests and the Buddhist nun were, in fact, elected.

*Scheduled*

Snow delayed all of my plane connections to Pennsylvania, so I arrived at the MCC headquarters in Akron at 2:30 a.m. At 4:00 a.m., I finished reading the thick stack of materials, including the schedule of speaking commitments already made for me. Within the next two days, I gave six presentations on Vietnam besides two mass media interviews. On the third morning, another newspaper interview preceded my leaving for a packed, nine-day speaking tour in New York, Virginia, and Washington, D.C. I balked.

Long days and short nights had taken their toll. My suitcase lay open and unpacked. Suddenly, the feeling of being overloaded overwhelmed me. I did not have enough time to finish packing before the interview, and the schedule allowed no time for packing after the interview. Determined not to be exploited by MCC again, I located Vern Preheim, the Asia Secretary.

"I'm sorry," I said, "but I won't make the train for New York today."

"Why not?" He looked surprised. Although not responsible for my work load in Vietnam, he had just caught the brunt of my frustration.

"I'm not packed up yet, and I'm supposed to be interviewed in just a couple of minutes, and there won't be any time to pack after the interview. There's no way I can get ready in time, and I feel worn out."

"Have you started packing yet?" he asked.

"Yeah, I've started, but in Vietnam I felt swamped under a work load with no escape until after the change of government. Now I'm feeling swamped the same way. I'm tired of trying to work at top efficiency all day and all night. I'm sorry but I can't do the interview and meet the train on time."

"You've got to try to catch the train today because leaving tomorrow would put you in too late for the appointments."

"I know." I sighed. "I'm sorry, but I don't know what to do."

"How much more time do you need to pack?"

"I don't know," I said. "It's hard for me to figure out what all I'll need for my presentations. I suppose another fifteen minutes would do it."

He glanced at his watch. "Okay. You go finish your packing. We'll cut the interview short. I really don't want to cancel it, though, because this paper reaches an audience that some of the others don't. Try to pack as fast as you can. You'll make it. Then you can relax on the train."

"Yeah. Okay. Thanks." I took a deep breath. The extra minutes he had given me looked like a lifesaver. Semi-organized confusion reigned in the suit bag and briefcase as I squeezed them shut. Then the interviewer popped her questions at me. And I beat the train.

Vern's reprieve allowed me to meet the schedule and conquer it. Five speaking engagements per day was common. One day in Virginia held seven. After delivering the morning chapel talk at Eastern Mennonite College that morning, I scurried to a nearby town for a television interview. Whisked back to Harrisonburg, I spoke at a faculty and student luncheon at the college. An afternoon discussion session in the Discipleship Center, followed by a visit with out-of-town Vietnamese, brought me to suppertime when I was involved in a round-table, student discussion. That evening, I was the featured speaker for the World Affairs Club at the college.

*The Heart of Capitol Hill*

As the plane landed in Washington, D.C., mixed emotions tugged at me. Crime-laden, big city life confronted me. I dared not walk alone on the streets at night. The crimes, however, were not confined to the streets which—like spokes of a wheel—converged on Capitol Hill. I had seen destruction caused by bomber pilots in Vietnam; now I saw where the other Pilates washed their hands on the Hill.

I recalled a proverb: "All politicians should serve two terms—the first one in office, the second one in jail." The words of Khalil Gibran also struck me: "The nets of the law are designed to catch petty criminals; on the larger criminals we bestow great honors." Jesus wept over Jerusalem; surely he was also weeping over Washington, D.C., I thought.

Don't be too cynical, I told myself. After all, you do have a more positive perspective than the cynical taxi driver in California.

I had read and reread John H. Yoder's thin volume dealing with Christian witness to government. I recalled his encouragement to view politicans as human beings who needed loving concern as well as admonition. I opposed stereotyping Vietnamese; logically I could not stereotype U.S. politicians, either.

Delton Franz, head of the MCC Peace Section Office in Washington, D.C., accompanied me to meet "Sonny" Montgomery, a Representative from Mississippi. A hawk during the U.S. military involvement in Vietnam, Montgomery was now head of the Congressional Committee on MIA's.

Montgomery's huge office with a high ceiling like a chapel felt intimidating. I saw rows of medals decorating his military uniform in a portrait photograph hanging prominently on the wall behind his desk. With his unmistakably Southern drawl, he nudged me with questions as he listened to my story.

Privately, he had softened his hard line. An aide, who had accompanied him to Hanoi early in 1976 to discuss U.S. soldiers still listed as missing in action, told me that Montgomery had quietly admitted, "I was for this war from beginning to end. But now I've been to Hanoi, and I've met the people there. And, if I had it to do all over again, I don't think I'd be for the war."

*Ignore the Pain?*

Since Max had just arrived in the U.S. on May 7, 1976, his news about Vietnam, including the elections, updated my experiences by several weeks. During the next ten days, he and I shared the presentations and interviews.

Max recounted his conversation with Nhung on election day in Vietnam at the end of April. "I asked her how she felt and she said she had voted first thing that morning and that she felt great. She seemed so excited. I asked her what she did after that. She said, 'I've been walking all over Saigon, and it looks so different. It belongs to us (Vietnamese) now.' "

After Max and I had given several presentations at one Mennonite college, a signed statement appeared on the bulletin board. I read it silently.

> So far a lot about Vietnam has been heard through magazines, through international reporters, and MCC workers. It seems like Vietnam is a "rosy world" through the description of foreign observers, especially the MCCers who seem to claim themselves the most reliable source. . . . They have done a good job of collecting information, helping Vietnamese . . . and giving fantastic objective interpretation of what they had seen. . . .
>
> So much has been heard about Vietnam from the Americans, the outsider (as admitted by Jim Klassen during the talk with the Peace Society on May 13), but not much from the insider, the Vietnamese. We, the small group of Vietnamese students on campus, have been so quiet, mysteriously quiet—why? Does our silence mean agreement with what has been spoken? Does that mean we don't care, we ignore Vietnam because we have a better life here. . . ? Or does that mean we don't know anything?. . .
>
> We hope none of the these is the reason for our silence.
>
> Our beloved country and its people has been suffering so much and too much at any period in the past and present, under any government including the present one! Our hearts are grieving, the scar is still there, the bleeding hasn't stopped yet. We would feel better off if the scar is not touched. But unfortunately . . . some kind of surgeons . . . are so conscientious and curious that they linger their hands on the scar, attempting to heal it. As they do it they "sound their trumpet before them" and it seems that they forget what Jesus taught, "When you give your 'concerns,' do not let your left hand know what your right hand is doing" (Matt. 6:3).
>
> We are in a crisis; we need a serene environment (please!); we get headaches with all the noise on the Vietnam topic. . . .

Max and I painted a rosy picture? We had specifically mentioned the massive unemployment, the unstable economy, the rice shortage, the U.S. boycott, the tons of buried explosives, the difficulties of reconciliation, and families who were still divided. In my introductory comments, I acknowledged my role as an outsider in Vietnam. Words spoken under pressure a year earlier still rang in my ears: "You're a foreigner. You don't understand."

Yes, I had white skin, blue eyes, and blond hair. But I felt the pain and agony of the Vietnamese, not only in Vietnam, but also in the statement posted on the college bulletin board.

I had also felt a dehumanization of secretaries, file clerks, and assistants in the Akron MCC office. One busy administrator there admitted to me, "I don't really have time to learn their names. They come, and they go. They're mostly short termers, you know. I think of them like cogs in a machine: as long as they do their job without complaining, things run smoothly."

Reality had squeezed suffering into the marrow of my bones. I had seen tears roll. I had also touched hearts patiently bearing pain without tears.

Sweeping the war under a carpet solved no problems. "Tough" soldiers who thought they could bury their actions, merely delayed having to face reality.

Grass grows impartially over the graves of the fallen. The living, though, bear the responsibility for building a better future— even when progress comes slowly. Consequently, as soon as the petitions titled "Lest We Forget . . . An Appeal for Reconciliation" rolled off the press, I carried a copy in my Bible. The Appeal, coordinated by the American Friends Service Committee, called on the U.S. Congress and Administration to act in four areas: recognition, reconstruction, amnesty, and rehabilitation. I wondered, how long will it take the U.S government to act for Vietnam or even for its own citizens? Providing reconstruction aid to Vietnam and restoring diplomatic relations with Vietnam would have eliminated many headaches of the Vietnamese college students.

*Questioning the Media*

The students' reference to Matthew 6 on the bulletin board revived an inner struggle for me. Jesus said, "When you help a needy person, do it in such a way that even your closest friend will not know about it" (Matt 6:3). Why should I travel so many miles to share the experiences that I had in Vietnam? In the face of rigid "religious" ideas about protecting the "holy" from normal mortals, why should I tell anyone I baptized new believers in Vietnam? Perhaps small clusters of Christians could understand my perspective, but why should I say a single word to the impersonal mass media?

At the change of government in Vietnam in 1975, members of my family had faced similar issues. A reporter from Wichita sat waiting to interview my mother when she got home from work.

"Are you Mrs. Klassen?" He whipped out a pad and pencil.

"Yes, sir."

"I'm Bartel from *The Wichita Eagle,* and I'd like to ask you a few questions about James."

"I'm sorry, sir, but that's not a story for the papers."

"But I've been waiting here all afternoon. I even called my office in Wichita, and they told me to wait until I had the story before coming back."

"I'm sorry to disappoint you," mother insisted, "but James stayed to be faithful to his Lord; he didn't stay in order to make headlines."

"I know. That's why we need his story. We have too many of the other kind of stories in the news. We need to hear his story."

Finally, she granted him an interview. When other reporters requested interviews, she responded, "The papers have already carried the story."

Why was I willing to share my story hour after hour, day after day, week after week upon my return to the U.S.? Why was I willing to challenge distorted perspectives? Why was I willing to tell others about the joy and the sorrow of my friends in Vietnam? Jesus had instructed his followers, "Let your light shine before people, so that they may see your good works and give glory to your Father who is in heaven" (Matt. 5:16). Consequently, I felt urged to share my experiences with people across North America to help them understand that the good news of reconciliation transcends national boundaries. I hoped that my sharing would also help bring a better future for my Vietnamese friends. What could I accomplish in brief encounters or formal presentations that lasted only five minutes, or fifteen minutes, or an hour? Perhaps I could only sow a few seeds, but I believed God would sustain the seeds I sowed.

*Catching Distortions*

In August 1976, Max and I met in Denver, Colorado, to serve as resources for a Peace Conference there. While checking programs for Vietnamese refugees, the two of us met the priest who headed the Roman Catholic work in the area. He had stayed in Vietnam for three months after the change of government, but we had never met him there during that time. We soon realized that our perspectives differed radically.

"You need to be realistic," he scolded. "You were there. You know that all church meetings had to be registered and then the communist soldiers started coming to them."

Max let me answer. "Yes, we were there," I responded gently. "Our church meetings were registered, too, but it was no problem. I myself was teaching weekly Bible classes in English and in Vietnamese, and we were never hassled. Our Christian Fellowship conducted three baptismal services during my last year there, and we never had any static. No soldiers came to any of our meetings."

"Well, they were Catholic soldiers from the North," the priest admitted.

Surprised by his concession and wondering whether he had deliberately attempted to distort the truth, I replied, "In my opinion, if there were Catholic soldiers from the North in Saigon, then naturally they would want to attend worship services there. It's clear now that there were Catholics and Protestants on both sides of the lines in Vietnam, and they had guns. Surely, God must be especially sad to see people—who claim to know about his love—pointing guns at each other and pulling the triggers."

"But the communists are godless atheists. Don't you think we have a responsibility to stop them?" The edge in his voice was gone.

"Don't you think God is more powerful than any government?" I asked. "I'll never say it's easy to be a Christian in Vietnam today. But, if you're serious about following Jesus, then it isn't easy to be a Christian in the United States today, either. And I'm sure that you're aware of the Vietnamese archbishop from the North who went to Rome to participate in the ceremonies making him a cardinal this past summer."

Our vigorous discussion continued, but I never forgot how the priest's initial selection of facts twisted the truth. The day was

August 6, the awesome anniversary of the U.S. bombing of Hiroshima.

## *If I Were You*

Just a month later, MCC convened a conference in Chicago for voluntary agencies and church mission groups that had formerly worked in Vietnam. One skeptic at the conference compared Vietnam to another situation: "Today there's as much freedom of religion in China as a tiger has in a cage." However, during the day and a half of discussions, an unusual source endorsed the ongoing Mennonite relationship with Vietnam.

A big-boned man represented the Christian and Missionary Alliance (C. & M. A.). I had met him in spring at the C. & M. A. headquarters in Nyack, New York, when I shared my experiences there. The C. & M. A. leaders had not been surprised at my report of church activity in the North: they themselves had helped found the churches there! Nevertheless, because the C. & M. A. missionaries had supported the U.S. in the war, they kept silent about the churches in the North, thereby fostering an image of the communists as only atheists.

In Chicago, the room hushed as the C. & M. A. Asia director spoke.

"After April 1975, we tried to reestablish contact with the church leaders in the North. We sent two letters, but we never got any response. Finally, we sent in verbal greetings with a delegation that visited Hanoi."

He looked down and paused. His voice thickened. "They sent back an oral message. 'Where have you been these past twenty years?' they asked us. 'We've been here all the time,' they said. 'Why weren't you supporting us before? Faith without works is dead.' "
He paused again.

His deeply lined face conveyed his feeling as he continued. "We feel bad that we haven't had more contact with them since 1954."

At the end of the conference, the C. & M. A. Asia director, who had served as a missionary in Vietnam, let us feel his heartbeat once more. "I'll admit the C. & M. A. has a hang-up with the step-by-step process of communist governments to get rid of church influence," he said. "But given your situation, it is good for MCC to maintain your relationship with Vietnam and encourage the church there. If I could, I would."

*What Is Truth?*

Six weeks later in California, Max and I faced a strong negative reaction from a Vietnamese audience. I introduced our presentation in Vietnamese with an Oriental legend about blind men and an elephant.

> "The elephant is like a spear," said one who had grabbed a tusk.
> "No, the elephant is like a rope," claimed another blind man, holding the tail.
> "Oh, no, you're both wrong," argued the third as he felt one of the elephant's legs. "The elephant is like a huge pillar."
> "No, no," said another one who held onto an ear. "You're all wrong. The elephant is like a giant fan."
> And so on. Each speaking from his own perspective. This afternoon we will be sharing some of our experiences with you, but we realize that it is not the whole picture. Obviously, even though we can speak some Vietnamese, we still are not Vietnamese. But we did stay for a year after the change of government, and we are happy for this opportunity to share some of our experiences with you.

Max and I painted a verbal picture in broad strokes and then showed slides we had taken. At each of our public presentations, we liked to allow time for the audience to ask us questions. I had just opened the question-answer period when a Vietnamese man jumped to his feet.

"Thank you very much," he began politely. "The words you spoke were very interesting, and the pictures you showed were very beautiful." Then he raised his voice. He spit the words at us. His face reddened with anger. "But we don't need any more communist propaganda! The communists probably told you exactly what to say! Your pictures—they're a lie! They don't really show how hard life is in Vietnam! Don't you have any other pictures?"

"Excuse me, sir," I responded gently when he paused to catch his breath. "I'm not a photographer, and I did not take many pictures. You said the pictures were too pretty. Maybe. But I also did not take any pictures of the Saigon slums and the street boys when Thieu was in power. I have a hard time taking pictures like that. But perhaps you will recall that in our verbal presentation we did mention problems in Vietnam. Let me tell you respectfully, sir, that we are telling the truth about what we experienced. No communist told us what we should say. Like I said in my introduction about the elephant, obviously there are many perspectives, and we are simply sharing ours."

"Well, I tell you I've heard enough! I don't need any more of your communist propaganda! I think the best thing that we can all do now is go home. This meeting is now adjourned."

No one dared to argue with him. After a brief, stunned hush, the puzzled audience milled around to say good-bye. A few people, mostly university students, lingered to apologize to us and to ask questions.

"What if someone wanted to go back to Vietnam?" one neatly dressed student asked shyly. I had heard that tone of voice before: the very person asking the question probably hoped to return to Vietnam.

"The government might expect that person to spend a block of time getting oriented to the new situation," I replied, "but I don't think there would be any reprisals. The biggest problem right now is that there aren't any diplomatic relations between the U.S. and Vietnam."

Later, Max and I learned that the man who challenged us had directed Thieu's propaganda program. Obviously, then, if he accepted the truth of what we said, he would deny the validity of his own efforts.

### Problems in the Promised Land

Although a multitude of kind sponsors in the U.S. helped Vietnamese refugees with housing, employment, medical care, finances, and countless other details, the refugees still faced formidable adjustments and obstacles. Unfortunately, some sponsors complicated the situation. So did some refugees.

"We ran because of American propaganda," a Vietnamese woman lamented when I visited her family near Lake Michigan. "But my husband has a strong spirit. He would not desert his homeland. Life here in the U.S. is hard, especially without him. He used to make the decisions, but I'm responsible for taking care of the family. I'm not only worried, I'm sad. And the winters are cold. I don't have any close friends. And the churches here are so pushy."

Her children, delighted with their ice cream cones, raced to the car in the shopping center parking lot. She and I ambled along the sidewalk.

"It's really a mess, Jim." She sighed. "If we go to church, then people think we're just doing it to please our sponsors. If we don't go to church, people think we're ungrateful. What are we supposed to do?"

"I don't know. That really is a headache."

"No, actually, that's one of the smaller problems we face," she countered. "If you want a headache, then listen to this. My sponsor wanted me to get a job right away after we got here. But there's no future in the job she had in mind. I wanted to get a college degree so I could have an adequate income to support my children. My sponsor threatened to take away the old car she had given me. 'Fine,' I told her. 'Take it. I don't need it. Material things don't matter to me anymore. I've lost my homeland, my husband, my friends, my home, my job—so much that's precious to me. Your car? Take it. I don't need your help if that's the way you feel.' "

The U.S. refusal to establish diplomatic relations with Vietnam complicated communications between refugees and family members still in Vietnam. Although many refugees let me read letters describing hardships in Vietnam, other times refugees insisted that relatives and friends in Vietnam dared not write the truth about the situation there. I also learned that refugees sometimes did not accurately descibe the situation they faced in the U.S.

"I'm working nights as an aide now in a home for the elderly," the Vietnamese woman continued. "Of course, I can't write back to Vietnam and tell anyone that I have to work here. I'd be too embarrassed to admit that I have to work. And if I told them the kind of work I do, I'm sure they would faint."

Because letters served as the primary link for people in the United States with people in Vietnam, rumors plagued that activity. A Vietnamese pastor on the East Coast of the United States warned a Vietnamese friend of mine that if she wrote to her family in Vietnam, the Vietnamese government would cut her family's rice rations. I had never heard of any rations being cut when families in

Vietnam received mail from the U.S. Besides, I knew that the pastor's own children had been writing to their grandparents in Vietnam: I had been in Vietnam when the grandparents happily received their letters.

*Roots and Flowers*

In the States, I met a few Vietnamese whom I had known in Vietnam. I served as a special link to two participants in the MCC exchange program, Ly and Phuong-Hang, bringing greetings directly from their family members. Ly and Phuong-Hang had expected to return to Vietnam after one year, but the lack of diplomatic relations between the two countries after the change of government in Vietnam made the scheduled return to Vietnam impossible.

Phuong-Hang had married an MCC exchangee from Germany; Ly was still single. Ly's elderly mother, to demonstrate her love for Ly, had made a special trip to Ho Chi Minh City before I left. Ly's father, a high school principal, had been struck with a sudden illnes and had died when Ly was only a year old.

In another state, Mrs. Hieu, her four children, and her mother—all of whom had evacuated from Vietnam in 1975—also eagerly awaited news about Vietnam from me. Mrs. Hieu wondered about other things, too.

"Jim, you never prayed before meals when you ate with us in Vietnam. Why do you pray before meals here?" Mrs. Hieu asked while visiting with my parents and me in Kansas. Although she had already plied me with questions about my religious faith since she had come to the U.S., her question suprised me.

"There I was a guest in your home, just like you're a guest in our home now," I explained. "I was trying to fit in without creating too many problems for you. And although it's common here to fold your hands, bow your head, and close your eyes to pray before eating, I don't think that's the only way to pray. A common Jewish way to pray is to raise your hands and look up. As far as I know, I prayed before every meal I ate in your home in Vietnam—but I did it silently and with my eyes open. My prayers were short, but sincere."

I was praying with my eyes open right then as I spoke to her, praying that she would understand and that the Lord would bless her in her search.

"Some people would probably say I was copping-out," I continued. "What I wanted to do, though, was to share my beliefs with you without imposing them on you. Rather than burdening you with a strange custom at every meal, I felt it was more important for you to understand my concern for peace and reconciliation and to see that it was related to my commitment to follow Jesus."

"But we would have let you bow your head and pray before meals."

"Oh, I'm sure you would have," I agreed, "but why should I have made you feel awkward when Jesus could understand my gratitude without making you go through that? As I understand it, the important thing about following Jesus is not rituals, but a lifestyle. For example, Jesus had more to say about money than about prayer. Jesus also stressed loving everybody, including so-called enemies, and I felt if you understood that, it was more important than forcing you to sit through a little ritual before every meal. And I would have prayed silently anyhow, so I simply did it with my eyes open."

Because she lived 800 miles from Kansas and still wanted more answers, I encouraged her to meet friends of mine who were members of the Fellowship of Hope. I knew I could not force friendships to happen. On her own, she became friends with other members of the Fellowship.

Barely two years later, the telephone rang late Saturday night on October 14, 1978. Her voice sounded radiant. "Jim, do you know what?"

"No, sorry. I can't guess," I replied.

"Tomorrow I'm getting baptized and am joining the Fellowship of Hope."

"Fantastic! Congratulations! May the Lord bless you!"

# Chapter 17

# WHEN THE SPIRIT SAYS WRITE

*Salt*

In 1978, the scorching summer sun bore down relentlessly on Mennonite World Conference participants traveling to and from the conference center in Wichita, Kansas. At that center, I saw a bearded man in burlap braving the heat in a lonely vigil to carry a sign around the circular building. Using the words of Jesus, the sign asked, "Are you the salt of the earth?"

Across the parking lot from the conference center, the Internal Revenue Service Office conducted business as usual. Would Mennonites from around the world ignore the impact of U.S. tax dollars which paid for military weapons jeopardizing all life on earth? No. I took a turn in the 24-hour peace vigil in front of the IRS Office. The mimeographed handouts summarized our message.

it is time to cease paying for war
    while praying for peace
it is time to turn from fear and despair
    to love and hope
it is time to turn from faith in massive weapons systems
    to faith in the love of God . . . which includes our enemies
IT IS TIME TO SAY NO TO TAXES FOR MILITARY PURPOSES
    -military spending is inflationary
    -military spending squanders earth's resources
    -military spending is a denial of faith in God
it is time to hear and live by the words of Jesus

The next day, vigil members filed into the Mennonite assembly. One carried a sign declaring, "It's a sin to build a nuclear weapon." On the podium, a representative began reading a special message. "My people (says the Lord) . . . I am your security. . . . Be not afraid." Translators rendered the message of peace—the heart of the gospel—in French, German, and Spanish.

### Rerun

One month later, I started running again. 3:30 a.m. Jonah in Jimshoes. I was running from words on paper, unwritten words.

I had memorized a chorus when I was as tall as a half-grown sunflower.

> I'm gonna sing when the Spirit says sing . . .
>     and obey the Spirit of the Lord.

Although song leaders substituted *pray* and *shout* for *sing,* no one had ever substituted *write.* Should I write when the Spirit said, "Write"?

As 1978 ended, I still struggled with the implications of writing. Ten years after the marathon about going to Vietnam, I tried Jonah's shoes again. They fit perfectly. I ran hard, but I had a hunch about the outcome.

"Jim, write a book about Vietnam."

"But, Lord," I replied, "I don't know how to write. Speaking: that I can do—radio, TV, interviews, forums, schools, churches, civic clubs. That's been hard enough. But please don't ask me to write. Oh, maybe I could write another short article or two. But certainly not a book."

"Yes, a book."

"But, Lord," I repeated, "I don't know how to write a book."

"Don't you think you can learn?"

"But, Lord," I pleaded, "writing a book takes discipline."

"Wouldn't that be good for you?"

"Oh, but, Lord, there are enough books on Vietnam," I declared.

"Are there? How many books do you know of that deal directly with the church's perspective during the years you were there?"

"But, Lord, who would buy the book I'd write?"

"If I ask you to write, don't you think I'll help with that, too?"

"Yeah, but, Lord," I countered, "writing means I have to bare my soul, even more than I already have. That's a terrible risk to take."

"I know."

"But, Lord, it hurts to be honest. If I paint an honest picture about the mess governments make, then I'll have to paint an honest picture about Christians, too. And if I do that about others, then I also have to be honest about myself and let people see I'm just a normal mortal. Being so honest hurts."

"I know."

"But, Lord," I lamented, "there's so much propaganda about Vietnam. Who really cares about the truth?"

"I do."

"Yes, Lord," I admitted, "I know you do. But who would read the book?"

"All I'm asking you to do is write it."

"Yes, I know, Lord," I argued, "but if I write a book, I can't just write about myself." I put my heart into this—my most convincing—point. "I've got to include my friends, but they shared with me in confidence. How could I dare to quote them in the book?"

"Ever hear of people called by something other than their given names?"

Well, certainly I had. Was that question supposed to be an answer? I had run out of questions. I had run out of excuses. I stopped running.

Jonah in Jimshoes. Was it easier to lay the shoes aside the second time? No. Writing a book loomed as an awesome task.

*Good-bye, Jonah*

How should I begin? In writing college orations, I always had needed a title first. Nine possible titles for the book sprang into my mind. Less than two weeks later, five more possible book titles made their debut. The title wave slowed to a trickle, averaging one new title every two months. Finally, on April 30, 1979, I rolled a sheet of scrap paper into my typewriter and centered my latest proposal: "JIMSHOES IN VIETNAM." Below it I typed the subtitle: "Orienting a Westerner." I started typing! What a relief!

I paused to look at the road ahead. I saw only one way to organize the pile of "raw material" in my journals: type it, using a separate sheet of paper for each entry in the journal. After that, I planned to coordinate the entries with other documentation. Given a variety of other involvements— including intensive legal research to challenge the Internal Revenue Service with my Christian pacifism—typing the journal entries spanned the next two years. I called it "doing my homework." As a constant reminder of my commitment to writing, I let my hair grow long—until another reminder replaced it.

At night, during the day, at home, on the road, my thoughts often turned toward writing. Sometimes I scribbled notes on scraps of paper.

> Basic assumptions
> —God is love
> —Jesus is Lord
> —Christians should follow him
> —and they will be evaluated—MCC, Bethel, Alexanderwohl
> —I, too, will be evaluated by the same standards
>
> Why say "Mennonite"?
> —capsule way of referring to my Christian commitment
>     and historical roots for biblical interpretation
> —still have questions about that identity
>     but perhaps it's better than
>     "American," or "Kansan," or "Christian"
> although none of those would be entirely incorrect either
>
> Peace
> —what is it?
> —what kind of commitment?
> —with whom?
> —has it come or hasn't it?
>
> Wars may come and wars may go,
>     but true peace with God and with people
>         can never be achieved with military power
> Whether in the presence of war or in the absence of war,
>     peace is an act of faith,
>         not a cheap hope
> —but faith based on a willingness to live with integrity
> —faith more realistic than
>     the false faith that bombs bring security
>         or that bullets bring peace

I was not in VN as a psychologist, sociologist, or anthropologist
I was not in VN as a politician, theologian, or historian
I was not in VN as a philosopher, missionary, or mechanic
I was not in VN as a farmer, pharmacologist, or student
I was not in VN as a poet, economist, or cook
     I was in VN as a Christian pacifist
       I was in VN as a friend

Some Vietnamese thought I was CIA
     "Father, forgive them, they don't know what they are saying"
Some Alexanderwohlites thought I was Communist
     "Father, forgive them, they don't know what they are saying" . . .
Praise the Lord for those Vietnamese friends
     and others around the world
       who remained my friends
         in spite of significant political changes in VN
Thank God for steadfast friends and family
But the problem of ambiguity
     will not stop me from speaking and acting
       for truth and peace and love
Perhaps not many will understand this book
     and an even smaller number will be sympathetic
       and of the sympathetic ones, only a handful will act.
       God bless them.
The rest will read the words of this book . . .
     —like "good Christian tourists" who take a multitude of slides
       but never see through the slides to . . . help alleviate
       the war and poverty which their cameras recorded.

The random notes helped frame the larger canvas. As I typed, I relived the events. I sometimes chuckled at the memories. Tears sometimes blurred my vision, forcing me to pause because I was too stubborn to wipe them. Occasionally, touching the frustrations drove me to type fast, and then I prayed that anyone seeing those words would continue reading to learn of the final reconciliation. Other times, like a concert pianist, my fingers clicked smoothly on the keyboard, confident that the words would contribute to peace and good will on our planet, both for the present and for the age to come.

Most of the experiences lay engraved on the surface of my mind, ready for instant replay. I felt blessed with a good memory and reams of documentation. Because I strove for accuracy, I prayed that my writing would reflect at least the basic meanings—if not the exact words—from the original conversations.

Deciding whether to let experiences stand by themselves or whether to add "editorial" comments confronted me constantly. Although I assumed that readers could usually sense my perspective without explicit remarks, I sometimes acquiesced to the urge to comment on the events.

The assorted shapes, sizes, and colors of scrap paper holding my random scribbles looked like gaudy ornaments when integrated with the uniform pages of typed journal notes. My heart pounded as I reread words I had zigzagged into an upper corner of a yellow piece of scrap paper during the wee hours of the morning when the idea of writing this book first seeped into my consciousness:

> Pray for me
> Pray for my friends
> Pray for those who call themselves God's children
> Pray for those who don't
> Pray for VN
> Pray for the U.S.
> Pray for the world
> Pray for Jesus' sake.

# Chapter 18

# FOOTNOTES BEHIND HEADLINES

*Squeezing Vietnam*

"For the past several years, there have been so many storms and so much bad weather in Vietnam," lamented one Vietnamese refugee woman when I visited her during the summer of 1979. "Many people think it's because of the sins of Vietnam, so we are praying for Vietnam." Earlier she had said all the rice in Ho Chi Minh City was rationed and none was available on the open market.

She, like many others, ignored or failed to comprehend related factors. Did she connect the drop in rice production to the Thieu-U.S. policy which had deliberately created ten million refugees within Vietnam between 1965 and 1973 by moving farm families off the land? Did she know that by 1975 the United States was shipping more than half a million tons of rice to the Thieu government per year? Did she realize that the U.S. abruptly terminated food shipments to Vietnam at the end of April 1975? Did she know that 90 percent of the irrigation system in central Vietnam had been bombed with U.S. bombs?[1]

Vietnam still faces a multitude of problems. Like the Vietnamese woman implied, praying should help. So would reconstruction aid from the U.S. But even though the United States promised 3.5 billion dollars to Vietnam,[2] the U.S. has not yet sent even one penny. A U.S. trade embargo since April 1975 prohibits all U.S. trade with Vietnam. U.S. delegates to international financial institutions, including the World Bank, voted against all Vietnam projects and pressured other delegates to vote against them, too.[3]

The refugee woman mentioned the bad, stormy weather in Vietnam. During December 1975, my last Christmas there, the weather had turned cold—the coldest many of my friends could remember. Flooding and then severe drought had hit Central Vietnam in 1976, followed by the coldest winter in 30 years which froze tender rice seedlings in the North. Coupled with that bleak picture, two typhoons and prolonged drought in 1977 had produced serious food shortages.[4]

The next year, 1978, the problems multiplied. More than 400,000 refugees from the Pol Pot regime in Kampuchea poured into Vietnam. The border conflict with Kampuchea turned another million Vietnamese into refugees in their own land as they fled the contested area. That fall the worst flooding in the history of Vietnam hit, destroying enough food to feed one third of the country for a whole year. At least four million Vietnamese felt the direct effects.[5]

1979. Same sad song. Drought this time. Plus insects. The food shortage was the worst since 1945, the year of Japanese occupation when approximately two million Vietnamese starved.[6] A letter from a Vietnamese friend of mine during the winter of 1979 said, "Vietnam is experiencing a famine."

People in the United States who decried Vietnam for the lack of food and medicine in the study-work camps failed to realize that all of Vietnam faced the same shortage.[7] Headlines about "boat people" from Vietnam ignored the food shortage and the economic crisis there. Since the United States routinely granted refugee status only to people fleeing communism or the Middle East, refugees from Vietnam claimed political reasons as the basis for leaving.

In spite of the headlines, I occasionally glimpsed another picture, even through refugees. In the fall of 1982, I received a long distance call.

"I'm calling about my husband's brother," the voice said over the phone. "He's so depressed in the refugee camp. We're terribly concerned about him. When the U.S. delegation came to the camp and interviewed him, he said he left for economic reasons. Really stupid. So the U.S. would not accept him. Apparently no one had told him he was supposed to say he left for political reasons. I hope you can help us. We really want to get him out of that camp."

Many refugees paid with gold to leave Vietnam, indicating that someone in the extended family was well-to-do. With economic resources like that, naturally life in Vietnam no longer looked attractive. Poor families, however, had no choice: they had to stay; they had no way to pay the price to leave.

Because many refugees carried expensive jewelry which could be converted into cash in "the promised land" to establish their "new life," refugee boats became lucrative targets for pirates. Consequently, refugees often arrived in the U.S. with empty hands, having been robbed at sea.

In a dimly lit Chinese restaurant in a southern U.S. port, I sat across the table from an elderly Vietnamese refugee as she shared her story.

"We paid seven ounces of gold in order to (secretly) leave Vietnam," she related. "But the communists were suspicious; they thought we might be trying to leave. They surrounded our house and even came inside to check, so the boat left without us. The second time, too. So we lost fourteen ounces of gold without being able to leave. The next time we paid, we were able to leave.

"But on the trip, Thai pirates came. I was terribly scared. I yanked off some of my jewelry and put it into a little powdered milk can—I don't even know whose can—but that's all I was able to save. What they took from me alone would have been enough to support one person for a lifetime."

By contrast, a young refugee family in the central region of the U.S. lived a far simpler life. I had translated for the family and doctors, sponsors, and employers. In spite of laudable efforts by the husky, hardworking father, his income never covered monthly expenses. One evening, the young father confided in me, "We brought along a little gold when we left Vietnam, and we've got it hidden just in case we ever need it."

In another rural community, a Vietnamese woman suffered from unemployment, a major physical disability, and separation from her husband. She surprised me, too. "I don't ever tell anyone," she said, "but I've got a beautiful gold necklace hidden away. It helps me feel secure."

The U.S. government enjoyed the publicity that the "boat people" received and the cooperation of the church organizations in sponsoring the refugees. In fact, the U.S. government gave sponsoring organizations $500 for each refugee from Southeast Asia that they placed. Besides allocating those U.S. funds for administration, travel, and health care, the sponsoring organization often designated part of that $500 as a cash grant for the refugee upon arrival in the U.S. Six months after I agreed to work "for MCC" as a translator in Kansas, I sadly learned that my wages depended on those U.S. government grants.

My superiors in MCC seemed insensitive to political implications of that funding. When I asked whether anyone raised ethical questions about the grants, the MCC Refugee Resettlement Coordinator said, "No, no one has seen any problems." Yet early in May 1980 in Hesston, Kansas, I heard him describe the Hmong refugees from Laos to prospective sponsors. "These Hmong had a slash-and-burn lifestyle in the hills. Although a few have craft skills, most of them are primarily subsistence agriculturalists relying on hand labor, except that many of them were recruited and paid by the CIA to fight in the secret war against the Pathet Lao." No political overtones? No ethical questions when the church uses grants from the U.S. government to settle CIA mercenaries?

What about Vietnam? In 1979 a representative from the United Nations reported, "If Vietnam were to receive sufficient economic aid, the refugee problem would disappear."[8]

How did MCC respond? Although MCC continued to send delegations and material aid to Vietnam, two front-page headlines on July 12, 1979, summarized MCC's position: "MCC Acts to Restrict [its own] Aid to Vietnam," and "MCC Coordinator to Travel Urging More Congregations to Sponsor Asian Refugees."

Instead of sending the aid it promised to Vietnam, the U.S. government paid church and civic organizations to sponsor Vietnamese refugees in the United States. Using "Voice of America" (VOA) radio broadcasts to report only glowing success stories of refugee resettlement, the U.S. enticed other Vietnamese to leave Vietnam by boat and sent the U.S. Navy Seventh Fleet into the South China Sea on a "humanitarian" mission to pick them up.[9]

Vietnam and the United Nations agreed in May 1979 to let ten thousand people leave Vietnam per month by plane if they had con-

firmation of acceptance from the country of their destination. The
U.S., however, preferred to tempt people to leave by boat; "fleeing"
by boat served U.S. propaganda purposes far better than orderly
departures by plane. The U.S. also ignored the U.N. request to stop
VOA radio broadcasts of one-sided refugee success stories.[10]

The 500,000 "boat people" received huge headlines, but the 50
million Vietnamese still in Vietnam faced hunger, poverty, and a
U.S.-China coalition that supported Pol Pot in the hills of Kampuchea. I sometimes wondered how many people cared about my
hungry friends in Vietnam.

The "boat people" were pawns. Vietnam itself faced a no-win
situation: condemned as an uncaring society if it let people leave by
boat, and condemned as a tightly closed society if it refused to let
people go. I translated for "boat people" as an elementary courtesy
to these new neighbors in the U.S., but I believed that Vietnam
needed more help than the "boat people" did.[11]

Jerry Elmer, field secretary for the American Friends Service
Committee, reported on his meetings with members of the National
Security Council (NSC) during 1979 and 1980.

I left . . . convinced not only that the Carter Administration is
deliberately misrepresenting the situation in Indochina for political
reasons, but is deliberately pursuing a policy to create additional
refugees.

Our six-person delegation to the White House urged the Carter
Administration to normalize diplomatic and trade relations with
Vietnam . . . for the safe and orderly emigration of Vietnamese who
wish to leave . . . thereby eliminating the need for flight in leaky and
unsafe vessels.

Normalization of relations would also provide an avenue for the
U.S. government to pursue with Vietnam outstanding issues between
our two peoples, such as the return of MIA remains to the United
States. . . .

Our delegation . . . urged the Carter Aministration to provide
emergency food aid to Vietnam. Two members of our delegation had
been in Vietnam in recent years. . . . Both reported acute food
shortages . . . growing . . . worse.

When we asked Mr. Sullivan (an NSC staff member responsible
for China and Southeast Asia) about United States policy toward
Vietnam, he replied, "United States policy is exactly to squeeze . . .
Vietnam as hard as we can, to force Vietnam to rely only on the Soviet Union; then Vietnam will find that the Soviet Union cannot meet
all of its needs."

Such a path has predictable and known consequences.

First, a U.S. policy to "squeeze" Vietnam will surely increase the flow of . . . refugees from Vietnam, since so many of the refugees are fleeing as a result of hunger and economic deprivation in their homeland.

Thus while the United States works to exacerbate the conditions leading to the refugee exodus . . . (it) also denounce(s) the Vietnamese for allowing the refugee flow to continue.

Second, such a policy will increase hunger, malnutrition, and the diseases associated with them, in Vietnam. Indeed, according to Sullivan, the United States sees its political interest in thus "squeezing" Vietnam.

Third . . . (it) will drive Vietnam . . . closer to the Soviet(s) . . . politically, economically, and militarily . . . Vietnam will see no alternative. . . .

Our delegation to the White House expressed shock that U.S. policy seemed designed to deliberately create more refugees, to deliberately create more economic dislocation and hunger in Vietnam.

"If Vietnam experiences economic hardship," Sullivan responded, "I think that's just great."[12]

Then the U.S. government took an even harsher stance—as if the war had not ended. William Shawcross, renowned for his authoritative book on Kampuchea, documented the Reagan Administration position regarding Vietnam in 1981.

While General Haig was touring China and Southeast Asia . . . he and his staff stated their policy of "bleeding" Vietnam in . . . chilling form. Assistant Secretary John Holdridge said it was no use normalizing relations with Hanoi. ". . . we will seek, if we can, to find ways to increase the political, economic, and yes, military pressures on Vietnam. . . ."

Renewed American military involvement (even indirectly) in Vietnam was made the more grotesque by the fact that Holdridge made his statement in Peking. The United States government is slipping . . . into a military and political partnership with China against Vietnam—when less than fifteen years ago the United States repeatedly declared it was in Vietnam for the purpose of keeping "Red China" out of the region.[13]

## The U.S. and China

Based on the assumption that "conflict can be comprehended without being hallowed,"[14] the following comments present a brief summary of the Vietnam-Kampuchea conflict. Instead of establishing diplomatic relations with Vietnam, the U.S. opened diplomatic relations with the People's Republic of China (PRC) which was backing the Pol Pot regime in Kampuchea. When Kampuchea attacked Vietnam's western border, Vietnam proposed submitting the dispute to the United Nations, but Kampuchea refused. Fearing even worse long-term instability created by China's open support of Pol Pot, Vietnam quickly gathered momemtum to overthrow Pol Pot in Phnom Penh. Both the U.S. and the PRC have supported seating Pol Pot in the United Nations.[15]

The recent ties between the United States and the People's Republic of China, however, opened the eyes of Christians in the United States: God had continued working in China.[16] Why do many U.S. Christians doubt God's ability to work in Vietnam? Isn't God greater than any human government?

*Miracles in Vietnam*

I listened to a young Vietnamese refugee, a musician, share his spiritual pilgrimage in church. He testified that the communist government in Vietnam had worked like a refiner's fire, helping him clarify his values. Then in June 1983, he came to visit me.

"Heard you're working on a book," he said. "What are you writing about?"

"About my experiences and the church in Vietnam. Other books have been written about Vietnam, but not much about the church there, particularly about the church's response to the change in government."

"I think Satan tries to use every government," he replied.

"I agree. I usually say that it's not easy to be a Christian in Vietnam, but at the same time, if we are serious about following Jesus faithfully, then it's not easy to be a Christian here in the United States, either."

"I lived under the communists for several years, and they do have some really good points," he shared openly. "And people here are surprised to hear that the church is growing. But I think it was just the power of prayer. Many miracles happened which would probably seem incredible to a lot of people. The Tran Cao Van Church has about a thousand members. Once the pastor said, 'By Christmas we're going to have a hundred new members.' So every night the members got together and prayed. 'Okay, this week let's pray for two new members'—and at the next church service two new members joined. 'Okay, let's pray for five new members'—and exactly five came forward. By Christmas, there were ninety-nine. Christmas Eve one family went home from the service, and the husband swore at the whole family, but the next morning he was back at church and accepted Christ, making exactly one hundred."

He continued. "The church has between seven and eight hundred active members because some have left for New Economic Zones or have left the country, but the church is still strong. Every night we got together and prayed."

"Every night?" I asked.

"Every night. Like the early church, or Pentecostal meetings—no set program, just sharing and singing. And we'd divide up by two's to pray together and share. I really miss that. There was power there."

He explained further. "I saw miracles happening. For example, drug addicts could just quit. I witnessed to one like that in our door-to-door program. After a week, he finally said he'd go to church with me, and on the way to church he accepted Christ. The next morning when I met him, his whole family had become Christians because he had such a moving testimony. Of course, it was the work of the Spirit."

He paused. His eyes watered. Then he continued. "How I miss that group! Now some of those friends are scattered across America. We're convinced that the Lord has something special in mind for us—not money, or big houses, or fame—but a special witness. Like a special crystal glass about to fall off the table and get smashed by the fall, that's how it is with the 50 million Vietnamese, my people. I think the Lord wants to train me as a missionary. My older brother could have come with me, but he declined. He said the Lord needed him in Vietnam, so he stayed. Before I left, he counseled me, 'Don't get caught up in all that easy money in America.' "

*For Whom?*

Easy money? Not for most people in the U.S. Earning money requires a sacrifice. People with low wages scrape along, sometimes making ends meet, sometimes not. People with higher salaries often get caught in a rat race, sacrificing family time for fatter paychecks.

Easy money? Not for most refugees in the U.S. I recalled visiting with a Vietnamese refugee a thousand miles away. That man had come from northern Vietnam where socialism had structured the economy for more than 30 years. "I couldn't believe it," he had told me. "When I first arrived in America, I was unemployed for three months. I never was unemployed in Vietnam. In (North) Vietnam there is no unemployment. Now I'm laid off. I never knew it would be like this. I'm fed up with being at home, but I don't know enough English to look for a job. I simply have to wait for my sponsors to find something."

Low wages shattered the American dream of climbing the ladder of economic success for another frustrated refugee in Kansas. "I can't understand it," he had lamented to me. "I've been working at the same place for almost a year and still haven't gotten a raise."

*Depression*

A Vietnamese friend of mine, along with a niece and two cousins of his, drove 800 miles to visit my parents and me in our simple home in Goessel, Kansas. Late that night, he and I stood conversing alone beneath the single bare light bulb which was centered in the sloping ceiling of my upstairs bedroom. It was past 1:00 a.m. Everyone else had already gone to sleep.

"Jim," he confided, "I'm going to make it here as far as material things go. But sometimes I get so terribly depressed in my spirit. Americans know so much about material things, but not much about spiritual things."

He had sensed the un-Christian materialistic greed, shortsighted pride, and the cutthroat competition permeating the U.S. Unfortunately, my friend had not yet felt the heartbeat of faithful Christian groups here and there across the land, living by the spirit of love, joy, peace, and humility.

A Vietnamese woman had shared her burden with my parents and me while her charming, preschool-age daughter played contentedly with a battery-run toy. Occasionally interrupting the woman's stream of words, I translated into English for my parents.

"How I miss my elderly mother!" she exclaimed at one point. "Not a day goes by without my thinking of Vietnam. Sometimes I think I'll go crazy."

The headlines about refugee resettlement in the United States naturally focused on economic successes rather than the loneliness of separation from strong family networks and from millenniums of traditions in Vietnam. U.S. propaganda broadcasts to Vietnam also avoided mentioning hardships and uncertainties the refugees faced at sea, in the refugee camps, and in the U.S. A Vietnamese periodical published in the U.S., however, still prints brief requests from people trying to locate friends or family members. The requests for information are printed free of charge and fill a page in each issue.

The Vietnamese woman's concerns skyrocketed when her mother, brother, sister, and family left Vietnam. Based on two letters from a friend who had left on the same boat with her family members, she described the situation.

"My brother—the one in Indonesia now with my mother— has always had bad luck. In 1975, the boat he was on ran out of food and water after seven days, so it turned back to Vietnam. This was the fourth time they tried leaving. All of their goods were stolen in Thailand, but no lives were taken. Finally, they got to Indonesia. We've sent four letters, two telegrams, and a hundred dollars to them in the camp there, but there's no guarantee that they got it."

Then a letter from her brother confirmed the lack of communication. Its strong words crushed her heart.

> One hundred people here have already died from malaria. If (you haven't written or sent money because) you're angry with me, don't take it out on me. Save your anger for the next life because we need your help now. Mother is seriously ill. . . . If I would have known about all these hardships in advance, I never would have left Vietnam.

Arrival in the "promised land," apparently, was expected to erase all memories—pleasant as well as painful ones. Both kinds of memories remained. I translated for a sponsor interviewing a young refugee couple in Kansas.

"Now that you've been here three months, what do you think of the U.S.?"

"I don't know very much about America yet," the young refugee woman replied immediately, "but I'm so homesick for my family that I could burst into tears at any moment."

The persistent pain has multiplied for others, too. As after every war, U.S. families having soldiers "Missing In Action" (MIA) in Vietnam still face a gaping uncertainty. Exploiting MIA concerns to avoid restoring diplomatic relations with Vietnam, the United States government has used the families like pawns in an international political struggle against Vietnam. (Vietnam is also using MIA information as the only ace they have in the political game with the U.S.) Even after diplomatic relations are restored, MIA information will probably still be sparse: the U.S. Army still cannot account for more than 19,000 MIA's from World War II.[17] In Vietnam, most of the U.S. MIA's were pilots, requiring complicated searches over rugged terrain.[18] While Vietnam struggles to produce enough food for its own people, who has the time and the resources to search the countryside for information about missing foreign soldiers? Nevertheless, since April 1975, as an overture for restored diplomatic relations, Vietnam has continued to release information and has sent the remains of several dozen bodies to the United States. Vietnamese MIA families, however, have even less hope regarding their loved ones: did U.S. soldiers keep records of the Vietnamese they were shooting and bombing?

*A Plea*

The suffering can never be erased completely. Indelible tears have written too much history. One fragile option remains, sitting quietly in the footnotes, hoping some day to lift its questions into the hearts of multitudes. Who will transcend the barriers with a friendly hand? Who will help build a better, brighter future? Will the church?

> The Archbishop of Ho Chi Minh City (formerly Saigon) made a special appeal to U.S. Catholics recently to work for the normalization of relations between the United States and Vietnam.
> Archbishop Nguyen Van Binh also called upon Catholic Relief Services to return to Vietnam to help attend to human needs in that nation.
> "Please give our best greetings ... to all U.S. Catholics.... Please ask them not to forget us. We need their assistance. The most important thing is the relations between our countries. My hope is ... normal relations between the U.S. and Vietnam. That would help in many ways....
> "I would like very much for the U.S. Catholic Relief Services (CRS) to give assistance to our country under the present govern-

ment. We are short of many things. We need CRS to help with food aid for typhoon victims . . . supplies for our school children, help for our hospitals. . . ."

Binh's comments reflect the views of many southern Vietnamese Catholics who observed the massive Catholic Relief Services program during 1954-1975 (the period the Vietnamese now call the "U.S. War"). CRS gave massive aid for the Catholic exodus to South Vietnam in 1954 and continued that aid throughout the war years. . . .

The number of Catholics in Ho Chi Minh City (formerly Saigon) is growing, Binh said, estimating 450,000 Catholics in the city.

"There are enormous crowds in the churches on Sundays," he said. "Many people have converted."

. . . Seminaries are training new priests. In Ho Chi Minh City, for example, 20 new seminarians entered last year.[19]

If Archbishop Binh's call for assistance produces a healthy, positive response, then the difficult life of Christians—both Catholic and Protestant—would be eased. Indeed, with substantial aid, everyone in Vietnam could breathe more easily. Alleviating hardships, not causing them, should be a hallmark of Christian discipleship. Because God sends rain on the just and the unjust, Jesus called his followers to a similar, impartial love.

Politicians come, and politicians go. Yet hundreds, thousands, millions of people have lost their lives at the whim of politicians. Surely Christians, shod with the Gospel of Peace, should be willing to sacrifice at least as much in constructive ways for the eternal kingdom of the Prince of Peace. Jesus declared: "My kingdom does not belong to this world; if my kingdom belonged to this world, my followers would fight" (John 18:36).

*Responding*

The choice is yours. The decision—"the cost of discipleship"—touches every area of your life: your reputation and bank account, your values and ambitions, your family and vocation, your today and your tomorrow. You decide.

"Christ changed us from enemies into his friends and gave us the task of making others his friends also" (2 Cor. 5:18). That is good news for Vietnam, for the United States, for the whole world. Everyone needs more friends, not more enemies. Be a friend—wherever you are—for Jesus' sake. Won't you?

# Chapter 19

# EPILOGUE

*Fundamentals*

The preceding pages have traced a decade and a half of my life. God's grace brought me safe this far; I trust it to lead me on. Seeing God work in the past reassures me that God will continue to work in the present and future.

Vietnam changed me and helped clarify my theology. Although I could converse in Vietnamese, I lacked schooling in Vietnamese theological jargon. The jargon seemed unnecessary in my setting: nearly all of the new believers in the Phan Thanh Gian Fellowship came from Buddhist homes. As I led the Bible studies and shared my life with the Fellowship, I tried to convey an uncomplicated message: the Bible is the foundation of my faith, and it points to Jesus who leads us to the heart of God. I stressed three points. (1) God is Sovereign (1 Timothy 6:15). (2) God is love (1 John 4:16). (3) We ought to obey God (rather than anyone else— Acts 5:29), following Jesus in a ministry of reconciliation and service motivated by love.

*Pacifism and Politics*

When I went to Vietnam, I thought I could be apolitical. I soon learned that all of my actions carried political overtones. The overtones even tainted language study. Two kinds of foreigners developed a fluency in Vietnamese—missionaries and CIA agents. "How well you speak Vietnamese!" people often told me. I was always grateful if they added, "You must be a missionary." Unfortunately, the distinction between missionaries and CIA agents was blurred because many non-Mennonite missionaries strongly supported the U.S. military in Vietnam and willingly shared information with U.S. government personnel.

In fact, even preaching and teaching about Jesus, the Prince of Peace, carried direct political implications. The Thieu police force arrested people for advocating peace because being neutral was illegal.[1]

My living under the Thieu government was a highly political act, just as political as living under the Provisional Revolutionary Government after April 1975. Consequently, I understood that living under any government—even the U.S. government—is a highly political act. Recognizing that, I still say, "Jesus is Lord," and let the political implications fall where they may.

Not taking certain actions can also carry political overtones. Refusing to register for the draft or refusing to pay taxes for war is neither more nor less political than registering for the draft or paying taxes for war.

My experiences related to Vietnam have confirmed my belief that Christian pacifism is the Jesus way. The heart of the good news has been torn out whenever peace and love and reconciliation are "doctrine" instead of lifestyle. To be saved is to be reconciled. Those who are reconciled live in peace and love.

*Invited to Forgive*

A heart which lacks room for forgiveness also lacks room for Jesus. Finding their roots in the Old Testament, Jesus and the writers of the New Testament insist that loving God without loving others is impossible. In fact, I must forgive Richard Nixon. Love does not always erase the memory of wrongs, but love prevents those wrongs from building barriers to present and future relationships. Consequently, love brings hope precisely because love is willing to absorb suffering rather than inflict it.

Of course, life involves pain. This book has only hinted at the horror of war. For graphic details of face-to-face combat, other first-person accounts even describe U.S. soldiers who saved the ears of dead "enemies" in Vietnam as trophies (e.g., *A Rumor of War, Nam, With Everything We Had*). As a sensitive person empathizing with others, I felt the agony around me squeezing its question marks into the marrow of my bones. And the questions linger. Why is the power of evil so pervasive? Will the U.S. ever help Vietnam rebuild?

Oppressors and oppressed on both sides of the barbwire barricades—literal or figurative—need to hear the good news. One Vietnamese poet wrote,

> Even as they strike you down
> with a mountain of hate and violence
> even as they step on your life
> and crush it like a worm,
> even as they dismember, disembowel you,
> remember, brothers and sisters, remember,
> People are not our enemy.[2]

Instead of addressing evil directly, killing people only produces more problems. Only love is strong enough to change people, and if people do not respond to love, then one consolation remains: the Lord weeps, too.

Jesus, with His clear vision of the truth, might have forced others to follow him. He did not. In a hundred—or a thousand—ways, he invited them to follow. Ultimately he gave his life to invite others to follow him. Peace and love and reconciliation is the way of Jesus. As his follower, I, too, cannot force anyone to follow. I can only invite.

*Challenges*

I believe that the research, production, and use of nuclear weapons is a sin. Only one nation—the U.S.—has ever used nuclear bombs, and that use in World War II was unnecessary because Japan was ready to negotiate even before the bombs were dropped.[3] War itself is sin. The U.S. military establishment receives approximately 50 percent of the revenue generated by income tax. I have tried to challenge the distorted priorities that shift tax revenues from constructive, humanitarian projects. Once I claimed a Nuremberg Principles tax deduction to receive a 50 percent refund; the IRS complied, so I sent the refund to MCC. Then the IRS demanded that I repay the amount refunded; eventually the IRS took the amount from me.

Throwing away his Styrofoam cup and paper plate at a picnic, a Vietnamese in the U.S. laughed uneasily. "Now we waste stuff like the Americans do. In Vietnam, every scrap of paper is important." The U.S. has only 6 percent of the world population, yet the U.S. uses 40 percent of the world resources.[4]

Sometimes, though, I feel tired of confronting injustice, evil, corruption, greed, oppression, nuclear weapons, propaganda, war, and fear. Sometimes I wonder who challenges the tyranny of so-called "urgent" tasks that devour the time needed to nourish lasting values?

### What Changed?

In Kansas, I ate imported bananas; in Vietnam I ate fresh bananas. In Kansas, I drank fresh water straight from the tap; in Vietnam, I seldom drank unboiled tap water. But life is more than food and drink.

I enjoyed living on the flat plains of Kansas; surprisingly, I enjoyed the rugged scenery of Pleiku and the spellbinding beach of Nhatrang. But every corner of creation has its share of beauty, and life is more than geography.

Vietnam gave me the opportunity to learn new cultural patterns and become bilingual. A Vietnamized, ethnic German, pacifist farm boy from Kansas was a strange combination. Perhaps I would always be a foreigner, but I would not always be a stranger. That reality humbled me. Returning to Kansas with a pair of rubber tire sandals, I realized that my family and my friends around the world had made me feel at home.

My experiences in Vietnam, particularly the decision to stay through April 1975, generated the ability to relax in God's love. The final verses of Romans, chapter eight, summarize the basis of that serenity which defeats fear.

> For I am convinced that neither death nor life, neither angels nor demons, neither the present nor the future, nor any powers, neither height nor depth, nor anything else in all creation, will be able to separate us from the love of God that is in Christ Jesus our Lord.

### Beyond Culture Shock

"Did you experience culture shock when you returned to the U.S.?" The question came countless times publicly and privately.

"No, I never did," I responded. "For one thing, I didn't have time for it! Immediately after I arrived back in the U.S., I started traveling around talking about my experiences in Vietnam. For several months, I didn't even have time to watch TV news. People were interested in Vietnam, and I was bubbling over. I still am long-winded when it comes to talking about Vietnam!

"I also had a very supportive family to come back to," I continued. "I think that's really been important, too. Of course, I tried to prepare myself for 'reentry': that was 1976—the year of the big bicentennial celebrations. I thought about how U.S. citizens might be responding to that. I always had to chuckle to myself about all the excitement, though, because 200 years is just a drop in the bucket compared to the history and traditions of Vietnam which go back nearly 5,000 years. Whenever I think of the bicentennial activities, I also have to think how narrow that perspective is, since the Native Americans (the Tribes) were here long before that."

"But isn't life dull in the States compared to Vietnam?" friends asked.

"No." I shook my head. "I've found life here in the U.S. full of adventures, too. Challenging the IRS, teaching math, coaching the largest forensics squad in the history of Bethel College, translating, even preaching once in a while—good night!—that's enough adventure for me. The one thing I really miss is the small-group Fellowship, but I'm trying to find a group like that here. Certainly I enjoyed Vietnam, but I can't live back there in some kind of 'golden age.' The challenge now is for me to work with those experiences creatively—to use them like a foundation and build on them."

Heavy-handed, illegal U.S. actions in Nicaragua, El Salvador, and Grenada, concerned me by their similarity to U.S. involvement in Vietnam. U.S. political leaders, however, seemed to ignore the similarities and preferred to focus on the Soviet Union's presence in Afghanistan or Israel's presence in Lebanon. Even before I returned to the U.S. from Vietnam, the U.S. had already crept into Angola, and that involvement confronted me in an unusual way.

"What do you think about those Vietnam missionaries over in Africa now?" an elderly man asked me after a worship service in Kansas one Sunday morning.

"Hmmm, I hadn't heard. I don't know," I replied.

"Yeah, seems like they're involved in that fighting over in

Africa." He shook his head. "After Vietnam was over, then they went over there."

Suddenly, I understood! 'Ah, you mean 'mercenaries.' "

"Oh?"

"Yeah, they're guys paid to fight in the war. I had heard about them, but they aren't missionaries. At least I haven't heard of any missionaries going to fight as mercenaries in Angola."

"Well, I see." He nodded. "I was puzzled by that, and since you had been there, I thought I'd ask you about it." He sauntered away.

The most unusual—and exciting—link to Vietnam for me still lay ahead.

*Jonah, Again?*

Many times God's blessings have far exceeded my expectations. I enjoy the challenge of detecting what God has done and is doing in my life. Discerning God's will for major commitments in my future, though, has been incredibly difficult. Jonah in Jimshoes. Twice. In 1981, I tried running once more, but this time, I had an additional advantage.

Barely three months before this third "marathon" with the Lord, Marian Franz preached in my home church, listing four tests of a call from God.

> First, you try to run away.
> Second, you argue that you aren't the right person.
> Third, it refuses to go away.
> Fourth, it is impossible.

I listened intently. I nodded. I jotted notes. Her sermon reassured me. It sounded as if she had read the first chapter of this manuscript! One, two, three, four points. So clear. So succint.

Then one night in August 1981, for some strange reason, I could not fall asleep. Being single had carried more advantages than disadvantages. I had felt that perhaps sometime in the distant future I might ask the Lord if I should start thinking about marriage. If the answer was affirmative, then I would ask about choosing someone who would consider becoming my wife.

That night in August, though, I lay on one side. No sleep. I lay on my back and soon rolled onto my other side. Still no sleep. In short, as I lay there, I felt all my "maybe's" about marriage being uprooted! Impossible! The text of a letter to Tran thi Ly, who is now my wife, slowly formed in my mind.

Ly and I had first met eight years earlier in Nhatrang when she came to ask my help in translating a nursing test. Then she had come to the U.S. as a participant in the MCC cultural exchange program, but was unable to return to Vietnam. After I returned to central Kansas, we had occasionally met each other again while she studied at Hesston College. As friends, we kept in contact after she found employment as a registered nurse in the area. Then she had moved to Louisiana.

That "night letter" expected me to ask what she thought about me and about marriage. I ran! There was no way I would ask her those questions. Jonah in Jimshoes. Again. After three weeks, I finally stopped running and wrote the letter to Ly with instructions to burn it if she already had a fiancé.

As with the earlier "calls," this call needed to be tested to determine whether or not it really was God's will. Ly and I did not automatically fall in love. Initially, we only agreed to consider marriage and pray about it—as two good friends with a special concern.

We wrote our own covenant for our wedding ceremony on December 26, 1982.


> Ly/Jim, the words I share with you now
>     are neither new nor shocking,
>     but they are said sincerely and joyfully
>         in the presence of God and our loved ones today
>         as a public statement of my commitment.
> I love you Ly/Jim,
>     with a strong—yet gentle—love,
>     and I believe God has called us to walk through life
>     as husband and wife.
> I pledge myself to continue to seek God's will,
>     just as a little river seeks the boundless ocean.
>         I have given my life to Christ for eternity
>         and want you to help nourish that vision.
> I pray that the home we establish may be a part of God's kingdom
>     where we—and others—can experience
>     peace and healing,
>     joy and forgiveness.

> We do not know exactly what the future holds,
>     but as your husband/wife,
>     I promise to love you faithfully in every circumstance of life
>     until death parts us.
> Ly/Jim, I accept you as my wife/husband and lifelong companion
>     united in the call to love mercy,
>     to do justice,
>     and to walk humbly with God now and forever.

God has blessed our life together, and the encouragement of family and friends from around the world—literally—has also blessed us. Ly and I each had full, rewarding lives when we were single, but our marriage has brought us a new sense of joy and adventure—enough to fill a book, figuratively speaking, because I do not plan to write that book! We have also felt a unity of purpose. In fact, her sacrifices, which replaced my long hair as a reminder, have enabled me to finish this book.

As I reflect on these experiences, my advice to others sounds negative: "Don't go! Don't do it! Don't—unless you feel the call. Don't follow Jesus. Don't join the church. Don't serve humanity. Don't get married. Don't challenge the IRS. Don't oppose nuclear weapons. Don't—until the holy fire burning inside you gives you no other choice. Test the call with your special pilgrims on the narrow way. Then, once the decision is clear, do not hesitate."

*Other Friends*

I had journeyed to Vietnam, not to destroy, but to build. I initially imagined that I would build with a hammer and screwdrivers in Pleiku. Trading those tools for a typewriter and chalk required fundamental readjustments for me. In every case, however, I hoped to build relationships which could transcend the differences of culture, geography, nationalism, race, and creed.

A year or two after I left Vietnam, three friends of mine—leaders in the Phan Thanh Gian Fellowship—left Vietnam on separate boats. They found each other in California. In August 1980, before I was married, I bought a bus pass to visit them. (Having left Vietnam by plane through a family reunification program, Mr. Hieu lived there with his family, too.) We had been in touch by letter and phone, but meeting face-to-face carried more risk. I still considered them close friends, but wondered whether they felt that way.

When I arrived, their friendly smiles and warm welcome immediately reassured me. The ties remained strong. I sandwiched a question into the rapidly flowing conversation: "What about the Fellowship in Vietnam?"

They paused, reluctant to answer. The invisible lot fell to Kha.

"You probably knew that Long passed away." Her voice was low-pitched.

"Yes, I had heard that," I replied.

"After he passed away, there was a new pastor at the Center on Dien Bien Phu, so the group thought they'd try it there again."

"Fine. How'd it work out?" I asked.

Her answer implied that things had not gone well at the Center. "Well, gradually we started meeting with Cuong at the Su Van Hanh Church instead."[5]

"That's okay, too," I responded. "I really have a lot of respect for Cuong. In fact, I still remember the little farewell message that he sent me just before I left Vietnam."

"It means the Fellowship is not meeting separately any more," she said to clarify, as if I had not understood the implications.

"That's no problem as far as I'm concerned. The crucial thing is not the name 'Mennonite,' but what's crucial is faithfulness to Jesus."

Signs of relief spread across their faces.

"The Mennonite emphasis on service is still strong," Ngoc added.

"Great!" I exclaimed. "I'm really pleased to hear that."

One afternoon the next week, I visited the Episcopal Church building where Thuy taught English to students learning it as a second langauge. While she was teaching, I visited in Vietnamese with several other Vietnamese teachers in the teachers' lounge. As usual, when they learned I stayed in Vietnam through the change of government, the conversation quickly focused on politics.

"You mean you lived there a whole year with the communists?"

"Yeah, I didn't leave till April 1976."

"So, what do you think of the communists?" the same woman asked.

"They're people, too," I answered simply.

"Sure, but they're so terribly corrupt," commented a male teacher.

"Maybe," I half-agreed, "but in my opinion they aren't nearly as corrupt as the previous government. Although one of my friends is a strong anticommunist, he really respected Ho Chi Minh for loving Vietnam and living a simple life. But my friend had no respect for Thieu: when Thieu couldn't exploit Vietnam any longer, Thieu packed up his gold and left Vietnam."

"But the communists are so cruel," asserted a woman with heavy makeup.

"Were you there in April 1975?" I asked her. "You should remember the rumors: anybody who had worked for the Americans was going to get shot, anybody who spoke English was going to be killed. All kinds of rumors. But there never was any bloodbath."

"But they're so hard on the rich people," she protested.

"Sure," I acknowledged. "They're trying to level out society. Under any government there are going to be people with power and people without power. Now in Vietnam the rich haven't got much power anymore. Here in the U.S., it's just the opposite. A couple of years ago, I translated for a Vietnamese man in Kansas who didn't know any English. He was thrown in jail because his bank account was overdrawn by 50 dollars. In Kansas that's a felony. At the same time, though, one of President Carter's rich assistants said he himself had regularly overdrawn bank accounts, but he wasn't in jail."

Thuy arrived in time to hear the last part of the conversation. "Jim and I always argue when it comes to politics." She sighed. "He's so stubborn."

"Well," I commented, "as a Christian, I belong to God's government which is higher than any human government. From that perspective, I believe there are advantages and disadvantages to every human government."

On the city bus en route to visit mutual friends for supper, Thuy shared her story with me in Vietnamese.

"The Lord sure has been good to me. I've seen some hard times, but the Lord has seen me through. For example, when we left by boat"—she was referring to her supposedly secret departure from Vietnam—"other people had been spreading the word about us, 'You know what? They're about to leave!' But nothing happened to us when we left."

She continued. "When Thai sea robbers confronted us, I had to translate. They looked terribly cruel, but nothing happened to me. I felt the Lord protected me. The Malaysian Coast Guard also looked mean, so we simply requested to go to a refugee island we had heard about. 'Oh, yes, there is one,' they said, but under the guise of taking us, they towed us out to sea."

"That's awful."

"One boat was leaking badly, and the motor went out on another boat. We had been crowded already, but we took those people aboard anyway. What a relief when we reached Indonesia! I didn't have any money, so I went begging for food. One Indonesian woman made food for me to sell. Then some refugees asked me to start some English classes: 'We'll pay you for it.' So I did."

Like an indelible trademark, Thuy always talked fast. "Now I'm here—but my family is all in Vietnam. They're all Buddhist, so I let them know how God has protected me. I'm really grateful to God for my job teaching English at the church so I can also send money to my family."

She had come to the United States in order to help support her family in Vietnam. Although she perhaps would not say it directly, she—like others—is a victim of the U.S. refusal to send reconstruction aid to Vietnam.

One evening as I was dining with a missionary couple who had served in Vietnam, the woman remarked, "Now Vietnamese girls have to come to the U.S. to support their families. It's an ironic parallel to just a few years ago in Vietnam when many girls had to become prostitutes to support their families."

*Final Reflections*

The refugees are a grim reminder that the agonizing impact of the war lingers. Suspicion, too, continues to be part of the legacy of war. When I first returned from Vietnam, skeptics who acknowledged the validity of my experiences nevertheless asked me, "Under a communist government, what will Vietnam be like in five or ten years?"

Not being a fortune-teller, I could only ask a parallel question:

"What will the U.S. be like in five or ten years? Will it have learned anything? Will it be invading other countries covertly or overtly?"

And what about the church in five or ten years? Will it be oppressive, or will it follow the pattern of the Prince of Peace who came to serve?

We all stand at the crossroad. Will we build or destroy?

I am grateful that Mennonite Central Committee continues to send delegations and material aid to Vietnam. That relationship provides reassurance to Vietnamese Christians—and others—that God's love transcends boundaries.

While living in Vietnam, I hoped and prayed that my presence would have more positive results than negative ones. I tried to be sensitive, but I often made glaring mistakes. Writing or talking about my experiences in Vietnam is a way of reliving them and evaluating them. I have striven for accuracy in this book at every point. But above all, I have written this book with a prayer that describing the flowers and barbed wire of the fifteen years it covers may encourage faithfulness to the Prince of Peace for the glory of God in everyday struggles, in this land or another, under any form of government, through all sociopolitical changes, for richer or poorer, in sickness or health, till the end of our days. Let us love mercy, do justice, and walk humbly with God both now and forever.

# BRIEF GLOSSARY

Anabaptist—nickname which sought to discredit 16th-century Christians in Europe who believed that baptism and church membership were only for adults who voluntarily confessed their faith and then lived a peaceful, holy life. (Ana: again. Anabaptist: rebaptized.)

*Ao dai*—traditional Vietnamese costume for men and women, a snug top (like a blouse or shirt) with long tails slit up to the waist on either side, worn with slacks.

ARVN:—(abbr.) Army of the Republic of Vietnam.

*Bo doi*—soldiers of the People's Liberation Army, the so-called "communist" soldiers.

Cadre—civil service worker in a leadership position.

Christian and Missionary Alliance (C. & M. A.)—first Protestant denomination to begin missionary work in Vietnam (in 1911), founded the Evangelical Church of Vietnam.

Central—one of the geographical and cultural divisions of Vietnam (along with "North" and "South").

Chan Y Vien Tin Lanh—Evangelical Clinic, functioned as a hospital (with beds). MCC and the Evangelical Church of Vietnam sponsored one Evangelical Clinic in Nhatrang and one in Pleiku. MCC also sponsored a clinic in Gia Dinh.

Chopper—slang for helicopter.

Democratic Republic of Vietnam (DRVN)—the government of Vietnam organized by Ho Chi Minh in 1947; after the Geneva Accords of 1954, it governed the northern part of Vietnam.

*379*

Geneva Accords—peace agreement in 1954 after the DRVN defeated the French at Dien Bien Phu. It called for countrywide elections in 1956 after temporarily dividing Vietnam at the 17th parallel to avoid further hostilities between Vietnamese who had fought with the French and Vietnamese who had fought with Ho Chi Minh. Although the United States did not sign the Geneva Accords, the U.S. made a unilateral declaration that it would "refrain from the threat or the use of force to disturb them," a pledge which it did not keep.

Gia Dinh Center—Mennonite church center, sanctuary, parsonage, clinic, and grade school in Gia Dinh, a city which bordered Saigon/Ho Chi Minh City.

Gia Dinh Mennonite Church—Mennonite congregation meeting in Gia Dinh.

Hanoi—capital of the Democratic Republic of Vietnam. Capital of the Socialist Republic of Vietnam after reunification.

Hoc tap—study-practice or study-work program; in general, the principle of putting academic studies to practical use; specifically, orientation sessions for civilians and soldiers of the former Thieu regime as part of a broad literacy and educational program established after the change of government.

Ly—Tran Thi Ly, translator for Nhatrang Nursing School, participant in MCC cultural exchange program, wife of the author.

Mennonite—Christian denomination (named after a 16th century Dutch reformer) stressing peace and service as an integral part of following Jesus.

Mennonite Central Committee—relief and social work organization supported by all branches of Mennonite churches and Brethren in Christ churches in the United States and Canada.

Mennonite Mission—Vietnam Mennonite Mission, established in 1957 by the Eastern Mennonite Board of Missions and Charities.

Menno Simons—a 16th-century reformer who emphasized Christian discipleship and pacifism and who led struggling Anabaptist communities in the Netherlands and northern Germany. (He did not found this Christian movement, but its members later became known as "Mennonites" in honor of his work.)

MIA—(abbr.) Missing In Action, (1) a soldier killed in action, but whose body was not recovered; (2) a soldier not yet confirmed dead, but whose current location is unknown.

Montagnard (French)—a tribal group living in the highlands in Vietnam.

My Lai—village near Quang Ngai where U.S. soldiers massacred Vietnamese men, women, and children.

Nam—(abbr. often used by U.S. soldiers) Vietnam.

New Economic Zones—areas of virgin land designated by the government for agricultural development by city dwellers volunteering to settle there.

Nhatrang—city on the coast of Central Vietnam, approx. 200 miles northeast of Saigon/Ho Chi Minh City, home of Nhatrang Evangelical Clinic.

Nhatrang Bible Institute—founded by the Evangelical Church of Vietnam to train church leaders and evangelists.

North—one of three geographical and cultural divisions of Vietnam (the other two being "Central" and "South").

North Vietnam—often designated the Democratic Republic of Vietnam.

*Nuoc mam*—fish sauce—used instead of salt; diluted with water, vinegar, sugar, and crushed garlic.

NVA—(abbr.) North Vietnamese Army.

Paris Peace Agreement—(Paris Accords) i.e, Agreement on Ending the War and Restoring the Peace in Vietnam, signed on January 27, 1973.

Pathet Lao—organized the revolutionary government in Laos.

Phan Thanh Gian—major street in Saigon/Ho Chi Minh city, renamed Dien Bien Phu after the change of government.

Phan Thanh Gian Center—building which housed the MCC office, Mennonite Mission office, Mennonite Student Center, and which provided living quarters for a household and a meeting place for the Phan Thanh Gian Fellowship.

Phan Thanh Gian Fellowship—group of Christians who used the Phan Thanh Gian Center as its meeting house, first baptisms performed at Tet 1975, Executive Committee elected November 1975.

Piaster (French)—a Vietnamese dollar.

PLA—(abbr.) People's Liberation Army.

Provisional Revolutionary Government (PRG)—organized in southern Vietnam in 1960 to challenge the Republic of Vietnam (RVN) following the refusal of the RVN to allow countrywide elections in 1956.

Republic of Vietnam (RVN)—a Saigon-based government created, financed, and defended by the U.S.; competed with the PRG for control of Vietnam south of the 17th parallel until April 30, 1975.

Revolution—radical sociopolitical changes needed to reunify Vietnam and establish a sound economy; specifically, the organized resistance to the Republic of Vietnam.

Saigon—capital city of Republic of Vietnam, renamed Ho Chi Minh City after the change of government.

Socialist Republic of Vietnam (SRVN)—established in 1976; formal reunification of Vietnam occurred July 2, 1976.

South—one of three geographic and cultural divisions of Vietnam (along with "Central" and "North").

South Vietnam—often designated the Republic of Vietnam.

Tet—Lunar New Year, most lavish celebration in Vietnam.

Tet Offensive—military action against all the major military installations of the Republic of Vietnam at Tet 1968.

Tin lanh—good news, gospel, evangelical.

Viet Cong (VC)—(abbr.) Vietnamese communist, negative term often designating anyone opposing the Thieu regime.

Vietnam Christian Service (VNCS)—a relief and social work organization established by MCC, Lutheran World Relief, and Church World Service.

work camp—social service project organized by Max primarily to help with refugee housing; also promoted cross-cultural understanding between ethnic Vietnamese university students and Montagnard refugees.

# NOTES

**Chapter One**
    1. Emmet John Huges, "The High Cost of Fantasy," *Newsweek* (December 13, 1965), p. 25.
    2. Arnaud de Borchgrave, "Then and Now—The Difference," *Newsweek* (March 14, 1966), pp. 41-42.
    3. Walter Gormly, "Americans Can't Name Vietnam Enemy," *The Mennonite*, LXXXI (July 5, 1966), p. 448.

**Chapter Two**
    1. "Nixon Orders Bombing Cut, Carrier Pullout," *Pacific Stars and Stripes* (October 26, 1972), p. 6.
    2. UPI Article, "North Air Strikes Reduced by Rains," *The Saigon Post* (October 26, 1972), p. 1.

**Chapter Four**
    1. Seymour M. Hersh, *The Price of Power: Kissinger in the Nixon White House* (New York: Summit Books, 1983), p. 605: ". . . . Nixon had agreed to end the war without consulting Thieu. . . . Nixon had not once but twice reassured Hanoi that the peace agreement was 'complete.' " See also Gareth Porter, *A Peace Denied: The United States, Vietnam, and the Paris Agreement* (Bloomington: Indiana University Press, 1975), pp. 124, 129-130; *Vietnam: A History in Documents*, ed. by Gareth Porter (New York: New American Library, Inc., 1981), pp. 412-413; for a blurred account which also acknowledges this fact, see Henry Kissinger, *White House Years* (Little, Brown and Company: Boston, 1979), pp. 1397-1398.
    2. Hersh, *op. cit.,* p. 607; Porter, *A Peace Denied, op. cit.,* pp. 130-131, 133, 144; *Vietnam: History in Documents*, ed. Porter, *op. cit.,* p. 415.
    3. Porter, *A Peace Denied, op. cit.,* pp. 127-128, 130: "Nixon's refusal to put pressure on Thieu meant that he was giving the Saigon government veto power—just what Kissinger had pledged to the DRV he would not do. . . . the decision had been made by Nixon *before* Kissinger's trip to Saigon. . . . It was not Thieu who sabotaged the October agreement and derailed the scheduled signing, but Nixon. . . . Thieu had been expected to 'demand some revisions in the text that we could get.' Thus Kissinger's aim in the October meeting (with Thieu) was not to get Thieu to agree to sign the draft on schedule, but to minimize the changes. . . ." See also *Ibid.,* pp. 131-135. Hersh, *op. cit.,* pp. 589, 592, 595, postulates a Nixon-Kissinger disagreement over approving the agreement (and over pressuring Thieu to sign), but then Hersh cites a supportive note from Nixon to Kissinger (p. 590) and includes a footnote (p. 605) which says, "Many of Kissinger's closest NSC aides. . . doubt that Kissinger . . . would have dared to go so far as to accept a peace offer without Nixon's approval."
    4. Porter, *A Peace Denied, op. cit.,* p. 131-134; for a weak analysis, but similar conclusion about Kissinger's credibility on October 26, see Tad Szulc, "How Kissinger Did It: Behind

the Vietnam Cease-fire Agreement," *Foreign Policy*, No. 15 (Summer 1974), p. 59; Hersh, *op. cit.*, p. 607.

5. Porter, *A Peace Denied, op. cit.*, pp. 149, 151-152; Szulc, *op. cit.*, pp. 59-60; Kissinger, *op. cit.*, pp. 1417-1418; Hersh, *op. cit.*, pp. 613-614.

6. Flora Lewis, *The New York Times*, CXXII (January 25, 1973), p. C23. (Although Kissinger at that time publicly denied making the demands as Lewis reports, Kissinger finally acknowledged his actions as noted in footnote 5.)

7. Porter, *A Peace Denied, op. cit.*, pp. 156-157; *Vietnam: History in Documents*, ed. Porter, *op. cit.*, pp. 419-422; Hersh, *op. cit.*, pp. 618-619, 623.

8. Hersh, *op. cit.*, p. 624: "Kissinger . . . understood that the North Vietnamese were being punished for insisting that he and Nixon sign an agreement that had been negotiated two months earlier and considered complete. . . . Nixon's and Kissinger's memoirs are replete with the fiction that Hanoi, faced with B-52 bombing, capitulated and returned chastened to the Paris talks. Hanoi did return to Paris, but only after Nixon and Kissinger made it clear that the October agreement would once again be on the table, without additional demands. . . . " See also Porter, *A Peace Denied, op. cit.*, pp. 164-165; Kissinger, *op. cit.*, pp. 1458-1459.

9. Lewis, *op. cit.*, p. C23.

10. David Rosenbaum, *The New York Times*, CXXII (December 26, 1972), p.10.

11. *Ibid.;* "The Battle for the Skies over North Vietnam," ed., by Lt. Colonel Gordon Nelson and Major Norm Wood, *Airwar—Vietnam* (New York: Arno Press, 1978), pp. 277-290; "Criminal Bombing Raids," *Viet Nam Courier* (February 1973), p. 10.

12. Szulc, *op. cit.*, p. 67.

13. "Aggression, Subversion, and a Divided Commission (1962)," *Vietnam: History, Documents, and Opinions on a Major World Crisis*, ed. by Marvin E. Gettleman (Greenwich, Conn.: Fawcett Publications, Inc., 1965), p. 188, citing *Special Report . . . of the International Commission for Supervision and Control in Vietnam* (Vietnam No. 1 [1962], Command Paper, 1755). . . London: Great Britain Parliamentary Sessional Papers, XXXLX (1961/62), pp. 4-11, 21-22; "Agreement on the Cessation of Hostilities in Vietnam (July 20, 1954)," *Vietnam: History, Documents, and Opinions, op. cit.*, pp. 141-144, citing *Further Documents Relating to the Discussion of Indochina at the Geneva Conference* (Miscellaneous no. 20 [1954], Command Paper, 9239) . . . London: Great Britain Parliamentary Sessional Papers, XXXI (1953/54), pp. 27-38; "The Close of the Geneva Conference (July 21, 1954)," *Vietnam: History, Documents, and Opinions, op. cit.*, p. 156, citing *Further Documents Relating to the Discussion of Indochina at the Geneva Conference* (Miscellaneous no. 20 [1954], Command Paper, 9239) . . . London: Great Britain Parliamentary Sessional Papers, XXXI (1953/54), pp. 5-9.

14. Dwight D. Eisenhower, *Mandate for Change: 1953-1956* (Garden City, New York: Doubleday and Company, Inc., 1963), pp. 338, 372.

California: Center for the Study of Democratic Institutions, 1965), p. 15.

16. *Credibility Gap: A Digest of the Pentagon Papers*, compiled by Len Ackland (Philadelphia: The National Peace Literature Service, American Friends Service Committee, no copyright, published ca. 1972), p. 39.

17. Porter, *op. cit.*, pp. 18-19.

18. *The Pentagon Papers* (New York: Bantam Books, Inc., 1971), p. 235.

19. *The Pentagon Papers, op. cit.*, p. 238; *Credibility Gap, op. cit.*, p. 61.

20. Robert McAfee Brown, Abraham J. Heschel, and Micheal Novak, *Vietnam: A Crisis of Conscience* (New York: Association Press, 1967), pp. 31-32, 78; Joseph Buttinger, *Vietnam: A Political History* (New York: Praeger Publishers, 1968), p. 485.

21. Franz Shurman, Peter Dale Scott, and Reginald Zelnik, *The Politics of Escalation in Vietnam* (Greenwich, Conn.: Fawcett Publications, Inc., 1966), pp. 83-87; David Kraslow and Stuart H. Loory, *The Secret Search for Peace in Vietnam* (New York: Vintage Books, 1968), p. 98-101; Porter, *Peace, op. cit.*, pp. 49-50.

22. Shurman, Scott, Zelnik, *op. cit.*, p. 86.

23. Porter, *A Peace Denied, op. cit.*, pp. 184, 187, 199, 278; *Vietnam: History in Docu-*

*ments,* ed. Porter, p. 424; "The Watergate Connection," *Time,* Vol. 105 (May 5, 1975), p. 14.

**Chapter Six**

1. In an unpublished June 1985 memorandum, Don Sensenig, MCC Refugee Resettlement Coordinator, reported that Pastor Sau had been killed under the new regime.

2. Holmes Brown and Don Luce, *Hostages of War: Saigon's Political Prisoners* (Washington, D.C.: Indochina Mobile Education Project, 1973), pp. 36-43.

3. Frances Fitzgerald, *Fire in the Lake: The Vietnamese and the Americans in Vietnam* (Boston: Little, Brown and Company, 1972), p. 317.

4. Jacqui Chagnon and Don Luce, *Of Quiet Courage: Poems from Viet Nam* (Washington, D.C.: Indochina Mobile Education Project, 1974), p. 114.

5. Murray and Linda Hiebert, "The Ravages of Our Secret War," *Sojourners,* Vol. 7 (February 1978), p. 28; *Refugee and Civilian War Casualty Problems in Laos and Cambodia,* Hearing before the Subcommittee to Investigate Problems Connected with Refugees and Escapees of the Committee on the Judiciary, United States Senate, Ninety-first Congress, Second Session, May 7, 1970 (Washington: U.S. Government Printing Office, 1970), pp. 80, 93, citing Daniel Southerland,"What U.S. Bombing Feels Like to Laotians," *Christian Science Monitor* (March 14, 1970), and Carl Strock, "The Long March: Laotian Tragedy," *The New Republic* (May 9, 1970).

6. Porter, *A Peace Denied, op. cit.,* pp. 174, 181-183, 240.

**Chapter Ten**

1. Wayne Oates, *Confessions of a Workaholic* (New York: The World Publishing Company, 1971), p. 60.

**Chapter Twelve**

1. *The Pentagon Papers* (New York: Bantam Books, ., 1971), pp. 55, 59-60.

2. John Pilger, *The Last Day* (London: Mirror Group Books, 1975), p. 28.

3. *Pentagon Papers, op. cit.,* p. 64; *Credibility Gap, op. cit.,* p. 56.

4. *Pentagon Papers, op. cit.,* pp. 57, 61-62, 65; Sheer, *op. cit.,* pp. 26-28.

5. Buttinger, *op. cit.,* pp. 419-420; Sheer, *op. cit.,* p. 26; Pilger, *op. cit.,* p. 28. Two other bloodbath massacre campaigns contributed to the panic in the South in 1975. (1) Richard Nixon referred to a bloodbath of half a million people in North Vietnam following 1954, but that alleged bloodbath was a lie. The September 15, 1974, *Indochina Chronicle* cited an article in *The Washington Post* on September 12, 1972, based on research by Gareth Porter:

A charge by President Nixon and others that the North Vietnamese murdered up to 500,000 of their own people when they took over the country in the 1950's is a "myth,". . . . The prime source for President Nixon, author Bernard Fall, and others in describing the alleged massacre during the North Vietnamese land reform from 1953 to 1956 is a book. . . entitled "From Colonialism to Communism," by Hoang Van Chi. Chi's book—published in 1954—was financed and promoted by such U.S. agencies as the Central Intelligence Agency. . . .

That September 15, 1974, *Indochina Chronicle* also carried an article based on an interview with Colonel Nguyen Van Chau, a Vietnamese Catholic who was director of the psychological warfare for the Saigon army during the presidency of the late Ngo Dinh Diem. According to Chau, "The alleged 'Communist Bloodbath' in North Vietnam after the 1954 Geneva Accords was '100% fabricated' by intelligence services in Saigon financed by the U.S. Government." (2) A careful analysis by D. Gareth Porter in the June 24, 1974, *Indochina Chronicle,* shows that the alleged massacre of civilians by the NLF in Hue in 1968 was a lie invented by Douglas Pike, an influential U.S. propagandist. To document a "massacre" by the communists, Pike's statistics took the casualties from the heavy fighting, artillery fire, and U.S. B-52 bombing and then attributed the deaths to the NLF. The *Chronicle* concludes,

". . . the official story of an indiscriminate slaughter of those who were considered to be unsympathetic to the NLF is a complete fabrication. . . . Understanding the techniques of distortion and misrepresentation practiced by Saigon and U.S. propagandists in making a political warfare campaign out of the tragedy of Hue is as important today as it was when U.S. troops were still at war in Vietnam.

6. Buttinger, *op. cit.,* pp. 419-420.

7. Sheer, *op. cit.,* p. 30.

8. AP Article, "US Spendings in Indochina 30 Times Those of Red Powers," *The Saigon Post* (June 3, 1974), p. 1.

### Chapter Thirteen

1. Due to fear, opportunism, and loyalty to Britain, 100,000 Loyalists fled from the United States in 1776, and their property was confiscated in the name of liberty. See Kent Britt, "The Loyalists," *National Geographic,* Vol. 147 (April 1975), pp. 512, 514, 521.

2. *Vietnam: The Legacy of the War,* compiled by Le Anh Tu (Philadelphia: American Friends Service Committee, 1976), p. 3.

3. *Ibid.,* p. 3.

4. *Pentagon Papers, op. cit.,* p. 8.

### Chapter Fourteen

1. Don Luce, "Letters," *The Nation* (July 14-21, 1979), p. 34; "Newsletter" (Dorchester, Mass.: Friendshipment, no copyright, published ca. 1979), p. 1; *Vietnam: Legacy of the War, op. cit.,* p. 2.

### Chapter Sixteen

1. Because the phrase *third party* was controversial rather than descriptive, this book has not used that phrase to refer to non-communists who were also anti-Thieu.

### Chapter Eighteen

1. *Vietnam: Legacy of the War, op. cit.,* pp. 1,3; Don Luce and John Sommer, *Viet Nam: The Unheard Voices,* (Ithaca: Cornell University Press, 1969), pp 174-185; *Credibility Gap, op. cit.,* p. 77; "Newsletter" (Dorchester, Mass.: Friendshipment, no copyright, published ca. 1979), p. 1; "Newsletter," (Philadelphia: American Friends Service Committee, summer 1977), p. 2. Note: although the factors cited in this chapter were basic in creating the food shortages and economic problems, "Vietnamese... government officials have been remarkably frank in telling the world that their policies in the years immediately after the war contained many errors.... They acknowledge readily that they tried to use wartime fervor as a substitute for careful management": see *Southeast Asia Chronicle* (April 1984), p. 1.

2. "Letter from Nixon to Pham Van Dong, February 1, 1973," *Vietnam: A History in Documents, op. cit.,* p. 427, citing *Aid to North Vietnam,* Hearing before the Subcommittee on Asian and Pacific Affairs of the Committee on International Relations, House of Representatives, 95th Congress, 1st Session, (Washington: Government Printing Office, 1979), Appendix 2, p. 25.

3. Bill and Peggy Herod, *The Sino-Vietnamese Conflict and U.S. Policy* (Dorchester, Mass.: Friendshipment, ca. 1979), pp. 3, 13; Linda Gibson Hiebert, "The Roots of Uprootedness," *Sojourners* Vol. 8 (September 1979), p. 7.

4. Carol Bragg, *Vietnam Two Years Later* (Philadelphia: American Friends Service Committee, April 1977), p. 3; "Rice for Vietnam" (New York: Friendshipment, no copyright, published ca. spring 1977), p. 2; *Far Eastern Economic Review,* (Feb 2, 1979), p. 16ff; "The Congress and Indochina," *Resource* (June 1978), p. 1; "Newsletter" (Philadelphia: American Friends Service Committee, summer 1977), p. 1.

5. Herod, *op. cit.,* p. 17; Linda Gibson Hiebert, "The Roots of Uprootedness," *op. cit.,* p. 7; Barbara Fuller, "Power Plays in Southeast Asia," *CALC Report,* (April 1979), pp. 18-19; *Thai Binh* (November 1978), p. 1.

6. Doug Hostetter, "Response to Baez," *CALC Report,* (July 1979), p. 13; *ABC World News Tonight* (August 13, 1979), 5:00 p.m. CDT; Buttinger, *op. cit.,* p. 190.

7. Some people have spent nine years in a study-work camp; that is too long. (The U.S.

has already waited ten years to establish diplomatic relations with Vietnam; that is too long, too.)

8. Quoted in *Vietnam and Human Rights* (Los Angeles: U.S./Vietnam Friendship Association of Southern California, no copyright, published ca. 1979), p. 22; Stickney, "News Release" (Philadelphia: American Friends Service Committee, June 26, 1979), p. 2. The U.S. helped Germany and Japan rebuild. If the U.S. would help Vietnam rebuild, then we could see whether the refugee problem would disappear. As the situation is now, even Tin, the former MCC office assistant, is interested in leaving Vietnam under the Orderly Departure Program.

9. Linda Gibson Hiebert, "The Roots of Uprootedness," *op. cit.,* p. 7; *Thai Binh* (June 1979), p. 3; *Thai Binh* (August l979), p. 12; *Vietnam and Human Rights, op. cit.,* pp. 19, 24.

10. *Ibid.*

11. Despite differences in our perspectives on politics, the MCC Refugee Resettlement Coordinator views his work like I viewed my translating, and he also supports programs to assist Vietnam.

12. Jerry Elmer, "A U.S. Policy That Creates Refugees," *The Pawtucket Evening Times* (June 30, 1980).

13. William Shawcross, "In a Grim Country," *New York Review of Books,* XXVIII (September 24, 1981), p. 71.

14. G. Ernest Wright, "Introduction," *The Anchor Bible: Joshua* (Garden City, New York: Doubleday & Company, 1982), p. 37.

15. *Vietnam and Human Rights, op. cit.,* p. 17; Herod, *op. cit.,* pp. 10-11, 17-21; James F. Leonard, "Time to Unseat Pol Pot," *Indochina Issues,* No. 36 (April 1983), p. 4; Paul Quinn-Judge, "The Khmer Resistance: State of the Union," *Indochina Issues,* No. 40 (September 1983), p. 3.

16. Jonathan Chau, "The Church in China," unpublished address to the General Conference of the General Conference Mennonite Church at Estes Park, Colorado, July 18, 1980.

17. Robert Reid, AP article, *The Newton Kansan* (August 21, 1979), p. 8.

18. John A. Dvorak, *The Kansas City Times* (March 14, 1977), p. 4; Robert K. Musil, *The Nation* Vol. 1223 (October 9, 1976), pp. 331ff.

19. Don Luce, "Archbishop Asks U.S. Catholics: 'Aid Vietnam,' " *National Catholic Reporter* (May 8, 1981), p. 2

**Chapter Nineteen**

1. Law/Decree 93/SL/CT of the Republic of Vietnam enacted in 1964 stated,

> Article 1. By this Decree are outlawed private persons, parties, leagues, associations that commit acts of any form which are directly or indirectly, aimed at practicing Communism or Pro-Communist Neutralism. Article 2. Shall be considered as Pro-Communist Neutralist a person who commits acts of propaganda for and incitement of Neutralism. . . .

Cited in Holmes Brown and Don Luce, *op. cit.,* p. 48.

2. Thich Nhat Hanh, "Recommendations," *Of Quiet Courage, op. cit.,* p. 145.

3. Japan was trying "to negotiate a surrender on all our (U.S.) terms except the retention of the Emperor—which, after using the bomb, we were to allow anyway." Ian G. Barbour, *Christianity and the Scientist* (New York: Association Press, 1960), p. 21; for the setting and the U.S. desire for the (unattained) unconditional surrender, see Louis Morton, "The Decision to Use the Atomic Bomb," *Foreign Affairs,* Vol. 35 (January 1957), pp. 339, 343-344, 345, 349, 353.

4. Doris Janzen Longacre, *Living More With Less* (Scottdale, Pa.: Herald Press, 1980), p. 17.

5. Rumors were and still are part of the agony of Vietnam. For example, during the worship service one Sunday in 1983, the author heard a Vietnamese pastor say that the Tran Cao Van Church in Ho Chi Minh City had been closed by the government, but a Vietnamese in

the congregation interrupted the pastor to say that, although the closing of the Tran Cao Van Church looked imminent, the government had not yet closed it. Another example: the Fall 1984 issue of the *Indochina Journal* carried the following notice: *"Correction:* We. . . printed in the last issue an appeal calling for the release of 4 Vietnamese religious leaders, including Cardinal Trinh Van Can. But he may not have been arrested, according to a reliable source."

In 1976, Cuong was pastor of the Su Van Hanh Church; when or under what circumstances he might have transferred to the Tran Cao Van Church is not known. In an unpublished June 1985 memorandum, however, Don Sensenig, MCC Refugee Resettlement Coordinator, reported, "The young pastor, Cuong, of the Tran Cao Van Church, has been in prison for two years, and has suffered mistreatment."

# THE AUTHOR

James R. Klassen served in Vietnam with Mennonite Central Committee (MCC) from October 1972 to April 1976, voluntarily staying through the change of government in April 1975. As an administrative assistant for MCC, he coordinated medicines for three clinics; on loan to the Vietnam Mennonite Mission, he taught Bible classes in both the Gia Dinh Mennonite Church and the Phan Thanh Gian Mennonite Fellowship.

Upon his return to North America, he traveled across the continent to share his Vietnam experiences in hundreds of lectures, interviews, forums, seminars, colloquiums, and retreats.

Reared in a Mennonite home on a farm in central Kansas, Klassen learned that love included admonition as well as affirmation. His father served as a deacon in the church, his mother as a Sunday school teacher.

Klassen won numerous 4-H and FFA awards and was high school valedictorian. From a one-room country grade school through college, Klassen also distinguished himself as a public speaker in county, state, regional, and national contests. Bethel College awarded him the Thresher Forensics Award in 1969; Pi

Kappa Delta, a national honorary forensics fraternity, awarded him Highest Distinction.

In 1969, at the end of a turbulent decade in U.S. history, Klassen graduated from Bethel College (North Newton, Kansas) as a mathematics major and a philosophy minor with a B.A. degree. (In 1976 he was corecipient of the Bethel College Young Alumnus Award.)

As part of his pilgrimage to take the Bible seriously, Klassen studied at the Associated Mennonite Biblical Seminaries, earning a Master of Divinity degree in 1972.

In central Kansas, he taught mathematics part-time at both Bethel College and at Tabor College and served as Vietnamese Language Consultant for the MCC Central States Region. His freelance work included translating in court for Vietnamese defendants who spoke no English. Klassen studied part-time at the New Orleans Baptist Theological Seminary and Notre Dame Seminary and taught English as a Second Language in Harvey Louisiana.

Klassen's published writings include contributions to six books. He has also written feature articles, meditations, and poetry, which have been published in *With, The Mennonite, Gospel Herald, Mennonite Brethren Herald, Sojourners,* and other periodicals. Two articles have been published in German and Vietnamese. Klassen lived in Vietnam for three and a half years; writing this book has spanned twice as many years.

On December 26, 1982, Klassen and Tran Thi Ly were married, demonstrating in a special way that God's love transcends cultural boundaries. Together they helped found Joy Christian Fellowship in Metairie, Louisiana. Ly is a registered nurse and served as a deaconess in the Vietnamese Baptist Church in Marrero, Louisiana. Klassen and his wife currently reside in Carrollton, Texas, and attend the Dallas Mennonite Fellowship and the Beckley Hills Vietnamese Church in Dallas, Texas. He is a member of the board of directors of Mennonite International Refugee Assistance (MIRA) in Dallas, which works primarily with refugees from Central America.

Thus far, Klassen has retained his membership in Alexanderwhol Mennonite Church (Kansas), where he was baptized on June 10, 1962.

Someone once told me that quantity buying reduced the price. "If I buy ten, then what's the price?" I asked.

"I've only got those two left."

"Okay, what's the price if I buy them both?"

"Five hundred for two, two hundred and fifty for one."

Some people enjoyed bargaining. I hated it. Conversing in Vietnamese still posed enough headaches for me. Bargaining in Vietnamese seemed impossible, but I tried anyway. "That's terribly expensive. How about four hundred for two?"

"Nope. Can't do it." She shook her head. "Five hundred is already my lowest price. You speak Vietnamese very well." She grinned.

"Thank you, but I only know a little bit. How about four hundred fifty?"

Even though I towered above her like a giant, the hunchbacked woman refused to budge. "Like I told you, mister, five hundred is my lowest price. I can't reduce it any more than that."

"Okay, I'll take them both." I handed her five hundred piasters, the equivalent of a dollar. She wrapped the elephants in an old newspaper.

A few days later when I was again scurrying through the central market, more ceramic elephant toothpick holders caught my eye. These were even brighter and more detailed than the ones I had bought.

"How much for ten of these?" I held a shiny, dark brown elephant.

"Six hundred piasters."

"No, not for one. I want to buy ten." Sure, these are nice, I thought, but they can't be that expensive since I only paid five hundred for the two inferior ones. Can't he understand my Vietnamese?

"That's right," the young guy insisted. "Six hundred piasters for ten."

"Six hundred piasters is the total for ten of these?" I echoed.

"Yes, ten. Six hundred piasters."

"Okay, I'll take ten," I replied, too overwhelmed to bargain. These nice ones cost only twelve cents apiece; the old woman had soaked me for fifty cents apiece on the ugly ones.

The following week, errands took me to the central market once more. I rounded a corner and stopped short. Elephant toothpick holders—better than my first ones, but not as nice as my cheap ones—lay on a counter. You really don't need any more, I told myself, so don't bargain, don't buy—just ask the price, once, clearly, in Vietnamese, and move on.

"Would you like to buy something?" A young girl behind the counter noticed that I had stopped.

"How much for ten of these?"

"Two hundred and fifty."

"No, not one. How much for ten?" I emphasized.

She grabbed a pencil and a scrap of paper, writing the numbers as she spoke. "Ten of these cost two hundred and fifty piasters."

Oh, no! Ten nice elephants for the price of one! What could I say?

I heard myself tell her, "Okay, I'll buy ten."

*Intermission 2*

In July, ready for Kansas, I left Saigon for my second break during 1974. A delay in Hong Kong dragged on. Forty-five minutes. Another forty-five. Another hour. The passengers on the Korean Air Lines flight clustered around a representative who finally brought official news.

"The problem is being fixed," he said. "We expect to begin boarding in about forty-five minutes, but we will not make it to Seoul in time to catch the flight to Hawaii. We will put you up in Seoul overnight at airline expense and are booking you on your same schedule one day later. If you must contact someone at your destination, we will cable them."

I asked the representative to telegram my parents. They never received the message, and I forgot my toothbrush in Seoul.

I faced another delay in Denver, just an hour by jet from Wichita, Kansas, where I hoped my parents were waiting. A bomb threat forced security guards to search the plane, the passengers, and all the luggage. How ironic, I thought, for a plane to receive a bomb threat in the U.S. instead of in war-torn Vietnam. I finally arrived in Wichita one day and three hours late.

At their wedding on the hottest day in Kansas that summer,